The City as a Technical Being

On the Mode of Existence of Architecture

By Peter Trummer

ORO
EDITIONS
Novato, CA

for

Oona

&

Seth

Contents

Foreword

By Graham Harman

This book by Peter Trummer is a rich compendium of ideas bearing on architectural history and theory. Although I have known Trummer for nearly a decade, and have had frequent enthusiastic discussions with him during that period, the work surprised me in a number of ways. The reader will soon find that Trummer plants one foot firmly in the debates that perturb contemporary philosophy, ranging from Object-Oriented Ontology (OOO) to the rather different orientation of Gilbert Simondon (1924-1989), that great recent thinker of technology and individuation. Yet Trummer's book is no intellectual collage. One of the things he does specially well, after honorably revealing the sources of his various concepts, is to show us the ways in which he departs from the evident deficiencies of those sources.

He does this from the opening pages of the book. When pondering the meaning of building, Trummer recounts two usual answers to this question. One approach treats architecture as produced by the hand of the individual genius; another sees it as a continual recurrence and repurposing of a repertory of stock architectural "types" (most famously in the work of Aldo Rossi)[1]. For Trummer there are numerous reasons to be suspicious of individual charisma in architecture, and they are not the expected egalitarian political reasons. To some extent, Trummer has simply seen too many "starchitects" at close range to believe in the mystique of their wizard's wands. He also holds, with George Kubler, that each of us is dealt a historical hand that largely dictates our personal range of options. But above all, Trummer is under the influence of Roland Barthes's meditations in the 1960s on "the death of the author."[2] Although Barthes was speaking primarily of written texts, comparable arguments hold for the architectural object. My own way of putting it would be to say that whether a given object is created by individual genius, collective effort, or environmental chance is less important than the features of the object itself. Any product will partly outrun the biographical or social factors that are too often used to explain it away. As for theories that link building with type instead, Trummer refuses this option for a different reason: the impossibility, starting from any pre-existing funds of types, of accounting for anything new. Instead of the solo prowess of a star human, or the classical fund of types, Trummer finds a new point of origin for building in the city itself. The skyscraper, for instance, is neither the achievement of a heroic individual nor a collage of pre-existing *eidei*. Rather, the skyscraper was first spoken into existence by that crucible of forces that is the city.

Trummer's embrace of the city as the locus of archtiectural form does need to ward off some possible misunderstandings. Having abandoned the self-contained individual force of both humans and buildings, it might be assumed that he turns in the alternate direction of human collectives and social contexts. True enough, the idea of the city quickly implies that we are dealing with a space of transient events rather than durable objects, and of relational forces rather than autonomous forms. But Trummer rejects this well-trodden path, turning again to Kubler for the needed moral support. In Trummer's words: "objects are not only part of a network of signals and a space of communication, but also themselves the initiators of other objects." Stated differently, the city is not so much a network of relations as a breeding ground for what Kubler calls "prime objects." Like prime numbers in mathematics, which cannot be reduced to any factors other than (a) one, and (b) themselves, prime objects resist decomposition into smaller familiar components. They must be regarded as new types in their own right. Along with the skyscraper, already discussed by Trummer, we can easily provide examples from other fields. The scientific article can be viewed as a prime object, perhaps first appearing in the work of the chemist Robert Boyle.[3] What we now call classical music is a prime object that may have been born in 1781, in the Russian quartets of Joseph Haydn.[4] The philosophical genre of the dialogue was introduced with unsurpassable brilliance by Plato, and has remained a familiar recourse for the writer of philosophy though none have managed to write dialogues of the same quality.

In any case, we now come to the philosophical side of Trummer's book, which is substantial. In order to characterize the status of the city more closely, he turns to Simondon, a philosopher often seen as in close proximity to the more prominent Gilles Deleuze. Architecturally minded readers are well aware of Deleuze's influence on their profession from the early 1990s onward. Against the angular disruptions and decontextualized rifts of Deconstructivism, the Deleuzean architect turned toward continuous gradients while smoothing out right angles and propounding curved, even blob-like topologies. The fortunes of Deleuzean architecture rose in unison with those of Deleuzean philosophy itself. While Deleuze was initially viewed as an entertaining, clown-like prankster amidst the gang of new French philosophers, within a few decades many were proclaiming him a great thinker for the ages, vastly superior to the likes of Jacques Derrida and Michel Foucault. With this new acclaim for Deleuze came a flood of translations of his books, along with a quickly increasing secondary literature. Simondon's fate in the Anglophone world was different. Here, for a host of accidental reasons, only readers of French had direct access to Simondon until quite recently. His classic *On the Mode of Existence of Technical Objects* was not officially published in English until 2017.[5] As for his weightier treatise *Individuation in Light of Notions of Form and Information*, not until 2020 did it see the light of day in our language.[6] Until then, readers hungry for a taste of Simondon's ideas were often left to scour the writings of a gifted young interpreter, Alberto Toscano in London.[7] With the sudden availability of Simondon's writings in English, a golden second opportunity arose for the Deleuzean architectural writers of the recent past to reformulate their principles: especially Sanford Kwinter, who appears to have entered a phase of Simondonian evangelism.

Simondon is famous for his critique of *hylemorphism*, the Aristotelian model of objects as made up of both form and matter.

Though I find many readers too quick to accept his account of Aristotle, there is admittedly something appealing about Simondon's vision. The established current of philosophies of substance –running from Aristotle through St. Thomas Aquinas, G.W. Leibniz, and more recently OOO itself– pays close attention to the structure of already existent and fully formed objects. The usual pitch for Simondon is that he does not limit himself in this way, but asks instead about the *process* of individuation by which a given thing emerges from the flux of its environment and takes on a never fully stable identity. In making his argument, Simondon brings forth an arsenal of curious terminology: metastable, transduction, disparation, allagmatic, ontogenesis. But while much could be written about the points of disagreement between Simondon and Deleuze –and Simondonians in Europe are quick to do so– the architectural reader who is already familiar with Deleuze can safely assume a shared general orientation between the two. If you liked Deleuze, you will no doubt like Simondon.

The most famous and influential aspect of Simondon's theory of individuation is his account of technology, with his book on the topic ranking among the most imaginative contributions to the field. And here we return to Trummer, the author of the present book. What is unique to Trummer's approach is his attempt to read the city itself as a technical object, one governed by the same processes of individuation that Simondon examined in such cases as steam engines or amplifiers. Trummer further individuates his theory of the city as a technical object by playing it off against real and possible rival interpretations: Lewis Mumford's city as mega-machine, Félix Guattari's city as proto-subjective machine, and the possibility of interpreting the city as what Timothy Morton calls a hyperobject. By the end of this process, the reader is left with a vivid new sense of what a city both is and can be. No longer a mere set of buildings erected in contiguous three-dimensional space, the city begins to feel more like a field of vibrating force from which new "prime objects" might unexpectedly emerge. I was not expecting a Simondonian school of urban theory to arise, but Trummer has provided the basis for one. Los Angeles has not looked the same since the first time I read this book.

Nonetheless, in these few pages I have not been able to do justice to Trummer's argument. Among other things, I have had to leave out his novel interpretation of "Sculpture in the Expanded Field," which is among the most important writings of Rosalind Krauss.[8] Trummer's deployment of the form/function dyad atop the structuralist diagram of Krauss enables him to find unexplored alternatives in the vicinity of this well-established pair. It also brings Trummer into close conversation with some prominent topics of OOO on the subject of architecture: zero-form and zero-function, referring to the de-relationized versions of form and function.[9] But our greatest debt to Trummer, as readers, will be to his reconception of the city in Simondonian terms. Trummer would be the first to admit that he has only begun to dig on this hilltop.

Graham Harman
February 2023

[1] Aldo Rossi, *The Architecture of the City*.

[2] Roland Barthes, "The Death of the Author."

[3] Steven Shapin & Simon Schaffer, *Leviathan and the Air-Pump*.

[4] Charles Rosen, *The Classical Style*.

[5] Gilbert Simondon, *On the Mode of Existence of Technical Objects*.

[6] Gilbert Simondon, *Individuation in Light of Notions of Form and Information*.

[7] Alberto Toscano, *The Theatre of Production*.

[8] Rosalind Krauss, "Sculpture in the Expanded Field."

[9] Graham Harman, *Architecture and Objects*.

Bibliography:

Barthes, Roland. "The Death of the Author," *Image, Music, Text*, trans. S. Heath, pp. 142-148. New York: Hill & Wang, 1977.

Harman, Graham. *Architecture and Objects*. Minneapolis: University of Minnesota Press, 2022.

Krauss, Rosalind. "Sculpture in the Expanded Field," *October 8* (Spring 1979), pp. 30-44.

Rosen, Charles. *The Classical Style: Haydn, Mozart, Beethoven*. New York: Norton, 1998.

Rossi, Aldo. *The Architecture of the City*, trans. D. Ghirardo & J. Ockman. Cambridge: MIT Press, 1982.

Shapin, Steven & Simon Schaffer, *Leviathan and the Air-Pump: Hobbes, Boyle, and the Experimental Life*. Princeton: Princeton University Press, 2017.

Simondon, Gilbert. *Individuation in Light of Notions of Form and Information*, trans. T. Adkins. Minneapolis: University of Minnesota Press, 2020.

Simondon, Gilbert. *On the Mode of Existence of Technical Objects*, trans. C. Malaspina & J. Rogove. Minneapolis: Univocal, 2017.

Toscano, Alberto. *The Theatre of Production: Philosophy and Individuation Between Kant and Deleuze*. London: Palgrave Macmillan, 2006.

Abstract

The city is the largest human artifact. It is made by us, yet simultaneously it makes us, as well as all other nonhuman entities. It is therefore a primary discursive subject for many disciplines. The particular discourse to which this book on the city contributes is the discipline of architecture. It explores a simple question: How does the city effect the mode of existence of its buildings?

The tradition within architectural history that identifies the city as the origin of our buildings poses a challenged to us, as architects, to theorize about the city's form and use in order to rationalize our own actions. This book responds to that disciplinary challenge. In opposition to other disciplinary approaches to the city and its architecture, however, I do not argue for *type* (Rossi, Ungers) as the deepest aspect of the architecture of the city. Neither do I use the *function* (Venturi & Scott Brown, Koolhaas) of the city to explain its material organization, nor consider *matter* (Jacobs, Banham) to be deeper than the real city. Instead, I argue that the mode of existence of architecture is inherent to the city itself, which originates its architecture as part of its being as a *technical object.*

The concept of the technical object that I use to define the city is taken from Gilbert Simondon's theory of *mechanology*. In this book I re-originate Simondon's approach into the discipline of architecture, thus presenting the city not simply as a milieu in which its buildings emerge, but as a technical object with the capacity to converge its elements and *individuate* new ones—that is, architecture. Simondon shows how the individuation of technical objects, in this case the city and its architecture, occurs through a process of *concretization.* In a thorough reading of the physical and intellectual history of the city, I visualize how urban elements like walls, streets, or plots, as well as buildings themselves, fuse their properties and give rise to new architectural and urban entities.

I conclude with the assertion that the city is an overdetermined *technical being*. The convergence of the qualities of one urban element into another is not simply the cause of all the emergent artifacts of the city. It is the city's internal necessity. It is in the very nature of the city to *tune* its architecture.

Introduction

The background against which this book unfolded was a series of questions that have occupied my mind from the beginning of my architectural education and have never since vanished. What actually is architecture? What do I do when I "do architecture"? And how does architecture come into existence? With this book I aim to present the preliminary conclusions I have reached so far through my experiences as a student, practicing architect, educator, and simply someone who loves to be in architecture and to be among it, in the city.

The first answer to the question, "What is Architecture?"[1] I received from a text by O. M. Ungers under the very same title. Ungers argues that not all buildings can be seen as architecture. If every building is architecture, then architecture would not exist. To define the line between what is and is not architecture, Ungers refers to a debate between Le Corbusier and Otto Häring that happened at the CIAM Conference in La Sarrez, Switzerland in 1928. For Le Corbusier, architecture was defined by the reality of the built environment in which buildings are embedded and constrained, whereas Häring defined architecture as *Baukunst*, in which architecture is liberated from the constraints of reality. Architecture should be free and hyperreal, he argued. Considering this debate, Ungers concludes that a distinction is to be made between what we call *building* on the one side and architecture on the other, since the first is bound by arbitrariness (*Willkür*), while the second is bound by the tyranny of ideas.[2] How beautiful, I thought, not only does this distinction draw a line between architecture and the built environment, it also moves architecture toward the arts and away from the sciences. I would say that this line of discrimination defines the essence of architecture, namely, that architecture is the discipline of ideas in buildings, or, as Peter Eisenman has radicalized the distinction: "The *real architecture* only exists in the drawings. The *real building* exists outside the drawings."[3]

Understanding architecture to be a discipline concerned with the idea of building, whether built or unbuilt in reality, led me to the next question: From whence does the idea come? Within the discipline of architecture I have found two opposing answers to this question. An idea is credited either to the genius of the author—the architect as an artist—or to a type, an *eidos*, meaning the idea within an element, thing, or object, which itself serves as a rule or model.[4] But throughout my life as an architect, I have been suspicious of both answers.

Author

Kant argues that "*Genius* is the talent (natural endowment) that gives the rule to art."[5] But I distrust the idea of the architect as genius, a singular creative spirit suspended from the real world and equipped to produce originality. Perhaps I witnessed too much mystification of "star-architects," only to end up working and thinking with some of them—whereupon the demystification started. I recall reading Egon Friedell's *A Cultural History of the Modern Age (Kulturgeschichte der Neuzeit)*, in which he states that Michelangelo was one of these few specimens, who are completely detached from their time and produce a world for themselves: "He was seen as the perfecter of classicism, the initiator of the Baroque, the last gothic man, and father of expressionism."[6] It is not that, as George Kubler writes, Bernardino Luini and Guilio Romano were not talented. They just had bad luck. When they came on stage the play was already over.[7] "To the usual coordinates fixing the individual's position," writes Kubler, "there is also the moment of his entrance, this being the moment in the tradition—early, middle, or late—with which his biological opportunity coincides. . . . Without a good entrance, he is in danger of wasting his time as a copyist regardless of temperament and training."[8] I have always sympathized with Kubler's idea.

Roland Barthes' essay "The Death of the Author" left similarly influential traces in me, especially its questioning of the originality of the author. "A text consists of multiple writings, issuing from several cultures," Barthes writes, "the unity of a text is not in its origin, it is in its destination; but this destination can no longer be personal. . . . The reader [is] a man without history, without biography, without psychology."[9] I have hardly seen a building that was not in some way influenced by, collaged, or copied from previous works of art and architecture. I remember Jacques Rancière's embrace of the power of collage as one of the great techniques of modern art. In *Aesthetics and Its Discontents*, he writes, "collage can be realized as the pure encounter between heterogeneous elements, attesting *en bloc* to the incompatibility of two worlds."[10] To use one of the most famous examples in architecture, who would have thought to link together the Greek temple and standardized mass-production? No one, before Le Corbusier.[11] I have never seen an architect doing something other than copying what already exists.

Type

Just before I began work on my my master's degree thesis I came across an issue of *Arch+* titled *ChaosStadt*. At the time I did not understand it. The volume has nothing to do with what I thought I knew city planning to be.[12] The essays it contains, with titles like "Grossstadtarchitektur," "The Object and The City," "The City of Big-Forms," and "Delirious New York," presented me for first time with the idea that architecture is a product of the city—the second disciplinary accounting of the source of an idea.

Having until that time considered architecture in terms of a singular object floating above a ground, I suddenly started to speculate on what it means that architecture is informed and even brought into existence by the city. At the time, perhaps the most prominent idea to bring the city into the foreground of our understanding of architecture was that put forth by Anthony Vidler in his 1976 essay, "The Third Typology."[13] Writing in an age of postmodern rationalism and influenced in particular by Aldo Rossi's *The Architecture of the City*, Vidler states that all architecture can been seen through a progression of three typologies: first was nature, then mass production, and finally the city. For Vidler, then, to design a building is nothing more than to reassemble, collage, or paste together existing archetypes that the city has produced throughout its history. Let's take for example the Trieste City Hall project by Aldo Rossi, which Vidler mentions in his text.[14] Rossi collaged two types from the history of the European city, a city hall and prison, to form what Vidler calls an "ambiguous condition."[15] The City Hall became an open arcade, itself a familiar type evolved from the stoas of early ancient cities. In *The Architecture of the City*, Rossi defines the concept of type "as something that is permanent and complex, a logical principle that is prior to form and that constitutes it,"[16] and goes on to argue, "type is the very idea of architecture, that which is closest to its essence. In spite of changes, it has always imposed itself on the 'feelings and reason' as the principle of architecture and of the city."[17]

I was drawn to this argument that the author of architecture, as understood through the concept of type, is not a human subject but instead an object like the city. But although architects such as Rossi, Robert Venturi, Rem Koolhaas, or Ludwig Hilberseimer have placed the city in the foreground of their architectural production by using preexisting architectural types for their projects, to me this begged another question: How does a new type emerge? The emergence of the skyscraper, for example, can neither be explained as the creation of a genius nor as a copy of an existing type. The only thing we know is that it was originated by an object called the city.

Prime Object

The initial idea for this book came to me when I saw the original caption to a diagram of a skyscraper from 1909 that appears in Koolhaas's book *Delirious New York*. The caption, which is cropped out in the book, is the most intriguing part of the diagram: "Buy a cozy cottage in our steel constructed choice of lots, less than a mile away above Broadway, only ten minutes by elevator. All the comforts of the country with none of its disadvantages. -Celestial Real Estate Company."[18]

What suddenly I saw when I read this caption was how the formal qualities of the city, namely the subdivision of its lots, were fused with the formal qualities of a building such that a floor plan has become an interior property and the elevator guarantees, like a street, individual access to each of these properties, all of which is made possible by the emptied-out floor plans resulting from moving the previously gridded steel-column structure to the facade. What I

"Buy a cozy cottage in our steel constructed choise lots, less than a mile above broadway, only ten mniutes by elevator. All the comforts of the country with none of its disadvantages." - *Celestial Real Estate Company*

FIGURE 1. THE THEOREM OF THE SKYSCRAPER, 1909

saw was how two formal objects met, with one—the city—passing into and modulating the quality of the other—the building—to produce a radical new building out of qualities that reside in the original two entities.

For me, one of the best descriptions of the emerging qualities of the new comes from George Kubler in his book *The Shape of Time*. What Kubler presents in the book as a formalist reading of art history reads to me as a thesis that defines the genesis of objects, most notably through his idea of the *prime object*.[19] Kubler published the book in 1962 and subtitled it *Remarks on the History of Things*. He states in his preamble that art history in the twentieth century was dominated by Ernst Cassirer's definition of art as symbolic language.[20] This idea of reading a work through its meaning has also dominated the disciplinary field of architecture since at least the Second World War, perhaps starting with Robert Venturi and Denise Scott Brown's reading of all architecture as either ducks or decorated sheds.[21] Or we can take Charles Jencks' diagram on the genealogy of postmodern architecture: to omit Le Corbusier and Mies van Rohe in his diagram, at a time when they were still practicing, was a clear sign of the move away from the modernist tradition of the function-first argument.[22] Since World War II, the understanding of a building as a system of signs, either as symbols, icons, or indexes, can be traced in nearly all works of architecture.

As Kubler writes in his preamble, the emphasis on meaning that had come to a high neglected the study of art on the basis of formal relations. Though unfashionable for his time, in the book he makes clear that there is no art without form: "Every meaning requires a support or a vehicle or a holder."[23] What irritated Kubler about the tradition of formalism, however, was the use of a biological metaphor as the explanation for styles. Kubler notes how Alois Riegl used the term "will-to-form" to define a time period—in Reigl's case, the *spätrömische Kunstindustrie*—by types of formal organization. It was eventually Heinrich Wölfflin who, comparing fifteenth and seventeenth century Italian art, developed five polar oppositions in the realization of form, called *Grundbegriffe*[24], which allowed scholars to classify the morphological qualities in a continuous period as styles. What Kubler found misleading, even in the work of his teacher Henri Focillion,[25] who used this biological metaphor as well, was that such formalism bound the mutation of objects to the genetic lifecycle of plants: "Its first leaves are small and tentatively shaped, the leaves of its middle life are fully formed; and the last leaves it puts forth are small again, intricately shaped. All are sustained by one unchanging principle of organization common to all members of that species."[26]

Kubler thought that a metaphor from the physical sciences would fit the history of art much better than a biological one. He saw the arts as a magnetic field and believed that artworks send out signals through the vast history of things. He states that in dealing with art, we are dealing "with transmission of some kind of energy; with impulses, generating centers, and relay points: with increments and losses in transit: with resistances and transformers in the circuit. In short", he continues, "the language of electrodynamics might have suited us better than the language of botany."[27] For Kubler, objects are not only part of a network of signals and a space of communication, but also themselves the initiators of other objects.[28]

Gottfried Böhm mentions in his introduction to the German edition of Kubler's book that one of the reasons for such a research on the evolution of forms of all things might be the fact that Kubler's research was on precolonial and colonial cultures in the Americas.[29] It is an aspect that is not unimportant, since, as Böhm argues, *The Shape of Time* was the first methodological writing in art history that aimed to distance itself from the European humanist tradition.[30] What is important to me here is not only Kubler's distancing from the European tradition, but also the way he goes about doing it in the book. Namely, it is neither the biography of the author nor interpretations of other readers that he lets speak about the inanimate art object. It is the object itself.

Now, what does that have to do with the idea of the *new*? What Kubler demonstrates in his signals-driven history of things is that every important work of art is a solution to some kind of problem, which spans throughout its history as a formal sequence. This formal sequence Kubler calls a *form-class*.[31] What intrigues me is his idea that at a certain moment in time there emerges out of a form-class a prime object.[32] Such prime objects, he argues, no longer can be explained by their antecedents.[33] Kubler compares prime objects to prime numbers in mathematics. "No conclusive rule is known to govern the appearance of either," he writes, "prime numbers have no divisors other than themselves and unity; prime objects likewise resist decomposition in being original entities."[34] They become a new original, or as I will demonstrate, a new diagram, a new whole with unprecedented qualities. Let us come back the example of the emergence of the skyscraper referred to above. The 1909 diagram—pieces of land with houses stacked within a steel construction and connected by an elevator—shows how the qualities of the city pass into a building to produce a new architectural entity: a prime object of architecture.

What I argue in this book is that the city and its architecture might have a life unto themselves. To support this argument, I use Gilbert Simondon's theory of mechanology, which he formulated in his book *On the Mode of Existence of Technical Objects* to describe the evolution of engines, electronic tubes, triodes, turbines, and telephones.[35] Through the lens of mechanology I examine how prime objects emerge throughout our history of the city, through what I call the *tuning* of qualities of one object into another, by which new architectural diagrams come into existence. The city tunes architecture twofold. First, architecture is the formal outcome of the city's various modalities and regimes. For the skyscraper these were infrastructural and economic: the problems of density and an increase in real estate values forced a new building to emerge. But secondly, and perhaps more importantly, what I want to highlight in this work is that the city tunes architecture—that is, is generates new architectural prime objects—with its own formal properties as well, meaning that from the formal qualities of the city unfold all of its architectures.

The book comprises four Chapters. The first chapter provides a disciplinary context of the city and its architecture. The second chapter defines what kind of technical object the city is. The third chapter presents various individuated cities through our urban history. And the fourth chapter dives into a series of examples of how the city tunes its architecture.

Chapter 1: The City as the Origin of Architecture

After a brief introduction to Simondon's mechanology and a speculative preview of how it could apply to the city, the first chapter establishes the disciplinary context for the present investigation of city as a technical being. In order to visualize the deviation of this position from other disciplinary approaches, I introduce a fourfold diagram, modified from the one used by Rosalind Krauss in her canonical essay, "Sculpture in the Expanded Field." The diagram serves as a guide to contextualize and differentiate the various positions that theorists, architects, and historians have taken to read the built environment of our cities, especially in the twentieth century. The diagram is based on a binary opposition of *form* and *use* and gives rise to four deeper levels: matter, type, function, and the technical object. Under the headings of each of these main levels follows a narrative series of significant authors within the discourse that contextualizes each of their positions.

Grouped under "Matter" are Jane Jacobs' *Death and Life of Great American Cities*; Reyner Banham's *Los Angeles: The Architecture of Four Ecologies*; Ildefons Cerdà's *General Theory of Urbanization*; and Sanford Kwinter's essay "Landscapes of Change: Boccioni's 'Stati d'animo' as a General Theory of Models." What all authors have in common is the idea that the material forces within the city give rise to the articulation of buildings and their use. Where their positions differ is in the kinds of forces each considers as being dominant. While for Jacobs it is mainly the economy, it is for Banham the ecologies of the territory. And whereas for Cerdà it is the material organization of the city, as he indicates in his use of the word *urbs*, it is for Kwinter thermodynamic processes, in the most abstract sense, the ones far from equilibrium, which give rise to the formations of the city.

In the subchapter "Type" are presented positions that argue for type, or the essence of forms, as being the deepest layer of the architecture of the city. Perhaps unsurprisingly, some of the most prominent theoretical works can be found here, like Aldo Rossi's 1966 *The Architecture of the City*, *The City within the City* by Oswald Mathias Ungers from 1977, and the 1978 *Collage City* by Colin Rowe and Fred Koetter. Their work holds in common the autonomy of forms within architecture. Their positions differ, however, in the degree to which these formal autonomies can become pedagogical models. And where Rossi is concerned above all with typology, or essential form, Ungers' position is rather that of a morphologist, while Rowe's formalism perhaps became the most applied urban design practice due to his followers' formulation of a new kind of contextualism.

Added to the "Type" subchapter is a book that is commonly understood in opposition to formalism: *Genius Loci: Towards a Phenomenology of Architecture* by Christian Norberg-Schulz, from 1980. The reason I add this to the list is Schulz's reading of the city of Rome. What he sees in the figure/ground formation of the Roman

Campagna, the landscapes surrounding Rome, is the formal essence of ancient Roman architecture.

In the subchapter "Function" I discuss a series of mid to late twentieth century authors who ask: What can architecture do? What can it be beyond just a building? Such a question consider function to be the deepest layer of the city. The most prominent position in the group is perhaps that defined in *Learning from Las Vegas*, by Robert Venturi, Denise Scott Brown and Steven Izenour from 1972. Seeing the city as a system of signs, they formulate their famous semiologist position by describing architecture as being either a "duck" or a "decorated shed." Two points of view have attributed to the architecture of the metropolis of New York City the role of causing unforeseen events. Manhattan's functional essence is presented through the writings of both Rem Koolhaas, in his *Delirious New York* of 1978, and Bernard Tschumi, in his *Manhattan Transcripts* of 1981. While Koolhaas casts the unforeseen events into the surrealist tradition by applying Dalí's paranoid critical method, Tschumi's line of thought belongs rather to the Situationist tradition formulated in postwar France.

The chapter ends with the formulation of the thesis of this book. I contend that the diagram of the expanded dialectic between form and use unfolds a fourth reading of the city. Namely, this is the reading of the city as a technical object, and its aim is to re-originate Simondon's mechanology in the discipline of architecture. In particular, I emphasize that not only is the city as a technical object the milieu for the genesis of its architecture, but that due to its inherent qualities of *overdetermination*, *convergence*, and *hypertely*, its elements continuously *individuate* to give rise to all kinds of new material formations—that is, architecture.

Chapter 2: The City as a Technical Being

Following the introduction of the idea of understanding the city as a technical object, the second chapter provides a twofold explanation of what this could mean to the discipline of architecture: first by way of an example of applying a mechanological methodology, and second by providing a framework for how the idea of the city as a technical being differs from other readings of the city as a machinic entity.

To give a first taste of seeing the city as a technical object I introduce as an example the plan of a traditional Mousgoum village in Cameroon. In its layout, all elements of future cities are already present and can be found in a stage of material convergence. What I show through a series of drawings is how formations of the material organization of this village emerge through the fusion of its various elements. Many of its architectural and urban outcomes can be found still today in our cities.

The second part of chapter 2 focuses on what kind of technical object the city is. After an explication of Simondon's idea that technical objects have their own evolution driven by their inner *technicity*, which is based in their hylomorphic interiority that always will be inaccessible to us humans, his thinking is brought into discussion with readings of the city as a machinic apparatus. To differentiate the Simondonian idea of the city as a technical being, his work is contextualized with that of three other thinkers. One is Lewis Mumford and his idea of the city as a megamachine, the second is Félix Guattari's idea of the city as a proto-subjective machine, and the third is the city as a hyperobject, which is a speculative title based on the writings of Timothy Morton.

While all three thinkers have ideas that allow us to read the city as a machine entity, these positions differ radically in regard to what degree and how this technical object, as it is framed, relates to the human subject. For Mumford it is clear that we humans operate as a megamachine—in his mind we, as citizens, are the machine. Guattari thinks that we can form with machines new social and technical ensembles, which can act as a new kind of proto-subjective apparatus. The application of Morton's ideas to the city suggests that we humans will never have access to such a sublime hyperobject. What this contextualization serves to show about Simondon's ideas is not only that he is one of the earliest post-humanist thinkers, but also that he gives technical beings their own mode of existence, their own *being*, to which as humans we have no access, but of which nonetheless we are part. This hybridization between the technical and the biological world that is unified in our largest artifact: the city.

Chapter 3: The Five Individuated Cities

The third chapter introduces the five individuated cities that have emerged throughout our urban history, from its beginnings after the Ice Age until today: *the city as an enclosure*, *the city as a grid*, *the city as a line*, *the city as an archipelago*, and *the city as a solid*. To follow the stages of these human aggregations, I use Henri Lefebvre's diagram on the history of urbanization as a script. The decision to use this context is twofold. First, Lefebvre provides us with a framework of human settlement by revising the timeline to show the degree of worldwide urbanization, from zero to one-hundred percent. Second, and even more importantly here, is the fact that Lefebvre uses this linearity to show how each city performed throughout history a sociopolitical function.

The aim of this chapter is to demonstrate the lack of correlation between the form of each of these five individuated cities and their sociopolitical function, and to show that the opposite is actually the case. Each city, like any other technical object, is an overdetermined entity. Once individuated it gives rise to a multiplicity of functional and formal expressions. This chapter focuses on these multiple specializations, through which cities gives us a glimpse of their hidden inner qualities.

We find that the city as an enclosure originated as a city of *walls within a wall*, but mutated soon after to entail *a territory within a wall*. In the early twentieth-century a new enclosed city emerged. This time the wall tuned its qualities, becoming itself *a territory as a wall*. The city as an enclosure has also mutated its function. Once being *the political city* it mutated later into *the mercantile city*. Its properties have been further specialized to become a city of *the common*, and tragically, has also tuned its legal status as *the camp*, the function of the state of exception.

The famous city as a grid, began formal as *the grid of four squares*, segregated by the intersection of two lines of infrastructure. *The grid with a void* is the most common model, and throughout history we find many *grids within grids*. It is not surprising that the city as a grid functioned best for what Lefebvre calls *the second circuit of capital*, but its function within regimes of *biopolitics* is perhaps closest to its origination.

The third kind of individuated city described in this chapter is the city as a line. This linear city appeared in dual forms: *megastructure* and *megafrom*. The linear city has tuned its functionality perhaps more extremely than any other. Not only can it be found as *the* model for a *socialist city*, it also functioned as the model for the city of *the open* society, as developed notably in the postwar decades by Alison and Peter Smithson. It was also the city envisioned by Edgar Chambless for his peculiarly totalizing *cooperative* of Roadtown. In fact, its inherent capacity to specialize its function to radically new performances was there from its beginning, as when Arturo Soria y Mata proposed the linear city as *a geoist city*, whereby he merged socialist and liberal ideas.

The city as archipelago is described in this chapter mainly through its appearance in the twentieth century. Its distinct forms are as *the territorial archipelago*, for example those proposed and built under the garden city movement; as *the morphological archipelago*, most notably OM Ungers and Rem Koolhaas's vision for Berlin; and as *the gridded archipelago*—Manhattan. Curiously, Lefebvre never explicitly mentions the archipelago city, however, he does addresses the inner *polycentrality* of cities. The city as an archipelago functions predominantly as city for *the welfare state*, but it has re-emerged in recent history as *a political form* to countervail fast global urbanization.

The last individuated city presented in this chapter is the city as a solid. It is latest individuated city, and in fact only one exists as a complete administrative municipality with all its citizen literally living in one building. But this is no reason to exclude the city as a solid from the history of urbanization, as it holds the qualities of a city even where it does not administratively function as one. As a technical object, its form occurs as a gigantic mass, either *the gridded mountain* or *the voided mountain*, or today in its underground versions, *the iceberg* and *the earth-scraper*. This latest city plays a dominant role within various stages of capitalism. It has assumed its function as *the financial syndicate* within early twentieth-century laissez-faire capitalism; as a new kind of spatial experience in form of *hyperspace* within late capitalism; and today it functions as a *financial asset* within our contemporary global finance capitalism.

The aim of this chapter is to identify specific cities as technical beings, and in particular their inner capacity to tune their forms and their functions. As a concise historical compendium of the city as a technical object, this chapter not only demonstrates that there is no correlation between its manifold forms of expression, but also that this overdetermined capacity is only possible because technical objects such as the city have hypertelic qualities—that is, they can tune themselves and therefore their architecture.

Chapter 4: The Architecture Tuned by the City

The fourth chapter, structured into three main parts, is dedicated to the architecture of the city and how cities tune their buildings. An exemplary mechanological reading of the typology of the Greek theater begins this chapter, following which the first section applies that method to the presentation of a newly emergent architectural ensemble within our cities: *the city on a single roof.* This emergent city type is described in terms of its process of concretization, which is inherent to all technical objects. Concretization is the process in which qualities of various elements fuse, step by step, with qualities of other elements. Through a series of drawings, this speculative convergence series identifies how the city merges the properties of its parts with the properties of buildings until a new architectural ensemble, equipped with radically new qualities, arises.

The second part of chapter 4 aims to place Simondon's idea of the mode of existence of technical objects into the history of the discipline of architecture. While we can find throughout the history of urbanization various theories that use the city as an argument for its architectural formation, the question asked here is how a mechanological methodology deviates from previous theories. As points of comparison I present five theories of architectural ensembles: Leon Battista Alberti's definition of the city as a house and the house as a city; Emil Kaufmann's distinction between heteronomous and autonomous architecture, which he used to define the baroque ensemble versus pavilion system, respectively, in order to identify a formal differentiation between premodern and modern architectural ensembles; Saverio Muratori's argument that the association of architectural ensembles between various scales are essentially bound to territorial formations; and finally architectural ensembles as poché, as described by Colin Rowe, with his unification of the figure-ground relationship of modern and premodern architecture into a building that acts as pure background. Architectural ensembles according to Simondon is a history of convergence, meaning that the emergence of any of the above described buildings—premodern, modern or postmodern or contemporary—is a result of the specialization of the building's elements, by which properties of the city enter into its hylomorphic interiority.

To visualize such specialization, which is essential to the mode of existence of the architecture of the city, the chapter ends with three detailed descriptions of speculative concretization processes. These descriptions outline the fusion of elements of the city into the elements of buildings that finally gives rise to new architectural typologies. The first process of concretization is the convergence of a building with a street, in the second, a building converges with a square, and in the third, a building meets the qualities of the urban ground. This final concretization gives rise to the newest prime object of the city: the city on a single roof.

Conclusion

The conclusion gives a summary of the thesis. In recapitulating my research and attempt to apply a mechanological reading of the architecture of the city, one piece of Simondon's writings stands out as particularly crucial. He writes, "technical objects do evolve toward a small number of specific types then this is by virtue of an internal necessity and not as a consequence of economic influences or practical requirements. . . . It is not the production-line that produces standardisation, but rather intrinsic standardisation that allows for the production-line to exist."[36] This is the viewpoint, that the internal necessity of the technical object of the city gives rise to its architecture. It is not the buildings or any external milieu that form the city. Rather, it is intrinsic to the city to form its architecture and all its milieus.

The conclusion ends with a proposal of a new kind of disciplinary approach to the city and its architecture. This approach would be distinct from the disciplines of urban design, which considers *form* as the essence of the city, urbanism, which considers *matter* as the essence of the city, and urban planning, which considers the essence to be *function*. Instead, I propose that thinking the city as a technical being could give rise to a new discipline: *citology*, or how a city tunes its architecture.

On the End

This brings me back to my initial question. How does the idea of the new relate to architecture in general and to the discipline of architecture specifically? I think this framing of the new in the terms of the prime object clarifies the distinction I made in the beginning of this introduction, between architecture as bound to the tyranny of ideas and building as the outcome of the arbitrariness of what it is to build. In his book *Über das Neue* [On the New], Boris Groys shows that in any culture the new is that which moves from the profane space into the cultural archive. The essence of the cultural archive is the new, while on the other side the profane space is the domain of the "worthless, inconspicuous, uninteresting, extra-cultural, irrelevant, and ephemeral."[37] But this profane space is heterogeneous, consisting of different things. It is not the space where the new is collected, but instead where the new is actualized. It is this boundary between the profane space and the cultural archive where the difference between architecture and buildings rests, since it is that which is new in an architectural object, its prime character, that moves into the architectural archive, and not the building itself. Here it is important to note that perhaps only the discipline of architecture has such a clear distinction between what are called *project* and *practice*.[38] One of the finest definitions of the boundary between the two was made by Peter Eisenman when he said, "if one has a project, the architect defines a world around them and if you have a practice, it is the world who defines you."[39] Projects are stored in our cultural archive, while it is the work of practices that we are living in.

Although such a boundary became fundamentally in question, if not eliminated, through the work of postmodern philosophers like Barthes, Foucault, and Derrida,[40] Groys makes clear that some kind of boundary can never be completely eliminated: "the hierarchy of values refers to what cannot be compared with one another at all, since such a comparison is unusual, indecent, and completely unthinkable."[41] Without such a boundary to define the new, architecture simply would not exist.

What I think is well possible, and what this book aims to do, is to shift the boundary of what is considered as new. My intention is to place an object, like the city, at the forefront of this debate, as the engine of the new, in order to extend the "hierarchy of values" by adding nonhuman authors as well. In showing how all these things meet, I want to argue for what Graham Harman refers to as an architecture "without human beholders, not without human ingredients."[42]

Which brings me to my last note. The intention is not to write a new history of architecture, even though I might like to. I do not write through the eyes of a naive art historian or a pseudo-philosopher, or even as an architect. I want to innovate how to think architecture, or as I stated in the beginning, I want to know what architecture's being is. This kind of project will always be limited to a fragment of the architectural audience. Or it will be an audience of those who, like me, feel that they are a product of the city. So it might be that this book was written, as Groys says, to overcome "the inner limit of value between oneself as a person in the profane space and as the subject of valuable cultural activities. They create homogeneity between their own life and the historicity of the culture."[43]

[1] Unger's original lecture in the summer of 1964 was given in German, under the title "Was ist Architektur?" *ARCH+*, vol. 179, O. M. Ungers – Berliner Vorlesungen 1964-65 (July 2000), 12–19.

[2] In the original text of his lecture, instead of architecture, Ungers uses the word "Baukunst," for which there is no meaningful translation into English. For the argument here, "architecture" is understood through the discipline of architecture, as the representation of an idea. See Ibid., 12–19.

[3] Ansari, Iman. "Eisenman's Evolution: Architecture, Syntax, and New Subjectivity." ArchDaily, 2013. Accessed September 24, 2021 https://www.archdaily.com/429925/eisenman-s-evolution-architecture-syntax-and-new-subjectivity.

[4] The first example of this definition of type and model is beautifully explained by Laugier in his first chapter, "General principles of Architecture," where he describes nature as the rule for the "little rustic cabin," which he calls "the model upon which all the magnificences of architecture have been imagined." Laugier, Marc-Antoine. *An Essay on Architecture*. London, Printed for T. Osborne and Shipton, 1755. Accessed September 24, 2021. http://archive.org/details/essayonarchitect00laugrich, 9.

[5] Kant, Immanuel. *Critique of Judgment*. Edited by Werner S. Pluhar and Mary J. Gregor. (Originally published in Prussia in 1790). Indianapolis/Cambridge: Hackett Publishing, 1987, 307.

[6] Friedell, Egon. *Kulturgeschichte der Neuzeit.* 15th Edition. (1st Edition published 1976). München: Deutscher Taschenbuch Verlag, 2003, 216. My translation.

[7] Kubler, George. *The Shape of Time*. Remarks on the History of Things. New Haven/London: Yale University Press, 1962, 7.

[8] Ibid., 6.

[9] Barthes, Roland. "The Death of the Author (1967)." In *Roland Barthes. Image, Music, Text,* translated by Stephen Heath, 142–48. Great Britain: Fontana Press, 1977, 5-6.

[10] Rancière, Jacques. "Problems and Transformations of Critical Art." In *Aesthetics and Its Discontents.* Cambridge, UK: Polity Press, 2009, 58 and 46-47.

[11] Le Corbusier. *Towards a New Architecture*. Edited by Frederick Etchells. (First published by John Rodker, 1931). New York: Dover Publications, 1986, 134-135.

[12] I consider city-planning not belonging to the discipline of architecture, but to geography.

[13] Vidler, Anthony. "The Third Typology." In *Oppositions Reader: Selected Readings from a Journal for Ideas and Criticism in Architecture, 1973-1984*, edited by K. Michael Hays. New York: Princeton Architectural Press, 1998, 13.

[14] Ibid., 17.

[15] Ibid., 15.

[16] Rossi, Aldo. *The Architecture of the City*. Translated by Diane Ghirardo and Joan Ockman. Oppositions Books. Cambridge, MA: The MIT Press, 1982, 40.

[17] Ibid., 41.

[18] Cartoon by A. B. Walker originally published in Life, March 4, 1909, and without the original caption in Koolhaas, Rem. *Delirious New York. A Retroactive Manifesto for Manhattan*. New York: Oxford University Press, 1978, 69.

[19] Kubler, George. *The Shape of Time. Remarks on the History of Things*. New Haven/London: Yale University Press, 1962, 39.

[20] Ibid., 7.

[21] Venturi, Robert, Denise Scott Brown, and Steven Izenour. *Learning From Las Vegas, The Forgotten Symbolism of Architectural Form*. 2nd Revised Edition. Cambridge, Massachusetts: The MIT Press, 1977, 88-89.

[22] Jencks, Charles. *The Language Of Post-Modern Architecture*. 2nd Edition. London: Academy Editions, 1978, 80.

[23] Kubler, George (1962), 7.

[24] Ibid., 32; and Wölfflin, Heinrich. *Kunstgeschichtliche Grundbegriffe: Das Problem der Stilentwicklung in der neueren Kunst*. 19th Edition. Basel: Schwabe Verlagsgruppe AG Schwabe Verlag, 2004.

[25] Focillon, Henri. *The Life of Forms in Art*. Translated by George Kubler. Revised Edition (1996). (Originally published as *La Vie des Formes*, 1934). New York: Zone Books, 1992.

[26] Kubler, George (1962), 8-9.

[27] Ibid., 9.

[28] It is at this point where Kubler and Gilbert Simondon merge, as will be discussed throughout this thesis.

[29] Böhm, Gottfried. "Kunst versus Geschichte: Ein unerledigtes Problem." In *Die Form der Zeit*, edited by George Kubler, translated by Bettina Blumenberg. Frankfurt am Main: Suhrkamp, 1982: 8.

[30] Ibid., 8-9.

[31] Kubler, George (1962), 33.

[32] Ibid., 39.

[33] Ibid.

[34] Ibid.

[35] See plates 1-15 in Simondon, Gilbert. *On the Mode of Existence of Technical Objects*. Translated by Cecile Malaspina and John Rogove. (Originally published 1958). Minneapolis: Univocal Publishing, 2017: 85-99.

[36] Ibid., 29.

[37] Groys, Boris. *Über das Neue - Versuch einer Kulturökonomie*. Edition Akzente. München: Carl Hanser Verlag, 1992, 56. My translation.

[38] Eisenman, Peter. "Project or Practice?" Architecture Fall 2011 Lecture Series, Grant Auditorium, Syracuse University School of Architecture, September 30, 2011.

[39] Ibid.

[40] Groys, Boris (1992), 60. My translation.

[41] Original Text: "die Werthierarchie verweist ja gerade auf das, was überhaupt nicht miteinander verglichen werden kann, da ein derartiger vergleich unüblich, unanständig und völlig undenkbar ist." In Groys, Boris (1992), 61. My translation.

[42] Harman, Graham. *Architecture and Objects. Art after Nature*. Minnesota: University of Minnesota Press, 2022, 66.

[43] Original Text: "die innere Wertgrenze zwischen sich selbst als Mensch des profanen Raums und als Subjekt wertvoller kultureller Tätigkeiten. Sie (die Innovationen) stellen dabei Homogenität zwischen ihrem eigenen Leben und der Geschichtlichkeit der Kultur her." In Groys, Boris (1992), 62. My translation.

Chapter 1: The City as the Origin of Architecture

1.1. The City and Mechanology

City

The city is the largest distinct human artifact we know and remains humanity's greatest aesthetic project. It can be classified as belonging to the last stage of Gilbert Simondon's four-part chain of interdependent worldly individuations: the Physical, the Biological, the Psychic, and *the Collective*. This last stage of individuation—the emergence of collective structurations—or, as Manuel DeLanda usefully argues it, the production of assemblages of populations, networks, organizations, and markets along with associated infrastructures such as buildings, streets, and the various conduits for the circulation of matter, is the recipe for none other than our cities.

These urban assemblages are not only made by humans, they also, as Aristotle said, make us: "It is evident that the State is a creation of nature, and that man is by nature a political animal."[44] With the city, Aristotle claimed, the human is transformed from a natural animal into a political one. The city was not only the birthplace of the political-anthropological subject, a place that Hannah Arendt derives from the *bios politikos* that becomes the foundation for the *vita activa*—"a life devoted to public-political matters"[45]. The city also invented human modalities of relational exchange: language, laws, commerce, and so on.[46] We humans produce these modalities, but these modalities also are us.

Analogously, the city as both a physical entity and a modality of abstract operations is not, as such, composed of buildings as the first term. Rather, buildings are resultants, literally assembled—shaped and invented—by *subjectless forces* originating in or passing through the city itself. The city is the birthplace of most forms of architecture, from temples and courthouses to cemeteries and fortifications,[47] and as such it is an apparatus of production, a megamachine in the wonderfully simple formulation of Lewis Mumford.

Mechanology

One approach to understanding the emergent qualities of such apparatuses and the components that make them up is Simondon's theory of *mechanology*, which he presents in his 1958 book, *On the Mode of Existence of Technical Objects*. Simondon's reading focuses on the individuation of objects as the basis of a theory of emergence, relying primarily on the dynamics of how objects meet. One primary advantage of this approach is that it accounts for how nonhuman or "inanimate" entities can have a life and society of their own.

In the early postwar consumer society in Europe—the age of cybernetics and the rise of network theories—a strange automobile appeared, the Citroën DS 19. While semantic theorists like Roland Barthes were fascinated with the magical image and outward appearance of the new Citroën, addressing it as a supernatural being or quasi-sacred object, Simondon took a very different approach, literally raising the engine bonnet and wielding a screwdriver to disassemble the motor. Simondon was less concerned with the question of what technology does to us humans than with the question, In what does the technical consist? This was the aim of his mechanology. He sought to discover how techniques become gestalts—that is, how tools, instruments, and machines, at one extreme, and factories, laboratories, and networks, at the other, individuate distinct and novel entities.

To use one of Simondon's queries for example: How do two separate parts of an early engine—a cylinder head and cooling gills—

come to meet? Typically, a machine is considered, like architecture, to be an assemblage of heterogeneous elements, each having independent form, shape, material, and function in order to perform a single task on its own and a compound one in confederation. When cooling gills were first added to engine assemblies, they were seen as a geometric unit with a single function—to cool the cylinder head—while the head was seen as a separately functioning unit that provided a structural envelope for the piston to reduce the buckling of its parts. Over time, these separate objects merged together to become a new and unique object, exchanging their formal and material properties in order for each part to bear formal and functional aspects of the other. The result was a ribbed cylinder head, which

> "can be thinner than a smooth cylinder-head with the same rigidity. In addition, a thin cylinder-head allows for more efficient thermal changes than would be possible with a thick one. The bivalent structure of the gill-rib improves cooling not only by increasing the heat-change surface (this is the very function of the gill qua gill) but also by making possible a thinner cylinder-head (and this is the function of the gill as rib)."[48]

The development of the unique—unanticipatable—structure is not a compromise, but rather it represents both a concomitance and a convergence.

For Simondon, this machine is an example of what he terms *technical objects*: units of an emergent-something that bear their own genesis within as their parts undergo a permanent exchange of energy. Simondon's definition of technical objects applies to machines as well as tools, factories, and networks. The concept supports a materialist position according to which all objects express lives peculiar to themselves, and when objects meet they transfer and transform physical and aesthetic properties such that each becomes indistinguishable from the other. The form and function of the cylinder head unifies with the form and function of the gills.

Mechanology can be said to examine this mode of tuning the qualities of form, wherein the material, shape, or function of an object passes into and modulates the qualities of another, revealing a *new* that did not exist before. Indeed, the very nature of the being of things—machines, cities, and so on—is to tune. To tune is to make another, likely novel, object, to birth qualities that previously were unknown or did not exist. The city, again, is the biggest tuning apparatus we know. It tunes us and all its component architectures, a process that is by definition infinite.

Disciplinary Context

Countless books have been written about the city, and it seems safe to assume there is no discipline for which the city is not a subject of some research. In his book *The Architecture of the City*, Aldo Rossi classifies research on the city into two primary fields. One field deals with the city as the product of generative-functional systems. Its concern is the performance of architecture and urban spaces and therefore it sees the city as comprising political, social, and economic systems. The second field deals with the city as a spatial structure, and therefore is related traditionally to disciplines like geography and architecture.[49]

Although this division among disciplines may be important to the internal audiences to which each is addressing, it is completely misleading to anyone who tries to understand the ontology of the city, its *being* in the world. To work against such classification into spatial or functional categories would mean, for example, to ask how the work of Le Corbusier on the topic of the city[50] might be very close to Otto Wagner's work on *Die Groszstadt,*[51] even though their architecture looks completely different. Or we could ask how it is that Ebenezer Howard's Garden Cities of To-morrow have a similar size and function as Tony Garnier's Cité Industrielle,[52] while the two may not share any ideas. Or further still, it requires some imagination to compare Camilo Sitte's Vienna with Ildefons Cerdà's Barcelona.[53] Not only are those two projects spatially and functionally totally different, but also they originated from completely different positions in the field of architecture: one being an architect and painter, the other an engineer and military man. And yet I would argue they are the closest of the three pairs. What these unrelated pairs share with each other is their belief in what drives the appearance of the city. In opposition to looking for correlations between the use of these projects and their form, if we categorize their political, social, or economic performance it still might not be of any advantage, since these cities—Vienna, Barcelona, Paris, Lyon and London—all share the same sociopolitical apparatus of modernity and are captured by the enormous growth of their metropolis.

What distinguishes or unites the above examples is how they look at the city, which positions they take to understand the essence of the city's appearances. These underlying philosophical ideas are more important than any particular disciplinary approach. Such ontological viewpoints, or how one sees the world, may better indicate the real audience to whom a work is talking. Having said that, this book welcomes dialogue with any discipline that is interested in examining the world as a formation of convergences, or in the words of Simondon, through processes of *individuation*.

This book is rooted in the idea that the city is the origin of architecture—that is, that the city acts as a milieu in which buildings individuate. This idea can be traced through a collection of written projects appearing after World War II in reaction to the modern movement's understanding of the city as a problem to be fixed.[54] These works served to turn around the equation and to look not from the subject to the object city, but from the object city to its architecture. In order of publication, the most significant of these works are as follows:

The Death and Life of Great American Cities, by Jane Jacobs, 1961
The Architecture of the City, (L'architettura della città), by Aldo Rossi, 1966
Los Angeles: The Architecture Of Four Ecologies, by Reyner Banham, 1971
Learning from Las Vegas, by Robert Venturi, Denise Scott Brown, and Steven Izenour, 1972
The City within the City, by Oswald Mathias Ungers, 1977
Collage City, by Colin Rowe and Fred Koetter, 1978
Delirious New York: A Retroactive Manifesto of Manhattan, by Rem Koolhaas, 1978

Genius Loci: Towards a Phenomenology of Architecture, by Christian Norberg-Schulz, 1980
The Manhattan Transcripts, by Bernard Tschumi, 1981
Landscapes of Change, by Sanford Kwinter, 1992
The General Theory of Urbanization, by Ildefons Cerdà, 1865

Appended to the list is one book from the nineteenth century, by Cerdà, which can be considered as the origination of the collection's general approach.

What is common among the authors of the above works is the idea that architecture can be understood as a product of the city, while what differs is the ontological position from which they understand the being of this architecture of the city. In order to elaborate on these authors' positions and their differences, I introduce a fourfold diagram of the architecture of the city, which presents differing ontological interests in terms of matter, type, function, and a fourth concept of (architectural) object, which I expound using the idea of the technical object from Simondon's mechanology.

1.2. A Fourfold Diagram of the Architecture of the City

The diagram I use here to visualize ontological differences in discourse on the city is a reconfiguration of the fourfold diagram composed by Rosalind Krauss in her 1979 essay "Sculpture in the Expanded Field."[55] Confronted with artwork such as Mary Miss's 1978 *Perimeters, Pavilions, Decoys*, which she describes as "half atrium, half tunnel, the boundary between outside and in, a delicate structure of wooden posts and beams," and posing the question of whether it constitutes sculpture, Krauss proposes a fourfold diagram composed of binary oppositions.[56] She argues that behind these binaries an expanded field can be found in which artworks can be placed and categorized: landscape/architecture expands into site-construction, architecture/not-architecture into axiomatic structures, landscape/not-landscape into marked site, and not-landscape/not-architecture into sculpture. Through her diagram she then is able to interpret postmodern American art from the 1960s and '70s, including Richard Serra's steel works, Robert Smithson's *Spiral Jetty*, Carl Andre's *Cuts*, and Robert Morris's Green Gallery installations.

The fourfold diagram of the architecture of the city I propose here is built around a similar binary between two properties fundamental to all architecture, namely that they come in a *form* and have a *use*. But there are two key distinctions from Krauss's diagram. First, where she describes her diagram as expanding the binaries into a field, I employ the diagram here to find what is *deeper*—that is, the underlying commonalities, or ontological lenses, that allow each binary to exist in the first place. Second, the terms at the bottom of the diagram deviate from Krauss in that *not-* is replaced with *zero-*.[57] This term is borrowed from Graham Harman, who uses it to articulate all the qualities of objects that are beyond human relationships to them.[58] These qualities are not yet revealed to us, or as Simondon would say, they are not yet individuated.[59] Rather than define a binary between what is and is not, zero here refers to the idea that behind any form or use may lie an endless amount of new forms and uses we cannot yet imagine. The *zero-form* and *zero-use* give space in the diagram to speculate on nonhuman relationships, such as what I refer to throughout this book as the tuning of the qualities of the city and its architecture.

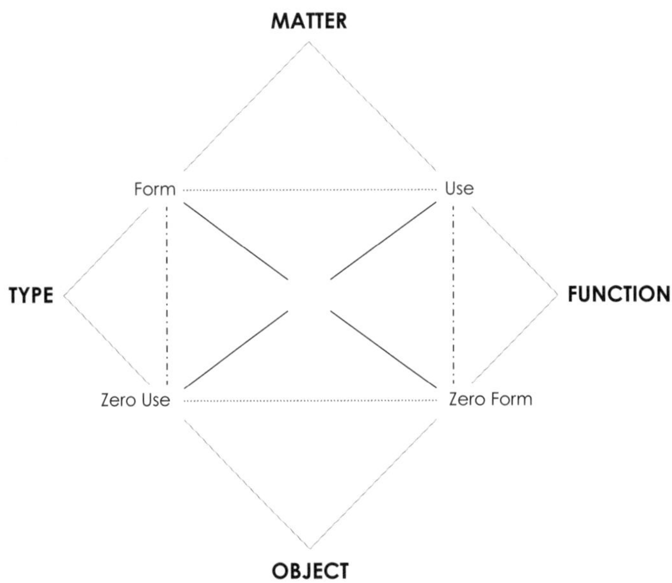

FIGURE 2. THE FOURFOLD DIAGRAM OF THE ARCHITECTURE OF THE CITY

The primary binaries between form, use, zero-form, and zero-use unfold in the diagram to four deeper essences. The first is *matter* and defines what a thing is made of. The second is *type* and defines a topological essence. The third is *function* and defines what a thing can do. The fourth and crucial one that unfolds from the diagram is what I will introduce as the *technical object*.

1.2.1. Matter: Deeper than Form and Use

When we think about matter as what sits deeper than the form and use of buildings, we generally refer to what buildings and cities are made of, their inner materiality. Furthermore, when we think about matter as such, typically we imagine the idea of a hylomorphic process in which matter moves into a form. But we can think of matter as a thermodynamic process as well.[60] Within this framework, cities behave far from equilibrium, the energy inserted into their contained environments giving rise to various new formations, for example as we can see in the way that economic power works as a major driving force of their appearance.

Below I discuss four thinkers whose work is representative of thinking matter as being deeper than the form and use of buildings. While Cerdà investigates the materiality of the city, Reyner Banham sees the city as a collection of ecologies for emerging architectural types, while Jane Jacobs and Sanford Kwinter both share the idea that the city is full of material processes and defines as such a milieu of all its material emergences.

The Empiricist

When Cerdà was asked to design the plan for the extension of Barcelona, he responded by writing one of the most important books on urban design: *The General Theory of Urbanization*.[61] In the book Cerdà systematically transforms the material reality of the city into condensed sets of data. His statistical analysis of the population of the emerging metropolis of Barcelona marks the beginning of scientific research on the material component of the city. Cerdà collected information on anything that the city would allow him to measure empirically, including illness, income, rent, and household expenses as well as geographical and infrastructural capacities.[62] The intention of his work was to consider the city not from the viewpoint of its citizens, but as a material organization of physical entities. To add emphasis to his thesis, Cerdà sought to invent an entire new discipline, which owing to him is today called urbanism.[63] Cerdà's terming was meant to shift away from the word *city* and its reference to citizens:

> since the genuine sense of *urbs* referred principally to the material part of the grouping of buildings, for all matters referring to the inhabitants [the Romans] used the word *civis* (citizen), from which they derived all the terms intended to express things, objects, happenstance, and qualities concerning the dwellers. The word *urbanus* (from *urbe*) referred to matters concerning the material grouping of the urb.[64]

In Cerdà may also be found the beginning of an understanding of (urban) matter as a dynamic environment, going beyond the purely statistical collection of data to include aspects of thermodynamics, such as thinking space not only as expressed by metrical properties but as having intensive properties as well.[65] For example, even while Cerdà still counted cars, he studied the flow of traffic and became aware that the urban space between buildings, the street, is a container in which the flow can expand and contract. A representation of this intersection of the metrical properties of the street and the intensive properties of flows can be seen in one of his diagrams in which he imagines the space of the street expanding when the flow of traffic increases toward the center and contracting when the flow decreases in the direction of the hinterland.

Cerdà's *General Theory* is not only concerned with material aggregates, but also with a modality of abstract operations. In the book Cerdà presents the five bases of urbanization as the necessary apparatus to execute his Extension Plan of Barcelona. The first is the technical base of urbanization, and it provides the metrical components of the "vitality" and "habitability" of the city. The second is the legal base of urbanization,[66] which should regulate the duties between property owner and the administration, especially when it comes to expropriating private land for the subdivision of the "interways."[67] The third is the economic base, which for Cerdà meant "the frank, fair, sincere, clear, intelligible exposition . . . of a complete economic system, thanks to which it is possible easily, equitably, and legally, to find sufficient means and resources to implement the work in question."[68] The fourth is the administrative base, which expresses the rules for the layout and the manner in which they are executed.[69] The fifth and final is the political base of urbanization: without political will, there would be only plans.[70] What Cerdà demonstrates with these five bases for his plan is that within the matter of the city is also embedded the modality of the flow of information through its material organism. Thus the city not only functions as a biopolitical apparatus,[71] but also provides a milieu for its architecture.

The Ecologist

The first thermodynamic thinker in architecture was perhaps Reyner Banham. Banham, the English historian from Norwich, a county town one hundred miles northeast of London that dates to the fifth century, became the preeminent theorist of design in the technological age. Alongside Lewis Mumford,[72] he was one of few theorists of his time to emphasize the idea that modernity is a machine-governed paradigm[73] Banham showed us through his writing the various machines that surround us, including those in which we live.[74] In his fascination for the machine, Banham bore witness to the shift from what he identified as "the first machine age" to "the second machine age." In the first machine age we were surrounded by machines, but in the second machine age we began to more directly control their power.[75] This was due especially to the rise of the affordable car. Instead of one horsepower we suddenly could have a hundred in our hand.[76] Which brings us to LA.

Banham was fascinated with Los Angeles, a city that was built by the first machine age and then exploded and emerged as a metropolis in the second.[77] For his seminal 1971 study of the city, *Los Angeles: The Architecture of Four Ecologies*, Banham had no historical reference for how to study the giant human artifact that is LA. It was clear to him that any historical methodology of reading the city, like its morphological formation over time, was useless. He did not want to end up, he writes, "like Socrates in Paul Valery's Eupalinos, to reject the inscrutable, to hurl the unknown in the ocean."[78] Banham saw the need to invent a method to study LA's fast urban fabric. He specifically wanted to understand what kind of architecture its technological environment produces. Therefore he borrowed a methodology from the life sciences, namely to think in terms of ecology. As Ernst Häckel defined it in the nineteenth century, "by ecology, we mean the whole science of the relations of the organism to the environment including, in the broad sense, all the 'conditions of existence.' . . . The physical and chemical properties of its habitat, the climate (light, warmth, atmospheric conditions of humidity and electricity), the inorganic nutrients, nature of the water and of the soil, etc."[79] While there is no evidence that Banham used this particular definition, it can be traced in his book when he claims, "no city has ever been produced by such an extraordinary mixture of geography, climate, economics, demography, mechanics and culture; nor is it likely that an even remotely similar mixture will ever occur again."[80] Banham shows how this mixture of environmental conditions and technological inventions produces four different ecologies that define L.A.'s new human environments: *Surfurbia, Foothills, The Plains of Id, and Autopia.*

The ecology of Surfurbia[81] is, for Banham, *the* public space of LA, emerging from the unification of the environmental condition of the beaches with the modern technological innovation of plastic foam and fiberglass surfboards. The surfboard is seen as a symbolic new mass-produced artifact,[82] its colorful layouts functioning to produce an environment for an artistic culture and a body lifestyle. The Foothills ecology[83] is located by Banham on the geological edge where the flat surface of the plain hits the hills. In this topographical beauty, the classic neighborhoods like Hollywood, West Hollywood, Beverly Hills, Bel Air, Brentwood, and Pacific Palisades meet the entertainment industry with outdoor theaters like the Hollywood Bowl and the Greek Theater. And where the hills become so steep as to require the innovation of cantilevered framed constructions on posts, LA produces its most sensational buildings, like the famous Chemosphere house designed by John Lautner in 1960.[84] Perhaps it is the ecology of the Plains of Id[85] where the technological and climatic conditions produce the most unique human environment. It is here where the carpark hybridizes with restaurants, banks, cinemas, churches, and anything else we can imagine, such that any experience can be a drive-in event: watch a movie, go to church, eat and drink, and never leave your car.[86] The Plains of Id is where new architectural typologies are born, like Milliron's Department Store designed in 1949 by Victor Gruen Associates.[87] Finally there is Autopia,[88] the highway network floating above the city. "The private car and the public freeway," Banham writes, "together provide an ideal—not to say idealized—version of democratic urban transportation."[89] Here, where the technological innovations of the affordable car and the freeway unite in a new human ecology of personal freedom, Los Angeles is most fully experienced by a door-to-door accessibility without any obstacles in between.

The Materialist

For an explanation of such new forms of urban life and architecture from an explicitly materialist viewpoint within the discipline of architecture, we can look to the writings of Sanford Kwinter. At the opening of an essay called "The Complex and the Singular," when Kwinter asks, "what would it change in our arts, our sciences, and our technics if time were conceived as something *real*?" he directs our attention deeper than the form and use of our lives toward wild matter.[90] Echoing Kubler's *Shape of Time*,[91] Kwinter argues that modernity's various time-based inventions, including the birth of the Cartesian "self," are, in fact, not real. "The forms of time expressed in these seemingly disparate historical developments are not, strictly speaking, 'real' at all," he writes, " but only chimeras of an emerging and very specific instrumental culture; they are, in a word, *abstractions*." Behind these abstractions is matter, wild matter, "a dense evolutionary plasma" as he calls it, similar to how Bruno Latour uses the term to explain what gives genesis to things in our world.[92] What Kwinter presents to us is a Bergsonian idea of the morphogenesis of form, whereby "reality…is a perpetual becoming. It makes or remakes itself, but it is never something made."[93] Kwinter describes how, if we think matter as vibrant plasma, borrowing from thermodynamics, the classical idea of what is possible as opposed to what is real is replaced by the "virtual," which is not yet "actualized."

Perhaps the most visual example of this idea comes in Kwinter's writings on Futurism. In an essay written in 1992 under the title, "Landscapes of Change,"[94] he introduces a thermodynamic idea of matter by presenting the three paintings by Umberto Boccioni that make up his Stati d'animo series: *States of Mind I: The Farewells, States of Mind II: Those Who Go, States of Mind III: Those Who Stay.*

What Kwinter argues is that in these paintings we find not just a representation of three scenes at a railway station, but in fact "three evental complexes, three morphogenetic fields, each arising within the same complex system of real matter and forces." Each painting is defined by a different phase or molecular structure within

FIGURE 3. UMBERTO BOCCIONI, STATES OF MIND: THE FAREWELLS, 1911.

FIGURE 4. UMBERTO BOCCIONI, STATES OF MIND: THOSE WHO GO, 1911.

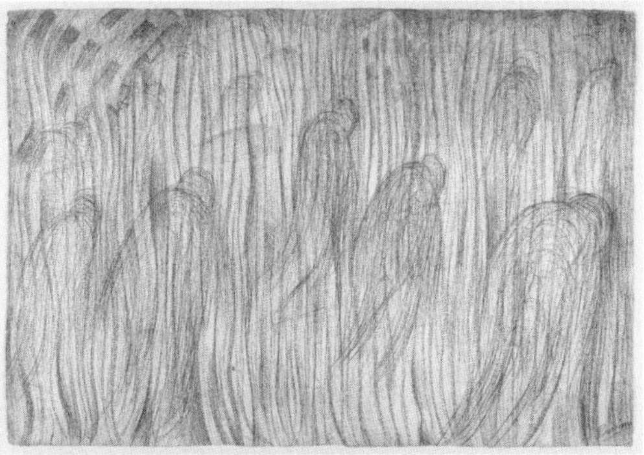

FIGURE 5. UMBERTO BOCCIONI, STATES OF MIND: THOSE WHO STAY, 1911.

thermodynamic processes of matter. The farewell scene expresses the turbulence and molecular aggregation of gases, the departing scene expresses the bifurcation and flow of liquids, and the scene of staying can be seen as the visualization of the inertia and laminarity of solids. What Kwinter introduces to architecture with his essay is the idea that all sorts of forms unfold by event-generating processes in which the smallest molecular parts become reorganized through an epigenetic landscape. One effect of this essay was that suddenly architects tried to understand buildings as outcomes of morphogenetic processes. Still today, every architectural school has more than one course on such a materialist reading into architecture: simulating material behaviors in rigid-body software, aggregation thinking, particle simulations, self-organizing form-finding processes under physical simulation engines, et cetera. What all these techniques have in common is that they understand architecture as based on the agglomeration of smaller parts, like molecules and atoms.

The Economist

There may be no more concrete of an example of what Kwinter describes as morphogenetic processes than Jane Jacobs' ideas about cities.[95] If architecture is the formation of material processes, for Jacobs, economics is the driving force behind this epigenetic landscape.[96] To put this in the terms of thermodynamics, we could say that the city is a container of material substance that is heated by the energy source of capitalism.

Jacobs is mostly known for her stance against the bulldozers of modernism and her defense of old neighborhoods. In the background of all her articulation on these subjects is her belief that, with their vibrant economic forces, "cities are natural generators of diversity and prolific incubators of new enterprises and ideas of all kinds."[97] It is in the relationships between the material composition, the various activities, the functional diversities, the social concentration, and the organization of flows that the production of diversity is stimulated. For Jacobs, then, the task of operating in a city is to actualize the potential of material compounds in this relational space of the metropolis, as in her example of the neighborhood park.[98] For Jacobs a park is not just an empty space, a piece of air, or a real estate feature in the city. For her the neighborhood park is the "bread and butter"[99] of a local community. Parks contain the behavioral processes of the community, and are dependent on a multiplicity of material factors and programmatic principles that drive their success as such. One of these is the diversity of uses and styles, which produce in Jacobs' eyes a multiplicity of moments of occupation and, therefore, a certain kind of safe and diverse space.

As far as what it means to see the city and its architecture as matter, the most succinct writing we have from Jacobs is a chapter of her book *The Death and Life of Great American Cities* titled "The kind of problem a city is."[100] In order to lay out this "problem," she refers to the three stages of scientific thought as defined by Dr. Warren Weavers:

(1) ability to deal with problems of simplicity;
(2) ability to deal with problems of disorganized complexity; and
(3) ability to deal with problems of organized complexity.[101]

Problems of simplicity are a two-variable problems: one quantity depends on another quantity. From the seventeenth to the nineteenth century, these problems predominated ideas for dealing with matter. To relate this to architecture, Ebenezer Howard's Garden City of To-morrow can be seen as addressing a problem of simplicity. Howard took the problem of urbanization and reduced the complexity of the city to an equation between quantities of jobs and quantities of homes. After 1900, the second stage of scientific thought occurred, which concerned problems with billions of variables. An iconic example is the problem of the billiard table, wherein it is unmanageable to handle the complexity of the movement of billiard balls colliding with one another on a table. According to Weavers, such problems of disorganized complexity could only be handled statistically. This was the idea behind the application of statistics by Cerdà for his study of Barcelona. Confronted with the enormous complexity of the new metropolis, he determined himself only able to analyze it statistically. It was in the 1930s, Weavers identifies, when the developments in the life sciences led to the realization of a middle ground, in which problems are neither reducible to two quantities nor encumbered by billions of variables. What emerged was an approach of thinking matter as a problem of organized complexity. In "The kind of problem a city is," Jacobs defines this as "dealing with a sizable number of factors which are interrelated into an organic whole."[102] And thus Jacobs concludes, cities are the kind of problems we find in the life sciences.[103]

1.2.2. Type: Deeper than Form and Zero-Use

The second group of thinkers represented in the fourfold diagram search the city to find something that is deeper than the form of its buildings as well as their zero-use—that is, their virtual, unactualized uses held within. This group's interest is in the architectural forms that are permanent and preexistent in the city. Such a priori forms, they contend, have the capacity to contain any use and program while their layouts provide the topological essence of the actual building itself. This disciplinary approach to the city became known as rationalism.[104] This was a realist movement, which, as expressed in the words of Aldo Rossi, believed that "life is much stronger than architecture."[105] The rationalists argue that behind every architectural object lies a type,[106] an idea, an eidos, or an essence by which all kinds of architecture of the city can be classified. While the topic of typological thinking in architecture is large and much has been written about it, I would like to emphasize that for typologists, the real building does not exist. What is real to them is just the eidos of which the building is a replica.To the rationalist, the type is real while the physical building is just the assemblage of its copies or replicas.

The central argument of the rationalists could be summarized by the claim that without the city[107] there is no type. This crucial shift toward thinking the city as the locus for architecture can be seen as a critique of the empiricism and positivism of modernist city planning of the 1920s and 30s, along with all its utopias.[108] The *rational* generation had to deal with the consequence of those modern utopias and their implications for the reconstruction of cities after World War II. Their critique of these reconstructions, closely linked to the 1968 revolts, declared that architecture was dead.[109] Amidst such crises the new movement found its footing. No more was this true than in Italy, due to the work of Ernesto Rogers and Saverio Muratori,[110] who in the 1950s had started a deep research into the architectural object and its evolution throughout the history of the city.

For the purpose of the argument I present here not the most important typological thinkers, but the most distinguished ones, as previously listed above, who use the idea of a topological essence to explain the formation of the architecture of the city. The four positions I discuss are those of the "real" typologist (Aldo Rossi), the morphologist (Oswald Mathias Ungers), the contextualists (Colin Rowe and Fred Koetter), and the phenomenologist (Christian Norberg-Schulz).[111]

The Typologist

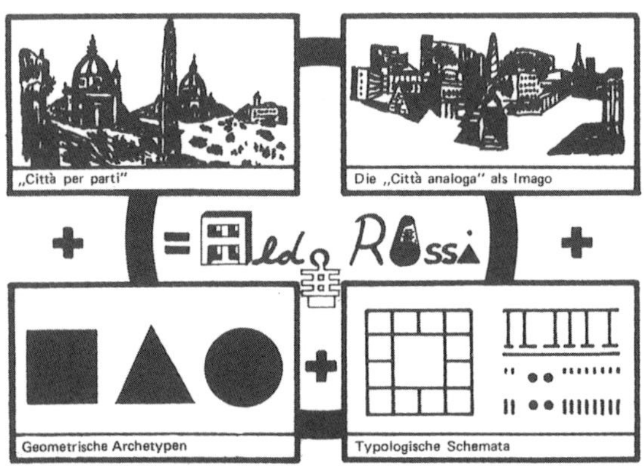

FIGURE 6. THE TYPOLOGICAL DIAGRAM OF ALDO ROSSI

For Aldo Rossi, the city is not made of architecture, the city is architecture.[112] The city, as a human artifact, is not merely the outcome of the construction of buildings over time or an assemblage of some forms. The city is composed of architectural types. In his book *The Architecture of the City*, Rossi argues that the morphology, or urban continuity of a city, may transform and that its buildings may change their function, sometimes radically, but that what stays constant is its formal type. Using examples like the amphitheater in

Nimes, France, in which the form of a Roman theater turned into the plan of a medieval city, or the Palazzo della Ragione in Padua, Italy, which changed program constantly throughout history, Rossi demonstrates that the structure, the built mass of both the theater and the palazzo, stays visible throughout their historical mutations. These structures carry for him a form of permanence. By permanence he means, "not only that one can still experience the form of the past in this monument but that the physical form of the past has assumed different functions and has continued to function."[113] Rossi does not reject function, per se. He just shows how the use of buildings can change over time while its topological structure stays the same. For Rossi, a building can take therefore any number of uses or programs—what I would argue is its zero-use. What he does deny is *functionalism* as it was used by modernist empiricists, who believed that "functions bring form together."[114] Rossi's critique is of what he calls "naive functionalism."[115]

But Rossi's thesis on the city is more than that. Noting that buildings appear throughout history in similar forms but in different shapes and with various functions, he looks for something deeper. This deeper idea, for Rossi, is type. By type, he means that forms have a topological principle, or an organizational essence, that does not change over time. A courtyard, defined as a void space within a building mass, is a topological essence. Rossi gives a beautiful example in his study of the social housing projects of Red Vienna in the 1920s and '30s. While many socialist cities in the early twentieth century, like Amsterdam, Frankfurt, or Tony Garnier's Cité Industrielle, tried to experiment with new building types by means of prefabricated modes of production, Rossi makes visible that the superblocks of Vienna present the constant formal diagram of the courtyard, which did not change throughout history even as its function changed, whether being used as a form for a Roman insula, a cloister in the Middle Ages, a Baroque palace, or a hospital and even horse stables in the Austrian Empire. It always performs the same form—a framed outdoor space surrounded by a wall of spaces. From this typological viewpoint, Rossi sees the city as the production of unchanged topological forms that repeat throughout history regardless of the forces, politics, or regimes shaping the city. What changes are the programs, functions, and events taking place within the forms, but not their type. Rossi's viewpoint of the city as architecture, namely as an assemblage of projects, leads him to conclude that cities like "Athens, Rome, and Paris are the form of their politics, the signs of their collective will."[116]

Finally, it is worth mentioning, especially to distinguish Rossi's position as a rationalist from others like Ungers, that the idea of types as being deeper than form and zero-use, is well visible in his design practice. In his Locomotiva 2 project for Turin, for example, a courtyard building is reduced to the geometric essence of a black square with a white square inside. Since the type was more real than how the form of this typology appeared on a specific urban site, Rossi in fact tried to build the most radical geometric abstraction of the type, to show its pure topological features.

The Morphologist(s)

If, for Rossi, what is real is the type, then for O.M. Ungers it is the model. By model, usually we mean a replica of a typological idea and how it forms the urban fabric—that is, the city's morphology. But that would not fully describe Ungers as a morphologist. In 1977, at the Sommer Akademie for Berlin organized by Cornell University, Ungers, along with Rem Koolhaas [117] and others,[118] formulated a thesis on the "the city within the city." The idea of their project for Berlin was drawn on the background of the declining population of West Berlin in the 1970s. At that time, West Berlin was an island within East Germany and for many the city was anything other than a desirable place to live. Addressing the conditions in big cities in Germany and around the world that had lost population due to "the exodus to suburban areas,"[119] Ungers and Koolhaas formulated an idea to reduce or "weed out"[120] areas of a city that are of low standards, obsolete, empty, or of no architectural value, and to keep areas of the city that contribute to its vitality. They proposed a city of enclaves, or archipelagos, each having a strong identity, like a mini-city.[121] "These enclaves", they write, "would not be selected on the basis of a particular taste or even for their aesthetic qualities, but only for the extent to which they embody, in a pure and legible form, ideas and

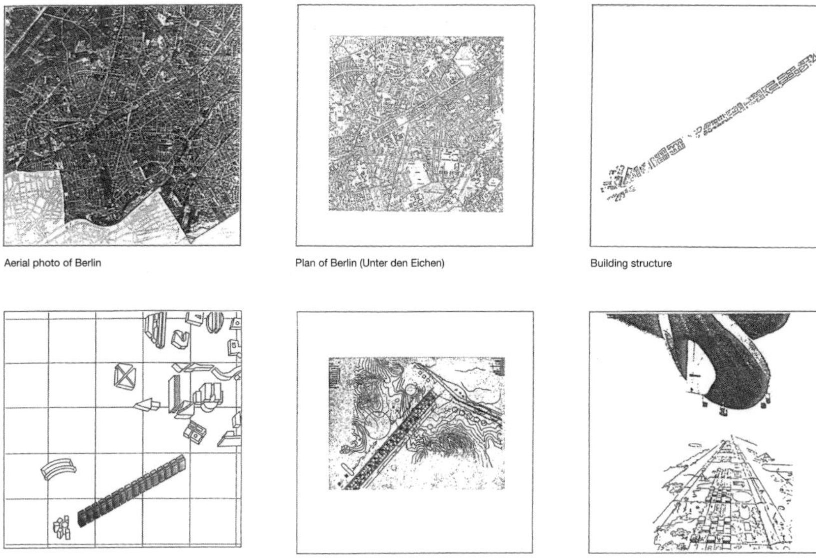

Aerial photo of Berlin — Plan of Berlin (Unter den Eichen) — Building structure

"Unter den Eichen" as a linear city (after the plan for Magnitogorsk) — Magnitogorsk linear city — Aerial view of Magnitogorsk

FIGURE 7. A MORPHOLOGICAL SEQUENCE BY O.M. UNGERS AND PETER RIEMANN

concepts, so that the history of architecture would coincide with the history of ideas once more."[122] The City in the City was born.

Much can and has been said about this project. It is perhaps the first project to consider the city no longer as a continuum. Many see in the archipelago a city of multiplicities and differences,[123] a postmodern condition in which the city has become more and more understood as an entity of multiple identities, what Henri Lefebvre calls *the ensemble of differences.*[124] But here I want to touch on a different aspect of the project, namely that Ungers and Koolhaas wanted to identify "ideas" within the urban morphology.

One of the key drawings illustrating this morphological approach can be found in one of the design studies of Berlin, drawn mainly by Peter Riemann, which were presented at the final exhibition of the Sommer Akademie. These studies, which are described as "morphological sequences"[125] in the 2013 book that presents Ungers's project, *The City in the City: Berlin: A Green Archipelago*,[126] identify the so-called islands of a future Berlin by transforming an image of the city until the formal character of an archipelago of islands emerges. These islands are seen as new models, their form expressing an inner structure, or an organizational principle. Therefore, they can be copied, and more importantly for Ungers and Koolhaas, they can be compared to ideas of the past. Take the island of Unter den Eichen, which can be found in Berlin's Lichterfelde. It is an analog to the linear city plan of Magnitogorsk proposed by the OSA group in 1930. It is a link to the past such as this to which Ungers and Koolhaas refer when they write that the history of architecture should coincide with the history of ideas again. And it is at this point that the use of architecture as a model becomes deeper that just its form or its zero-use. While Koolhaas, as we will see, has never emphasized these morphological principles in his work (perhaps only aside from OMA's project for the Roosevelt Island Housing Competition for New York), Ungers expressly re-originated the idea of the morphological sequence in his design practice. In a later theoretical work, Ungers describes his practice as a morphologist as "conceptualising an unrelated, diverse reality through the use of images, metaphors, analogies, models, signs, symbols and allegories,"[127] toward their becoming new pieces of architecture.

The Contextualists

FIGURE 8. THE TWO UNIVERSALS OF SPACE OF PETER EISENMAN

To understand the formal principles guiding the work of Colin Rowe and Fred Koetter, we can look to a simple diagram published in *Arch+* 37, an issue from 1978 edited by Nikolaus Kuhnert, Werner Wigenfeld and dedicated to the various positions within the rational movement. Juxtaposing two versions of the same figure/ground drawing of an abstract cube, the diagram is meant to represent the "two universals of space" in the work of Peter Eisenman. On the left a black figure—the silhouette of the cube—sits on a white (back)ground, and on the right a white figure—the cube with its edges articulated by line work—sits on a black (back)ground. The notion of these two opposite conditions as two universals of space, and their applicability to the architecture of the city, is revealed in the cover image of Rowe and Koetter's book *Collage City*, in which both conditions of the figure/ground diagram are applied to a plan of the city of Wiesbaden.[128]

FIGURE 9. FIGURE GROUND DIAGRAM OF WIESBADEN, 19TH CENTURY. COVER IMAGE FROM COLLAGE CITY, 1978.

On the left side of the Wiesbaden plan we can identify the idea of the neutrality of space, whereby buildings define a (back) ground for the figurative spaces of the city such as squares and streets. On the right side is the reverse: white figurative buildings float in an empty spatial black (back)ground. What Rowe and Koetter express with this drawing is that all cities are based on the same formal diagram, which is deeper than the individual form or zero-use of any one city. There is just one discrepancy, namely that in premodern or preindustrial cities the figure was space and the ground was architecture, while in the modern city the figure is the architectural object and the ground is the empty space between. These two reciprocal diagrams are described in the book through a comparison of the figurative void space of the Palazzo Uffizi by Vasari and the figurative object of the Unité d'habituation in Marseille by Le Corbusier. The first, an expression of a building for the public, is servant to its outside, while the second, an expression of a machine for living for the modern nuclear family, is servant to its inside. Rowe and Koetter then apply their idea of contextualism to reconcile these two buildings which seem not to share any common ground.[129] "If the Uffizi is Marseilles turned outside in," they write, "or if it is a jelly mould for the Unité, it is also void become figurative, active and positively charged; and, while the effect of Marseilles is to endorse a private and atomized society, the Uffizi is much more completely a 'collective' structure."[130]

What Rowe and Koetter were trying to find was a compositional strategy that could express this double-sidedness of object-building versus figurative-space, of modern and premodern ideologies, a simple formal device to unite these two universalities. What they came up with was the idea of urban poché: "a building itself may become a type of poché."[131] Poché refers literally to the solid black fill in a drawing. For Rowe and Koetter a poché-building acts in a twofold manner. This is best demonstrated by their example of Palazzo Borghese in Rome.[132] The building acts toward the city as a background by "repairing" the fragmented urban fabric and finishing the enclosure of a public space, while at the same time it acts toward its inside as the ground for an internal figurative courtyard. In short: a poché-building can be defined as a space between two figures. In fact, this condition is best visualized at Rome's Palazzo Farnese. The building is the ground to two figural spaces, one to its inside the other to its outside.

With the idea of contextualism, Rowe in particular aimed to critique ideologies of progress as expressed by both the utopian thinkers of the 1960s, like Archigram and Superstudio, and the holistic technocratic planners of postwar Europe.[133] His position was firmly that of the discipline of architecture, as well as a continuation of an aesthetic formalism, for example as formulated by Camillo Sitte.[134] Rowe's formal contextualism, as William Ellis summarizes, "understands change as the incremental, contingent subversion of the status quo (Popper), effected through a discourse between 'ideal' types and 'imperfect' contexts (Trilling)."[135]

The Phenomenologist

If you want to measure the sound waves of a door slam, you have to experience the door slam first.[136] I have not encountered a better description of Husserl's phenomenology than this general summary given by Graham Harman. Husserl notably turned our attention to things, since we have to experience them first before we can analyze them.[137] Phenomenology has since been seen as a critique of science and scientific methods, especially of the empiricism such as that employed by Cerdà, by which entities are understood only as bundles of properties, as just data. But how does this turn to objects have anything to do with type? Simply because of how phenomenology has been appropriated by the discipline of architecture,[138] especially through the work of Christian Norberg-Schulz.

When Norberg-Schulz wrote his book *Genius Loci: Towards a Phenomenology of Architecture*, his intention was to direct the idea of "the phenomenon" of place to one particular object: the landscape, meaning both the material qualities of its substances and how those substances can be translated into architectural form.[139] It seems as if Norberg-Schulz was trying to re-originate Martin Heidegger's essay "Building Dwelling Thinking" literally. After quoting Heidegger's essay "Hebel-Der Hausfreund,"—"the buildings bring the earth as the inhabited landscape close to man, and at the same time place the closeness of neighbourly dwelling under the expanse of the sky,"[140]—Norberg-Schulz himself concludes, "to be able to dwell between heaven and earth, man has to 'understand' these two elements, as well as their interaction."[141] Toward such understanding, he gives a very deliberate description of various landscapes: the romantic landscape of the north of Europe, the cosmic landscape of the desert, the classical landscape of the Greeks and the Romans, and the complex landscape of Central Europe.

Norberg-Schulz argues that the material qualities of the landscape move into architectural form. Take his example of Rome. When we think of Rome[142] we think of rectangular grids, military camps, and a city orchestrated around two main axes: the decumanus maximus and cardo maximus.[143] But how does it come to be, Norberg-Schulz asks, that Rome resists this abstract, geometric, absolute order, and rather comprises an agglomeration of single entities into large clusters?[144] He finds his answer in the geological and volcanic formations of the Roman Campagna. In this rustic landscape of the *forre*, where water has carved deep ravines and cliff walls in the volcanic crust, he sees the birth of Rome's narrow winding streets. And in the volcanic crater in the Alban Hills near the Valle del Sacco, he sees the origins of the Rome's buildings.[145] The hills emerge from the landscape like large urban masses which form a sharp edge on the top. The negative conical void of the crater subtracted from this mass is truncated by the flat surface of the lake inside the crater. There is no wonder how in this natural formation Norberg-Schulz saw the formal diagram of Rome's public buildings like the colosseum: a single gigantic enclosure of a wall architecture with its performative void as a stage inside.

1.2.3. Function: Deeper than Use and Zero-Form

This next group of scholars is united by the idea that what lies deeper than the use and the zero-form of the city and its architecture is their function. Function here does not just mean the use or the program a building is made for or contains. It means what a thing—in our case a building—can do.[146] To paraphrase the famous expression by Hegel in his Lectures on Aesthetics: architecture is not just a shelter, it is the expression of the culture of a nation.[147] Architecture in this example has a particular function for the nation state, besides its particular use and form. Which is to say that architecture is in relationship with much larger modes of operation, or *regimes*, as Félix Guattari calls them—varied "concrete abstractions" that lay behind our buildings and govern the milieus of our cities.[148] These abstract operations are very much the same as what Michel Foucault summarizes as an *apparatus*. An apparatus, as defined by Foucault, is the "heterogeneous ensemble consisting of discourses, institutions, architectural forms, regulatory decisions, laws, administrative measures, scientific statements, philosophical, moral and philanthropic propositions."[149] In his book *Discipline and Punish: The Birth of the Prison*, Foucault illustrates this idea architecturally with the example of the panopticon, in which the building acts as such an apparatus. A more general meaning of what concrete abstraction means to architecture is given by Pier Vittorio Aureli in his essay "Life, Abstracted: Notes on a Floor Plan." He states,

> The drawn plan is thus not just an abstraction of architecture but a concrete abstraction, since together with other forms of architectural notation, the plan translates many determinations—money, measures, code, gender, class, rituals,

beliefs, ideologies, environmental conditions, etc.—into a specific spatial layout. With its conventions of scale, measure, and view, the plan acts—much like money—as a "general equivalent" within which a multitude of determinations coalesce into a measurable "universal" datum.[150]

Many such concrete abstractions have emerged in the city and especially in our working environments, housing, etc., where socioeconomic processes have had the most impact on the architecture of the city.[151] Less than a focus on these regimes per se, what the three thinkers in this section have in common is the understanding that, through the milieu of the city, architecture functions—as objects of communication, events, or social condensers—and can therefore reach far beyond its use and zero-form.

The Semiologists

FIGURE 10. THE DUCK AND THE DECORATED SHED. FROM LEARNING FROM LAS VEGAS, 1972.

As Robert Venturi, Denise Scott-Brown, and Steven Izenour suggest in the subtitle of their book, *Learning from Las Vegas: The Forgotten Symbolism of Architectural Form*, a building can have a function that is much deeper than just the zero-form of a shed and any use or program it could contain. Modernism avoided any reinforcement of the function of buildings through symbolism—the function was in the form. But Venturi, in his book *Complexity and Contraction in Architecture*, had rejected this simplification of modernism, as articulated by Frank Lloyd Wright and Le Corbusier with their search for truths and use of architectural primitives.[153] He instead wanted to include in architecture "the richness and ambiguity of modern experience."[154] It is that richness and ambiguity that Venturi, Scott-Brown, and Izenour saw in the new roadside eclecticism of Las Vegas,[155] the expression of the complexities of their time.

Architecture as a symbol, like billboards along the Strip in Las Vegas, can function as an object of communication. "This architecture of styles and signs is antispatial;" they write, "it is an architecture of communication over space; communication dominates space as an element in the architecture and in the [urban] landscape."[156] I find the title of part two of the book, "Ugly and Ordinary Architecture, or the Decorated Shed," as the more poignant title, since the word *ordinary* indicates that there is an audience to whom these symbols are addressed. This audience is the contemporary urban collective of the United States in the 1960s and '70s. *In Leaning from Las Vegas*, architecture, especially the architecture of the city, becomes a medium and coexists with the history of semiology. Architecture has perhaps always corresponded to symbolic art forms. For Hegel, the purpose of architecture was always to find its meaning in "the external environment. . . . Buildings are mere means which presuppose an external end. Hut and church presuppose residents, people, images of gods, for which they are performed."[157]

Perhaps it was with this context in mind that Charles Jencks wrote *The Language of Post-Modern Architecture*. Indeed, we might easily divide all postmodern architecture into one of the three categories of a sign. As defined by Charles Pierce in his essay "Logic as Semiotic: The Theory of Signs," these categories are symbol, icon, and index.[158] Pierce's definition of symbol is of particular importance here. "A Symbol is a sign which refers to the Object," he writes, "usually an association of general ideas, which operates to cause the Symbol to be interpreted as referring to that Object."[159] He further states, "A symbol is a sign which would lose the character which renders it a sign if there were no interpretant."[160] As such, symbolic architecture needs an audience that can understand its symbols. That audience, as in *Learning from Las Vegas*, is the ordinary people of our cities, us.

What makes *Learning from Las Vegas* significant is how it takes the city of Las Vegas, which at that time nobody thought could belong to the discourse of architecture, and introduces it into the discipline by reading the history of architecture as a medium of communication. In a series of drawings in the book we see how the three elements of symbolic architecture—symbol, word, and architecture—are placed to make a building a medium of communication. Whereas the sign was in the Eastern bazaar the experience of the immediate space or in the church of the middle ages the storybook facade, the car culture of the American city brought about the new form of the decorated shed. The sign, once on the facade, migrated toward the highway and a new threefold architectural type emerged: the sign on the street, the ordinary shed, and the carpark in between. The Strip, through Venturi, Scott-Brown, and Izenour's analysis, becomes the icon of a symbolic architecture in a vast space of speed, in which people are reminded of places they have never been, never will be, but which they include in their ordinary "everyday."[161]

The Situationist[162]

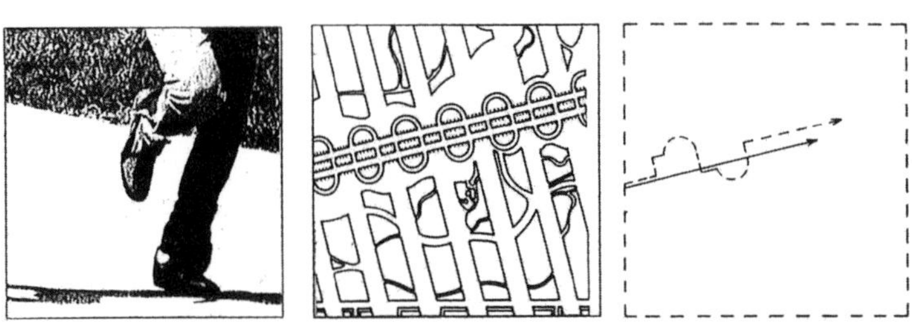

FIGURE 11. THE MURDER AND ITS VICTIM. FROM THE FIRST EPISODE – "THE PARK" – IN THE MANHATTAN TRANSCRIPTS, 1981.

Reading Bernard Tschumi's thesis on the city of New York, The *Manhattan Transcripts*, it is difficult not to imagine that he wrote it as a manifesto in the aftermath of the Situationist movement around 1968 in Paris.

Indeed, as the murderer hunts its victim through the park in one of the *Transcripts'* episodes, the slogan of Guy Debord and Jacques Fillon, "Architecture must become thrilling,"[163] could not be better inscribed in an architectural representation. The Situationist critique of modernism was against its belief in functionalism and technology, specifically as instantiated by Le Corbusier.[164] Just having finished the Unité d'habitation in Marseille in 1952, he could not have given the Situationists a better example for their critique of the what they saw as the reduction of life to its bare biological minimum, putting the nuclear family in a standardized box along a dark corridor. It was in particular the idea, held by Le Corbusier and the modern movement at large, that mankind needed in some way to be fixed, that the Situationists attacked. "With him," Debord writes of Le Corbusier, "moreover any remaining joy will fade. And love-passion-liberty."[165] For Debord and the Situationists, such thinking led to an architecture designed and built to meet just a minimum of life. "We don't just need to demand bread, we need to demand fun", they wrote in 1954.[166] The Situationists found their ideas in the writings of the Dutch cultural historian Johan Huizinga, who in his 1938 book, *Homo Ludens*, brought forward the idea that human culture is based on the idea of play.[167] Huizinga's ideas influenced the Situationists' development of the *derive*,[168] by which they meant to fuse "architecture and play."[169] The derive was central to the Situationist quest to bring back the enjoyment of life, the happiness of the unforeseen, the irrationality within us, and even to reinvent life and push it beyond just our pure biological existence.

For the Situationists, architecture should be used for play. That is the function of architecture, to trigger events that are deeper than a zero-form and its pre-given use or program. In *Manhattan Transcripts*, play is the unpredictability of the event. The architectural narrative, set in New York City, is staged in four episodes: The Park, The Street, The Tower, and The Block. Each episode deviates from the modernist coherence of form and function, replacing it with what Tschumi calls a Space-Event-Movement (S-E-M) model.[171] Events, for Tschumi, "have an independent existence of their own. . . . Events have their own logic, their own momentum."[172] He understands architecture as a non-formal discipline, one that orchestrates sequences of spaces to allow unpredictable events to occur. For example, take his Space-Event-Movement diagram in Episode 4: The Block. Tschumi writes of the diagram:

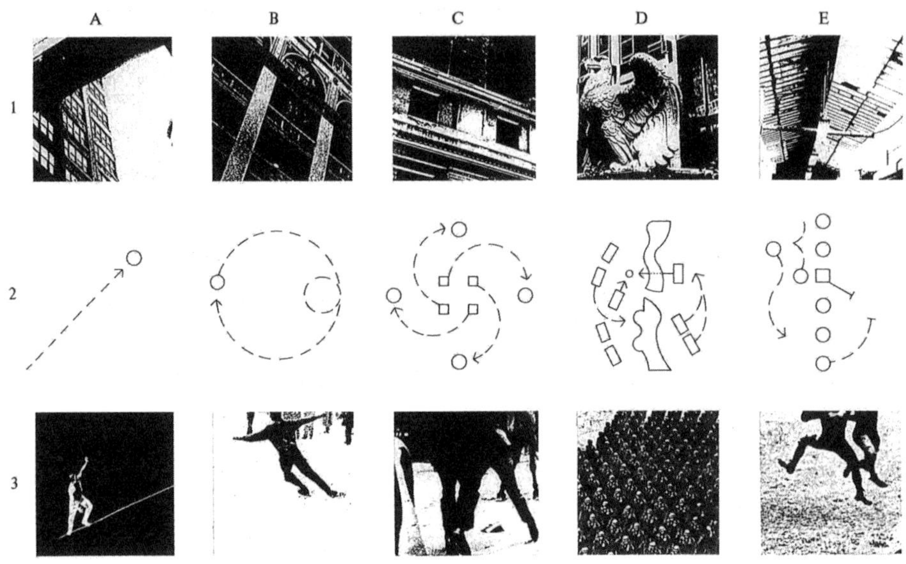

FIGURE 12. OBJECT(SPACES)-MOVEMENT-EVENT. FROM THE FOURTH EPISODE – "THE BLOCK" – IN THE MANHATTAN TRANSCRIPTS, 1981.

> The vertical relation of object [space], movement and event can also be combined, from a "functional" and homogeneous A1, A2, A3, where object-reinforces-movement (which) reinforces-event, or vice versa, in a sort of architectural tautology favored by most functionalist doctrines; or they can, alternatively, be fully disjunctive and heterogeneous, whereby A1, E2, B3 announces that there is no relation whatsoever between form, program and movement. Further scrambling can be applied in the guise of a sort of post-structuralist questioning of the sign, whereby movement, object, and event

become fully interchangeable, an A3, B1, C2 occurrence—where people are walls, where walls dance the tango, and tangos run for office. [173]

It is with this last sequence that I would argue Tschumi gave the discipline of architecture an object-oriented framework avant la lettre.[174]

The Surrealist

If you scroll through the book Delirious New York by Rem Koolhaas, you see fascinating images of early New York alongside stories that you cannot believe even belonging to the city. When I first saw the innocently conventional plan of a high-rise building on page 128 and read in the caption, "Eating oysters with Boxing Gloves naked, on the nth floor," the thesis of the book unfolded for me.

We can easily see the description of the ninth floor in the Downtown Athletic Club as another version of the idea of the event as being deeper then the zero-form and use of a floor plan. But I

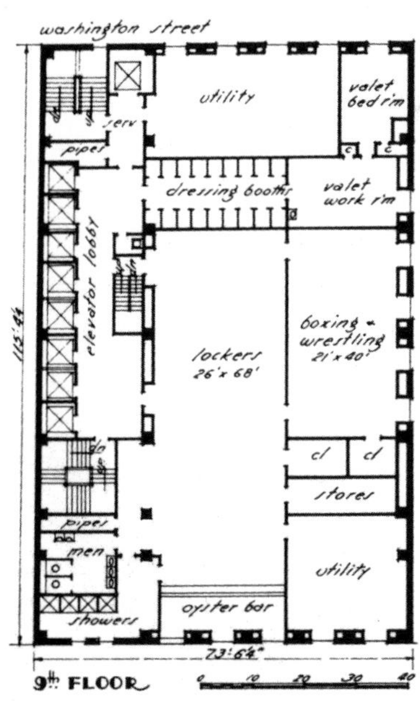

FIGURE 13. "EATING OYSTERS WITH BOXING GLOVES NAKED, ON THE NTH FLOOR." DOWNTOWN ATHLETIC CLUB, PLAN OF 9TH FLOOR, FROM DELIRIOUS NEW YORK, 1978.

would argue that for Koolhaas the city is more than that. The city's function is not just to produce unforeseen events, but in fact is to be an incubator, a social condenser,[175] generated by the irrationalities of the culture of congestion.

When in 1811 the commissioners of New York proposed to lay out a grid onto the island of Manhattan, with its thirteen avenues and 156 streets, the function of the city was defined. This function, for Koolhaas, is not the utilitarian speculation of money, but rather more conceptual: "In spite of its apparent neutrality, it [the grid] implies an intellectual program for the island: in its indifference to topography, to what exists, it claims the superiority of mental construction over reality."[176] Suddenly there was a city with 2028 islands on which anyone could turn such limited territory into "a maximum unit of urbanistic Ego."[177] These "urbanistic egos" very quickly received an architectural thesis and a type from Raymond Hood. As Hood imagined in his text "A City Under a Single Roof," a single syndicate could build a city with all the functions within one single envelope:

> In this plan the whole ground area is free for traffic—for automobiles, pedestrians and parking. The buildings are supported on columns which leave the space beneath them open. Only the stairways and elevator entrances come down to the street level. Below are as many stories of covered garage space as the foundations permit. From the second to the tenth floors are shops, stores and even theatres, served by connecting arcades at every floor. Office space occupies the level from the tenth to the twenty-fifth floors. From the twenty-fifth to the thirty-fifth are clubs, restaurants and hotels. Above that are the apartments.[178]

The architectural prototype for Hood's vision, in the eyes of Koolhaas and his Office for Metropolitan Architecture (OMA), was the hotel, a building that contains all the functions of a city, and in which the inhabitants are temporary occupants. Therefore we find at the end of *Delirious New York* a series of OMA hotel projects, like the Hotel Sphinx by Elia Zenghelis and the Welfare Palace Hotel by Koolhaas and Madelon Vriesendorp.

The image of a city of islands was first theorized by OMA in their drawing of The City of the Captive Globe from 1972, which also appears at the end of Koolhaas's book.[179] This became the image of the postmodern city: a city of ideological and capital egos, one next to the other, unified by a collective ground. This idea of an archipelago, of "cities within cities,"[180] expresses the city's potential as a producer of difference. It is the function of the city once forecasted by Jane Jacobs, when she wrote in *The Death and Life of Great American Cities*, "big cities are natural generator of diversity and prolific incubators of new enterprises and ideas of all kinds."[181] Koolhaas, who was fascinated by the idea of the social condensers of the Russian avant-garde in the 1920s, like Moisei Ginzburg's famous Narkomfin housing project, saw in Manhattan that this incubator of difference does not need to be designed. The invention of new forms of collective daily life, which Ginzberg encouraged through architecture,[182] unfolds naturally within the New York grid.

Koolhaas saw Manhattan's reality emerging without reason. For him Manhattan is a surrealist entity, a product of irrationality enforced by a culture of congestion. So it is no wonder that Koolhaas highlights Salvador Dalí's statement when he arrived on the island: "New York: why, why did you create my statue long ago, long before I was born ... ?"[183] Dalí saw New York as the materialization of his surrealist thesis of the Paranoid Critical Method (PCM). PCM was a psychological therapy turned in the opposite direction. While the paranoid method was used in clinics to simulate normality, Dalí turned it upside down.[184] "As the name suggests," Koolhaas writes,

> Dalí's Paranoid-Critical Method is a sequence of two consecutive but discrete operations: a. the synthetic reproduction of the paranoiac's way of seeing the world in a new light—with its rich harvest of unsuspected correspondences, analogies and patterns; and b. the compression of these gaseous speculations to a critical point where they achieve the density of fact: the critical part of the method consists of the fabrication of objectifying 'souvenirs' of the paranoid tourism.[185]

The paranoid tourist is New York itself, as when Koolhaas describes

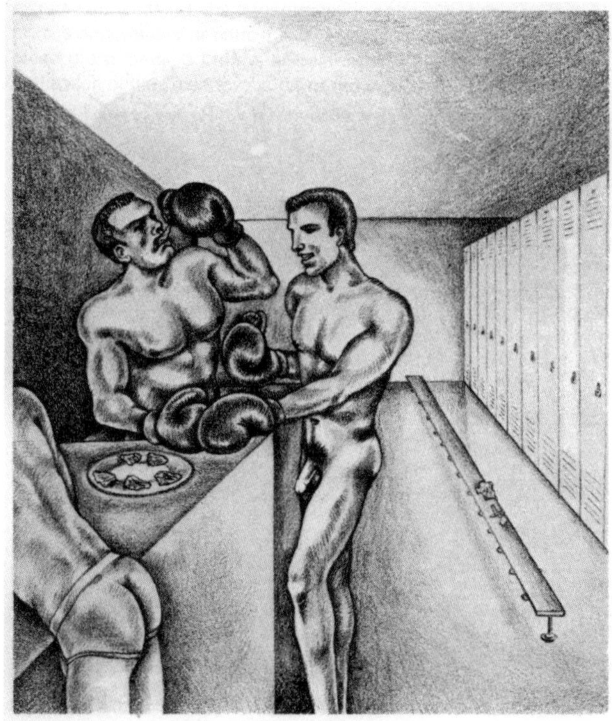

FIGURE 14. A MACHINE FOR METROPOLITAN BACHELORS. FROM DELIRIOUS NEW YORK, 1978.

the ninth floor plan of the Downtown Athletic Club: "It is not a locker room, but an incubator for adults, an instrument that permits the members—too impatient to await the outcome of evolution—to reach new strata of maturity by transforming themselves into new beings, this time according to their individual designs."[186] The Downtown Athletic Club is just one example of New York's PCM as expressed through the bachelor machine, whereby New York is the generator of a new fantasy of mankind, the producer of a new species within the electrified city. Or, as Cynthia Davidson summarizes Koolhaas's description of the bachelor machine, "high rise buildings like the downtown athletic club are the announcement of the split of mankind in two specimens: the metropolitan, who uses the full potential of modernity to achieve the perfection or completeness of the nonexistent, and the rest of all humans."[187]

Summary

Before I introduce the last conceptual category of the fourfold diagram, which I use for the methodology of my reading on the architecture of the city, I want to shortly summarize the three concepts of the diagram thus far. What each has in common with the others is the idea that the city is the milieu for its architecture. Where they differ is what each considers to be deeper than the form and the use of buildings. By form I mean the shape in which things appear to us. By use I mean the programmatic purpose a building fulfills.

Under the category of matter, I have presented positions that consider what a thing is made of as being deeper than its form and use. Materialists argue that behind the formations of the architecture of our cities lies vibrant matter with its energy and thermodynamics. These positions aim for an autonomy of matter. Under the category of type, I have presented positions that consider topological essence as being deeper than form and zero-use. Zero-use, because all typologists share the idea that form can take on any uses—an endless number of possible functions, programs, or activities. These positions aim for an autonomy of type. And under the category of function, I have presented positions that consider what a thing can do as being deeper than its use and zero-form. Zero-form, because all such relationists share the idea that any use can go into any form—an endless number of possible shapes. These positions aim for the autonomy of function.

The remaining concept in the diagram is the idea that objects are deeper that zero-form and zero-use. Which means that what is deeper than both appearance and use is the autonomy of being an object, and specifically the technical object as Simondon describes it: "pluri-functional, overdetermined; in it each structure exists not only as organ, but as body, as milieu, and as ground for other structures."[188]

1.2.4. Object: Deeper than Zero-Form and Zero-Use

The idea that the object might be deeper than the form and use of any architecture is not new to our discipline. In the mid-1970s, at the height of postmodernism, Peter Eisenman introduced the idea of turning our attention toward the object when he wrote that "objects are seen as ideas independent of man."[189] While I completely agree with this statement, the present book diverges from Eisenman's conclusion and its consequential pedagogical model for the discourse of architecture.

The Neo-Formalist

In his 1976 essay, "Post-Functionalism," Eisenman sketches the clear divide within the architectural discourse of postmodernism, between the commitment to the idea of type on one side and the idea of function on the other. The discourse on type, he argues, is placed within a humanist tradition of dialectics: "an oscillation between a concern for internal accommodation—the program and the way it is materialized—and a concern for articulation of ideal themes in form."[190] The idea here is that demands for new programs and functions, as in the nineteenth century in Europe, can only be answered by formal types. Eisenman describes as an example the French hotel, a type often cited by Colin Rowe. The French hotel emerged as a new functional type in the nineteenth century, its internal organization of spaces designed to accommodate new functional demands. Such demands were, in particular, the private compartmentalization of rooms and the improvement of services necessary to accommodate new forms of travel—visitors to the city with shorter stays and more needs. At the same time, this new interiority was "masked by a rigorous, well-proportioned external facade,"[191] in order to act as a recognizable type on its exterior. This approach to architecture sees the answer to new sensibilities in the return to an autonomous disciplinary approach, whereby ideal formal principles, whether proportional systems, the planar sequence of spaces, or a pre-given *parti*[192] as presented in J.N.L. Durand's "Lessons on Architecture," are the solution to the problems of new interior concerns. In this respect all postmodern typologists aim to find the solution in the past, and thus to keep alive a humanist dialect.

After the typological approach in the nineteenth century, Eisenman argues, the increasing complexities of program at the beginning of the twentieth century led to the modernist doctrine of "form follows function." This belief in function became enormously popular in post–World War II England. Referring to "the English Revisionist Functionalism of Reyner Banham, Cedric Price, and Archigram," Eisenman argues, "this neo-functionalist attitude, with its idealization of technology, was invested with the same ethical positivism and aesthetic neutrality of the prewar polemic."[193] What Eisenman argues, in other words, is that this functionalism is not a new position but a continuation of the moral imperative he terms "ethical positivism." He sees the 1960s English avant-garde as an idealist view of reality: "in fact, functionalism is really no more than a late phase of humanism, rather than an alternative to it."[194]

What Eisenman focuses on in his critique is that neither of these architectural approaches incorporate the true sensibility of modernity as it was manifested in other disciplines throughout the nineteenth century, including mathematics, music, painting, literature, film, and photography: "It is displayed in the non-objective abstract painting of Malevich and Mondrian; in the non-narrative, atemporal writing of Joyce and Apollinaire; the atonal and polytonal compositions of Schönberg and Webern; in the non-narrative films off Richter and Eggeling."[195] Stuck in humanist, idealist positions, architectural functionalism lacks what Eisenman calls modernity's "changed mental attitude toward the artifacts of the physical world,"[196] which he describes specifically as the "displacement of man away from the center of his world. He is no longer viewed as an originating agent. Objects are seen as ideas which are independent of man."[197]

In opposition to the humanist dialectic of form and function, Eisenman replaces it with a modernist dialect of form and form.[198] What he means is that there are two formal tendencies. One is to describe architecture as a compositional arrangement of what he calls a "pre-existent geometric or platonic solid."[199] The other is to see "architectural form in an atemporal, decompositional mode, as something simplified from some pre-existent set of non-specific spatial entities. Here, form is understood as a series of fragments—signs without meaning dependent upon and without reference to."[200] What Eisenman proposes with his form/form dialectic is that architecture may be composed by an author through geometric compositions, but at the same time a building exists as a "self-referential sign,"[201] meaning that its sign(s) refer only to the object itself rather than outwardly to some other referent.

Although in his essay Eisenman does not mention Kant's idea of the thing-in-itself,[202] his argument is very close to Kant's, which holds that regardless of how much we humans may try to understand things by the way they appear to us through our senses and our minds, we will never have real access to them. Kant argues that if we strip away the affects of a work of art, as would do the empiricist, and if we further believe the work of art is not reducible to deductive principles of reason, as thought by the rationalist, then what is left is form. A similar notion that formal ideas of objects are embedded in architecture as self-referential signs leads Eisenman to formulate a new kind of formalism in response to the two humanist positions—the rationalists with their type and the positivists with their function.

Eisenman's turn toward objects falls within the tradition of formalism invented by art historians in Germany, Switzerland, and Austria in the late nineteenth and early twentieth centuries. The work of scholars like Heinrich Wölfflin,[203] Adolf von Hildebrandt,[204] Alois Riegl, [205] and many others became especially known in architecture through the work of August Schmarzov[206] and Emil Kaufmann,[207] just to mention a few, and was continued by Rudolf Wittkower and Colin Rowe in England. Through his close formal reading of architecture as a self-referential sign, Eisenman has tried to find ideas that reinforce a discourse on architecture as an autonomous discipline. His particular formalism aims to understand the author through what he calls a "project," which he demonstrates, for example, in his book on Palladio.

In the book, a close reading through formal analysis of the architectural traces within Palladio's villas, Eisenman reveals a hidden project based on the two touching columns in the "portico" of the Palazzo Chiericati in Vicenza.[208] What this little, fragmented self-referential sign indicates is that Palladio's work can be read as the

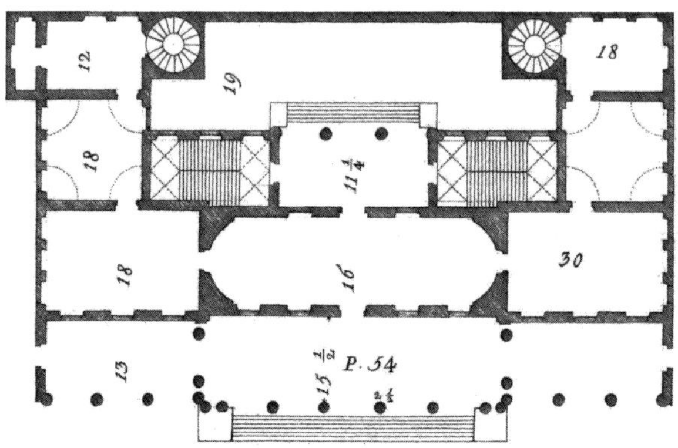

FIGURE 15. ANDREA PALLADIO, PALAZZO CHIERICATI, VICENZA, ITALY, 1550–1680.

construction of a heterogeneous space.[209] The portico, usually placed in the front of villas, as in Villa La Rotonda, is moved into the transition space and unfolds as an intersection, a heterogeneity of two architectural spaces. This idea of spaces in motion allows Eisenman to put forward the argument that, through the work of Palladio we witness the first traces of overcoming the homogeneous space of the Cartesian grid, with its endless expandability and human centricity, and enter into a new area of a topological spaces[210] and differential geometries, as thenceforth has been discussed in architectural discourse up to today.

In "Post-Functionalism," while Eisenman is concerned with the displacement of the human subject from the center of the world as the prime sensibility of modernity, he also turns the formal ideas within objects back to us humans again. But this conclusion could have gone the opposite direction as well. Instead of trying to meet objects with humans, we could ask the question: What if objects meet with other objects? This is the question I ask in this book; one object will be the city, the other will be its architecture.

The Mechanologist

In order to show how those two objects meet, I will use as my methodological approach Simondon's mechanology. In *On the Mode of Existence of Technical Objects*, Simondon formulates a way of seeing machines, tools, factories, and networks as technical objects: units of an emergent-something that bear their own genesis within. He stresses that such machines have their own existence and are not just artificial beings.[211] What guarantees their genesis is that they exchange energy and information among themselves or between themselves and their milieus.[212] Simondon's intention was to change society's perception of man and machine. What he witnessed at the time of his writing in the 1950s was that attitudes toward technical objects were like those toward foreigners or strangers: affected by fear and xenophobia.[213] Technical objects were seen either as primitive tools or as aliens with autonomous existences. For him, these were both fictional constructs based on ignorance and a refusal to accept that technical objects contain a human reality. "This strange or foreign being is still human," he writes, "and a complete culture is one which enables us to discover the foreign or strange as human. Furthermore, the machine is the stranger; it is the stranger inside which something human is locked up, misunderstood, materialised, enslaved, and yet which nevertheless remains human all the same."[214] Machines are us and we are machines.

Through his writings Simondon established a discipline that studies the fundamentals of the evolution of technical objects apart from or in addition to the technical sciences. This is the disciplinary approach of mechanology, in which he distinguishes three kinds of machines: the element, the individual, and the ensemble.[215] The machine as an element is a machine that is not in conflict with mankind, but rather is seen as a fulfillment of human desires. "This is the climate of eighteenth century optimism, which introduces the idea of continuous and indefinite progress, bringing about the constant improvement of man's lot."[216] At the level of the element, a machine becomes an extension, and improvement, of the human body. The machine as an individual, however, is the machine that becomes man's competitor. "Because man had centralized technical individuality within himself at a time when only tools existed; the machine thus takes the place of man because, as tool bearer, man used to do the job the machine now does."[217] This was the age of thermodynamics, the emergence of the factory, the expansion of energy, the conquering of the world by the steam engine, and the era when the machine started to replace us humans as labor. Finally, emerging in the twentieth century is the machine as a technical ensemble, wherein "thermodynamic energeticism is replaced by information theory." The machine as a technical an ensemble we know in the form of our digital networks.

Individuation

The main question that guides Simondon's mechanology is: "How does something appear, how is something capable of becoming individuated, how does a given structure, a given form emerge?"[218] In order to formulate his thesis on the mode of existence of technical objects, Simondon uses a number of ideas that are encapsulated in one main concept: his idea of *individuation*. Individuation is the process by which all technical objects emerge. It defines the genesis of a machine, from the abstract technical object to the concrete. In order for technical objects to individuate, their elements need to be in constant causal exchange of information and energy, such as I described earlier with Simondon's example of the cylinder head and cooling fins.[219] Once an element, an individual, or an ensemble reaches unity, which Simondon refers to as concretization, its individuation is finalized.

Individuation is not limited to the internal parts of machines. It also takes place between technical objects and their milieus. As Simondon writes:

The [technical] object necessitates a certain kind of milieu in

FIGURE 16. CONCRETIZATION OF THE ELECTRONIC TUBE. FROM SIMONDON'S ON THE MODE OF EXISTENCE OF TECHNICAL OBJECTS, 1958.

> order to function properly, because it is energetically coupled to its milieu; this case is almost identical to that of the division into tower and towed; for instance, a clock synchronised by a grid loses all capacity for functioning if it is brought from America to France, because of the different frequency (60 Hertz and 50 Hertz); an electrical motor requires a grid or generator; a synchronous single-phase motor is more finely adapted to a determinate milieu than a universal motor; in this milieu, it functions even better, but outside of this milieu it becomes worthless. [220]

Technical objects individuate therefore in a twofold manner: internally among their individual parts and externally in their relationships to a milieu. Simondon concludes that technical objects are not simply running through a kind of evolution governed by adaptation and headed toward a perfected final result, but rather that concrete technical objects continue to exert influence through exchange of energy and information: "each structure exists not only as organ but as body, as milieu, and as ground for other structures; in this system of compatibility whose systematicity [*systematique*] takes form just as an axiomatic saturates, each element fulfills not only a function in the whole [*ensemble*] but a function of the whole."[221]

Many readers place Simondon and his idea of individuation in the intellectual tradition of materialism, specifically because his concept of emergence, of *becoming something*, was for him an explicit critique of the old idea of hylomorphism.[222] In hylomorphic terms, when we think of how matter meets a form—for example, how wood meets a table, or marble meets Michelangelo's *David*—the form is always seen as the mold, idea, or type[223] into which matter is pressed. Within such thinking, form and matter are seen as abstract entities[224] without any potential for convergence—that is, they do not magnetically pull toward each other or ever unite. Simondon argues against this Aristotelian idea, demonstrating that both matter and form have morphogenetic potential. To illustrate this he gives a beautiful description of the relationship between the clay and the mold that come together to produce a brick, in which the mold affects the formation of the clay while the matter of the clay has an effect on the mold:[225]

> If one takes fine sand that is wet and then one puts it in a brick mould: with the release from the mould, one will obtain a sand heap and not a brick. If one takes clay and then passes it to the rolling mill or the spinneret: one will obtain neither plate nor wire, but an accumulation of broken layers and course cylindrical segments. The clay, conceived as supporting an indefinite plasticity, is the abstract matter. The right-angled parallelepiped, conceived as a brick form, is an abstract form. The concrete brick does not result from the union of the clay's plasticity and the parallelepiped. So that there can be a parallelepipedic brick, a really existing individual, it is necessary that an effective technical operation institutes a mediation between a given clay mass and this notion of the

> parallelepiped. However, the technical operation of molding does not itself suffice. Moreover, it does not institute a direct mediation between a given mass of clay and the abstract form of the parallelepiped; the mediation is prepared by two chains of preliminary operations which make matter and form converge toward a common operation.[226]

This common mediation means that the form of the mold and the matter of the clay translate energy between one another. What Simondon is arguing, then, is that matter and form are not just affected by one another through an outside force, but that there exists a reciprocity of forces within this process of individuation of the brick, "an operation common to and at the same level of existence between matter and form."[227]

The materialist aspect of Simondon's work is significant given how his work has entered the discipline of architecture and urban design. Theorists Sanford Kwinter and Jonathon Crary introduced Simondon to the English-speaking discipline of architecture with their 1992 translation of his essay "The Genesis of the Individual."[228] At the time, architecture was influenced by the philosophical works of Gilles Deleuze,[229] such as *Difference and Repetition or A Thousand Plateaus* with Félix Guattari, for which Simondon's critique of hylomorphism acted as background. Awareness of Simondon's ideas in relationship to Deleuze could be seen especially when the idea of "folding" entered the discourse of architectural design practice.[230] With his reading of the baroque through the idea of *the fold*,[231] Deleuze replaced a hylomorphic reading of art history with "*le pli*" as an abstract machine, in which the modulations of forces of matter through time define an emergence of forms through the infinity of bifurcations within an epigenetic landscape

A similar shift toward understanding urban formations through the modulation of social, political, and other material forces was presented for the first time in *Zone 1/2: The Contemporary City*,[232] the inaugural edition of *Zone* edited by Kwinter and Michel Feher in 1986. It was the eve of globalization, when such materialist viewpoints were used more and more to argue for the emergence of formations within the city through the forces of capitalism, and the wide spread of communication systems triggered some to think no longer in terms of spaces of places but of spaces of flows.[233] It is therefore no surprise that the dominant viewpoint with which Simondon's work was introduced into the discipline emphasized in particular looking at the flow and forces of matter that form the underlying milieus of our cities. Perhaps there is no better example of this than Manuel DeLanda's book *A Thousand Years of Nonlinear History*, in which he charts the emergence of medieval cities from a network of flows of money, goods, and communication, rather than by the conventional viewpoint that cities are formed throughout history by agricultural revolutions. "What matters is not agriculture per se," DeLanda writes,

> but the great increase in the flow of matter-energy through society, as well as the transformations in urban form that this intense flow makes possible. From this point of view cities arise from the flow of matter-energy, but once a town's mineral infrastructure has emerged, it reacts to those flows, creating a new set of constraints that either intensifies or inhibits them.[234]

The influence of materialist readings such as Simondon's work on architectural education in those dawning years of globalization and neoliberalism can be seen in the shift away from semiological and formalist pedagogies toward technological and materialist ones. The dominance of deconstructivism was replaced by a materialist approach.[235]

1.3. Thesis

I have located Simondon's idea of the technical object within the fourfold diagram as being deeper than zero-form or zero-use. Indeed, there exists a technical object that was the origination of all our machines. That object is the city.[236] The city manifested what Lewis Mumford called the *megamachine*.[237] The megamachine emerged out of new forms of human organization in early civilizations, including the specialization of individual craftsmanship, the division of labor, the overproduction of agriculture, the power of kings, and top-down lines of communication, to produce architectural giants that had never existed before, such as the Egyptian pyramids. For Mumford, the megamachine is the archetypical "Big Machine" and itself consists of an ensemble of machines: the political, the economic, the military, and the bureaucratic. The city is our first megamachine.[238]

My thesis is that the city as a technical object acts as a twofold background for all its architecture. First, throughout its history the city has converted its abstract physical elements, as all technical objects do, into concrete architectural formations. Second, the city itself appears throughout its history in various forms, including, as I will chart in this book, the Wall City, the Grid City, the Linear City, the Archipelago City, and the Interior City. Thus, far from being merely a generic background, the megamachine of the city acts at various times and places as a particular milieu for the emergence of its architectural formations, which therefore concretize in specific political, economic, and social modalities.[239]

Throughout this book I will discuss how one object meets another by passing its aesthetic properties of form, shape, function, and material into it, thereby modulating its qualities to ultimately reveal a *new*[240] that did not exist before. In our case, the new emerges as a building, or architecture, originated by a technical object, the city. With its emergence 5000 years ago through the building of a wall to divide a territory between inside and outside, the city established the physical qualities of its technical objectness. Due to the overdetermined quality of all technical objects, the wall thus began a genesis of architecture that continues to flourish. From the initial point of the city establishing the distinction between inside and outside, a speculative history of architecture is possible: If we imagine the formal and functional qualities of the wall changing in one particular way, reducing its physical presence to just a boundary, then a plot of land, or a real estate, is in the making. If, conversely, we imagine a heightening of the wall's formal qualities, intensifying its wall-ness into a full enclosure, then a house, a building, or an interiority is in the making. Through a further process of convergence, the piece of land and the house may fuse together, uniting the house with the piece of land into various architectural formations, from the Roman insula to the courtyard house, and including all kinds of building forms that have appeared in which rooms aggregate within a defined territory. Such a convergence runs on until it reaches it limits, for example in the beginning of the modern metropolis, when the single floor plate could not incorporate newly specified needs and suddenly the high-rise building emerged.

Key to the thesis I want to present here is the idea that all architecture emerges out of the mutation of the physical components of the city. From its origin to today, the city has tuned its object qualities to allow radically new architectural entities, or building types, of all kinds: villas, stoas, basilicas, forums, theaters, monasteries, hotels, housing slabs, high-rise buildings, mat-buildings, megaforms, megastructures, shopping malls, atrium buildings, pencil towers, and up to today's completely new typologies, like the City on a Single Roof. In order to further examine this process and to show that objects, like the city, are deeper than their zero-form and zero-function, I have extracted three key mechanological concepts for my methodology:

- technical objects are *overdetermined*
- technical objects *converge*
- technical objects are *hypertelic*

These three aspects from Simondon's work center on the idea that the genesis of technical objects is fundamentally based on the qualities of technical objects themselves and not caused by flows of energy.

Overdetermination

"A perfected technical object is an individualized technical object in which each structure is pluri-functional, overdetermined,"[241] writes Simondon. For him, this is because technical objects cannot be reduced such that their structure (form) performs a defined corresponding use (function).[242] It follows that they also cannot be reduced in the other direction, such that a particular usage results in a definite corresponding form. As he writes:

> The same result may be obtained from very different functionalities and structures: a steam engine, a gasoline engine, a turbine, and an engine powered by springs or weights are all equally engines, but there is a more genuine analogy between a spring engine and a bow or a cross-bow than between the spring engine and a steam engine; the engine of a pendulum clock is analogous to a winch, while an electric clock is analogous to a door bell or a buzzer.[243]

Technical objects are overdetermined because in their form (structure) lies an endless amount of usages, while at the same time a particular function can be performed throughout a multiplicity of forms.

The fact that technical objects are overdetermined is necessary for their evolution, as this is what enables them to change over time. It is this quality that allows them to evolve and contain an endless amount of zero-forms and zero-functions, because, as Simondon argues, "in any given epoch there is no infinite plurality of possible functional systems; there are far fewer technical species than there are usages to which technical objects are destined."[244] Only an overdetermined technical object allows for change and becoming something else, because there will always be more usages than things.

Convergence

In order for objects to change, or to become something else, objects can converge.[245] What Simondon argues is that objects can converge their functions in a structural unit and at the same time can converge their forms in a structural unit. What this means is that, due to their overdetermination, elements of a technical object have the capacity to converge either their function or their form by exchanging aesthetic properties like shape or material. And not only do functional and formal properties converge, they can even be replaced by each other. "In the technical object there is a reversibility between function and structure; over-determination of the system of structures within the regime of their functioning makes the technical object more concrete by stabilising its functioning without adding a new structure."[246] Simondon demonstrates in his various examples that every new object starts as an abstract form and converts its form and function over time into a new concrete technical object. This is the process he defines this as concretization,[247] which turns technical objects toward new finite specialized entities. This idea is similar to what George Kubler calls the "signals" of the work of art, meaning that artworks send out signals across time that converge with other ideas to generate new prime objects.[248] This quality of convergence is one of the main qualities of technical objects, as Simondon argues: "if technical objects do evolve toward a small number of specific types then this is by virtue of an internal necessity not as a consequence of economic influences or practical requirements; it is not the production-line that produces standardization, but rather intrinsic standardisation that allows for the production-line to exist."[249]

Hypertely

Once a technical object becomes a concrete entity it has the tendency to specialize.[250] Simondon refers to this characteristic tendency as hypertely, which he breaks down into two basic types: "one corresponds to a fine-tuned adaptation to well defined conditions without breaking the technical object up and without a loss of autonomy; the other corresponds to a breaking-up of the technical object, as in the case of the division of a unique primitive being into tower and towed. The first case preserves the autonomy of the object, whereas the second case sacrifices it."[251]

In the first kind of hypertely, the technical object undergoes a change by adapting and specifying its formal, material, and functional properties to extremes within its own autonomy. As we know from the process of concretization, there will always be a loss of information in the elements, due to the overdetermination of every individual element within a technical object. This loss of hidden qualities allows for the technical objects to tune toward specialization. The second kind of hypertely of technical objects splits them apart. Simondon compares it to a kind of parasitism in biology, in which adaption is not related to the internal qualities of an object but to its external ones.[252] This is demonstrated in Simondon's earlier mentioned example of the particular milieu needed for a technical object to exist:

> a clock synchronized by a grid loses all capacity for functioning if it is brought from America to France, because of the different frequency (60 Hertz and 50 Hertz); an electrical motor requires a grid or generator; a synchronous single-phase motor is more finely adapted to a determinate milieu than a universal motor, in this milieu, it functions even better, but outside of this milieu it becomes worthless.[253]

In this second kind of hypertely the technical object loses its autonomy but increases its specificity, since there is no need for permanent convergence between all its parts.

All three qualities of technical objects—overdetermination, convergence, and hypertely—make it possible for technical objects to *tune* other objects, meaning that they allow new objects to emerge from their inherent qualities, which therefore makes these objects deeper than their zero-form and zero-function.

While my interpretation of Simondon's mechanological approach emphasizes the first part of my thesis—the city converts its abstract physical elements into concrete architectural formations—I want to end this first chapter with one more aspect that emphasizes the second part, which is that the city acts as a milieu for architectural formations. As mentioned earlier, for Simondon technical objects are not just individuated bodies but constitute milieus in themselves. They can be seen as grounds[254] for objects to emerge. The city is therefore not just an overdetermined object, but also can be described as the background for all its architecture. Simondon makes this point clear by criticizing the formalist positions of gestalt theory:

> What has escaped the attention of psychologists in their analysis of the inventive imagination aren't the schemas, forms, or operations that stand out as the spontaneously salient and striking elements, but rather the dynamic ground upon which these schemas confront each other and combine, and wherein they participate. Gestalt psychology, while recognizing the function of totalities, attributed force to form; a deeper analysis of the inventive process would no doubt show that what is determinant and plays an energetic role are not forms but that which carries the forms, which is to say their ground; the ground, while perpetually marginal with respect to attention, is what harbors the dynamisms; it is that through which the system of forms exists; forms do not participate in forms, but in the ground, which is the system of all forms or rather the common reservoir of the forms' tendencies, well before they exist separately and constitute themselves as an explicit system. The relation of participation that links forms to ground is a relation that bestrides the present and diffuses an influence of the future onto the present, of the virtual onto the actual. For the ground is the system of virtualities, of potentials, forces that carve out their path, whereas forms are the system of actuality."[255]

This argument addresses the idea that a mechanological approach to the city favors background[256] over foreground, or rather that the foreground is just another actualization of its background. But as I have mentioned above, this background is not neutral and does not define something generic. The city as background is already a specific form with various functional modalities and regimes.

This brings me to the next chapter, in which I present the city as a technical object and describe the various forms, their physical components, and the function of the *ground* of this megamachine, from which all architecture emerges.

[44] Aristotle. *Politics*. Translated by Benjamin Jowett. Batochhe Books Kitchener, 1999, Book I/Part1, 5. Accessed September 24, 2021. https://historyofeconomicthought.mcmaster.ca/aristotle/Politics.pdf

[45] Hannah Arendt footnotes in her quote Augustine *De civitate Dei* xix.2,19. Arendt, Hannah. *The Human Condition: A Study of the Central Dilemmas Facing Modern Man*. Garden City, New York: Doubleday Anchor Books : Doubleday & Company, 1959, 13.

[46] An extended list of the inventions of the city, as found throughout the book *The Culture of Cities* by Lewis Mumford: language, law, politics, culture, capitalism, double-entry bookkeeping, tragedy, drama, gambling, banking, planning, real estate, property, plans, geometry, bureaucracy, processions, tax, credit, tolls, armies, newspaper, luxury, traffic, manners, vulgarism, syphilis, ghettos, sanitation, pimping, pick-pocketing, printing, copying, standardization, privacy, cooperative ownership, grids, psychology, education, child care, healthcare monopolies, cooperations, mobs, society, guilds, institutions, modes of production, the police, magistrates, administration, prostitution, revolutions, proletariats, slums, social division of labor, the stranger, the burgher, the merchant, the craftsman, the robber, the spectator, the shopkeeper, the worker, the employee, the beggar, the flaneur, the thief, the atomic individual. See: Mumford, Lewis. *The Culture of Cities* (1938). San Diego, New York, London: A Harvest/HBJ Book, 1970.

[47] An extended list of buildings produced the city, as found throughout *The Culture of Cities* by Mumford: theater, temple, courthouse, academy, gymnasium, bank, hotel, insula, defensive walls, museum, dome and spire, hospital, bath house, storage building, prison, madhouse, palace, exchequer, casino, school, guild hall, town hall, cathedral, asylum, university, playhouse, shopping mall, burg, fortress, camp, warehouse, concert hall, ballroom, athletic club, gym, bourse, stock exchange, library, archive, quarantine, waste treatment plant, railway station, stadium, parking garage, barracks, arsenal and magazine, storehouse, dock, harbour, airport, urban villa, skyscraper, Unité d'Habitation, Temple of Love, datacenter, market, graveyard, the street, alley, boulevard, piazza, *campo de popolo*, square, hinterland, galleria, passages, garden, theme park, grand avenue, public green, park, pleasure garden, zoological garden, bowling grounds; architectural entities like the flat, the one-room apartment, office space, department store, drawing room, salon, corridor, private toilet, glass window, storage box, dormitory, and even fountain. See: ibid.

[48] Simondon, Gilbert, (2017), 15.

[49] Rossi, Aldo, (1982), 23.

[50] See: Le Corbusier. *The City of To-Morrow and Its Planning*. (First published in 1929 by Parson & Clarke Ltd. New York). New York: Dover Publications, 1987.

[51] See: Wagner, Otto. *Die Groszstadt: eine Studie über diese*. Wien: Anton Schroll, 1911.

[52] See: Garnier, Tony. *Une Cite Industrielle*, Edited by Riccardo Mariani, Rizzoli International Publications, INC. New York, 1990.

[53] See: Cerdà, Ildefons. *General Theory of Urbanization (1867)*. Edited by Vicente Guallart. (Originally published as *Teoria General de La Urbanizacion*, 1867) New York, Barcelona: Actar Publishers & the Institute for Advanced Architecture of Catalonia, 2018.

[54] See the work of Cerdà and Le Corbusier on the city in: Cerdà, Ildefons (1867) and Le Corbusier (1987).

[55] Krauss, Rosalind. "Sculpture in the Expanded Field." October 8 (Spring 1979), 30-44.

[56] Ibid., 30. In a footnote Krauss explains the origin of this diagram, referencing its use in mathematics known as the Klein group as well as its use by structuralists in the human sciences related to Jean Piaget. She describes the dimensions of the diagram as follows:

"1) there are two relationships of pure contradiction which are termed axes (and further differentiated into the *complex axis* and the *neuter axis*) and are designated by the solid arrows (see diagram); 2) there are two relationships of contradiction, expressed as involution, which are called *schemas* and are designated by the double arrows; and 3) there are two relationships of implication which are called *deixes* and are designated by the broken arrows." Ibid., 37. Thus there are six pairs of these various types of binary relationships.

[57] The word "zero" has been used several times before in the history of the arts, including the ZERO art movement in Germany or Barthe's *Writing Degree Zero*, to name just two. See Hillings, Valerie L., Daniel Birnbaum, and Margriet Schavemaker. *ZERO: Countdown to Tomorrow, 1950s - 60s*. 1st Edition. New York: Guggenheim Museum Publications, 2014, and Barthes, Roland. *Writing Degree Zero* (Originally published as *Le Degré Zéro de l'écriture*, 1953). London: Jonathan Cape, 1967.

[58] See: See Harman, Graham. "Zero-Person and the Psyche." In *Mind That Abides: Panpsychism in the New Millennium*, edited by David Skrbina, 253–82. Amsterdam: John Benjamins Publishing, 2009, and Harman, Graham. "Form and its Rivals." SCI-Arc, October 5, 2012. Accessed September 24, 2021. https://www.youtube.com/watch?v=fqLEmyjlq1M.

[59] See: Simondon, Gilbert. *L'individu et sa genèse physico-biologique (L'individuation à la lumière des notions de forme et d'information)*. Presses Universitaires de France - PUF, coll. "Epiméthée," 1964.

[60] See: Prigogine, Ilya. "The Physics of Becoming", Part II in *From Being to Becoming - Time and Complexity in the Physical Sciences*, New York: W.H. Freeman and Company, 1980: 73-150.

[61] See: Soria y Puig, Arturo. *Cerdà: The Five Bases of the General Theory of Urbanization*, Madrid: Electa, 1999.

[62] See: Fig.10 in Ibid., 31.

[63] See: Ibid., 79-94.

[64] See: Ibid., 83.

[65] See DeLanda, Manuel. *Intensive Science and Virtual Philosophy*. London, New York: Continuum, 2002.

[66] See: Soria y Puig, Arturo (1999), 101-406.

[67] Ibid., 229.

[68] Ibid., 374.

[69] Ibid., 408.

[70] See: Rossi, Aldo (1982), 161-163.

[71] See: Wallenstein, Sven-Olov. *Bio-Politics and the Emergence of Modern Architecture*. New York: Princeton Architectural Press, 2009.

[72] See: Mumford, Lewis. *Technics and Civilization*. Originally published 1934. New York: Harcourt, Brace & World, 1963.

[73] See: Banham, Reyner. *Theory and Design in the First Machine Age*. Originally published 1960. London: Architectural Press, 1977.

[74] See: Banham, Reyner. *Architecture of the Well-Tempered Environment*. Revised edition. Chicago: University of Chicago Press, 1984.

[75] Banham, Reyner (1977), 11.

[76] Ibid., 11.

[77] Banham learned to have horsepower in his own hand, as he wrote: "I learned to drive in order to read Los Angeles in the original." In Banham, Reyner. *The Architecture of Four Ecologies*. 1st Edition. London: Allen Lane Penguin Books, 1971, 23.

[78] Ibid., 23. Quote from Valéry, Paul. "Eupalinos or The Architect (1921)." In *Paul Valery: Dialogues*, translated by William Stewart, 56–152. Bollingen Series: 45.4. New York: Pantheon Books, 1956.

[79] Egerton, Frank N. "History of Ecological Sciences, Part 47: Ernst Haeckel's Ecology." *The Bulletin of the Ecological Society of America* 94, no. 3 (2013): 226.

[80] Banham, Reyner (1971), 24.

[81] Ibid., 37.

[82] Ibid., 49.

[83] Ibid., 95.

[84] Fig 42, in Ibid., 105.

[85] Ibid., 161.

[86] See: Banham, Reyner. *Architecture Documentary: Reyner Banham Loves Los Angeles*, 1972. Accessed September 24, 2021. https://www.youtube.com/watch?v=ymg0e4g7qeQ.

[87] See: Hardwick, Jeffrey M. *Mall Maker - Victor Gruen, Architect of an American Dream*. Philadelphia: University of Pennsylvania Press, 2004.

[88] Banham, Reyner (1971), 213.

[89] Ibid., 217.

[90] See: Kwinter Sanford. "The Complex and the Singular." Kwinter, Sanford. *Architectures of Time-Toward a Theory of the Event in Modernist Culture*, Cambridge, Massachussetts, London, England: The MIT Press, 2001, 3-31.

[91] Although Kwinter does not specifically refer to him in his essay, we can hear Kubler talking in the background.

[92] See: Harman, Graham. *Prince of Networks: Bruno Latour and Metaphysics*. Melbourne: re.press, 2009.

[93] Henri Bergson quoted in Kwinter, Sanford. "The Complex and the Singular." In *Architectures of Time-Toward a Theory of the Event in Modernist Culture*, First MIT Press paperback edition, Massachusetts Institute of Technology, (2002), 3.

[94] Kwinter, Sanford. "Landscapes of Change: Boccioni's 'Stati D'animo' as a General Theory of Models." *Assemblage* 19 (1992): 50–65.

[95] See: Jacobs, Jane. *The Economy of Cities*. The Vintage Book edition, New York: Random House,1970 and *The Nature of Economies*. The Modern Library. New York: Random House, 2000.

[96] "Abrams, Charles. "The Economy of Cities by Jane Jacobs." *New York Times*, June 1, 1969, sec. Book Review, BR3.

[97] Jacobs, Jane. *The Death and Life of Great American Cities.* New York: Random House, 1961, 145. This argument is, as we will see later, essential to Rem Koolhaas's understanding of the city as a bachelor machine.

[98] Ibid., 89-140.

[99] Ibid., 91.

[100] Ibid., 428.

[101] Ibid., 429.

[102] Ibid., 432.

[103] Ibid., 429-433.

[104] See: Delevoy, Robert L., Anthony Vidler, Leon Krier, Massimo Scolari, Rita Wolff, Karl Gruber, R. Krier, and Rodrigo Perez De Arca. Rational Architecture. *The Reconstruction of the European City*. Bruxelles: AAM Editions, 1978.

[105] Ibid., 18.

[106] See: Quincy, Quatremère de. "Type." In *Oppositions Reader: Selected Readings from a Journal for Ideas and Criticism in Architecture*, 1973-1984, edited by K. Michael Hays, 616–20. New York: Princeton Architectural Press, 1998, 616.

[107] See: Vidler, Anthony. "The Third Typology." In *Oppositions Reader: Selected Readings from a Journal for Ideas and Criticism in Architecture*, 1973-1984, edited by K. Michael Hays, 13–17. New York: Princeton Architectural Press, 1998.

[108] See: Fishman, Robert. *Urban Utopias in the Twentieth Century, Ebenezer Howard, Frank Lloyd Wright, and Le Corbusier*. Fourth printing. Cambridge, Massachusetts, London, England: The MIT Press, 1991.

[109] See: Kuhnert, Nikolaus, and Marc Fester, eds. "Der Tod in der Architektur". *Arch+*, vol. 37, 1978.

[110] Muratori, Saverio, "Studi per una operante storia urbana di Venezia." Roma: Instituto poligrafico dello Stato, Libreria dello Stato, 1960.

[111] It might be surprising to some within the discipline of architecture that I include Norberg-Schulz here. I will argue that his work is not part of the rationalist movement, but it can be considered to belong to the discourse of typological thinking.

[112] Rossi, Aldo (1982), 21.

[113] Ibid., 59.

[114] Ibid., 46.

[115] Ibid., 46.

[116] Ibid., 162.

[117] Koolhaas wrote the first version of the thesis. See Ungers, O. M, Rem Koolhaas, Peter Riemann, Hans Kollhoff, Arthur Ovaska, Florian Hertweck, Sébastien Marot, and Ungers Archiv für Architekturwissenschaft. *The City in the City: Berlin: A Green Archipelago: A Manifesto (1977).* Zürich: Lars Müller Publishers, 2013, 13.

[118] This is the list of collaborators in one of the first English translations of the text: O.M. Ungers (Berlin, Köln, Ithaca, N.Y.), Rem Koolhaas (London), Peter Riemann (Ithaca N.Y., Berlin) , Hans Kollhoff (Ithaca N.Y., Karlsruhe), Artur Ovaska (Köln, Boston). See Ungers, Oswald M., Rem Koolhaas, Peter Riemann, Hans Kollhoff, and Arthur Ovaska. "Cities within the City. Proposals by the Sommer Akademie for Berlin." *Lotus International* 19, no. L'isolato urbano | The urban block (1978), 82–97.

[119] See: "Thesis 3: The problem of the population drop," in ibid., 84.

[120] Ungers et al. (2013), 15.

[121] Ibid., 15.

[122] Ibid., 15.

[123] See: Koolhaas, Rem, and Zoe Zenghelis. “The City of the Captive Globe (1972).” Edited by Haig Beck. *AD Architectural Design* 47, no. 5 (1977).

[124] Lefebvre, Henri. “Continuities and Discontinuities.” In *Writings on Cities*, translated by Eleonore Kofman and Elizabeth Lebas. Cambridge, Mass, USA: Wiley-Blackwell, 2006, 109.

[125] See the morphological sequence drawings by Peter Riemann in Ungers, Oswald M., et al. (2013), 52-55.

[126] Ibid., 83-130.

[127] Ungers, Oswald M. *Morphologie. City Metaphors*. Köln: Walter König, 1982, 9.

[128] The diagram of Wiesbaden is drawn in reverse in relationship to the drawing of the two universals of space. Still they express the same meaning. In my further explanation I will use the black and white code in reverse: the building is considered to be drawn black and the space between them to be white. This kind of figure/ground representation is commonly used within the discipline of architecture.

[129] Schumacher, Thomas L. “Contextualism: Urban Ideals and Deformations (1971).” In *Theorizing a New Agenda. An Anthology of Architectural Theory 1965-1995:* edited by Kate Nesbitt, 2nd Edition, 294–306. New York: Princeton Architectural Press, 1996.

[130] Rowe, Colin and Fred Koetter. *Collage City*. Cambridge, Massachusetts, and London, England: The MIT Press, 1983, 68.

[131] Ibid., 79.

[132] Ibid., 76.

[133] Ellis, William. “Type and Context in Urbanism: Colin Rowe’s Contextualism.” In *Oppositions Reader: Selected Readings from a Journal for Ideas and Criticism in Architecture, 1973-1984*, edited by K. Michael Hays, 225–52. New York: Princeton Architectural Press, 1998, 228.

[134] Ibid., 228.

[135] Ibid., 228.

[136] Original quote: “If I hear a door slam, then I hear a door slam, and this experience must be described in all its subtlety; to explain this experience with a scientific theory of sound waves and eardrum vibrations is derivative, since all we encounter directly is the experience of the door slamming.” Quote by Graham Harman in Kimbell, Lucy. “The Object Fights Back: An Interview with Graham Harman”. *Design and Culture* 5(1), 2013, 103-117.

[137] See: "What Objects Mean for Architecture", in *Is There an Object Oriented Architecture? Engaging Graham Harman*, edited by Joseph Bedford. London, New York: Bloomsbury Academic, 2020, 23-24.

[138] See: Abraham, Raimund. *[UN]BUILT*. 2nd revised and enlarged edition by Brigitte Groihofer. Wien, New York: Springer, 1996.

[139] “We mean a totality made up of concrete things having material substance, shape, texture and colour. Together these things determine an environmental character, which is the essence of place.” Norberg-Schulz, Christian. *Genius Loci: Towards a Phenomenology of Architecture*. (Originally published as Genius Loci - Paesaggio, Ambience, Architettura, 1979). New York: Academy Editions Ltd, 1980, 6-7.

[140] Ibid., 10. Original German quote by Heidegger: “Die Bauwerke holen erst die Erde als die bewohnte Landschaft in die Nähe des Menschen und stellen zugleich die Nähe des

nachbarlichen Wohnens unter die Weite des Himmels" in Heidegger, Martin. *Hebel - der Hausfreund*. Günter Neske Verlag: Pfullingen, 1957, 18.

[141] Ibid., 23.

[142] Norberg-Schulz, Christian (1980), 138.

[143] Benevolo, Leonardo. *Die Geschichte der Stadt*. 5th Edition. (Originally published as Storia della Città, 1975) Frankfurt am Main: Campus Verlag, 1990, 256.

[144] Norberg-Schulz, Christian (1980), 138.

[145] Ibid., 143.

[146] For the question of "What can architecture do?" see Jeffrey Kipnis's writings on the work of OMA. Kipnis, Jeffrey. *A Question of Qualities: Essays in Architecture*. Edited by Alexander Maymind. New edition. Cambridge, Massachusetts: The MIT Press, 2013.

[147] Original quote: "Man kann in dieser Hinsicht sagen, dass ganze Nationen sich ihre Religion, ihre tiefsten Bedürfnisse nicht anders als bauend oder doch vornehmlich architektonisch auszusprechen gewusst haben". In Hegel, G.W.F. Vorlesung über die Ästhetik. 1835-1838. https://www.lernhelfer.de/sites/default/files/lexicon/pdf/BWS-DEU2-0170-04.pdf: 718.

[148] See: Guattari, Félix. "Regimes, Pathways, Subjects." In *The Guattari Reader - Pierre-Félix Guattari*, edited by Gary Genosko, Cambridge Massachusetts: Blackwell Publishers Inc. 1996. 95-108; and Guattari, Félix. *The Three Ecologies*. Translated by Ian Pindar and Paul Sutton. London, New York: Continuum, 2000.

[149] Foucault, Michel. *Power/Knowledge: Selected Interviews and Other Writings, 1972-1977*. Edited by Colin Gordon. 1st American Edition. New York: Pantheon Books, 1980, 194.

[150] Aureli, Pier Vittorio. "Life, Abstracted: Notes on the Floor Plan." e-flux Architecture, Architecture and Representation, October 2017. Accessed September 24, 2021. https://www.e-flux.com/architecture/representation/159199/life-abstracted-notes-on-the-floor-plan/

[151] A real example of such a concrete abstraction is the office landscape in 1950s Europe. The open-office floor plan, invented by the Quickborner team, changed the working process from a Taylorist, task-driven one into a project-based one. What therefore was needed was not the hierarchical layout of rows of tables to fulfill Fordist working procedures, but an open and flexible layout, whereby the various specific skills and knowledge of employees could become reorganized according to projects. See: Hookway, Branden. *Pandemonium: The Rise of Predatory Locales in the Postwar World*. 1st Edition. Princeton Architectural Press, 2000.

[152] There is perhaps no diagram in the discipline of architecture that more comprehensively reduces all buildings to just two kind of objects, a duck or a decorated shed.

[153] Venturi, Robert (2002), 16.

[154] Ibid., 16.

[155] Venturi, Robert, Denise Scott Brown, and Steven Izenour (1977), 8.

[156] Ibid.

[157] Hegel, Georg Wilhelm Friedrich. *Vorlesungen über die Ästhetik*, 1835-1838, https://www.lernhelfer.de/sites/default/files/lexicon/pdf/BWS-DEU2-0170-04.pdf: 713. My translation.

[158] See: Jencks, Charles. *The Language Of Post-Modern Architecture*. 2nd Edition.

London: Academy Editions, 1978, 49. Jencks does not mention Charles Peirce specifically in his text, but for my further explanation i use his definition.

[159] Peirce, Charles Sanders. "Logic as Semiotic: The Theory of Signs." In *Philosophical Writings of Peirce*, Revised Edition, 98–119. With an Introduction by Justus Buchler. New York: Dover Publications Inc., 1986, 102.

[160] Ibid., 104.

[161] Venturi, Robert, Denise Scott Brown, and Steven Izenour (1977), 53.

[162] Instead of a situationist, I could have easily labeled him a Letterist, or member of the French art movement founded by Guy Debord in 1952. Many of the texts like "Architecture and Play" were written in this period. Concepts like the derive were published first in *Potlatch*, a Letterist magazine. Since Debord joined the Situationist International in 1957, and since books were written about the Situationists and the city, including the Letterists' texts, I use that more unifying label for Tschumi's *Manhattan Transcripts.*

[163] Guy Debord and Jacques Fillion, In McDonough, Tom, ed. *The Situationists and the City: A Reader*. New York: Verso Books, 2009, 46.

[164] See ibid., 32.

[165] Ibid., 35.

[166] Bernstein, Conord, Dahou, Debord, Fillon, Wolman. "The Minimum Life" in *Potlatch* #4, 13 July 1954, translated by Gerardo Denis and Reuben Keehan, Accessed September 24, 2021. https://www.cddc.vt.edu/sionline/presitu/potlatch4.html

[167] See: Huizinga, Johan. *Homo Ludens - A Study of the Play-Element in Culture*. London, Boston and Henley: Routledge & Kegan Paul, 1949.

[168] See: "Architecture and Play", In McDonough, Tom (2009), 46.

[169] Ibid., 46.

[170] Tschumi uses two different words in the *Manhattan Transcripts*. In the diagram he uses the word "object" while in the text he refers to "space."

[171] Tschumi, Bernard. *Architecture and Disjunction*. Cambridge, Massachusetts: The MIT Press, 1996, 162.

[172] Tschumi, Bernard. *The Manhattan Transcripts*. (First published 1981 by Architectural Design). London: Academy Editions, 1994, XXI.

[173] Tschumi, Bernard (1994), 12.

[174] On the potential of metaphor see: Harman Graham. *Object-Oriented Ontology. A New Theory of Everything*. Pelican Books. New York: Penguin Random House, 2018.

[175] The "social condenser" was an architectural tool used by constructivist architects like Moisei Ginzburg and Ivan Leonidov to construct new kinds of communal life in the years after the Russian Revolution. "The need for a social-collective life, for the emancipation of women from the unnecessary household burdens—this is a manifestation of the will of the architect to take her place in the building of a new life, in the creation of a new organism—the Social Condenser of our time." Ginzburg 1927 "We need not merely new clubs, but clubs—inventions, insofar as these are not clubs for playing whist and dancing the quadrille, but clubs designed for brand new, previously unheard-of human relations, new 'Social Condensers' of our time." Leonidov 1928. In Murawski, Michał. "The Social Condenser: A Century of Revolution through Architecture, 1917–2017." *The Journal of Architecture* 22, no. 3 (April 3, 2017), 369–71.

[176] Koolhaas, Rem. *Delirious New York. A Retroactive Manifesto for Manhattan*. New York:

Oxford University Press, 1978, 15.

[177] Ibid., 15.

[178] Hood, Raymond M. "A City under a Single Roof." In *The Sphere and the Labyrinth: Avant-Gardes and Architecture from Piranesi to the 1970s*, by Tafuri, Manfredo, translated by Pellegrino D'Acierno and Robert Connolly. Cambridge, Massachusetts: The MIT Press, 1987, 193.

[179] The drawing comprises fourteen individual projects: Religion in ruins; A subconscious portrait of O.M. Unger's architecture; Two towers of Le Corbusier's Plan Voisin in the grass; The Cabinet of Dr. Caligari; The Waldorf-Astoria Hotel; Homage to Mies; Dalì's Architectural Angelus, 1933; Ivan Leonidov's Ministry of Heavy Industry; El Lissitsky's Lenin's stand; Outdoor indoor; Malevich's Architekton; RCA Building, Rockefeller Center, 1933; Homage to Superstudio; Trylon and Perisfera by Wallace Harrison." Koolhaas, Rem, and Zoe Zenghelis, (1977), 331-332.

[180] See: Ungers, Oswald M., Rem Koolhaas, Peter Riemann, Hans Kollhoff, and Arthur Ovaska (1978), 82–97.

[181] Jacobs, Jane (1961), 145.

[182] See: Wolfe, Ross. "Dom Narkomfin in Moscow, 1929 - Moisei Ginzburg & Ignatii Milinis' Iconic Constructivist Masterpiece." The Charnel-House, 2013. Accessed September 24, 2021. https://thecharnelhouse.org/2013/10/05/dom-narkomfin-in-moscow-1929/.

[183] Koolhaas includes a footnote with this quote from Dalí: "Salvador Dalí, 'New York Salutes Me!' Spain, May 23, 1941." In Koolhaas, Rem (1978), 220.

[184] Ibid., 201.

[185] Ibid., 202.

[186] Koolhaas, Rem (1978), 133.

[187] The quote used here was rephrased by Davidson while editing a text by me. See Trummer, Peter, "The City in the Age of Hyperobjects," in: *Log*, No. 45 (New York: Anyone Corporation 2019), 35-42. The original text by Koolhaas is as follows: "Skyscrapers such as the Club announce the imminent segregation of mankind into two tribes: one of *Metropolitanites*—literally self-made—who have used the full potential of all the *apparatus of Modernity* to reach unique levels of perfection, the second simply the remainder of the traditional human race." In Koolhaas, Rem (1978), 133.

[188] Simondon, Gilbert (2017), xv.

[189] Eisenman, Peter. "Post-Functionalism." In *Oppositions Reader: Selected Readings from a Journal for Ideas and Criticism in Architecture, 1973-1984*, edited by K. Michael Hays, 9–12. New York: Princeton Architectural Press, 1998, 11.

[190] Ibid., 9.

[191] Ibid., 9.

[192] An architectural parti can be generally understood as the underlying formal diagram of the plan or a section of a building. See: https://en.wikipedia.org/wiki/Parti_(architecture)

[193] Eisenman, Peter, (1998), 10.

[194] Ibid., 10.

[195] Ibid., 11.

[196] Ibid., 11.

[197] Ibid., 11.

[198] Ibid., 12.

[199] Ibid., 12.

[200] Ibid., 12.

[201] Eisenman, Peter. “Aspects of Modernism: Maison Dom-Ino and the Self-Referential Sign.” In *Eisenman Inside Out: Selected Writings, 1963-1988*, 111–20. New Haven, CT: Yale University Press, 2004, 111.

[202] “And we indeed, rightly considering objects of sense as mere appearances, confess thereby that they are based upon a thing in itself, though we know not this thing in its internal constitution, but only know its appearances, viz., the way in which our senses are affected by this unknown something. The understanding therefore, by assuming appearances, grants the existence of things in themselves also, and so far we may say, that the representation of such things as form the basis of phenomena, consequently of mere creations of the understanding, is not only admissible, but unavoidable.” In §32 of Kant, Immanuel. “Prolegomena to Any Future Metaphysics (1783).” Translated by Paul Carus. The Project Gutenberg E-Book, 2016. Accessed September 24, 2021. https://www.gutenberg.org/files/52821/52821-h/52821-h.htm.

[203] See: Wölfflin, Heinrich. *Kunstgeschichtliche Grundbegriffe: Das Problem der Stilentwicklung in der neueren Kunst*. 19th Edition. Basel: Schwabe Verlagsgruppe AG Schwabe Verlag, 2004.

[204] See: Hildebrand, Adolf von. *Das Problem der Form in der Bildenden Kunst*. Straßburg: Heitz & Mündel, 1893

[205] See: Riegl, Alois. *Spätrömische Kunst-Industrie*. (Originally published 1901). Bremen: Unikum Verlag, 2011.

[206] Schmarsow, August. “Das Wesen der Architektonischen Schöpfung (1894).” In *Quellentexte zur Architekturtheorie*, edited by Fritz Neumeyer. München: Prestel, 2002.

[207] Kaufmann, Emil. *Von Ledoux bis Le Corbusier - Ursprung und Entwicklung der Autonomen Architektur*. (Unchanged reprint of the 1933 Edition published in Verlag Dr. Rolf Passer, Wien/Leipzig). Stuttgart: Verlag Gerd Hatje, 1985.

[208] Eisenman, Peter, with Matt Roman. *Palladio Virtuel*. New Haven/London: Yale University Press, 2015, 11.

[209] Ibid., 11.

[210] Ibid., 14.

[211] Simondon, Gilbert (2017), 16.

[212] Ibid., 54.

[213] Ibid., 10.

[214] Ibid., 10.

[215] Ibid., 52.

[216] Ibid., 21.

[217] Ibid., 21.

[218] Ibid., xi.

[219] Ibid., 28.

[220] Ibid., 54.

[221] Ibid., xvi.

[222] See: Simondon, Gilbert (1964).

[223] See: de Quincy, Quatremère. "Type." In *Oppositions Reader: Selected Readings from a Journal for Ideas and Criticism in Architecture, 1973-1984*, edited by K. Michael Hays, 616–20. New York: Princeton Architectural Press, 1998. De Quincy used the idea of the mold to explain his idea of type.

[224] See: Simondon, Gilbert (1964), 2.

[225] Ibid., 2.

[226] Ibid., 2-3.

[227] Ibid., 5.

[228] See: Simondon, Gilbert. "The Genesis of the Individual." In *Incorporations*, edited by Jonathan Crary and Sanford Kwinter, translated by Mark Cohen and Sanford Kwinter, 297–319. New York, NY: Zone Books, 1992.

[229] See: Deleuze, Gilles. *The Fold: Leibniz and the Baroque*. Foreword and translation by Tom Conley. London: The Athlone Press, 1993.

[230] See: Lynn, Greg, ed. *Folding in Architecture: Revised Edition*. 1st Edition. (Originally published in 1993). Hoboken, New Jersey: John Wiley & Sons, 2004.

[231] "And when the folds of clothing spill out of painting, it is Bernini who endows them with sublime form in sculpture, when marble seizes and bears to infinity folds that cannot be explained by the body but by a spiritual adventure that can set the body ablaze. His is not an art of structures but of textures, as seen in the twenty marble forms he fashions." In Deleuze, Gilles (1993), 121-122.

[232] See: Feher, Michel, Sanford Kwinter, and Jonathan Crary, eds. *Zone 1/2: The Contemporary City*. 1st Edition. New York: Zone Books, 1985.

[233] Castells, Manuel. *The Rise of the Network Society*. Reprint of the 1996 First Edition. Chichester: Wiley-Blackwell, 1997, 407.

[234] DeLanda, Manuel. *A thousand years of non-linear history*. Edited by Jonathan Crary, Sanford Kwinter, and Bruce Mau. New York: Swerve Editions, 2000, 28.

[235] Kwinter, Sanford. "The Genius of Matter: Eisenman's Cincinnati Project." In *Re:working Eisenman*. London: Academy Editions, Ernst & Sohn, 1993, 90-97. And. "The Eisenman Wave." In *The master Architect Series: Eisenman Architects, Selected and Current Works*. Mulgrave, Victioria: The Images Publishing, 1995, 7-15.

[236] Guattari, Félix. "Über Maschinen." In *Ästhetik und Maschinismus: Texte zu und von Félix Guattari*, edited by Henning Schmidgen, 115–32. Berlin: Merve Verlag, 1995, 119.

[237] See: Mumford, Lewis. "The Design of the Megamachine." In *The Myth of the Machine: Technics and Human Development*, 188–211. San Diego, New York London: A Harvest/ HBJ Book, 1967.

[238] Simondon hints at this fact when he explains the technical object in comparison to mankind: "the pieces of the engine are like people who work together, each in their own turn, but who do not know one another. Moreover, this is precisely how the functioning of thermal engines is explained to students in the classroom, each piece being isolated from the others like the lines that represent it on the blackboard in geometric space, *partes extra partes*." In Simondon, Gilbert (2017), 27.

[239] Here I draw on Graham Harman's "guerrilla metaphysics," which holds that any two objects always meet within a third. "If two objects can interact at all, they must both already be suspended in the same ether, linked by the vicarious cause of a larger

object that they themselves both use as a base or alibi for their relationship. Simply put, causation requires a prior shared medium, since otherwise it would be impossible. This medium cannot simply be their own relationship, because this would result in tautology-we would be saying that entities can relate because they relate. Instead, objects must both belong to the same medium, have some sort of fascinated side-by-side relationship, before they enter into total vicarious relation and fuse directly into one another." In Harman, Graham. *Guerrilla Metaphysics: Phenomenology and the Carpentry of Things*. Chicago: Open Court, 2005, 189.

240 By *new* I refer to Kubler's idea of the prime object. Applying this idea to architecture, the new indicates topological changes within buildings. These changes are mainly recognizable in organization of spaces in plan and section or volumetrically. I will focus on such new architectural ensembles, which are driven by the elements of the city.

241 Simondon, Gilbert (2017),15.

242 See: "Chapter One: Genesis of the Technical Object: The Process of Concretization," ibid. 25-51.

243 Ibid., 25.

244 Ibid., 28.

245 Ibid., 26.

246 Ibid., 35.

247 Ibid., 20.

248 "In this category we are interested less in the natural signals of physical and biological science, than in the artifact signals of history, and among artifact signals we are concerned less with documents and instruments than with the least useful of artifacts—works of art." Kubler, George. *The Shape of Time. Remarks on the History of Things*. New Haven/London: Yale University Press, 1962, 20.

249 Simondon, Gilbert (2017), 29.

250 Simondon gives a detailed description of what he means by "overspecialization" when he writes: "a tire that can be used well in a cold climate may not be appropriate for a hot climate and vice versa; a plane made for high altitudes may be disadvantaged by the need to function temporarily at low altitudes, in particular for landing and takeoff. The jet engine, which is superior in very high altitudes to a propeller engine precisely because of its principle of propulsion, becomes difficult to use at a very low altitude; the great speed attained by a jet engine becomes a rather paralyzing aspect when it needs to touch ground; the reduction of wing area, which comes with the use of a jet engine, requires landing at a high speed (almost the cruising speed of a propeller aircraft), thus requiring a very long landing strip." In ibid., 53.

251 Ibid., 54.

252 Ibid., 53-54.

253 Ibid., 54.

254 See: "Technical invention: ground and form in the living and in inventive thought," In Ibid., 59-62.

255 Ibid., 60-61.

256 In a lecture for an architectural audience at SCI-Arc, Graham Harman presents a series of "thinkers of the background," including Martin Heidegger, Sigmund Freud, Clement Greenberg, and Marshal McLuhan. I consider Simondon as well to be a thinker of the background, and this book should be seen as a contribution to thinking the city

as the background for its architecture, wherein the background is not just a milieu or a form, but a technical being. See: “Form and Its Rivals.” Lecture by Harman Graham, SCI-Arc, October 5, 2012. Accessed September 24, 2021. https://www.youtube.com/watch?v=fqLEmyjlq1M.

Chapter 2: The City as a Technical Being

2.1. The Mousgoum Village

Every time I open my copy of Leonardo Benevolo's book *The History of the City* I pause on page seventeen, at an incredible drawing of a traditional Mousgoum village located in today's Cameroon.[257] It has always grabbed my attention, but for a long time I could not figure out what specifically affected me. I had no idea how to read the drawing beyond its immediate visual impact. It shows a plan of a wall in the shape of a near-perfect circle. But this is not just a wall. It is made up of rooms, or houses, with similar circular shapes as the larger wall itself. Within the enclosed space of the big circle float other rooms, two of them touching like magnets. The interiors are open, divided in half by a single wall, or have curved pocket walls attached to the outer walls, which generate a kind of concave-convex interiority. Each enclosed space seems to belong to only one person, contain only one function, or store only one thing.[258] The open space within the wall of the village has peculiar characteristics as well: while most of it is hatched with a different density of points, there are two distinct white figures on the ground. One is rectangular—not a perfect geometry like the circular shape of the rooms but having clearly four corners—and appears repeatedly throughout the open space. The other white figure has no particular shape. It meanders through the territory, connecting the entrance in the larger, primary wall with several of the openings of the individual rooms or houses. There are other details that I have always found strange. For example, the bracket-like lines in front of each house—a room in the making or a space attached to the house? I had no idea. I could not access this drawing, but at the same time I was attracted by its affect. Now, thirty years after I first encountered it, this drawing would be the single most important image if I were to reduce the thesis of this book to just one. There is no better drawing I have found to show the physical elements of the city in the process of concretization. Indeed, this drawing shows an early stage of the city, a precursor of all urban technical objects wherein overdetermined physical elements will converge into myriad new forms of architecture.

Mechanization of Life

Benevolo placed the drawing of the Mousgoum village[259] in his chapter on the Neolithic period, as an example of our first urban settlement forms. As implied in the name of the period, the Neolithic was a new time. It was the time when the ice that had crusted over much of the planet slowly receded and the earth as a new material entity emerged. It was perhaps the most exiting period of human evolution, to read Lewis Mumford's description of this age of erotic exuberance.[260] Life was full of discovery. Everyday a new plant was found, tasted, or cooked. We even started to play with them genetically. The Neolithic was the beginning of our domestication[261] and with it began the mechanization of our life.

With the end of the Ice Age, humans no longer had to occupy natural caves and exclusively hunt and gather food. The Neolithic period saw humans give form to their environments by means of agricultural plantation and the construction of houses and buildings for storage and other uses. As Mumford writes,

> the initial stages of domestication, though slow if one judges them by the pace of the last three centuries of mechanizations, were full of adventures adaptations and useful surprise. Each new addition to the diet, each increase in the size and quality of fruit, each new fiber that proved useful for spinning into thread and weaving, each new medicinal plant that dulled pain, healed wounds, or overcame fatigue, must have given

> far more genuine reason to rejoice and marvel than the latest motorcar or rocket model.[262]

Perhaps today we would say that life then was more exciting than Minecraft, where now we create the evolution of worlds digitally. It was a fruitful period, not just for plants but for humans as well. The Neolithic saw an erotic and sexual revolution in addition to a cultural revolution.[263] As Mumford explains in his book *The Myth of the Machine*,[264] this domestication affected the way we live, especially our daily routines, by way of the the crystallization of a new human trait of "industriousness," which he defines as "the capacity for assiduous application to a single task, sometimes carried over years and generations."[265] The agricultural revolution forced the first known specialization of work and dependence of an economy on the productivity of plants. Corn was money.

The expression of life in the archaic village culture became the dominating figure[266] of our existence, organized according to various forms of repetition: yearly sequences, seasonal cycles, daily routines. The process of growth and harvest governed our being. Life became mechanical. The wilderness of nature became controlled. As Mumford writes, "getting a living ceased to be an adventure: it fell into a settled routine."[267] But, he argues further, our daily routines had an even deeper origin than the domestication of agricultural production and the resultant settlement pattern of the village. That deeper origin was "the performance of a ritual."[268] In the ritual we find the first practices of repetitive behaviors in larger collectives. What makes the ritual specific, for Mumford, is that it is shared by communal groups, whereby it can be practiced with different members of other groups and people.[269] This means that rituals can be reproduced even when members change. The ritual aims for sequences, repetition, and order. It is thus one of the first and most essential forms of mechanization. Here we can recognize the idea of the technical object. Every member of the ritual knows their role and executes a specific task, without the necessity to know any other part in the act of the ritual. Mumford asserts that "one finds in the neolithic economy the beginning of a well-defined order; and this orderliness, this industriousness, transposes into physical structures much that had so long been confined to ritual and oral traditions."[270] We can conclude that the beginning of the city, as a technical object, is based in the village.

If we now look into the physical organization of this technical object, we might find in a hypothetical drawing of this Neolithic village not only a clearly legible manifestation of the mechanization of our human existence, but also one of the first models of our future megamachines. As Mumford suggests to us, the city may be just the last stage of such machines, its appearance as a technical object the outcome of a long process of individuation: "Before the city, there was the hamlet and the shrine and the village; before the village, the camp, the cache, the cave, the cairn; and before all these there was a disposition to social life that man plainly shares with many other animal species."[271]

A Speculative Process of Concretization

If the mechanization of life can be considered as the milieu of a village or city, then those mechanisms are the mediator between its various parts. The urban formations that compose the psychical background of this milieu carry many hidden qualities. Indeed, what we learn from Simondon is that technical objects are not just ensembles of organs but also are individuated, and thus have the capacity to act as the ground for new structures to emerge.[272]

In searching for a case study with which to visualize particular moments of mutation of the physical elements of a village toward new architectural and urban configurations as they appear in our cities, I hoped to find an example in which the elements of a city—walls, streets, houses, blocks, public space, and pieces of land—were present, yet appear in an abstract, not yet unified, stage, in order to analyze its process of concretization. I remembered the drawing in Benevolo's book. And after searching for the plan, I found not only the version that was used by Benevolo,[273] but also a scanned reproduction.[274] Before seeing this scanned image, either due to my unawareness at the time or because of the low resolution of the reprint of the drawing in Benevolo's book, I had not been aware of how the village was organized in any detail. What especially comes to the foreground in the scan I found is not only the figuration of the buildings, but also the origination of the territory within the village, in particular its subdivision.

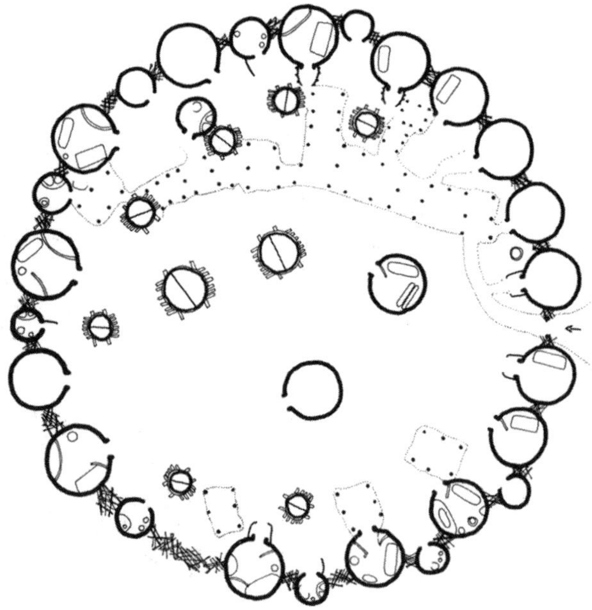

FIGURE 17. PLAN OF A HOMESTEAD IN A MOUSGOUM VILLAGE

Looking at the drawing today, with better trained architectural eyes, I see in it a city in the process of concretization, whereby its physical elements converge to produce new entities with qualities that did not exist before. It thus affords a clear means of visualizing a speculative process of concretization by which the village concretizes new urban architectural objects.

A Village: In Which a Wilderness Converges with a Wall

Where a wall meets a wilderness, it defines two sides: What is inside and what is outside. The wall cuts out an object from the world. In this case, that object is a circular, enclosed village. Extracted from a vast undefined wilderness, the village creates a world in itself, the world of the mechanized life of the village, or later, the city. From this fundamental convergence, two totally new and essential elements of any future city emerge.

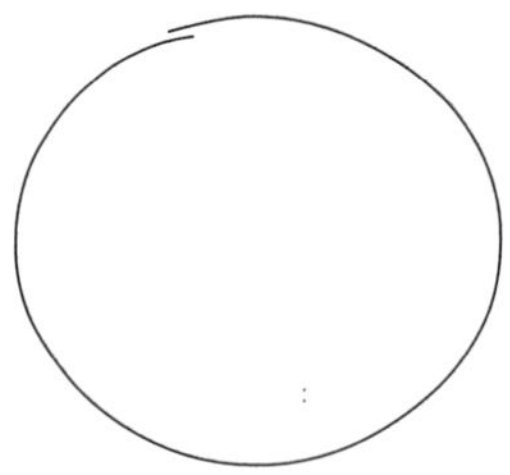

FIGURE 18. A VILLAGE

The first of these elements is a territory, which defines a piece of land and can be seen as the single property of the village. It is the common

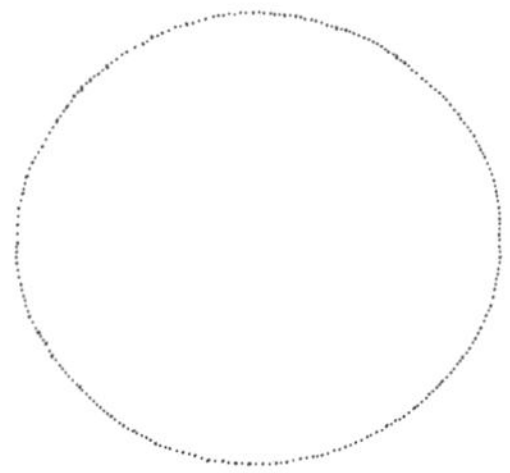

FIGURE 19. A TERRITORY

ground of the village, or what is often referred to as public space. The boundary of this new ground is defined by the projected geometry of the wall.

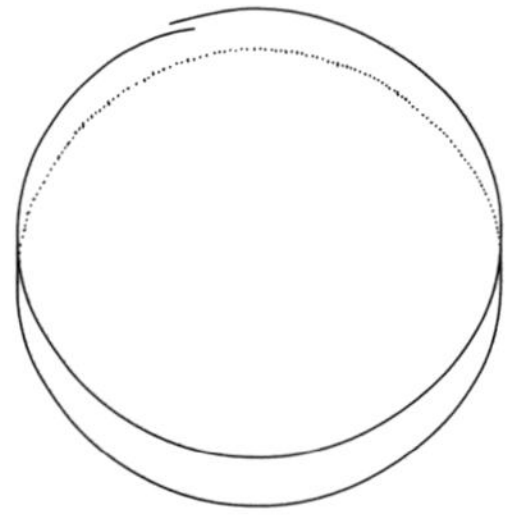

FIGURE 20. A SPACE

The second element is space—that is, the volume shaped by the plan of the territory multiplied by or extruded to the height of its wall, which forms an invisible three-dimensional space.

A Piece of Land: In Which the Territory of the Village Converges with a Rectangular Form

Due to the hypertelic qualities of technical objects, their individual elements have the capacity to specialize certain qualities more than others. One such quality is a wall's relationship toward the ground, which defines the boundary of a territory.

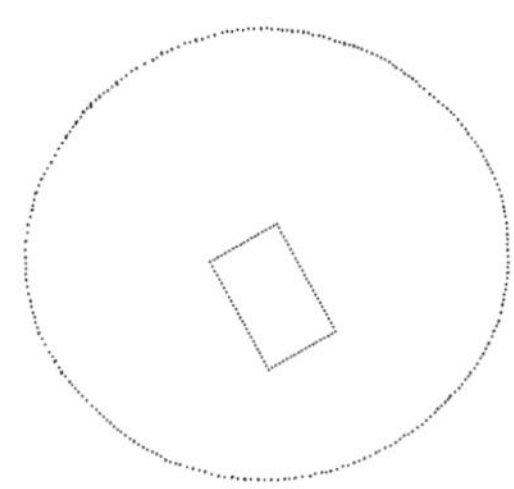

FIGURE 21. A PIECE OF LAND

Where a wall of the village converges with a rectangular form, a new territory arises. Such a territory has the formal properties of a piece of land similar to what we see in the subdivision of city blocks. In the lower part of the plan of the Mousgoum village we see rectangles each delineated by six points. These rectangles are like plots of land, miniature territories of a sort, which frame pieces of the common ground of the village much like other boundaries frame villages in a wilderness.

A House: In Which the Space of the Village Converges with a Wall

Whereas the village gives rise to plots of land by specializing its qualities in relation to the ground, it gives rise to houses by specializing those in relation to the wall. With the wall, the village frames both a two-dimensional territory and a three-dimensional space. It is from the convergence of that space with an enclosed wall that a house appears. On the south side of the Mousgoum village plan, between five and

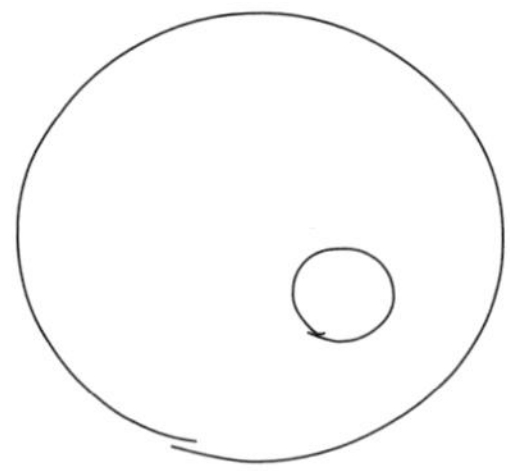

FIGURE 22. A HOUSE

six o'clock, we see this convergence drawn literally. It appears as if the house is a small copy of the village. The house forms a world within the world. So it comes as no surprise that art historian Steven Nelson quotes Madan Sarup to describe the houses of Mousgoum architecture: "To build a home is to build a discrete world."[275] As the space of this world converges with a wall it produces not just a boundary but a three-dimensional enclosed space, which multiplies throughout the plan of the village. This convergence gives rise to a new, unknown quality that did not exist before—namely, the window, since any topologically consistent transformation of a wall will maintain an opening, a hole, somewhere, in our case a light well at the top.

A Duplex House: In Which a House Converges with a House

FIGURE 23. A DUPLEX HOUSE

On the inside of the village, at eleven o'clock on the circle, we can see how two separate structures begin to collapse the space between each other. In the fusing of these two houses we can see the emergent early form of the duplex house, or even the beginning of the row-house.

In some of the detail drawings of the other Mousgoum homestead plans, a short corridor connects two structures, as we

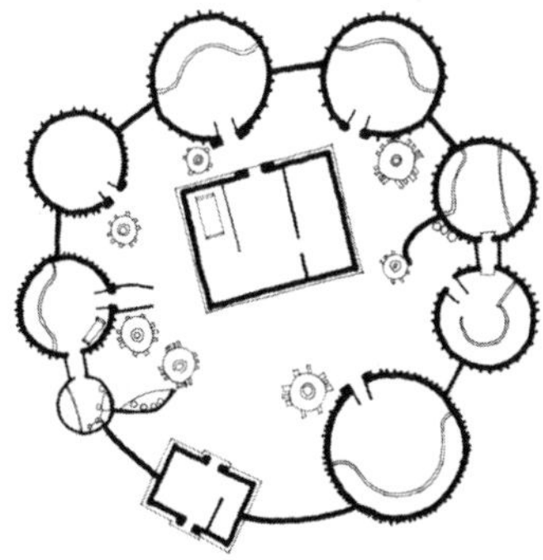

FIGURE 24. PART OF A HOMESTEAD IN A MOUSGOUM VILLAGE

can see in figure 24.[276] It is as if the doorframes were extruded and conjoined to form a tunnel-like corridor together, each structure losing its autonomy and assembling with the other. These kinds of convergences are not limited to just habitable elements. As we see in further examples, uses of various kinds unite.

A Real Estate:[277] *In Which a House Converges with a Piece of Land*

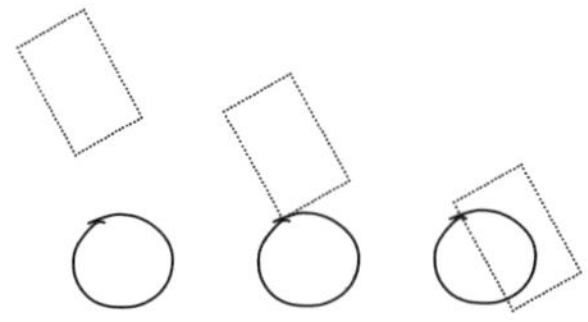

FIGURE 25. A REAL ESTATE

Where the two main properties of a village—its space and its territory—fuse together, they form what we would call today a real estate: a property with a building on it. In the south part of the plan, three houses indicate their relationship to three individual pieces of land. What can be witnessed here is a process of the concretization of a real estate.

Uniquely, while each house merges with one piece of land, its formal properties are unchanged. In contrast to the village, whose territory and space are congruent, in a real estate the qualities of the land and the building remain autonomous. It is a radically new urban artifact. From an architectural viewpoint, front yards, back yards, and private gardens appear, while from a functional viewpoint new sociopolitical formations emerge, since each piece of real estate can be owned or occupied by a different agent.[278]

A Housing Block: In Which Houses Converge with a City Wall

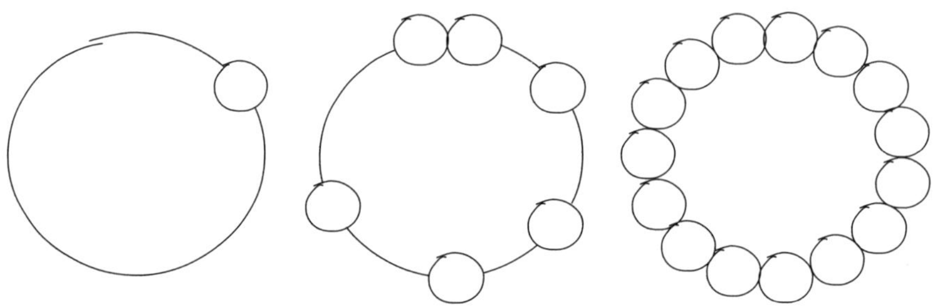

FIGURE 26. A HOUSING BLOCK

The most visible concretization in the Mousgoum village plan is the emergence of a what can be seen as a housing block.
When the enclosed, circular quality of the village wall converges with the spatial quality of the house, new topological qualities appear that give birth to a new architectural formation: the courtyard building, perhaps the most famous architectural type.[279] One of these new qualities is an interior outdoor space, topologically similar to the voided center of a donut. Produced by the circular arrangement of the houses to which it gives access, this territory is commonly known as a courtyard, which can only be shared by those same houses that frame it. While the houses are unified by their alignment along the wall, they produce effects that amount to more than just a variation on the row house. One such quality is the new interior relationship that emerges within this circular assemblage, a continuous indoor space known as an enfilade. In the form of a circle, such an inner corridor becomes in effect an endless interior space.

A Street: In Which a Territory Converges with Front Doors

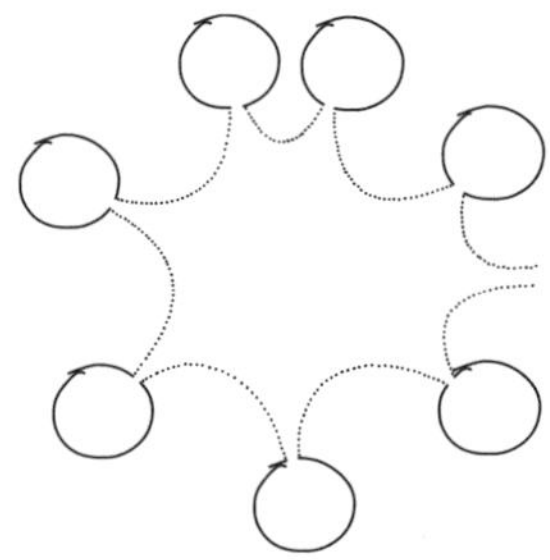

FIGURE 27. A STREET

The first bounded piece of land in the village was identified as a replica of the village wall and appeared in the shape of a rectangle. The second bounded piece of land has no particular shape at all. It is, rather, topological.

Outlined in the drawing by a dotted line, it starts at the entrance of the village and meanders across the northern part, reaching to unite the entrances of several houses. Here, a new component of the common ground of the village emerges, one that has all the characteristics of a street.

In his *General Theory of Urbanization*,[280] Cerdà defines a street as the space between the buildings and a public space. As such we can see in the Mousgoum village plan the emergence of the idea of a street where the delineated territory spans between the entrances of the houses as a space of circulation. This unique piece of land within the territory of the village further imparts qualities on the remaining space left over. This leftover space, of no particular form, is neither a piece of land for private purposes nor a space of circulation. It is, rather, the common territorial ground between them, the collectively shared space of the village, containing all the qualities of the parks and other communal spaces in our cities.

A Floor Plan: In Which a House Converges with a Street

In one of the houses in the west of the village, a convex space spans between interior walls. Throughout the village we can see some empty

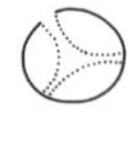

FIGURE 28. A FLOOR PLAN

houses while many others entail an interior form in which a space of circulation extends from the opening of the house and unites various rooms. What emerges is a floor plan, in which the idea of the street of the village converges with the territory of the house.

What the street does to the layout of the village, the space within the house does to the various elements of the floor plan, uniting and giving access to pieces of furniture or rooms as an interior street.

A City: In Which Pieces of Land Converge with a Territory of Circulation

FIGURE 29. A CITY

There is one final abstract form that can be found in this embryonic layout of an urban form, embedded in the plan though not immediately visible. It is the layout of any contemporary city.
If we closely read the territory of the street, that non-figurative space

between the houses, we find within it a pattern of invisible pieces of land. These repetitive lots are marked by six points, just as the lots in front of the houses in the south of the plan. If we were to connect these points and draw the outlines of these apparent lots, we could identify the beginning of a process of concretization for a layout of a city, whereby these discrete pieces of land converge with the territory of circulation.

If we consider the invisible pieces of land not as mere lots, but rather as entire city blocks, then an urban fabric emerges wherein these individual territories seem to be organized in a gridded formation. What would make this all a city would be the eventual relationship in which the convergence of these two distinct kinds of territory concretizes. The territories of the individual blocks assemble as islands while the continuous territory of circulation connects them in a unified space. The latter territory becomes our streets and public spaces of circulation, while the former territories become the blocks that organize our spaces of habitation.

All nine processes of concretization of urban formations: the house, the piece of land, the real estate, the duplex house, the housing block, the floor plan, the street, and the layout of a city, are all part of the same speculative genesis of a technical object called the city. They all emerge due to the fusion of their embedded aesthetic properties. Such a mechanological reading of urban forms, as precedes in the case of the Mousgoum village, allows us to frame these technical objects as forming the active background out of which radically new forms, functions, spaces, events, and prime objects can emerge.

What I wanted to demonstrate in this example of the Mousgoum village is that the city does not simply consist of architecture, but that it originates architecture. Technical objects, like the city, allow such processes of concretization to happen because their abstract elements can converge with each other due to their overdetermination. No architectural ensemble, ground element, or future individuated city can exist outside of technical objects, all are hidden within their backgrounds. Architecture is not part of the city, it is the city.

2.2. The Kind of Technical Object the City Is

The City: Our Greatest Work of Art

The city is, for Mumford, "man's greatest work of art."[281] "Mind," he writes, "*takes form* in the city; and in turn, urban forms condition mind."[282] Throughout the history of our urban life, the city has been the producer of our diversified activities, giving rise to all forms of specialization. For Jane Jacobs, it is a generator of diversity that incubates all kinds of new enterprises.[283] For Rem Koolhaas, it is an incubator not only for economic enterprises, but also for metropolitan bachelors, as it triggers events that would not be possible without its culture of congestion.[284] And finally, for Henri Lefebvre, the city is an assemblage of "differences."[285] There are many others for whom he city is *the* most important human artifact. At the core of these urban theories is the idea that the city allows for the emergence of the *new*: something previously unknown that is revealed to be already embedded in its qualities.

Such new forms of specialization and differentiation, or what Mumford identifies as a transformation of "the passive agricultural regime of the village into the active institutions of the city,"[286] cannot simply be explained by the city as a new form of density, accumulation of people, and exploitation of resources. What changed with the emergence of the city, he argues, was the will and need to exchange, to communicate, and to cooperate together.[287] This new pattern of active behavior, which is what is referred to by his concept of the mechanization of life,[288] is for him not only intensified by the city, it is the very reason the city came into existence. With the city, the boundedness to the biological life of the village was gone and radically new opportunities emerged:

> These opportunities and activities superimpose upon primary groups, based upon traditional acceptances and daily face-to-face contact, the more active associations, the more specialized functions, and the more purposive interests of secondary groups: in the latter the purpose is not given, but chosen: the membership and the activities are selective: the group itself becomes specialized and differentiated.[289]

Thus the city is not just man's greatest work of art, it is a very particular artifact as well. "The City", as Félix Guattari states, "is a mega-machine; it functions like a machine."[290]

The City as an Object

When Max Weber quantified the city he used a threefold definition. As a physical construct, the city is identifiable in opposition to the village when its buildings are standing densely "wall-to-wall" with each other. As a social construct, the city differentiates radically from the village since cities are "large localities" in which personal relationships between some people can be people totally absent. And finally, Weber argues, the city is driven mainly by commercial activities in opposition to the agricultural production of the village.[291] This threefold idea of the city gives us insight into what kind of object the city actually is. It is constituted by buildings: its physical structure; it is inhabited by people who don't know each other: its social structure; and both of those components are embedded in the forces of the economy. The city, it seems, is background and foreground at the same time. As a technical object, it operates as a machine in its inner parts and performs like a milieu as a whole. When Guattari argues that the city functions as a machine, he addresses specifically the aspect of the city as milieu. For him the city is a social-machine driven by capitalism.[292] Although Guattari does not mention Mumford in his essay "On Machines,"[293] his previously quoted statement mimics Mumford's formulation of the idea of the megamachine. As Mumford argues in *The Myth of the Machine*, the city and other gigantic projects like the pyramids were only possible because of the invention of the megamachine.[294] Enabled by the concentration of power at the beginning of our urban revolution, this human machine became, through patient work and disciplinary method, the archetype of all its future forms.[295] "This Megamachine," he writes, "was composed of a multitude of uniform, specialized, interchangeable but functionally differentiated parts, rigorously marshalled together and coordinated in a process centrally organized and centrally directed: each part behaving as a mechanical component of the mechanized whole."[296] Mumford cites the classic definition of the machine given by Franz Reuleaux: "A machine is a combination of resistant bodies so arranged that by their means the mechanical forces of nature can be compelled to do the work accompanied by certain determinant motions."[297] But the idea of the megamachine does not stop at describing the organization of work. Rather, it is, for Mumford, an "invisible machine"[298] that unifies multiple forms of technical objects: the military machine, the bureaucratic machine, the political machine, the economic machine, and the labor machine. All encapsulated within the boundary of the city.

Although Mumford never wrote directly about the city as a milieu for architectural emergence, he hints at it while discussing the convergence of pre-urban forms into the singular city, as happened between both social and physical components:

> What happened rather with the rise of cities was that many functions that had heretofore been scattered and unorganized were brought together within a limited area, and the components of the community were kept in a state of dynamic tension and interaction. In this union, made almost compulsory by the strict enclosure of the city wall, the already well-established parts of the proto-city—shrine, spring, village, market, stronghold—participated in the general enlargement and concentration of numbers, and underwent a structural differentiation that gave them forms recognizable in every subsequent phase of urban culture.[299]

Mumford shows how the formal and functional qualities of the early city served as the background, or milieu, that would give rise to new forms throughout the history of our cities. But what if the city as a technical object is a milieu not only for its human components but also for all its nonhuman inner components, its architecture?

Technical objects have the potential for their inner components to interfere or converge with each other,[300] thus allowing for new qualities and properties to emerge.[301] While this is often acknowledged for the human parts of the city, as we have seen, it is also true for nonhuman parts of the city as well. The city is not just a social machine, but also, as I will argue here, *a technical being*.[302] Subtly distinct from the technical object, Simondon uses the term technical being to underscore the innate quality of genesis that defines the technical object:

> The unity of the technical object, its individuality, and its specificity are the characteristics of consistency and convergence in its genesis. The genesis of the technical object partakes in its being. The technical object is that which is not anterior to its com- ing-into-being, but is present at each stage of its coming-into-being; the technical object in its oneness is a unit of coming-into-being. The gasoline engine is not this or that engine given in time and space, but the fact that there is a succession, a continuity that runs through the first engines to those we currently know and which are still evolving. . . . The technical being evolves through convergence and self-adaptation; it unifies itself internally according to a principle of inner resonance.[303]

The technical being, in other words, is the technical object considered as a unity, with its tendency for individuation and all the attendant qualities. It is the city and its own genesis borne within.

With the example of the Mousgoum village I have tried to show what it could mean to approach any urban form as a technical being, specifically by introducing a mechanological reading of urban elements and their capacity to converge into concrete architectural and urban formations. In the rest of this chapter I want to introduce the most important components that constitute the city, the largest technical being on our planet. This introduction is necessary to include before any description of the various processes of concretization, which will come in the last chapter.

When Jacobs wrote a full chapter in *The Death and Life of Great American Cities* about "The kind of problem a city is," she meant to clarify the kind of complexity the city represented for her research. Here, I want to clarify how the city as a technical being, as re-originated from Simondon's thesis, distinguishes itself from the various other definitions of the city as a machine. Broadly speaking, we can distinguish four ideas that see the city as a technical object:

- The city as a megamachine
- The city as a proto-subjective machine
- The city as a hyperobject
- The city as a technical being

While Guattari's idea of the city as a social, proto-subjective machine may differ from Mumford's megamachine, the idea of the city as a technical being stands out perhaps more starkly in that it underlines the major shift in thought about the city that occurred in the last two centuries since Cerdà first used the word urbanization—that is, the city is no longer seen as an object to which we humans have "access."[305]

2.2.1. The City as a Megamachine

Mumford describes the megamachine as "an invisible structure composed of living, but rigid, human parts, each assigned to his special office, role, and task, to make possible the immense work output of this great collective organisation."[306] Each individual is like a part in an engine, everyone working together in a chain of operations, fulfilling their function without knowing what the others do.[307] Perhaps there is no better description of the city as a machine than this. His statement reminds me of a passage in Otto Wagner's book Die Grozstadt, where he writes: "The number of city dwellers who prefer to disappear into the crowd as 'numbers' is significantly larger than the number of those who want to hear a 'good morning' or 'how did you sleep' from their neighbors in the family house who criticize them every day."[308]

This reduction to a number in a crowd, according to Mumford, runs through our entire human history, being already present in the ritual, dance, totem, taboo, religion, and magic that laid the groundwork for our mechanical history.[309] All of these things were brought together in the village. Thus our domestication, though tied the life of plants and the cycles of nature, was at the same time the beginning of the mechanization of urban life. As the Ice Age waned, the newly liberated ground allowed us to breed into a new specimen.[310] We became a species of reproduction and work became ritualized, as Mumford so clearly formulates the emergence of the megamachine. It is clear that with the city the management of our specialization and its repetitive operations rapidly accelerated. It was the overproduction of agricultural goods that forced this reorganization and formed our first cities.[311] Even Athens, the so-called city of free citizens, adapted parts of the megamachine. The Greek polis, next to the medieval city, was probably one of the few moments of urban history in which we tried to escape the megamachine through free citizenship and autonomous organization.[312] Although politically it may be seen in opposition to the megamachine, this was perhaps only possible because it always stayed, in terms of size, a village.

Mumford demonstrates the pervasiveness of this mechanization of life. After the fall of the Roman Empire, he points out, a new motto of the megamachine was introduced by the Benedictine order in the Middle Ages: "to labor is to pray."[313] This kind of mechanized behavior was no longer forced onto individuals, it was a moral value.[314] Mumford sees in the medieval cloisters the new pioneers of mechanization.[315] "Through its regularity and efficiency," he writes, "the monastery laid the groundwork for both capitalist organisation and further mechanization: even more significantly, it affixed a moral value to the whole process of work, quite apart from its eventual rewards."[316] The cloister established an autonomous, self-organized, religious community. To all the duties of discipline and punishment the Benedictine order added a new one: the daily work became a "Christian duty."[317] A new rhythm of living emerged: the twenty-four hour day.[318] This cycle deviated from the seasonal life of the village, eliminating our biological rhythm in a foretaste of our modern habits. Mumford further notes that this new form of discipline and regularity was sustained by the craft and trade associations of the Middle Ages, and also identifies another important element of mechanization that takes us from the cloisters to the medieval marketplace: the measurement of time.[319] What started with the bells of churches then moved to the clocktowers, from whence it become the mechanical clock in our pockets,[320] and later on our wrists. This was the origin of the automation of urban living that transformed the biological sequence of day and night into a pattern of synchronized human action. As Marx argues, "the clock is the first automatic machine, applied to practical purposes."[321] Before this model of automation could move into the factory, another mode of mechanization was needed: bureaucratic management and the emergence of the office. This new form of large bureaucracies appeared specifically in European capital cities. One invention in particular that gave fuel to the megamachine was double-entry bookkeeping.[322] This type of accounting, invented by the mathematician and Franciscan friar Luca Pacioli, gave rise to an enormous capital growth at the beginning of the industrialization of Western cities. First used by entrepreneurs in the late Middle Ages, like the Fugger family, it became a central part of the bureaucracies of the nation state, its laws and norms. As Mumford writes in *The Culture of Cities*: "The new Italian oligarchy was the first political power to order its finances in accordance with the principles of mercantile bookkeeping and presently the fine Italian hand of the tax-expert and financial administrator could be observed in every European capital."[323] "It was this cumulative mechanical organisation," he later concludes, "not the steam engine, that accounts for the upsurge of industrial energy after 1750."[324]

In one of the last chapters in the second volume of his *Myth of the Machine*, Mumford summarizes the evolution of the automation of life and its mechanical processes in the city with a quote from the satirist Samuel Butler: "Day by day the machines are gaining ground upon us: day by day we are becoming more subservient to them; more men are daily bound down as slaves to them, more men are daily devoting the energies of their whole lives to the development of mechanical life."[325] In fact, it seems, that with the emergence of our urban life and the automation of living we not only became enslaved by the machine, but are completely resigned to our slavery.[326]

The final stage of our free enslavement to machines takes shape for Mumford with emergence of the computer. While for Simondon the individualized machine is the competitor of our mechanical capacities, for Mumford the computer competes with our mental capacities.[327] "This final form," writes Mumford, "is an attempt to exercise control, not only of the mechanical process itself, but of the human being who once created it: turning him from an active to a passive agent, and finally eliminating him altogether."[328] It is therefore no surprise that he cites the work of the Austrian cybernetic theorist Norbert Wiener, who was one of the first to compare the computer's attributes to the human brain.[329] Wiener was referencing the fact that the computer could absorb information and, through feedback loops, adjust from mistakes as we do. Wiener, as Mumford mentions, was aware of the consequences of such an invention but still respected the autonomy of human responsibilities: "No-one was more concerned than he over the peculiar fascination automated systems would have for autocratic minds, eager to confine human reactions to those that conform to the limited data they are capable of programming."[330]

In his admiration for the city, which perhaps even exceeded his fascination with the garden city,[331] Mumford saw a bulwark against the dark history of automation and mechanization of life finalized by the computer and the new megamachines.[332] For him, there was one technical object that still could not be equaled by computer networks: the city. He writes:

> What [John Stuart] Mill realized at this early moment, and what Wiener later emphasized, is that the sum total of human potentialities in any community is infinitely richer than the limited number that can be installed in a closed system—and all automatic systems are closed and limited—even those computers that are capable of learning through further use of the material already provided. By reason of its very nature no computer can be as wealthy in life-experiences and tested information as a great city.[333]

The technical object, which once was an extension of us, a tool, a machine, and later our competitor, became us. We are the megamachine. We are the city.

2.2.2. The City as a Proto-subjective Machine

When Guattari mentions in his lecture "On Machines"[334] that the city is an example of a megamachine, his aim is to liberate the idea of the city and other such human machines from their "anathema," and to eliminate the idea of the machine as just the expression of all the inhumanities we have learned of from Mumford's history of mechanization. Concerned that contemporary ecological crises triggered by machinic catastrophes could lead us back toward a primitive stage of mankind in the hope that we might start all over again, Guattari targets a more progressive position. He turns to the work of Pierre Levy, specifically his book *Les Technologies de l'intelligence* and the idea of the "hypertext": the idea of the machinic interface, or of conceiving the machine as interface.[335]

Guattari refers specifically to the fifth dimension of Levy's description of machines:

> A machine is a cutting point and an interface. It translates (*traduit*), reveals (*trahit*), folds and unfolds for a machine below the flows from a machine above. It is itself composed of translation machines that divide, multiply and heterogenize it. The interface is the "foreign policy" dimension of the machine, through which it can enter new networks and translate new flows.[336]

What Guattari finds conceptually radical in Levy's idea of the machine as interface is his break with the ontological difference between "being and things."[337] "I would propose", he writes "that we attempt to consider that in the machine, and at the machinic interface, there exists something that would not quite be of the order of the soul, human or animal, *anima*, but of the order of a proto-subjectivity. This means that there is a function of consistency in the machine, both a relationship to itself and a relationship to alterity."[338]

What Guattari proposes, in other words, is that a machine is not limited to its materiality. "In techne" he continues,

> there are ontogenetic elements, elements of the plan, of construction, social relationships which support these technologies, a stock of knowledge, economic relations and a whole series of interfaces onto which the technical object attaches itself. From this, we can establish a link between a modern type of technological machine and the tools or the actual pieces of the machine, and think of these as elements connected to one another.[339]

This line of thinking may clarify that Guattari did not just want to expand a metaphorical idea of the city as a megamachine. While he agreed that the city is a social machine, his intention was rather to invent a new definition of the machine. This new understanding of the machine, and therefore of what a city can be, imagines a machine consisting of both human and nonhuman parts.

In his essay, "A Few Fragments on Machines,"[340] Gerald Raunig, an Austrian philosopher, gives a simple description of how we can understand Guattari's machines made of human and nonhuman parts. What Raunig argues is that both Guattari and Deleuze disagree with the linear argument of Marx, that there exists an evolution of man and the machine that reached from the tool, as an extension of man, toward the machine, which became independent of man. Deleuze and Guattari, he writes, wanted to eliminate this distinction of man and tool and conceptualize the idea "as one that refers to the pre-modern understanding of the 'machina,' in which the separation between the organic and the mechanical was irrelevant."[341] What Deleuze and Guattari describe in their book *Anti-Oedipus* is that there is no such difference, since what exists is "only a process that produces the one within the other and couples the machines together."[342] Their aim was to replace this opposition of machine and man and allow human and nonhuman entities to fuse together to form a new idea of the machine. Raunig uses a quote from *Anti-Oedipus* to define this new kind of technical object: "It is no longer a matter of confronting man and machine to estimate possible or impossible correspondences, extensions and substitutions of the one or the other, but rather of conjoining the two and showing how man becomes a piece with the machine or with other things in order to constitute a machine."[343]

It is this becoming a piece of the machine with nonhuman parts that I consider as the main idea of Guattari's proto-subjective machine. I have found no better example in which Guattari (and Deleuze) make this idea of becoming a subject more visible as in their example of the wasp and the orchid. In this famous passage, written in "Rhizome,"[344] they explain how with the wasp and the orchid we can seen a proto-subjective machine. "The orchid," they write,

> deterritorializes by forming an image, a tracing of a wasp; but the wasp reterritorializes on that image. The wasp is nevertheless deterritorialized, becoming a piece in the orchid's reproductive apparatus. But it reterritorializes the orchid by transporting its pollen. Wasp and orchid, as heterogeneous elements, form a rhizome.[345]

Crucially, Guattari and Deleuze tell us, what happens between the wasp and the orchid is "not imitation (at all) but a capture of code, surplus value of code, an increase in valence, a veritable becoming, a becoming-wasp of the orchid and a becoming-orchid of the wasp."[346]

To understand the city as a proto-subjective machine, we need only to replace wasp and orchid with citizens, its humans parts, and urbs, its nonhuman parts. Thus, to use the language of Guattari and Deleuze, in the city lies a becoming-human, while in us lies a becoming-city. The same can even be said about the architect and the city. Sanford Kwinter identifies in the relationship between the architect and the city a proto-subjective machine when he compares Rem Koolhaas to Chuck Yeager. Yeager, an American fighter pilot in the Second World War who was also the first to break the sound barrier, became one with his plane. He was, as Kwinter quotes one of Yeager's peers, "the only pilot (I've ever flown with) who gives the impression that he's part of the cockpit hardware, so in tune with the machine that instead of being flesh and blood, he could be an autopilot. He could make an airplane talk."[347] For Kwinter, Koolhaas was in tune with the city as Yeager was with a plane. Instead of "flying like a bullet," Koolhaas was stirring like a dogfighter through the late-capitalist city and becoming one with the metropolis.[348]

I am not a philosopher, but it seems that this proto-subjectivity is what Levy is referring to when he asks in an essay how the Kantian transcendental subject could be rethought through Guattari's machines.[349] The answer hints in the direction that we do not have a specific human trait; rather, we become. The city plays an important role in this becoming human and we may find machines of human and nonhuman parts already in early stages of our urbanization.

Throughout its history, as I have described above, new human modalities have continually emerged in the city. Such new human modalities, for example languages and laws, were generated through the process of urbanization, but at the same time influenced our actions to create new kinds of cities. Do we not hear in this the words of Aristotle? Is not the Greek polis for him just such a proto-subjective machine when he writes:

> Hence it is evident that the state is a creation of nature, and that man is by nature a political animal. And he who by nature and not by mere accident is without a state, is either a bad man or above humanity: he is like the 'Tribeless, lawless, heartless one,' whom Homer denounces—the natural outcast is forthwith a lover of war; he may be compared to an isolated piece at draughts.[350]

What kind of becoming lies in this Creek city-state machine? The polis is clearly a machinic interface between various pieces: nonhuman objects like the wall and human objects like laws and languages. Both types of elements create a very specific proto-subjective machine of action: a "vita activa," as Hannah Arendt calls it.[351] It is a machine in which the life of humans is devoted to public-political matters. "To be political," meaning to live through words and persuasion instead of wars, she writes, meant "to live in a *polis*."[352] In this proto-subjective machine of the polis, organic pieces and technical pieces unify. Humans and nonhumans create a world of becoming. This unification of the machine, before staging the becoming-political, is beautiful described by Arendt: "the Greeks, in distinction from all later developments, did not count legislating among the political activities.

In their opinion, the lawmaker was like the builder of the city wall, someone who had to do and finish his work before political activity could begin."[353]

Perhaps it is this proto-subjective machine of the Greek city-state that Mumford sees as an alternative to the ancient megamachine. For Guattari, it is clear that the city is this machinic interface between animate and inanimate pieces: a machine as an interface between walls, laws, and people. And we can conclude, therefore, that in the city lies the becoming-human and in us lies the becoming-city.

2.2.3. The City as a Hyperobject

While both Mumford and Guattari see the city as a function of the human world, or as a machinic unification of human and nonhuman, today we find a third position which contends that humans do not have full access to technical objects like the city. Timothy Morton calls such entities *hyperobjects*. In his book *Hyperobjects: Philosophy and Ecology After the End of the World*[354] he defines hyperobjects as entities that defy our traditional understanding of things due to their spatial and temporal scales. The biosphere, global warming, capitalism, real estate investments, nuclear waste, and ocean gyres are just some examples of hyperobjects. These objects have the capacity to continuously withdraw from us even as we know about them. Humans may be responsible for their existence and they may affect our daily lives, but at the same time, for Morton, we do not have conceptual "access" to them: "Hyperobjects are not simply mental (or otherwise ideal) constructs, but are real entities whose primordial reality is withdrawn from humans."[355] It seems as if they have a reality of their own.

We can say that the city is a hyperobject. We created it and live in it, but we have lost access to understanding it, especially its built elements. In the urban environment, as buildings emerge that we have not seen before, their formal structures have become stranger and stranger. To take just some recent developments: high-rise buildings built in New York City that are as thin as pencils, neighborhoods built in Africa without any inhabitants, towers built in China without roads, or, my favorite example, housing projects and villages built on the roofs of shopping malls around the world. These examples do not hint toward the mind of some genius architect who created them. Rather, it seems that they simply appeared. We can identify them but we cannot understand how they emerged. Yet time after time the city continues to give rise to such new kinds of buildings.

Morton's thesis touches a certain zeitgeist. His idea of the withdrawn object comports well with our current age of the Anthropocene.[356] This new geological period, the start of which many position around 1800 and the beginning of the Industrial Revolution, implies a new strata on our planet that we humans have created. This new surface is the result of our own inventions. Our modes of production and consumption have left marks and traces on the skin of the earth. With the Anthropocence, not only has the opposition between man and nature disappeared, but we have started to live on a surface of our own creation. Unfortunately, furthermore, this human creation is no longer within our control.

Perhaps it was this shift in the perception of our planet that buoyed a new philosophical movement known as object-oriented ontology.[357] OOO, as it is abbreviated, was originated by Graham Harman,[358] whose philosophy attempts to turn away from the human access of objects and toward the interior of objects themselves. Harman rejects what he calls the post-Kantian obsession—that is, the focus exclusively on the relationships between people and objects. Instead he wants to include the relationships between objects and objects, as he writes: "I hold that the interaction between cotton and fire belongs on the same footing as human interaction with cotton and fire."[359] OOO is the birth of an ontology of objects themselves.[360] Harman, in turning attention toward objects, points to the deep mystery that lies within them. For him, an object is much "deeper than any possible relations to it."[361] "To use a Hammer," he writes,

> and to stare at it explicitly are both distortions of the very reality of that hammer as it goes about just being itself, unleashed in the world like a wild animal. An airport is certainly something deeper than its colour and shape, but it is also much more than its current usefulness, and even more all *possible* uses of it. Any sort of human relation to objects will inevitably fail to grasp them as they are.[362]

It is the depth of objects such as Harman describes that causes them to "withdraw" from us humans.

According to Harman, in order to access objects, like cities or buildings, we typically either *undermine* or *overmine* them.[363] When we ask ourselves what something is composed of, we are undermining.[364] As he writes, "bolts and wires taken alone enjoy a rather minimal reality. In combination with thousands of other minutely engineered pieces, they blend into the composite visible equipment known as a bridge. But these tiny devices would bring about an utterly different state of affairs if reassigned elsewhere, whether as scrap metal or as segments of a bomb."[365] We need only to replace bolts and wires with columns and beams and we can clearly see an architectural history unfolding in front of our eyes, in which buildings are reduced to their material compounds. When we try to access objects by asking what they can do, what their function is, or what kind of events they generate, then we are overmining. [366] As Harman continues:

> the bridge as a whole is not a self-evident, atomic finality; rather, it functions in numerous different equipmental ways, swept up into countless larger systems. Usually, it enacts an official plan of efficiency, shaving ten minutes from the drive around a bay. But in certain regions of the world, separating hostile factions, it is monitored by snipers. The bridge can be the unforgettable site of a fateful conversation (nostalgia-equipment), the location of a distant relative's suicide (memorial-equipment) or perhaps it is simply stalked in a troubling insomnia. It is an object of study for architectural critics or material for sabotage by vandals.[367]

We can identify in the above lines many postmodern architectural positions that consider events as being deeper than buildings themselves.[368]

Through Harman's critique, we can see Mumford's city as megamachine and Guattari's city as proto-subjective machine from a new perspective. While Mumford's reading of the city clearly emphasizes the undermining mode of attempting to access the machine, as when he considers the chain of functional parts being replaced by humans, Guattari's idea clearly emphasizes the overmining of technical objects. He shows us what machines can do, what functions they have for us.

"Hyperobjects," Morton writes, "exhibit their effects *interobjectively*; that is, they can be detected in a space that consists of interrelationships between aesthetic properties of objects."[369] To define a city as such an (interobjective) hyperobject, then, perhaps fulfills the "modernist sensibility" that Eisenman found lacking in the 1960s functionalist avant-garde.[370] Not only might such a sensibility change our attitude toward the physical world, it also carries the promise of looking into the relationships of objects themselves.

How can we now examine those strange buildings, like the village on top of a shopping mall, through the lens of OOO? How do objects relate? What are their interobjective effects? Or, to ask the question repeated throughout this book, How does a city *meet* its architecture? To answer these questions, Harman points to the arts, and in particular to metaphor.[371] For him, humans and nonhumans access objects only indirectly, like in metaphors. Harman's most frequent example is a line taken from a text on metaphor by the Spanish philosopher Jose Ortega y Gasset: "the cypress is like the ghost of a dead flame."[372] Harman demonstrates that the cypress and the flame can only meet or fuse when their aesthetic properties radically change. "When they [cypress and flame] collide with one another," he writes, "their hard carapaces crack and the internal matter, in a molten state, acquires the softness of plasm, ready to receive a new form and structure."[373] Harman sees the arts, and in particular the artist, as initiating the unravelling of the hidden qualities within objects.[374] The architect, therefore, is privileged to be the originator of strange city-buildings. Furthermore, this emphasizes an idea particular to the discipline of architecture that buildings are unique single objects. Rafael Moneo describes this notion beautifully:

> On the one hand, a work of architecture has to be considered in its own right, as an entity in itself. That is, like other forms of art, it can be characterized by a condition of uniqueness. From this point of view, the work of architecture is irreducible within any classification. It is unrepeatable, a single phenomenon. Stylistic relationships may be recognized among architectural works, as in the other figurative arts, but they do not imply a loss of the singularity of the object.[375]

This idea of architecture as a singular object doesn't give us the complete picture of our new kinds of architectural objects. Pencil towers or villages on a single roof define something more than a unique individual building type. Something that points to a formal similarity. For Moneo, this is the second aspect of the discipline of architecture:

> On the other hand, a work of architecture can also be seen as belonging to a class of repeated objects, characterized, like a class of tools or instruments, by some general attributes. From the first hut to the archaic stone construction, primitive architecture conceived of itself as an activity similar to other kinds of craftsmanship, such as the making of textiles, pottery, baskets, and so on. The first products of this activity, which we in retrospect have called architecture, were no different from instruments or tools: building a primitive hut required solving problems of form and design similar in nature to those involved in weaving a basket, that is in making a useful object. Thus, like a basket or plate or cup, the architectural object could not only be repeated, but also was meant to be repeatable. In these terms it can be said that the essence of the architectural object lies in its repeatability.[376]

Who originates such repeated objects, such common features of architecture? What gives rise to new typologies, or to what Kubler calls prime objects?[377] If we accept Kubler's idea, that the *problem* to which an architect contributes with their work already exits, then they can only pick up signals that are pre-given. "The monograph upon a single work of art is like a shaped stone ready for position in a masonry wall," Kubler writes, "but that wall itself is built without purpose or plan."[378] If an individual building is like the shaped stone, then all shaped stones define what Kubler calls the formal sequence or form-class to which the individual author contributes with their work.[379] The city, then, is to the building what the wall is to the shaped stone.

Let us take for example the village on a shopping mall. As will be discussed in more detail in chapter 4, here the aesthetic properties of the mall merge with the aesthetic properties of the city, the subdivision of lots fusing with the roof of the mall. And thus the new formal characteristics of the building—the villages on a single roof—derive from the qualities of the city. The city does to architecture what the wall does to the stone: it acts as a background. It sends out aesthetic signals for the shaping of new kinds of objects. These background signals of the city define all the qualities of its architecture. They are the protean, common secrets from whence all prime objects originate. But this background, according to Kubler, has neither plan nor purpose, nor does it have a human author. The city, as a hyperobject, indeed seems to have a life of its own. Its own form of being.

2.2.4. The City as a Technical Being

To think the city as a technical being is to think a human creation as an autonomous being. Whereas OOO argues that we will never be able to access this kind of "tool-being,"[380] Simondon is one of few who try to give us an idea of the existence of technical objects, to answer the question: How do technical objects meet? In *On the Mode of Existence of Technical Objects*, he lays out his mechanology, which describes the individuation of technical beings.[381] Although he defines technical beings by looking into the interiority of objects, he stresses the importance of differentiating technical objects from biological beings. As Henning Schmidgen points out in his essay "Thinking Technological and Biological Beings,"[382] Simondon's mechanology aims to set apart "the essence of technological objects from the essence of natural objects."[383]

The way humans have typically thought about cities as technical entities, as in the case of Mumford's megamachine, is by reducing human organisms to machines. This was the general position articulated by cybernetics theorists like Norbert Wiener,[384] who in 1948 conceptualized machines as living systems. Schmidgen points out in his essay a mode of thinking that emerged in postwar France, specifically as articulated by Georges Canguilhem in a lecture from 1947 titled "Machines and Organism." "Canguilhem," writes Schmidgen, "argued for a biological philosophy of technology. Instead of continuing to reduce organisms to machines, Canguilhem suggested taking the historical fact of on-going machine constructions as a starting point."[385] That "fact of on-going machine constructions" is not just the starting point for Simondon, it is his thesis: "Concretization gives the technological object an intermediate place between natural objects and scientific representations."[386] This allows Schmidgen to conclude that "the technological object is not a living being. But it is an individual."[387]

What enables the city and its architecture—non-animated technical objects—to evolve, change, and allow new typological forms, or prime objects, to emerge, is what distinguishes them from biological beings. "Technical beings" Simondon writes,

> are different from living beings in many respects, but they differ essentially in the following respects: a living being engenders beings that are similar to itself, or that can become so after a certain number of successive reorganizations occurring spontaneously if the required conditions obtain; a technical being, on the contrary, does not have this capacity; it cannot spontaneously produce other technical beings similar to itself, despite the efforts of cyberneticists who have tended to force technical beings to copy the living by constructing beings that are similar to them: this possibility is currently a mere supposition and is without foundation; but the technical being has greater freedom than the living, afforded to it by its infinitely lesser degree of perfection.[388]

It is within this gap that technical beings can be distinguished from biological beings, within this greater freedom and lesser degree of perfection in technical objects, like the city, that the architect is able to appear as the "inventor"[389] of new architectural typologies.

Re-origination of Mechanology in Architecture

In order to re-originate from Simondon's mechanology the idea of thinking the city as a technical being, I will focus on two aspects: first, Simondon's idea of the evolution of the technical object in relationship to what can be called an inner or an outer milieu;[390] and second, the process that defines the becoming of an individual architectural object, namely the process of concretization.

The City as Background

Simondon's technical object does not appear in a vacuum. For him, every technical object is placed "at the meeting point between two milieus."[391] Schmidgen refers to these two milieus as the inner and outer *Umwelten* of technical objects.[392] The inner is what Simondon calls the technical milieu while the outer is for him the geographical milieu.[393] The inner milieu consists of all kinds of mechanical, electronic, and chemical processes, while the outer milieu might be defined as the environment in which technical objects operate. The geographical milieu, for example, can be the climatic conditions at the altitudes in which a technical object performs. It can be an electromagnetic field, with its frequencies and voltages, or a thermodynamic system, with its heat, radiation, and energy. In short, technical objects are conditioned externally by milieus. If we transfer this idea to architecture, then, buildings have two milieus, or *Umwelten*, as well. The inner, technical milieu can be considered to be various technical regimes. The outer, geographical milieu is the city.

The geographical milieu allows for a kind of disciplinary exegesis, whereby socioeconomic dynamics, climatic conditions, and geological forces in cities are seen to cause all kinds of new architectural modalities. This would mean that the genesis of any new type of building is driven by the intensive properties[394] of its milieus. Such a reading of the city would identify the properties of matter as the main forces for the genesis of architecture. This re-origination of the thesis of *On the Mode of Existence of Technical Objects* into the discipline of architecture would thus place Simondon's work in line with a tradition that Harman traces through Anaxagoras and Giordano Bruno, both of whom believed that a "boundless" or "unlimited" blob of matter called *aperion* "contains the seeds of everything."[395] But such a definition of the city as a milieu would not be sufficient to explain all the new emerging qualities of buildings, like the above cited high-rise pencil towers. As we saw in Simondon's example of the cylinder head and cooling fins, technical objects transform through their exchange of not only energy and information, but also geometric properties.[396] Technical objects do not meet exclusively through their material qualities, but also through their formal and functional qualities.

What I am arguing here is that the material qualities of the city are not the primary forces of novelty. The emergence of new building typologies is driven just as much by aesthetic qualities. Instead of understanding the city as a milieu, I would like to consider it as a background. A background full of formal and functional properties, with the potential to fuse, merge, and move into each other. As above, what Kubler's wall is for each new stone, the city is for each of its emergent buildings. It is the background that reproduces itself as architecture. This line of thought resonates with Benevolo's argument for the origin of architecture: "The city is an enclosure, or a series of enclosures, in which the art of manipulating medium and short distances—that which from then on would be described as 'architecture'—reached maturity, while the older art, which aimed at the occupation and modification of the landscape, was gradually forgotten."[397] What happened with the emergence of the city, in his view, is that all kinds of new architectural entities arose from the overdetermined potentials of the city's aesthetic qualities.

The idea that out of the city-as-background emerges all of its architecture is the core argument of this book. This idea is not in opposition to Simondon's thesis. In fact, it was he who gave me the hint to think the city as background in his comparison of his idea of technical beings with gestalt theory.[398] In the second chapter of his book, "Evolution of Technical Teality; Element, Individual, Ensemble," under the subheading, "Technical invention: ground and form in the living and in inventive thought," he writes:

> Gestalt psychology, while recognizing the function of totalities, attributed force to form; a deeper analysis of the inventive process would no doubt show that what is determinant and plays an energetic role are not forms but that which carries the forms, which is to say their ground; the ground, while perpetually marginal with respect to attention, is what harbors the dynamisms; it is that through which the system of forms exists; forms do not participate in forms, but in the ground, which is the system of all forms or rather the common reservoir of the formes' tendencies, well before they exist separately and constitute themselves as an explicit system. . . . . For the ground is the system of virtualities, of potentials, forces that carve out their path, whereas forms are the system

> of actuality. Invention is the taking charge of the system of actuality through the system of virtualities, the creation of a unique system on the basis of these two systems. Forms are passive in so far as they represent actuality; they become active when they organize in relation to this ground, thereby bringing prior virtualities into actuality.[399]

If we understand the city not just as milieu or *Umwelt*, but as gestalt theory suggests, as background, then this *ground* can be seen as the common reservoir for all its *forms*. The elements of the city—walls, streets, territory, the subdivision of land, public space, infrastructure, buildings—do not just compose the city. Their aesthetic potentials act as the ground that allows for the origination of new prime objects.

The Background as Architecture

As we know from Simondon, technical objects like the city can be described as a technical beings. These beings have the capacity for evolution. One of their evolutionary characteristics is that elements converge together to form new concrete entities. Simondon calls this the process of concretization.[400] If we apply this ontological idea to the city, all of its urban elements, like buildings, streets, and public space, can be considered the outcome of this process, meaning that the fusion of the formal qualities of the background drives the emergence of all new architectural typologies.

Let us take our common urban building typologies: the courtyard house, the urban block, the high-rise, the slab, the megastructure, the megaform, the mat-building, the hyperbuilding, the city under a single roof, as well as our newest, the pencil-tower and the village on a shopping mall. All these urban types can be understood as the convergence of existing elements of the city into new ones. They are prime objects. To revisit Kubler's concept: "Prime objects resemble the prime numbers of mathematics because no conclusive rule is known to govern the appearance of either. . . . Prime numbers have no divisors other than themselves and unity; prime objects likewise resist decomposition in being original entities."[401] The last statement here is essential. It is what makes prime objects unique to the discipline of architecture and to my own thesis. If buildings, as prime objects, resist being decomposed, then only one question is left: How do they become indivisible unities?

Simondon's mechanology has a clear answer for that. New unities, according to him, occur when the elements of technical objects converge from an abstract form to a concrete form. While in an abstract form each part of a technical object can be recognized, in its concrete form these are unified and appear as one. The reason for this, Simondon explains, is because technical objects have hypertelic qualities, which allow for an "exaggerated degree of specialization" within entities.[402] Due to the overdetermined functional and formal properties of any part of the city for example, new kinds of buildings with radically new features can emerge. In every element of a city, therefore, lies the potential to actualize unforeseen new technical objects. In order to visualize such a process of concretization we can imagine an abstract diagram, a formal arrangement of a loose composition of elements that converge with each other over time and turn into a more and more concrete unified architectural entity. This process of concretization unfolds, for Simondon, always as a series: "The technical object thus exists as a specific type obtained at the end of a convergent series. This series goes from the abstract to the concrete mode: it tends toward a state which would turn the technical being into a system that is entirely coherent within itself and entirely unified."[403] We can therefore conclude that the city as a background forms its architecture only once this "morphological sequence"[404] has reached a moment of coherence. A process of fusion is exhausted and a new urban original concretizes.

The word morphology suggests that this evolution of technical objects is biological. But the process of concretization is not at all biological, it is technical. The difference between a biological and technical evolution of art is discussed by Kubler near the beginning of his *Shape of Time*. He explains how the evolution of styles in art has always been treated using biological lifecycle references, using the plant metaphor as an example: "Its first leaves are small and tentatively shaped; the leaves of its middle life are fully formed; and the last leaves it puts forth are small again, but intricately shaped. All are sustained by one unchanging principle of organization common to all members of that species, with variants of race occurring in different environments."[405] The crux of this argument is that any new form is always bound within a continuous space and time. This essential characteristic of the biological metaphor has dominated the discourse of architecture beyond the history of styles. We have not only thought our architectural history in this way, but our buildings as well. Laugier was perhaps the most influential of many to have argued that a building should be a descendent of the primitive hut.[406] The biological metaphor has also been used for the morphological reading of our cities. Just think of the work of Muratori, who looked into the historical layers of Venice to identify the permanences in buildings over time.[407] And it has even dominated our recent disciplinary history. All kinds of new digital forms have been argued for with biological references and designed by means of animation techniques[408] or by simulating evolutionary processes though genetic algorithms.[409]

What Kubler offers us instead is a physical metaphor, suggesting we replace the biological metaphor with the language of electrodynamics.[410] He compares artworks—we can extend his metaphor to cities and buildings—to signals:

> These signals are like kinetic energy stored until the moment of notice when the mass descends along some portion of its path to the center of the gravitational system. One may ask why these old signals are not actual. The nature of a signal is that its message is neither here nor now, but there and then. If it is a signal it is a past action, no longer embraced by the "now" of present being. The perception of a signal happens "now," but its impulse and its transmission happened "then." In any event, the present instant is the plane upon which the signals of all being are projected. No other plane of duration gathers us up universally into the same instant of becoming.[411]

The city as a background transmits architectural signals, it is "there" and "then." But architectural signals are independent of any regular or biological time frame. They are, as Kubler describes historical time, "intermittent and variable."[412] They occur not at all continuously. These aesthetic signals of urban elements are the measure by which concretization unfolds. Such formal sequences, as Kubler calls them, unify and fuse the properties of the city. Urban elements meld together; walls, streets, subdivisions of land, public space, buildings of all different times, places, functions, shapes, and material properties, these all unify and radically change their inner character. What emerge are new urban building types, from the courtyard house to the village on a shopping mall.

What happens to buildings is the same as what happens to technical objects. With his series of images of the gasoline engine, the electronic tube, the triode, the telephone, electro-motors, and turbines,[413] Simondon gives us an inside look at the processes of concretization of these technical objects. Schmidgen describes the effect of the series:

> With respect to the 4-stroke combustion engine, he argues that its various components come closer over time, while certain parts get functionally 'overdetermined.' Thus, at a certain point, the cooling fins on the cylinder function no longer only thermically but also statically: they cool the cylinder at the same time as they give it additional stability. Simondon offers another example: in the development of electronic tubes, the passive components of this object became reduced, whereas its active parts were condensed. The rubber base grows smaller and eventually disappears. At the same time, the functional parts of the tube start to take ever more space within the glass ampoule.[414]

Not only does Simondon demonstrate how technical objects can take on new properties, he even shows us that at a certain moment some parts may disappear while others appear.

It is this topological shift of qualities, what Harman would call the cracking in the carapaces of these objects' inner matter,[415] that occurs when the elements of the city converge to form all kinds of concrete new typologies. To conceive of these topological shifts as a question of typology is to characterize architecture in terms of what Moneo calls its "deeper geometry."[416] It is its depth as a technical object.

This book is therefore an attempt to answer a hypothesis which Moneo formulated in his text "On Typology." When he asked himself the question of how to tackle the question of typology today, he made a remarkable statement: "The architectural object can no longer be considered as a single, isolated event because it is bounded by the world that surrounds it."[417] In other words, any future idea of typology must place the architectural object among other objects. The world that bounds architecture is the city: the origin for all its architecture. This background will never become exhausted since the city generates itself by constantly producing new architectural objects. The city is an overdetermined technical being.

Thus far I have introduced the idea of the city as a technical being and shown the application of a mechanological methodology with my reading of the Mousgoum village. In the next chapter, I will focus on the five individuated cities from throughout our urban history, and how their main components constitute these cities as overdetermined technical beings, allowing them to change due to the intrinsic hypertely of their form and function.

[257] Benevolo gives the location in the caption of the drawing. See Fig 22. In Benevolo, Leonardo, (1990), 17.

[258] Art historian Steven Nelson describes a homestead with a similar layout. Its representation in Nelson's book is diagrammatic, with a detailed description of the function of every architectural element. In Nelson, Steven (2007), 32.

[259] I use the spelling "Mousgoum" after Steven Nelson. See: Ibid.

[260] Mumford, Lewis. *The City in History: Its Origins, Its Transformations, and Its Prospects* (1961). San Diego, New York, London: A Harvest/HBJ Book, 1989, 12.

[261] Benevolo, Leonardo, (1990), 9.

[262] Mumford, Lewis. *The Myth of the Machine: Technics and Human Development*. San Diego, New York, London: A Harvest/HBJ Book, 1967, 154.

[263] Mumford, Lewis (1989), 11.

[264] See: Mumford, Lewis (1967).

[265] Ibid., 128.

[266] Ibid., 156.

[267] Ibid., 131.

[268] Ibid., 60.

[269] Ibid., 58-71.

[270] Ibid., 129.

[271] Mumford, Lewis (1989), 5.

[272] Recall that Simondon explains this capacity of technical objects, like our urban milieus, as being due to their overdetermination, pluri-functionality, convergence with other objects, and their hypertely.

[273] See: Fig 22. In Benevolo, Leonardo (1990), 17.

[274] See: Fig.17.

[275] Nelson, Steven (2007), 18.

[276] For further detail drawings of the Mousgoum settlements, see: Nelson, Steven (2007), 21 and http://socks-studio.com/img/blog/musgum-05.jpg.

[277] By *real estate* I refer here to its definition as a discrete land property with a building on it, or as Aldo Rossi defines it, an "inhabitable real estate." In Rossi, Aldo, (1982), 49.

[278] Rossi provides a possible classification of houses according to their socioeconomic context, distinguishing between four types: the pre-capitalist house, the capitalist house, the para-capitalist house, and the socialist house. Ibid., 50.

[279] See: "Typological Question" in Ibid., 35-45.

[280] See: "The street as a connective entity of way and buildings." In Puig, Arturo Soria y, ed. *Cerdà: The Five Bases of the General Theory of Urbanization*. Madrid: Gingko Press, 1999, 104-105.

[281] Mumford, Lewis. *The Culture of Cities (1938)*. San Diego, New York, London: A Harvest/HBJ Book, 1970, 5.

[282] Ibid., 5.

[283] Jacobs, Jane. *The Death and Life of Great American Cities.* New York: Random House, 1961, 143-151.

[284] Koolhaas, Rem, (1978), 132.

[285] Lefebvre, Henri. "The Right to the City" Chapter 2-17. In *Writings on Cities*, translated by Eleonore Kofman and Elizabeth Lebas. Cambridge, Mass, USA: Wiley-Blackwell, 2006, 131.

[286] Mumford, Lewis. *The Culture of Cities* (1970), 6.

[287] Ibid., 6.

[288] See: "Mass Production and Human Automation." In Mumford, Lewis. *The Myth of the Machine: The Pentagon of Power* (1970), 164-196.

[289] Mumford, Lewis. *The Culture of Cities* (1970), 6.

[290] Guattari, Félix. "On Machines." Edited by Andrew Benjamin. J*PVA Journal of Philosophy and the Visual Arts* 6, no. Complexity (1995), 8–12.

[291] See: Weber, Max. *Economy and Society: An Outline of Interpretive Sociology*. University of California Press, 1978, 1212-1213.

[292] See for example Deleuze and Guattari's description of Amsterdam. In Deleuze, Gilles, and Félix Guattari. T*housand Plateaus: Capitalism and Schizophrenia*, translated by Brian Massumi, 002 edition. (Originally published in French 1980). Minneapolis: University of Minnesota Press, 1987, 15.

[293] Guattari, Félix (1995), 8–12.

[294] See: Chapter 9 "The Design of the Megamachine" In Mumford, Lewis. *The Myth of the Machine: Technics and Human Development* (1967), 188-211.

[295] Ibid., 194.

[296] Ibid., 196.

[297] Mumford, Lewis. *Technics and Civilization*. Originally Published 1934. New York: Harcourt, Brace & World, 1963, 9.

[298] Mumford, Lewis. *The Myth of the Machine: Technics and Human Development* (1967), 188.

[299] Mumford, Lewis. *The Culture of Cities* (1970), 31.

[300] Simondon, Gilbert (2017), 53.

[301] Ibid., 26.

[302] Ibid., 59.

[303] Ibid., 26.

[304] Jacobs, Jane (1961), 428.

[305] See: Morton, Timothy. *Hyperobjects: Philosophy and Ecology After the End of the World*. Minneapolis: University of Minnesota Press, 2013.

[306] Mumford, Lewis. "The Design of the Megamachine." In T*he Myth of the Machine: Technics and Human Development* (1967), 189.

[307] See Simondon's comparison of engines and people. In Simondon, Gilbert. *On the Mode of Existence of Technical Objects* (2017), 27.

[308] Original quote in German: "Die Anzahl der Großstadtbewohner, welche vorziehen, in der Menge als 'Nummer' zu verschwinden, ist bedeutend größer als die Anzahl

jener, welche täglich einen "guten Morgen" oder "wie haben Sie geschlafen" von ihren sie bekrittelnden Nachbarn im Einfamilienwohnhaus hören will." In Wagner, Otto. *Die Groszstadt: eine Studie über diese*. Wien: Anton Schroll, 1911, 21-22. My translation.

309 Mumford, Lewis. "The Design of the Megamachine." *In The Myth of the Machine: Technics and Human Development* (1967), 71.

310 See: "The Breeder's Eye", In Ibid., 128-132.

311 See: "The Origin of the City in the Middle East", In Benevolo, Leonardo (1990), 20-58.

312 Mumford, Lewis. *The Myth of the Machine: Technics and Human Development* (1967), 241.

313 Ibid., 267.

314 Ibid., 263.

315 See: "Pioneer in Mechanization." In Ibid., 263-274.

316 Ibid., 266.

317 Ibid., 264.

318 Ibid.

319 See: Ibid., 265.

320 See: Ibid., 286.

321 Ibid.

322 Braudel, Fernand. *Civilization & Capitalism. 15th-18th Century*. Translated by Siân Reynolds, vol. III. The Perspective of the World. (Originally published as Le Temps Du Monde, 1979). London: Collins, 1984, 128.

323 Mumford, Lewis. *The Culture of Cities* (1970), 89-90.

324 Mumford, Lewis. *The Myth of the Machine: The Pentagon of Power* (1970), 165.

325 Ibid., 194.

326 See: "Forward to *Nowhere*", In Ibid., 193-196.

327 See: "Final Stage: The Big Brain" Ibid., 188-193.

328 Ibid., 189.

329 Ibid., 188.

330 Ibid., 189.

331 See: Introductory Essay by Mumford, Lewis. In Howard, Ebenezer. *Garden Cities of To-Morrow*. Edited by Frederic J Osborn. (Originally published in 1902 and in 1898 as To-Morrow: A Peaceful Path to Real Reform). London: Faber and Faber, 1946.

332 See: "The New Megamachine." In Mumford, Lewis. *The Myth of the Machine: The Pentagon of Power* (1970), 263-299.

333 Ibid., 191.

334 Guattari, Félix. "On Machines." (1995), 8–12. Originally published in French in *Chimeres* 19, (Spring 1993). The text is a transcript of a lecture Guattari gave in 1990 in Valencia.

335 See: Levy, Pierre. *Technologies de l'intelligence. l'avenir de la pensee a l'ere informatique*. Paris; Paris: POINTS, 1990.

[336] Levy, Pierre. "Fraktale Faltung oder wie Guattaris Maschinen uns helfen können, heute das Transzentale zu denken." In *Ästhetik und Maschinismus: Texte zu und von Félix Guattari*, edited by Henning Schmidgen. Berlin: Merve Verlag, 1995: 109. My translation. Original German version: "Eine Maschine ist Schneide- und Schnittstelle. Sie übersetzt (traduit), verrät (trahit), faltet und entfaltet für eine Maschine unterhalb die Ströme von einer Maschine oberhalb. Sie ist selbst aus Übersetzungsmaschinen zusammengesetzt, die sie dividieren, multiplizieren und heterogenisieren. Die Schnittstelle ist die 'aussenpolitische' Dimension der Maschine, wodurch sie in neue Netze eintreten und neue Ströme übersetzten kann."

[337] Guattari writes: "Pierre Levy uses an expression which I find very useful: 'trying to break down the ontological iron curtain between being and things.'" In Guattari, Félix (1995), 8–12.

[338] Ibid., 8.

[339] Ibid., 8-13.

[340] See: Raunig, Gerald. *A Few Fragments on Machines*. Translated by Aileen Derieg, 10/2005. Accessed September 24, 2021. https://transversal.at/transversal/1106/raunig1/en.

[341] Ibid., 5.

[342] Deleuze, Gilles, and Félix Guattari. *Anti-Edipus - Capitalism and Schizophrenia*. Preface by Michale Foucault. Tenth. Printing 2000. Minneapolis: University of Minnesota Press, 1983, 9.

[343] Deleuze, Gilles, and Félix Guattari. *Anti Ödipus - Kapitalismus and Schizophrenie.* Translated by Bernd Schwibs. Original title: L'Anti-Oedipe, 1972. Frankfurt am Main: Suhrkamp, 1977, 498. Quoted in Raunig, Gerald (2005).

[344] Deleuze, Gilles and Félix Guattari, (1987), 3-25.

[345] Ibid., 10.

[346] Ibid.

[347] Kwinter quotes Major Gen. Fred J. Ascani, from Chuck Yeager, (New York: Bantam Books, 1985). In "Flying the Bullet, or When Did the Future Begin?" Translated by Dieter Hoffmann-Axthelm. *ARCH+*, vol. 132, Rem Koolhaas / Projekte und Texte 1993-1996 (June 1996), 80–85.

[348] Ibid., 80.

[349] Levy, Pierre. "Fraktale Faltung oder wie Guattaris Maschinen uns helfen können, heute das Transzentale zu denken." In *Ästhetik und Maschinismus: Texte zu und von Félix Guattari*, edited by Henning Schmidgen. Berlin: Merve Verlag, 1995, 95.

[350] Aristotle. *Politics*; Translated by Benjamin Jowett. Batochhe Books Kitchener, 1999, Book one, Part two, 5. https://historyofeconomicthought.mcmaster.ca/aristotle/Politics.pdf.

[351] See: "The Term *Vita Activa*." In Arendt, Hannah (1959), 13-18.

[352] Ibid., 26.

[353] Ibid., 173.

[354] See: Morton, Timothy. Hyperobjects: Philosophy and Ecology After the End of the World (2013).

[355] Ibid., 15.

[356] See: Stromberg, Joseph. "What Is the Anthropocene and Are We in It?" *Smithsonian*

Magazine, January 2013. Accessed September 24, 2021. https://www.smithsonianmag.com/science-nature/what-is-the-anthropocene-and-are-we-in-it-164801414/.

[357] See Harman, Graham, (2018).

[358] It was first known as Object-Oriented Philosophy. See: Harman, Graham. *Tool-Being: Heidegger and the Metaphysics of Objects*. Chicago and La Salle, Illinois: Open Court, 2002, 217.

[359] Harman, Graham. *The Quadruple Object*. Winchester, UK, Washington, USA: Zero Books, 2011, 6.

[360] Harman, Graham, (2002), 1.

[361] See conversation between Bruno Latour and Graham Harman. In Latour, Bruno, Graham Harman, and Peter Erdelyi. *The Prince and the Wolf: Latour and Harman at the LSE*. Winchester: Zero Books, John Hunt Publishing, 2011, 37.

[362] Harman, Graham. *Guerrilla Metaphysics: Phenomenology and the Carpentry of Things*. Chicago: Open Court, 2005, 74.

[363] Harman, Graham, (2011), 7.

[364] See Ibid., 08-10.

[365] Harman, Graham (2002), 22.

[366] See: Harman, Graham (2011), 10-13.

[367] Harman, Graham (2002), 23.

[368] In particular, I recall a video presented in the main hall of the Italian pavilion at the 2014 Venice Biennale curated by Rem Koolhaas, which showed all kinds of scenes of events that architecture can provide.

[369] Morton, Timothy. *Hyperobjects: Philosophy and Ecology After the End of the World* (2013), 1.

[370] See: Eisenman, Peter. "Post-Functionalism." In *Oppositions Reader: Selected Readings from a Journal for Ideas and Criticism in Architecture, 1973-1984*, edited by K. Michael Hays, 9–12. New York: Princeton Architectural Press, 1998.

[371] See: Harman, Graham (2018), 66-73.

[372] The original metaphor Jose Ortega y Gasset used is from the Spanish Poet Lopez Pico. Ibid., 72.

[373] Ibid., 73.

[374] See: Harman, Graham. *Architecture and Objects. Art after Nature*. Minnesota: University of Minnesota Press, 2022.

[375] Moneo, Rafael. "On Typology." *Oppositions. A Journal for Ideas and Criticism in Architecture* 13 (Summer 1978), 23.

[376] Ibid., 23.

[377] See: Kubler, George, (1962), 39-53.

[378] Ibid., 33.

[379] See: Kubler, George (1962), 33-39.

[380] See: Harman, Graham, 2002.

[381] See especially part 1 of chapter 2: "Evolution of Technical Reality; Element, Individual, Ensemble." In Simondon, Gilbert (2017), 53-81.

[382] Schmidgen, Henning, (n.d.), 11–18.

[383] Ibid., 15.

[384] See: Wiener, Norbert. *Cybernetics or Control and Communication in the Animal and the Machine*. New York: Wiley, 1948.

[385] Schmidgen, Henning. "Thinking Technological and Biological Beings: Gilbert Simondon's Philosophy of Machines." *Revista Do Departamento de Psicologia* UFF, no. 17 (n.d.), 12.

[386] Simondon, Gilbert (2017), 49.

[387] Schmidgen, Henning (n.d.), 15.

[388] Simondon, Gilbert (2017), 71.

[389] Ibid., 71.

[390] Schmidgen, Henning (n.d.), 13.

[391] Simondon, Gilbert (2017), 55.

[392] Schmidgen, Henning (n.d.), 13.

[393] Ibid., 55.

[394] See: DeLanda, Manuel. *Intensive Science and Virtual Philosophy*. London, New York: Continuum, 2002, 58-61.

[395] Harman, Graham (2011), 9.

[396] Simondon, Gilbert (2017), 27.

[397] Benevolo, Leonardo. *The European City*. The Making of Europe: Series Editor: Jacques Le Goff. Translated from the Italian by Carl Ipsen. Oxford UK, Cambridge, Mass,: 1993: 2.

[398] See footnote 7. In Simondon, Gilbert (2017), 59.

[399] Ibid., 60-61.

[400] Ibid., 20. The process of concretization is explained in detail in chapter 1: "Genesis of the Technical Object: The Process of Concretisation." Ibid., 25-51.

[401] Kubler, George (1962), 39.

[402] Simondon, Gilbert (2017), 53.

[403] Ibid., 29.

[404] See Simondon's Illustrations of "Morphological Evolution" Plate 3-6. In Ibid., 87-90.

[405] Kubler, George (1962), 8-9.

[406] See: Laugier, Marc-Antoine. *An Essay on Architecture*. London, Printed for T. Osborne and Shipton, 1755. Accessed September 24, 2021. http://archive.org/details/essayonarchitect00laugrich.

[407] See: Muratori, Saverio, "Studi per una operante storia urbana di Venezia." Roma: Instituto poligrafico dello Stato, Libreria dello Stato, 1960.

[408] See: Lynn, Greg. *Animated Form*, New York: Princeton Architectural Press, 1999.

[409] See: DeLanda, Manuel. "Deleuze and the use of the genetic algorithm in architecture", In *AD-Architectural Design* 72(1) January 2002, 9-12.

[410] Kubler, George (1962), 9.

[411] Ibid., 17.

[412] Ibid., 13.

[413] See: Simondon, Gilbert (2017), 85-100.

[414] Schmidgen, Henning (n.d.), 14.

[415] See: Harman, Graham (2018), 73.

[416] Moneo, Rafael (1978), 23.

[417] Ibid., 44.

Chapter 3: The Five Individuated Cities

Underpinning this argument is the assertion that, deeper than the from and use of the city, are its qualities as a technical object. All urban forms emerge from these overdetermined qualities of the city itself. The argument I have tried to formulate in the previous chapters is that a city takes form through the fusion of the aesthetic qualities of its parts. In this chapter, I will introduce specifically the various emerging and mutating forms of the city and discuss their appearance in history.

Looking throughout our urban history we can distinguish between five individuated cities:

- The City as an Enclosure
- The City as a Grid
- The City as a Line
- The City as an Archipelago
- The City as a Solid

By visualizing each of these five through the lens of Simondon's mechanology, I aim to show their evolutionary difference from the idea that the form of the city is determined predominantly by socioeconomic forces. While such forces may be considered the milieu in which a city emerges, they cannot explain its formal appearance, or why a city is shaped as it is. Technical beings such as the city have their own genesis, a mode of existence that is driven by their inherent processes of concretization. Before discussing each of the

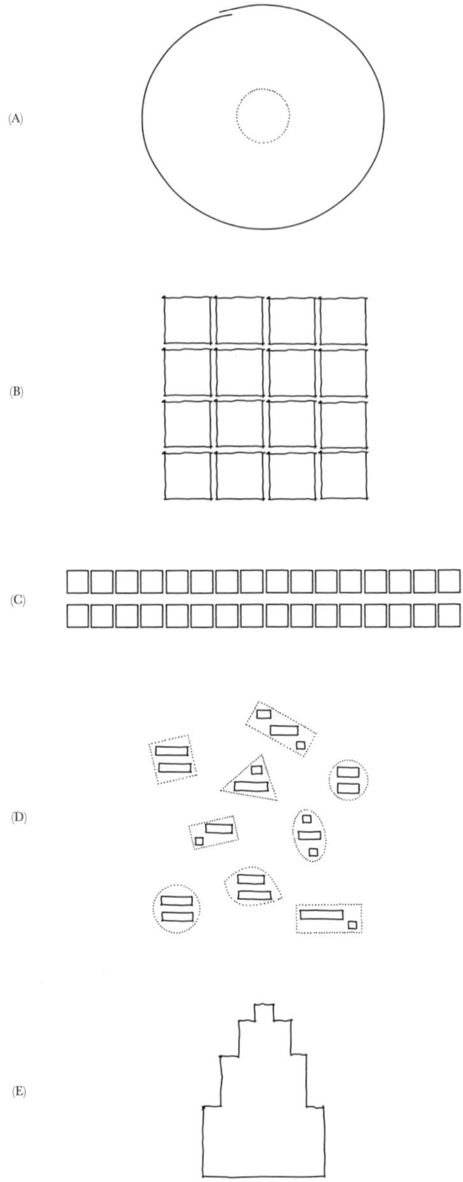

**FIGURE 30. THE FIVE INDIVIDUATED CITIES:
THE CITY AS AN ENCLOSURE (A), THE CITY AS A GRID (B), THE CITY AS A LINE (C), THE CITY AS AN ARCHIPELAGO (D), THE CITY AS A SOLID (E.)**

five individuated cities in detail, it is useful to further sketch the counterexample of the city as determined by socioeconomic forces.

The Urban Revolution

In 1970, shortly after his book *The Right to the City*,[418] Henri Lefebvre published another on the history of urbanization, called *The Urban Revolution*,[419] in which he presents the evolution of city-forms as a territorial transformation from a purely rural planet to a totally urbanized one. Lefebvre formulates a new idea of what traditionally has been understood as *urban society*.[420] Noting that what sociologists commonly refer to as urban society is any form of urban agglomeration, such as "the Greek polis, the oriental or medieval city, commercial and industrial cities, small cities, the megalopolis," he argues that "we have forgotten or overlooked the social relationships (primarily relationships of production) with which each urban type is associated."[421]

To better understand what Lefebvre means by "relationships of production," we can look to a subsequent book by him, *The Production of Space*,[422] in which he distinguishes between two circuits of capital, which drove our history of urbanization through economic production.[423] The first circuit of capital, for Lefebvre, is Marx's idea that investment is made into man, material, and machines in order to produce new products. Those products are then sold to the market, which creates profit. That profit is then invested further and a new cycle begins. To Marx's primary circuit of capital Lefebvre adds a second circuit. It is based on the economic venture by the capitalist of investing money into real estate—meaning the development of land, plots, and urban areas—of which the gained profit is invested further into real estate again.[424]

If we apply Lefebvre's idea of circuits of capital and their modes of production to our history of urbanization, the term *urban society* comes to mean a society that tends toward total urbanization. The history of the city is therefore the history of urbanization and its attendant social relationships of production, which have transformed our planet to be one hundred percent urbanized today. Lefebvre visualizes this idea with a simple diagram.

0 ———————————— 100%

FIGURE 31. LEFEBVRE'S DIAGRAM OF THE PROCESS OF URBANIZATION: FROM "PURE NATURE" ON THE LEFT TO THE COMPLETION OF URBANIZATION ON THE RIGHT

The diagram appears as a timeline. At its start, it marks the beginning of our urban revolution, the moment of our domestication, the moment we attached ourselves to the soil. The end of the line represents the beginning of the twenty-first century. For Lefebvre, however, the evolution of the city is more than a simple linear timeline, it is also spatial. While the timeline shows our process of urbanization, an exodus from the rural that over 5000 years led from a state of zero urbanization to a planet of total urbanization, this totality does not mean that the whole planet is urbanized by cities, or that all people live in cities. What it means, rather, is that no part of the world is not part of the economic processes that constitute our *urban fabric*. As Lefebvre writes, "this expression, 'urban fabric,' does not narrowly define the built world of cities but all manifestations of the dominance of the city over the country. In this sense, a vacation home, a highway, a supermarket in the countryside are all part of the urban fabric."[425] What started as an overproduction of agricultural goods accelerated throughout history. The growth and exchange of goods through which the city emerged has expanded, according to Lefebvre,

> from simple barter to the global market, from the simple exchange between two individuals all the way to the exchange of products, works of art, ideas, and human beings. Buying and selling, merchandise and market, money and capital appear to sweep away all obstacles. During this period of generalization, the effect of the process—namely the urban reality—becomes both cause and reason.[426]

Lefebvre sees the city therefore as a superstructure floating above the economic structure of production. With that in mind, I find the title of the German translation of his book particularly poignant.

Die Revolution der Städte, as it is called, literally means that the city, the technical object itself, is making a revolution.

In his reading of the history of our urban reality through social relationships of production, Lefebvre distinguishes between four kinds of historically emerging cities: *the political*, *the mercantile*, *the industrial*, and a final phase he calls the *critical zone*.

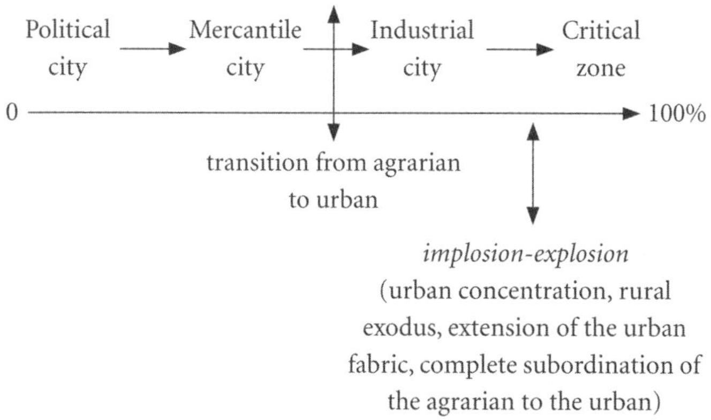

FIGURE 32. LEFEBVRE'S FOUR KINDS OF CITIES

The first, the political city,[427] mainly refers to cities that emerged at the beginning of our urbanization, due to vast exploration and the management of large-scale agricultural projects, especially in the Middle East around 5000 years ago. The mercantile city became the successor of the political city, according to Lefebvre.[428] It was the city of the late Middle Ages, in which the exchange of goods become the function of cities, given form by the urban marketplace. The industrial city is the third city to emerged on Lefebvre's line of urbanization. It is the city produced by new industrial capital.[429] Even when industrial cities were not located at the sources of energy such as mines, as Lefebvre notes, the accumulated capital soon moved into the cities. In this regard we can point out a secondary definition of the term *capital city*: the locus of large amounts of capital.

The last phase of urban agglomeration is what Lefebvre calls the critical phase.[430] It describes the spatial condition in which the rural implodes and the urban explodes. Form this moment onward the city expands its urban fabric endlessly and subordinates the agricultural land to become completely urbanized. It defines our urban exodus: the condition in which we live today. Although Lefebvre exhorts researchers "to identify and describe the various forms of urbanization and explain what happens to the forms, functions, and urban structures that are transformed by the breakup of the ancient city and the process of generalized urbanization," he allows that "until now the critical phase was perceived as a kind of black box. We know what enters the box, and sometimes we see what comes out, but we don't know what goes on inside."[431]

If we overlay Lefebvre's cities onto the five individuated cities introduced at the start of this chapter, meaning that we overlay concepts of cities driven by function (the former) onto those driven by form (the latter), we can identify some interesting discrepancies:

- In some cases, use and form seem to be congruent. For example, the political city of Lefebvre emerged simultaneously with the city as an enclosure. It can be argued that one enhances the other and vice versa.
- However, we also find that the same city form can take on different uses, or socioeconomic functions. While the city as an enclosure did not change in form since its origination, it did change in its use, in the late Middle Ages turning into Lefebvre's mercantile city.
- The same can be seen in the opposite direction. While the industrial city marks a particular point in Lefebvre's diagram, the change in modes of production that it represents did not also give rise to a unique form of the city. In fact, the opposite is the case: the industrial city can be found in various forms, from the city as a line to the city as an archipelago. The form of the city can change while its use stays the same.
- Finally, in regard to the "black box" of Lefebvre's critical zone, if we clear some of this fogginess and look at what has happened recently in our cities, it seems that it has produced definitely new city-forms, specifically the city as a solid, a gigantic "mountain"[432] of pure interiority.[433]

What really is going on inside that technical object we call the city? It is exactly this question, addressed by Lefebvre, which this book seeks to answer. What can explain the discrepancies and incoherences between the forms of cities and their uses, between the appearance of their physical structures and their socioeconomic performances? While I have explained the capacity of the city to take on various forms and uses as a result of a general quality of technical objects—namely, overdetermination—that label alone does not suffice to explain how this occurs. What I now want to discuss are the specifics of that inner capacity, what Simondon calls the hypertely of technical objects: the idea that individual parts of an object such as the city are able to specialize and converge, leading to the genesis of all its various forms and uses. This emergent diversity is due to the capacity of some those parts to tune their hidden qualities. They actualize what yet exists only virtually, tuning inexhaustible potentiality toward new concrete forms. This process of concretization, as we know, is not biological but technological. It works mechanologically. In various moments throughout our urban history, different parts intensified different qualities to cause the appearance of new forms and uses of our cities. It is precisely in those aesthetic qualities that we can discern hypertely. We can see how the city as an enclosure emerged from the village, by tuning its enclosure-ness to function as a polis. Similarly, the city as a grid can be seen to have emerged through the specialization of the interiority of the city as an enclosure, the very quality of interiority having led to increasingly more order within.[434] It is inherent hypertely that accounts for the differentiation of the linear city from the city as a grid, through the specialization of one element: the street. The city as an archipelago ran through a similar process of concretization, but rather than an infrastructural element, the hypertelic components were the island regions formed by the mesh of the grid. More recently, we can see how the city as a solid arose from the fusion of the of the city as an enclosure[435] with the island qualities of the city as an archipelago.

The city as a technical object seems to individuate throughout its history by mutation, fusion, unification, specialization, and convergence of its inner parts, tuning new functions and taking on new forms in a manner that confounds any linear chronology. It is as if the city sends the electromagnetic signals described by Kubler across time to allow new cities to individuate. I have found five unique ones, and I assume another is right now in the making.

3.1. The City as an Enclosure

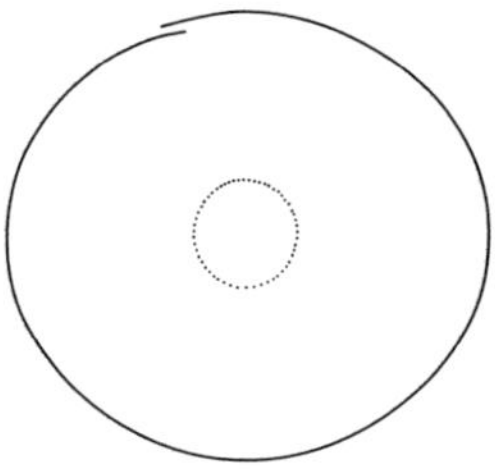

FIGURE 33. THE CITY AS AN ENCLOSURE

The city as an enclosure can be considered perhaps the most common model in our history of urbanization. If we place it on our timeline, we realize that it sits not just the beginning, but also can be found today. Appearing first around 4500 BCE in Mesopotamia,[436] it clearly emerged out of the formal properties of the village enclosed within a fence. The city as an enclosure initially functioned as a fortification, a model for defense, as at the early city of Uruk. Amidst agricultural overproduction following the last ice age, new centralized powers formed, with the city and its fortified walls becoming the figure of a new political entity. The city as an enclosure was used later as a model for the Greek polis.[437] It was also repeated throughout the Roman Empire for all new settlements and military camps across that vast territory.[438] If we look at today's urban morphology of Turin, we can still find the layout and the scale of a Roman settlement at its center. The city as an enclosure can be seen as a model in the history of cities in Asia as well, often occurring not as a city surrounded by single wall but as a multiplicity of enclosures.[439] The city as an enclosure dramatically affected the European landscape as the foundation for all new cities in the Middle Ages. After the Roman camps that were the first wave of originating new cities in the European territory, the second one happened in the medieval period.[440] This was a moment when technical innovations initiated an overproduction of agriculture, which allowed craftsmanship and trading to flourish. The intensification of commerce allowed people to liberate themselves from the feudal landowners and originate autonomous, self-governed cities. In a short time these new cities formed a vast network of trade throughout the Europe, which still can be found in the infrastructural connections between European cities today. However, this first model of our cities largely disappeared with the emergence of the

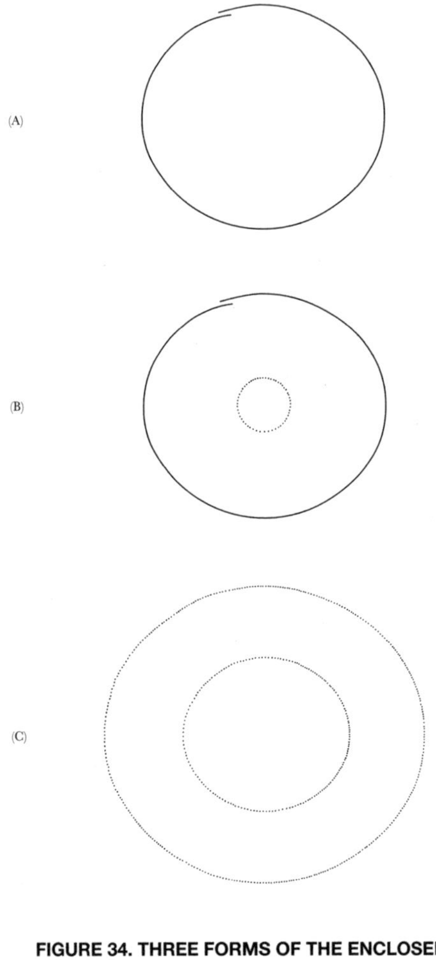

FIGURE 34. THREE FORMS OF THE ENCLOSED CITY:
WALLS WITHIN A WALL(A), A TERRITORY WITHIN A WALL(B),A TERRITORY AS A WALL(C).

industrial age, the ending of wars, and the sprawling growth of urban populations throughout the continent. I would argue it reappeared as a mutated typology in Ebenezer Howard's garden city, an enclosed city without a wall.[441] And today it is used as a model for both gated communities and refugee camps around the world.[442]

The Forms of Enclosed Cities

a. Walls within a Wall

The first form of the city as an enclosure is, in fact, a city of multiple enclosures, or more simply: a city of walls within a wall. This city has two kinds of spaces. The first defines an inner city, comprising a centrally framed core, while the second defines an outer city, a walled, ringlike space surrounding the inner city. This kind of city occurred in early West Asian cities like Ur, Uruk, and Babylon,[443] but it can be found as a model for ancient Chinese cities as well, like Beijing.[444] The formal difference between this first kind of walled city and many later enclosed cities can be observed in their spaces of circulation: while in European cities the spaces of circulation, like streets and squares, are continuous throughout their interior, in East Asian cities the streets are interrupted and broken by walls. The idea of a city of such onion-like layering of space surrounding a central walled core is still present in the urbanization of Asian cities today. For instance, Beijing still expands in rings of space, whereby the walls of the ancient city are replaced by streets and infrastructure.

b. A Territory within a Wall

The second form of the city as an enclosure contains a territory within its wall. Here, the inner walls of our previous form of enclosed city tune one specific quality—namely, those walls mutate into a boundary. Thus, although the layout of a single wall enclosing the city suggests that the territory within is continuous, the inner boundary frames a distinct territory within that broader territory of the city. This inner territory is a very particular kind of piece of land. For one, it can be found in the agora of the ancient Greek polis, which Mumford identifies as "an open space, publicly held and occupiable for public purpose, but not necessarily enclosed," and "an amorphous and irregular form. . . . somehow an open square."[445] Marking that square were boundary stones called *Horoi*, with inscriptions like, "I am the boundary of the Agora."[447] Horoi marked not just the agora but all kinds of boundaries between various properties, both public and private. They were even used as mortgage stones.[448]

In terms of architecture, the empty space of this inner territory can be loosely surrounded by buildings, as it is in Greek cities like Athens,[449] or as in later examples it can be densely surrounded, like at the Roman Forum.[450] This type of inner void multiplied throughout the history of urbanization, turning into the marketplace, *campo*, and *piazza* of the medieval European city,[451] or the *grande place* of baroque Paris.[452] In all of these cases, what generally is understood as public space is an empty location that designates a territory free of private interests. Its edges are marked for rites and laws to be performed within. Beginning in the 1950s, however, this inner territory took a new form when it fused with the privately administered, quasi-public interiority of buildings. Two new architectural types emerged: the shopping mall as invented by Victor Gruen and the atrium building by John Portman. But more about them later.

c. A Territory as a Wall

The third form of the city as an enclosure is bounded not by a wall, but rather by a territory as a wall. Throughout our urban history, we can find many cities that have a limit yet are not walled. One example is Çatalhöyük in present-day Turkey.[453] Surrounded by a plateau, it was a city of buildings but no roads, where roofs were the public space. The early Minoan city of Knossos on Crete similarly had no defensive walls. Why would it? As Mumford writes, "what indeed was this mountainous island itself, girt with the sea as its moat, but a vast citadel?"[454] And perhaps the most famous example of a territory as a wall is the Venetian lagoon, an aqueous boundary of the island city.[455] A territory as enclosure furthermore defines most cities that were planned with a system of bastions, the vast, surrounding defensive territory that became necessary after the invention of the canon.[456] With bastions we can see how third form of the city as an enclosure entails the specialization of a specific quality of the wall, its thickness expanding to the size of a territory and its height diminishing to become just a boundary.

The reemergence of a territory as a wall can be seen in Howard's garden cities. Mumford appreciated the garden city movement for its fulfillment of a democratic solution to city planning. For him, small communities are the only solution to Plato's desire: "There is no greater good in state than that the citizens should be known to each other."[457] But what is unique in the form of the garden city is that the ideal, circular city is framed by a productive territory. This boundary territory carries all the agricultural function needed to sustain the city and its autonomy. Thus, what once was the hinterland outside the city wall, as in both previous forms of the city as an enclosure, becomes in this third form the wall itself; one sort of territory is walled by another.

The Functions of Enclosed Cities

As discussed earlier in regard to Lefebvre's diagram, the form of the city as an enclosure can take on different functions, having coincided first with his idea of the political city and then later with the mercantile city. I would like to add to those two cities of Lefebvre two more: *the camp* and *the common.*

a. The Political City

Demarcating an inside and an outside, a wall is a political boundary. The reason Lefebvre, among many others, calls the first city the political city is that it emerged out of the need for a form that would act as a political center, or a center of power, to manage and organize the transformation that was occurring along the fruitful riverbanks after the end of last ice age, namely the expansion and overproduction of large-scale agriculture. This is the city of Mumford's megamachine, with its rigidly hierarchical organization that uses humans as mechanical plug-ins to run the military, bureaucratic, and production machines. While this idea of the political city is best summarized by Lefebvre when he writes, "ownership of the land becomes the eminent right of a monarch, the symbol of order and action,"[458] as we know from the writings of Mumford, Hannah Arendt, and others, the city as an enclosure also performs as a different kind of political city. Specifically, it was the first autonomous form of self-governance, the birthplace of democracy. The Greek city-state was therefore the birthplace of us as political subjects, the setting for Arendt's *vita activa*, in which human life is devoted to public political matters.

b. The Mercantile City

By mercantile city we mainly mean the economic structures of centralism and state monopolies which European states invented between the sixteenth and nineteenth centuries to maximize their profits from colonialism and imperialism. Such policies of growth were introduced after "medical localism and autonomy were eliminated," as Mumford writes.[459] Lefebvre describes the transition from the political to the mercantile city thusly:

> the city would no longer appear as an urban island in a rural ocean, it would no longer seem a paradox, a monster, a hell or heaven that contrasted sharply with village or country life in a natural environment. It entered people's awareness and understanding as one of the terms in the opposition between town and country. Country? It is now no more than—nothing more than— the town's "environment," its horizon, its limit. Villagers? As far as they were concerned, they no longer worked for the territorial lords, they produced for the city, for the urban market.[460]

In such a description we can start to understand how it is that the city as an enclosure could tune new uses while its form remained the same.

In the Middle Ages the enclosed city supported the autonomy of its citizens, effectively granting the right to function as a trade zone, which allowed for the market to take its place in the inner void of the city. Braudel explains: "No town is without its market, and there can be no regional or national markets without towns."[461] This counted for the mercantile city in baroque times as well, with just one difference, which was that one city, namely the capital city, grew larger than the rest and its economic model extended beyond its immediate territory. The shift in function from a political city to mercantile city changed the performance of not only the inner void of the enclosed city, but also its external territory. In other words, as Lefebvre points out, the relationship between the city and its hinterland changed.[462] While in the beginning the city as an enclosure was fundamentally different from its natural surroundings, it then turned its adjacent territory, its hinterland, into a part of the city itself. Such an incorporation of the surrounding territory as a part of the enclosed city was fully actualized several centuries later through the introduction of the garden city diagram. The city and its surroundings became one as the wall was tuned to become a territory.

Beyond those territories as boundaries, the vast space between medieval mercantile cities was a one of the circulation of goods, people, and money. "The 3000 towns of all sizes in fifteenth-century Germany," Braudel writes, "acted as so many relay-points, four or five hours' journey apart in the south and west of the country, seven or eight hours apart in the north and east."[463] Perhaps this territory of relay-points in the nineteenth century fused with the qualities of fast infrastructures like trains to give rise to the linear city. What can be said for sure is that the beginning of long-distance trade and these networks of enclosed towns initiated what today we call the global economy.[464]

c. The Camp

The city as an enclosure can also be used as a camp. In his book *Homo Sacer: Sovereign Power and Bare Life*,[465] Giorgio Agamben examines the question: What really is a camp? What kind of juridical-political structure is embedded in the camp, a kind of city as an enclosure, that allows for atrocity to occur? Agamben concludes that the decisive factor is that a *state of exception* is extended onto the entire civilian population.[466] He shows that the a camp did not emerge from any common law but rather from martial law. Nazi concentration camps had their origin in a Prussian law called the *Schutzhaft*,[467] which allowed the police to execute a preventive act and take individuals into so-called protection.[468] What Agamben shows is that this execution of a "protective custody" under a state of exception happened throughout modernity. He points out that the first concentration camps in

Germany were in fact the work of Social Democrats, who used the law to intern communists as well as Jewish refugees from Eastern Europe in 1923.[469] The city as an enclosure provides a complementary spatial form for the camp's requisite state of exception, which in his 2005 book on the subject Agamben aptly summarizes as a "no-man's land between public law and political fact."[470]

d. The Common

If we were to place Howard's garden city diagram on Lefebvre's diagram of the evolution of urbanization, it would sit right at the point of the implosion-explosion.[471] The garden city was developed to counter the increasing concentration of urban population and the rural exodus in late-nineteenth and early-twentieth centuries. While Lefebvre argues that no new sociopolitical forms of the city emerged after industrialization, I would instead argue that new urban mutations have become actualized. The garden city is one of them. As a technical object, I consider it a fusion of a walled city and its surrounding territory. The use of its inner void space turned away from political or commercial performance and was tuned to become a well-irrigated garden.[472] The garden city thus illustrates an individuated use of the form of the city enclosed by a territory as a wall: the city as a collective property, or common.

In his book, *Garden Cities of To-morrow*, Howard's vision for his garden city of tomorrow starts with a an acquisition of property by a trusted group of founders:

> The reader is asked to imagine an estate embracing an area of 6,000 acres, which is at present purely agricultural, and bas been obtained by purchase in the open market at a cost of £40 an acre, or £240,000. The purchase money is supposed to have been raised on mortgage debentures, bearing interest at an average rate not exceeding £4 per cent.[473]

Four men hold this land in trust to allow the people of the garden city to build on it. The central idea being that through such a form of investment people could gain a common ownership of a large territory.[474] It would allow them to establish an autonomous form of public services in which a municipality would govern and maintain this collective property. While the dominant trend since the beginning of our urbanization has been to subdivide the territory between the wall into private and public ownership, Howard's vision eliminates these two opposites and replaces them with a single cooperative ownership. "The change required," he writes, "would be simply a change of landlords. Separate ownership would merge in the joint-stock ownership of the public. Instead of being in the possession of individuals, the country would be held by the great corporate body-society."[475]

3.2. The City as a Grid

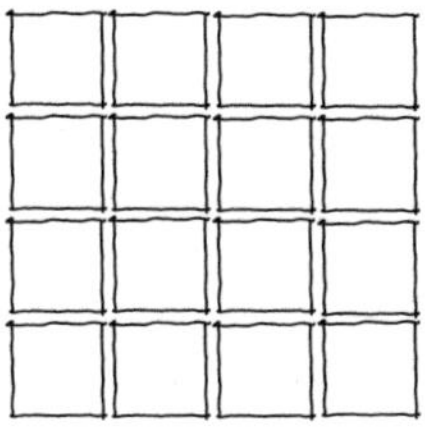

FIGURE 35. THE CITY AS A GRID

The city as a grid can be seen as the emergent city form of the nineteenth century. It accommodated the fast growth of urban populations in the beginning of our industrialization by means of capitalism, or more specifically through the speculation of land.[476] For Mumford, the city of the capitalists does not have a form. Rather, capitalism "accounts for the steady loss of form that went on after the eighteenth century."[477] Perhaps this explains why the city as a grid is also absent from the diagram of Lefebvre, who describes the industrial age as having produced a kind of "non-city."[478] The city as a grid can be seen in almost total opposition to its precursor. Rather than being hemmed in by walls, it allows for endless expansion. The city as a grid is limitless. Although it has a particular form, it has neither a boundary nor a shape. And yet the city as a grid is the final individuated city in our history of urbanization in which the urban fabric, like the city as an enclosure, can be considered as a unified whole.

Amsterdam, with its *Grachtengordel* of the seventeenth century, was the first such city to transition from the protectionism of the mercantile city toward the commercial competition of real estate. The most famous layout for a gridded city is the 1811 Commissioner's Plan of New York, which subdivided the land of Manhattan into parcels of twenty-five-feet by one-hundred-feet lots ready for speculation. The most recognized grid to have been laid down on a piece of land in Europe is Cerdà's Extension Plan of Barcelona. Along with being a practical demonstration of the ideas of Cerdà's *General Theory of Urbanization*, the city as a grid became the signifier in Europe of what Benevolo refers to as the "post-liberal city."[479]

The city as a grid was not an invention of industrialization. In fact, the grid first appeared inside the walled city to give order to its interiority. While we should not be surprised to find a grid in many Roman cities[480] due to their functions as military camps, it may seem less obvious that we can find grids in Greek cities as well. A new Greek polis, such as Milet,[481] Priene, or Olynth, typically had a gridiron scheme known as a Hippodamian plan.[482] The city as a grid is the form of most newly founded cities, as seen especially in the colonial cities of the Americas.[483] It is, however, by no means just a colonial phenomenon, having become a generic layout that can also be found in Asian cities such as Guangzhou[484] or Kyoto.[485]

Finally, there is a grid that turned into a city. This is the Jeffersonian Grid of the United States.[486] Overlaid onto the vast territory of the western US, this grid subdivided a "wilderness" into sections of one square mile, further subdividable into forty-acre parcels. A fundamentally agricultural grid, only through Frank Lloyd Wright's Broadacre City project did it become urbanized. Wright's vision for his anti-urban city grew out of a belief that true democracy can only be established when free individuals can explore their own piece of land. With Broadacre City, Wright wanted to make manifest a Jeffersonian politics signified in his capitalist desire: "That Government is best Government that is least Government."[487] It is obvious that he wanted to make the city disappear.[488]

The Forms of the City as a Grid

In a certain sense, the city as a grid has just one form. It is a field that is virtually boundless. But within that field we find different topological features:

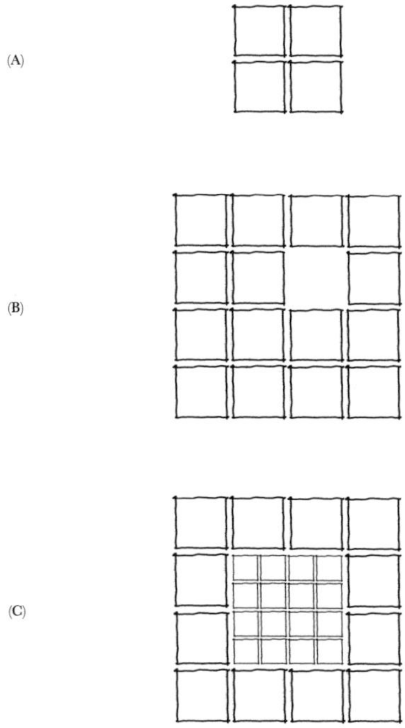

FIGURE 36. THREE FORMS OF THE GRIDDED CITY: THE GRID OF FOUR SQUARES(A), THE GRID WITH A VOID(B), GRIDS WITHIN GRIDS(C).

a. The Grid of Four Squares

While the city as an enclosure divides a territory into inside and outside, the city as a grid subdivides its ground into spaces of occupation and a unifying space of circulation. This idea can be seen in the earliest Egyptian hieroglyphs representing the city: a cross dividing the ground of a city into four parts.[489] The topological principle of this diagram allows each part to contain any function while maintaining access. This sort of atomized grid has been found in an Assyrian relief as well,[490] and it was materialized in one of our earliest cities. Babylon, a city designed around 2000 BCE, was divided into four parts by the Euphrates and its canals, all perfectly straight and geometrically perpendicular to each other.[491]

The idea of originating a city at the intersection of two perpendicular streets characterizes almost all early gridded cities.

The Romans called this *centuratio*: a geometric apparatus to subdivide land into equal square plots.[492] Using a measuring instrument called a *groma*[493] to identify the right angle of the two main axes of the new city: the decumanus maximus and the cardo maximus.[494] These main axes were much wider than all other streets, marking the center of city. Throughout the history of urbanization, the intersections of two distinct circulation paths have been used continuously as the origin points for cities. This can be seen especially in European cities of the Middle Ages, where the grid form often was enclosed by a wall, demonstrating the potential for two individuated city types to be coincident with one another. At that time the intersection of the axes of circulation was no longer an abstract point but would become a specific object, such as a bridge or a marketplace.

b. The Grid with a Void

While the single cross is the nuclear idea of the city as a grid, when repeated it becomes the idealized form. Rosalind Krauss identifies the uniqueness of the grid in its defining flatness and the pure relationship of its inner parts: "Flattened, geometricized, ordered, it is antinatural, antimimetic, antireal. It is what art looks like when it turns its back on nature. In the flatness that results from its coordinates, the grid is the means of crowding out the dimensions of the real and replacing them with the lateral spread of a single surface."[495] Applied to the city, this idea of the grid points to an endless urban fabric based on the inner logic of its subdivision. In the city as a grid we can distinguish between two kinds of properties. The first consists of a series of rectangular pieces of land—city blocks—which are further subdivided into equally sized plots. At a minimum, one plot boundary is concomitant with the boundary of the city block. Enclosed and compartmentalized, these are assets that can be bought and owned. They are privately exploited. The second kind of property is a continuous piece of land that is publicly owned and serves as an infrastructure of the city, providing access to all of its properties. This is the street.

Dividing the city into private islands[496] unified by a public territory running between, the grid has specialized throughout its history one particular quality above all. This quality was a shift or reversal, wherein one or more rectangular privatized islands are enfolded as part of the public property of circulation. This merger can happen by simply erasing one or more blocks, while in other instances the boundary of the blocks stays and only its use merges with the public realm.

In his book *The History of the City*, Benevolo points to the beautiful examples of this kind of grid with a void that can be found in the original sixteenth century plans of Caracas and Quito, where the voids emerged by one of the blocks remaining without buildings.[497] Further examples abound across time and space. Often multiple blocks are unified to generate a larger park or public space within a grid.[498] There is perhaps no better example than New York's Central Park. Not only is it one of the largest voids, it intensifies the thesis of the grid as well. The huge park goes beyond being anti-natural—it fakes the natural as well.[499] At Monpazier, a village in the north of France founded in the thirteenth century by King Edward I of England, the grid appears to have a standard central void, where one of the blocks is left empty and unifies with the surrounding streets.[500] But from the top view, or what today we call Google Earth, it seems as if this void is entirely enclosed by buildings. What is unique about this void is that, due to the fusion of two city forms, the city as a grid and the city as an enclosure, an architectural object emerges that produces a kind of space that is both void and building, public and private at the same time.

c. Grids within Grids

The city of grids within grids is perhaps the most common model. The gridded city is almost always composed of more than one grid. Even a city like Manhattan, which seems based on a single continuous mesh formed by twelve avenues and 155 streets, has within it an embedded hierarchy of grids. For example, fifteen major cross streets along with some avenues form a larger grid within the grid. A city made of multiple grids such as this is mainly due to historical growth. Turin, for example, originated as a Roman grid, which extended in baroque times into grids of larger block sizes that were further added to by many subsequent urban interventions.[501] Grids are enmeshed with other grids of different times, different sizes, and different kinds. In Vienna, the baroque streets formed a radial grid whose inner fields were filled in by rectangular grids over time, as manifested by Otto Wagner's *Die Grossstadt* wherein he squeezed a rectangular mesh into a radial grid without triangles.[502]

When grids overlap and merge they can produce a Moiré effect, such as can be found in Cerdà's Barcelona plan. The grid of the inhabitable *manzanas* overlaps with the large diagonal grid of the regional infrastructure network.[503] A pure version of such grids within grids can be found in Belo Horizonte in Brazil or John Reid's 1795 plan for Washington, D.C. The most conceptual, and contemporary, version of a city generated by overlapping grids is Peter Eisenman's Piranesi Variations project for the Campo Marzio in Rome.[504] Like many of his earlier indexical projects, Eisenman used an archaeological technique and overlapped different grids and plans of Rome from different times. Through the impositions of a major four-square diagram subdivided by a nine-square diagram, his aim was to project "a dynamic interaction between history and the present, architecture and the urban" onto the Campo Marzio, which "has no one place, no one time, no one scale."[505]

The Functions of the City as a Grid

The city as a grid is by all measures a technical object: totally overdetermined and full of properties with the potential to specialize and allow new kinds of cities to emerge. While it has primarily just one form, it has multiple functions. I want to focus here on two for which the grid has specialized: its function within what Lefebvre identifies as the second circuit of capital, and its biopolitical function.[506]

a. The Second Circuit of Capital

"It was the time to buy real estate in Manhattan."[507] As written in these remarks by the Commissioners regarding their new gridded layout for Manhattan, the motto at the turn of the nineteenth century was clear: Invest in Urban Assets. What thenceforth increased exponentially as a consequence of industrialization was in fact a process that had started already in seventeenth-century Europe. With its accumulating capital, the new bourgeoisie began to invest not only in modes of production needed to produce industrial commodities. They started a new circuit of capital: the selling and buying of real estate. Estates and land, which until that time had been owned by feudal lords, passed slowly but surely into the hands of urban capitalists.[508] Writing in *The City in History*, Mumford notes that "the individual lot and the block, the street and the avenue" became treated "as abstract units for buying and selling, without respect for historic uses, for topographical conditions, or social needs."[509] A new entity was born: the urban asset.

It was thus that the grid tuned its full potential. There was no better form for this new kind of capitalism than the endless grid, infinitely repeatable and able to be subdivided into an endless amount of self-similar rectangular shapes: short frontage and long depth. This was the unit to make profit with, in New York[510] and in many other gridded cities to come. The real estate model of New York, which may be considered as *the* capitalist city with the greatest grid of all time,[511] was actually already a practice in the baroque urban extensions of European cities like London or Berlin. What appeared with the establishment of the grid as a vast collection of urban assets was that, as Lefebvre writes, "Urban Land, too, now became a mere commodity like labor: its market value expresses its only value."[512] Indeed, Lefebvre's second circuit of capital was borne by the city as a grid.[513]

Lefebvre argues in his writings, especially *The Production of Space* and *The Urban Revolution*, that the city's main function is its role as the major player in the second circuit of capital—the speculation of real estate that, as he was arguing in the 1970s, had overtaken industrialization as the dominant production of capital.[514] For Lefebvre, too many readers of Marx were concerned only with the first or principal circuit of capital. Through his concept of the second circuit of capital, he sought to critically advance traditional Marxist readings of the city:

> As the principal circuit—current industrial production and the movable property that results—begins to slow down, capital shifts to the second sector, real estate. It can even happen that real-estate speculation becomes the principal source for the

> formation of capital, that is, the realization of surplus value. As the percentage of overall surplus value formed and realized by industry begins to decline, the percentage created and realized by real estate speculation and construction increases. The second circuit supplants the first, becomes essential.[515]

What Lefebvre emphasizes in his work on the function of the city is one particular and seemingly unfinished aspect of Marx's work: land as an element in the capitalist mode of production.[516] Lefebvre tells his reader that in addition to the two elements of capital and labor that Marx mentions in *Capital*, there is a third: earth. Capital is not just profit and wages, it is rents as well.[517] The grid was the perfect layout for this second circuit of production. The grid subdivides the ground and accommodates the three levels to which capitalism extends its development, as identified by Lefebvre: the land, the underground,"and lastly to what might be called the *above-ground* sphere, i.e. to volumes or constructions considered in terms of their height, to the space of mountains and even of the planets."[518]

b. Biopolitics

"Modern architecture is an essential part of the biopolitical machine," writes Sven-Olov Wallenstein.[519] Indeed, the biopolitical function of the city is not exclusive to the city as a the grid. In fact, I would argue that biopolitics is inherent to the city, which from the beginning functioned for the well-being of its citizens. Nonetheless it can be said that the grid was part of the origination of biopolitics. Or at least for Michel Foucault it was. In his lecture at the Collège de France on 11 January, 1978 Foucault lines out his concept of *bio-power*:

> By this I mean a number of phenomena that seem to me to be quite significant, namely, the set of mechanisms through which the basic biological features of the human species became the object of a political strategy, of a general strategy of power, or, in other words, how, starting from the eighteenth century, modern western societies took on board the fundamental biological fact that human beings are a species. This is roughly what I have called bio-power.[520]

Foucault argues that at the beginning of political centralism in Europe, around the seventeenth and eighteenth centuries, governments were in search of new layouts for cities that would give rise to this new bio-power. The spatial translation of this politics was a new kind of space: a space of circulation. "Broadly speaking," he explains, "what was at issue in the eighteenth century was the question of the spatial, juridical, administrative, and economical opening up of the town: resituating the town in a space of circulation."[521]

What Foucault tries to show in his lectures of that year—published as *Security*, *Territory*, *Population*, his first book on governmentality—is how the grid became the dominant layout to accomplish that new space of circulation. Many cities that were built in the seventeenth century were based on the gridded layout of the Roman military camp, which, according to Foucault, was used not to signify the importance of the camp as a territorial manifestation, but rather to draw on the concept of the camp serving as a disciplinary instrument for troops.[522] The form of the camp functioned as a biopolitical apparatus. As an example, Foucault analyzes the plan of the French new town of Richelieu, whose main street divides the city into rectangular blocks of varying size. Streets meet in right angles and are parallel "but at different distances from each other, some closer, others further apart, such that the town is subdivided into rectangles of different sizes, going from the larger to the smaller. The biggest rectangles, that is to say, where the streets are furthest apart, are at one end of the town, and the smallest, with the tighter grid, are at the other."[523] People were accommodated in the biggest rectangles where the circulation of air was most assured. At the opposite end, stores and other commerce were located where the spacing of the grid is much tighter and, as Foucault explains, an intensification of circulation is needed. What Foucault demonstrates here is the hypertelic quality of the grid that allows for its spaces of circulation to specialize for various levels of flow. In fact, these ideas about the design of circulation were not altogether unprecedented in the construction of the Roman camp. Vitruvius wrote of the importance of the location of a new camp to guarantee the well being of its future inhabitants:

> First comes the choice of a very healthy site. Such a site will be high, neither misty nor frosty, and in a climate neither

> hot nor cold, but temperate; further, without marshes in the neighbourhood. For when the morning breezes blow toward the town at sunrise, if they bring with them mists from marshes and, mingled with the mist, the poisonous breath of the creatures of the marshes to be wafted into the bodies of the inhabitants, they will make the site unhealthy.[524]

According to Foucault, using the model of the Roman camp for this circulation space of goods, people, troops, water, and air ensured four biopolitical functions.[525] First, it served sanitary purposes by providing spaces of ventilation for the city's crowded dwellings. Second, it constituted trading routes for all kinds of goods. Third, the layout of the camp connected its inner streets to the territorial outside, or hinterland, and thus to other cities engaged in trade, while also preserving its customs controls. Finally, its specific layout served as a method of surveillance to counteract the city increasingly becoming a site of crime, as it could no longer be closed up at night due to the imperative for trading to continue.

In summary, the biopolitical function of city as a grid is to govern the human species as a biological entity—a population within an urban milieu. As such, the grid serves just one of two particular biopolitical scales defined by Wallenstein:

> On the lower or micro-level it works by individualization, or more precisely by *producing individuality* as the focal point of all the different techniques for monitoring the body politic, which now fractures into a *living multiplicity of individuals*. In this sense, individuality is produced by those very disciplinary techniques that at the same time *discover* it as their proper object. But this process also makes another object visible on the higher or macro-level, namely *population*, which is how individuals appear when they are treated as statistical phenomena, and when they become endowed with a collective health and collective forms of reproduction and life.[526]

Without question, the city as a grid serves the macro scale of biopolitics, and the best example of this is definitely Cerdà's 1862 Extension Plan for Barcelona.[527] As I previously discussed in the first chapter, Cerdà's plan, along with his *General Theory of Urbanization* published five years later, is understood as the first plan to use a survey of statistical data to arrange its layout.[528] Cerdà's work can be seen as ground-zero when it comes to what is needed to govern urban space. He anticipated Foucault's four biopolitcal functions with his five governmental bases of urbanization: the technical, the administrative, the political, the legal, and the economical.[529]

As we have learned from Simondon, not only can form can take on various functions in technical objects, but the opposite is true as well. The same function of a technical object can be specialized into different forms. Such is the case for the city and its biopolitical function. As we will see later, the other, micro-scale of biopolitics is fused with the city as an archipelago.

3.3. The City as a Line

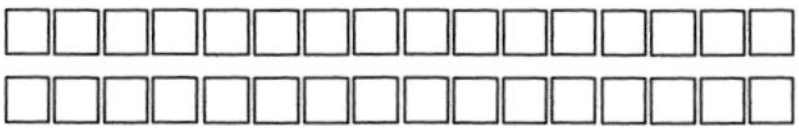

FIGURE 37. THE CITY AS A LINE

The city as a line might be for a phenomenologist one of the most natural forms of human settlement.[530] We humans long have settled along paths, streets, rivers, and other topographical edges. And yet this individuated city is not discernible in Lefebvre's diagram. Although the city as an enclosure and the city as a grid do not always have a clear correlation between form and use, we do find moments in our history of urbanization, as I have discussed above, when both enclosures and grids specialized their formal features to accelerate a particular socioeconomic performance of the city. In contrast, the linear city individuated initially out of its predecessor, the grid, by converging with an industrial object: the train. It emerged out of a technical object.

The city as a line fuses aspects of the grid with what Lefebvre, referencing the conurbation of Germany's Ruhr Valley, describes as the shapeless form of the industrial city.[531] The linear city originated from these two city types and was located between them, its functional idea being to place the various uses of the city along an infrastructural axis running between other cities or towns. It could even span a continent. What is unique about the linear city is that its emergence was not like the embryological process of biological evolution. Rather, it appeared concurrently in two different locations. To borrow an analogy from quantum physics, we could say that the city as a line appeared like quarks: in a pair, quark and antiquark. On one side, there was Arturo Soria y Mata's concept for La Ciudad Lineal, first published in 1882,[532] and on the other side, Edgar Chambless's Roadtown of 1910.[533] Soria y Mata designed his linear city for territory around Madrid, proposing to link villages together by a continuous metro line with *manzanas*, or blocks, lining both sides. Chambless, for his part, published Roadtown in an eponymous book as a general proposal for urbanizing the countryside in the United States.[534] In it he imagines an endless building placed atop a railroad running from the Atlantic to the Pacific. Both proposals originated two kinds of linear cities at the same time: one is *megastructure*, wherein buildings are attached along an infrastructural entity; the other is *megaform*, in which an infrastructural element is united with a building by being placed in its interior.[535]

Although Chambless's proposal was never realized and Soria y Mata's only partially, the linear city remained an influential model throughout the twentieth century. It was the basis for N. A. Milyutin's Sozgorad, the socialist city of Russia, with its famous programmatic diagram of parallel functional stripes as for Stalingrad.[536] The linear city proposed in the competition entry by Ivan Leonidov's OSA group for a new city in Magnitogorsk in 1930 became the blueprint in 1972 for OMA's project Exodus, or the Voluntary Prisoners of Architecture. Ernst May also proposed a linear city for Magnitogorsk, even though he was a pioneer of the city as an archipelago, as we will see later. The linear city can be seen in Le Corbusier's Plan Obus for Algiers from 1933 and his Cité linéaire industrielle in France from 1942. Ludwig Hilberseimer also used the linear layout for the belts of "city aggregates" he proposed in his 1955 book, *The Nature of Cities*.[537] His plans for restructuring the American landscape have many familiarities with Soria y Mata's linear city. Indeed, the linear city became very popular after World War II, with many architects using it as the urban model of the welfare state at that time, notably in the work of Alison and Peter Smithson in England and the Metabolists in Japan. There have been speculative fictional linear cities, such as Raimund Abraham's Glacier City of 1964 and his Megabridge of 1965.[538] And we must not forget the 1969 Continuous Monument by Superstudio. Even Peter Eisenman and Michael Graves designed a linear city for New Jersey in 1965.

Reyner Banham, in his 1976 book *Megastructure: Urban Futures of the Recent Past*, refers to such linear buildings the size of whole cities as "dinosaurs of the Modern Movement." Gracing the cover of Banham's book is Paul Rudolph's Lower Manhattan Expressway project from 1970, in which the city as a line became once again its topological signature: a high speed infrastructure clustered with individual housing aggregates and carving through an existing city fabric or vast territory.[540]

Few linear cities have actually been built, most of them staying utopian even if meant to be realized. This may be the case with one of the newest as well. Saudi Arabia is currently planning to build a one-hundred-mile linear city. It is intended to host one million people and extend from the Red Sea to the mountains in the northwest, "a futuristic city with no cars, no streets, and zero net carbon emissions," and "residents ferried about by autonomous mobility solutions and ultra-high-speed transit."[541]

The Forms of the Linear City

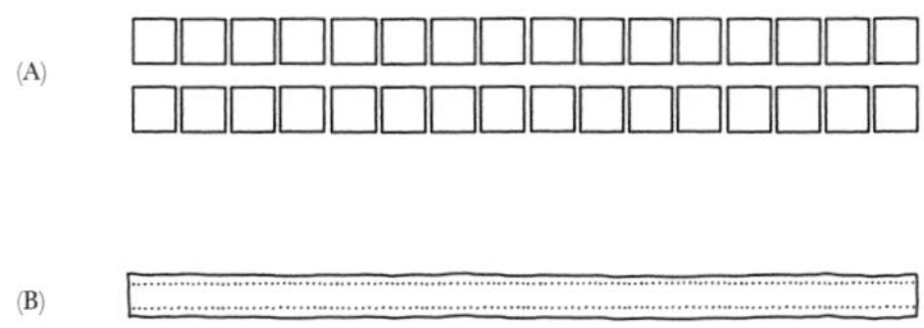

FIGURE 38. TWO FORMS OF THE LINEAR CITY: MEGASTRUCTURE(A), MEGAFORM(B).

As mentioned, the linear city individuated out of the convergence of the city as a grid with the infrastructural element of the train. In one of its forms—the linear city megastructure—it is a street from the grid that converges with the railroad, and in the other—the linear city megaform—it is a high-rise.

a. Megastructure

The city as a grid is based formally in the relationship between its many subdivided blocks and the single continuous space of circulation that unites them. This unifying territory forms the grid of streets, which contains all infrastructural qualities of a city and gives access to the individual blocks and smaller plots. It is this aspect that Mumford saw taken to an extreme in Soria y Mata's La Ciudad Lineal, the ultimate specialization of the infrastructural qualities of the grid:

> The gridiron plan reached its ideal culmination in Señor Soria y Mata's proposal for a Linear City. Himself a transportation engineer, he boldly proposed to make the new city a function of a spinal rapid-transit system, projecting a continuous urban belt parallel to the transportation lines, to connect the connect the older historic centres [in the countryside surrounding Madrid].[542]

The topological principle of this linear form emerges through the hypertelic potential of the urban grid itself, such that a single street and its adjacent city blocks are extracted from the larger grid and fuse their linear quality with a train line. What results is a megastructure of a central railway with blocks attached in series on either side. In La Cuidad Lineal, Soria y Mata called these blocks *manzanas*. They were rectangles, between 80 and 100 meters wide by 200 meters long, and based on land modules of 20 by 20 meters.[543] The formal quality of the megastructure emphasizes the topological arrangement of discrete urban elements, either being an urban block, a single property, or an individual building along a single line of infrastructure, like charms dangling off a bracelet.

b. Megaform

Kenneth Frampton defines a megaform as "a continuous urban mass extending predominantly in a lateral or horizontal direction rather than vertically; a form in which, unlike the megastructure, the mass is not broken down into a series of structural subsets."[544] And even though in the same essay Frampton describes Chambless's Roadtown as a "naive" urban proposal, he admits that the endless extrusion into the countryside may be one of the most original megaforms.[545]

What distinguishes a megaform from a megastructure is its topological difference, or the relationship between its parts. In regard to our two original linear cities, this difference can be seen in how each form converges with the train. While the megastructure fuses the high-speed infrastructure with the qualities of a street in a grid, the megaform melds the infrastructural object of the railroad with the qualities of a high-rise tower. Chambless writes that his Roadtown is based on the idea "to lay the modern skyscraper on its side and run the elevators and the pipes and the wires horizontally instead of vertically."[546] His linear city is a horizontal skyscraper with an endless amount of floors, in which the elevators have been replaced by a high speed train, the shaft a railroad tunnel. Topologically, the megaform is therefore radically different from the megastructure. Rather than being docked to the railroad's infrastructural spine, each architectural object encompasses it, like pearls strung on a necklace. These are lined up so closely, however, that the megaform appears as a continuous unified entity. But this is not the only unique hypertelic quality of the skyscraper when it meets Roadtown. Its floor plates reveal another virtuality, as they become the physical articulations of the property boundaries and make the linear city an endless urban artifact.

The Functions of the Linear City

a. The Geoist City

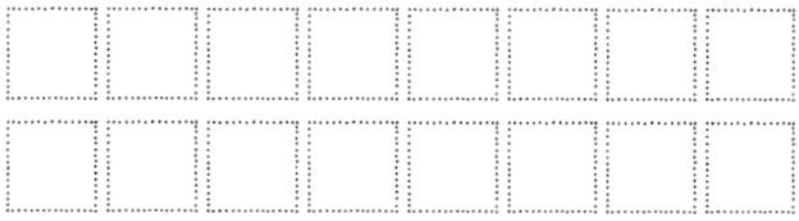

FIGURE 39. THE TERRITORIAL MEGASTRUCTURE OF SORIA Y MATA

In the 1903 version of his linear city, Soria y Mata proposed building linear cities all over Spain with the aim to distribute land among the poor. Soria y Mata's aim with these linear connections between the old historical villages was to intensify the qualities of the agricultural land surrounding cities like Madrid while giving the poor the opportunity to generate their own revenue. He added a policy attached to the new properties along the transit line, designating them for mainly agricultural use while allowing individuals the opportunity to bid on and purchase the plots with the provision that they not be leased or resold. The policy was to give poor people at least temporary ownership of the land, in the form of this 1500-meter-wide strips, by expropriating it from the former owners. The new occupants would not be allowed to sell or lease the land within the first three years without paying a fine. They could exploit the ground of their new land in the form of harvesting and owning its products, but would not have full legal ownership of their property, as they would be obligated to pay annually a certain amount of money to the former owner.[547]

Manuel Martín Rodriguez has demonstrated how Soria y Mata's proposal is deeply indebted to Henry George's idea of the single tax, today known as Geoism.[548] In his book *Progress and Poverty*, George lays out his economic ideology.[549] He argues that people should pay taxes for the land from which they extract resources. Those resources, for George, are common goods and therefore belong to everyone. They are pre-given. At the same time, he argues, people should own all of the value of the products that they produce from those pre-given resources. As George explains his reasoning: "a single tax on the value of land would hardly lessen the number of conscious taxpayers, for the division of land now held on speculation would much increase the number of land holders. But it would so equalize the distribution of wealth as to raise even the poorest above that condition of abject poverty."[550] La Ciudad Lineal can therefore be seen as a unification of the two Geoist tenets. On one hand no one should ever own a piece of territory, as is the case with the urban lots of the gridded city, but on the other hand occupants should be free to produce and exploit the goods they gain from that piece of land.

Therein lies the function of Soria y Mata's linear city, one of which was partially built and can still be traced in the current fabric of Madrid. He wanted to give added value not to the landowner but to the people who urbanize and civilize it. The people who contribute to a country, a land, or a city should "reap the harvest of what we have sown," as he wrote in 1901.[551] For him, in order to unfold this vision it was necessary to expropriate the old urban fabric along with its society and to turn them both into new ones.[552]

b. The Cooperative City

The linear city would not be a properly overdetermined technical object if it did not take on various different uses. Indeed, in Edgar Chambless's proposal for Roadtown, it takes on a visionary use of an entirely different kind than the one described just above. Rather than a collection of many individual agricultural plots, Chambless's megaform is a nearly total cooperative.

Proposed in the early twentieth century, the city of Roadtown functions in principle as a cooperative for all its needs: from production to consumption, public and private facilities, and the high-tech infrastructure and railroad that unite it all. As we read through Chambless's book, *Roadtown*, we find all kinds of ideas for cooperative enterprise, including amusement centers, athletic fields and swimming pools, as well as entertainment like resorts, museums, art galleries, lecture halls, and dance halls.[553] In addition to those public facilities are cooperative facilities for care and education, such as hospitals, nursery homes, kindergartens, schools, and colleges. Books can be ordered by telephone from the library, which also houses an audio collection for the efficiency of learning by ear instead of eye.[554] There are even cooperative stores, kitchens, and laundries. And all is connected to cooperative infrastructures like the railroad, power plants, and the communication network of telephones, dictographs, and telegraphones.[555] Of course, Roadtown is envisioned to be a cooperative working environment, in its factories, workrooms, and department stores. Individual producers and merchandising would turn cooperative as well.[556] Eventually, all products would be bought and sold through one central cooperative organization. In this seemingly autarkic city, so-called Roadtown Associations of worker collectives would preclude any future strikes.[557]

Aside from its limitless horizontal extrusion, what little unique architectural character there is at Roadtown can be found in the entrances to the houses, which are accessed from above or below.[558] With the cooperative in control of building all the homes, individuality moves to the interior.[559] "City people have theaters, libraries, churches and crowds, but they do not have neighbors with common interests." Thusly Chambless prefaces his sketch of daily life in Roadtown, before continuing,

The Roadtowners who get the food at the same kitchen, and

hear the same band play, and sell their products cooperatively, and promenade on the same endless roof garden, and send their children to the same instructors, are going to get acquainted if they so desire. The entire Roadtown will be in connection by the loud speaking telephone, and folks can call on each other on a stormy night without so much as getting out of their comfortable rockers.[560]

Chambless believed his cooperative linear city would be "a new arrangement of civilization, a new plan for all commerce and all city building."[561] He likens Roadtown's "revolutionary humanitarian principles" to those of the single tax reform and socialism:[562] "The lamb of socialism shall lie down with the leopard of individuality and a child of the common good shall lead them."[563] But the longer you read on about what this cooperative city can do, the more you wonder whether it is not a religion. And, in fact, the last part of the book is titled, "The Roadtown religion," in which the dogmatic principles of the megaform are listed point by point.[564]

c. The Socialist City

As discussed, technical objects have the capacity not only to fuse one particular form with various functions, but to do the reverse as well: a certain function can be concretized in various forms. This is particularly the case with the socialist or social-democratic city. It does not appear only in the form of the city as a line, but rather converges with many other forms, as we will see in particular with the city as an archipelago.[565]

The main argument for the linear city as the socialist city par excellence was made by N. A. Milyutin in his 1930 book, *Sotsgorod: The Problem of Building Socialist Cities*. As the chairman of the Commission for Planning in communist Russia, Milyutin was attempting to answer the question of how the ideas of Marx, Engels, and Lenin could be articulated architecturally and urbanistically.[556] What would be the layout for the new social and collective life, in which workers, farmers, and especially women[567] would be liberated from the microeconomic forces of the Western, petty-bourgeois household? The main points of Milyutin's critique of the capitalist city are its expression of centrality[568] and its grid. A critique of centrality, for Milyutin, is given historically: the capitalist city manifests its spatial centrality due to the location of the market, the locus for the trade and exchange of goods.[569] His critique of the grid, meanwhile, turns on its role in the liberal city of the nineteenth century. For it was the subdivision of the gridded city into urban assets that allowed the capitalists to exploit the proletariat through enormous rents in times of huge demand for housing.[570]

In the socialist idea of a planned economy, and in the USSR's first five-year plan from 1928 to 1932, Milyutin saw the opportunity to overcome the failure and dangers of the Western city. "Skyscrapers," he writes, "are the epitome of capitalism."[571] Their presence instills the most capitalist forms of living. The righteous answer is therefore the antithesis: decentralization or, as Milyutin names it, "de-urbanization."[572] This idea was already projected by Marx and Engels in one of the ten points of their *Communist Manifesto* of 1848: "Combination of agriculture with manufacturing industries; gradual abolition of the distinction between town and country, by a more equable distribution of the population over the country."[573] The ideal form for such a new decentralized city was for Milyutin the city as a line—both the most rational and radical solution. With the linear city, not only were distinctions between countryside and city abolished and people more distributed, but more importantly, the mode of production, living, and communal life were unified in the most efficient way. Milyutin uses an example of the thermodynamics of a power plant to explain the main principle of his linear city. "A well-planned steam-powered power plant," he writes,

> is structured as follows: Next to the transport routes are the fuel reservoirs, next to them are the steam boilers, which are supplied with fuel via vertical and inclined transport devices. Behind the row with the boilers are the machines that convert the steam into mechanical energy. Behind these machines is a row of dynamos that produce electrical energy. After that come the distributors, then the transformers and finally the transmission paths. This arrangement ensures that machines of one type are always arranged in a clear line. This

significantly shortens the transmission and distribution routes for fuel, steam and energy.[574]

Milyutin calls his concept the "functional-assembly-line system."[575] In this city system any extension always would occur in parallel to guarantee the shortest and most direct form of communication. His ideal linear city consists of six parallel programmatic zones.[576] Each zone is mono-functional: the first zone is for the railway line; the second for production with communal enterprises, warehouses, and educational facilities for science and technology; the third is called the "Green-belt" and functions as the main traffic band for all kind of vehicles; the fourth zone is for the residents and is split into three bands—social facilities, residential buildings, childcare; the fifth zone is a park and hosts all the leisure and recreational facilities, like sports fields and pools; and finally in the sixth zone are located state-run farms, called *sovkhoz*, with their fields of fruit and vegetables.

The fact that Milyutin explains the form of his linear city mainly by way of the metaphor of the assembly line is an obvious invitation for a mechanological reading of his plan. I would argue that this socialist linear city specialized the hypertelic quality of the directionality of the grid. Milyutin's linear city is not just some urban programs lined up along an infrastructure. In the famous plan for Magnitogorsk by Leonidov's OSA group,[577] its linear city is made of a grid structure with three rows, each containing a specific programmatic character. While it is a grid, it attenuates in one direction at the expense of the other. Milyutin goes even further., eliminating one direction completely and stretching the other to the extreme. The gridded arrangement of roads and blocks vanishes and endless parallel mono-functional zones emerge. The socialist linear city therefore is not simply an urban assembly line, but rather the convergence of two qualities: the functional qualities of Tony Garnier's Cité industrielle concretized within the formal qualities of the grid city.

d. The Open Society[578]

Following the Second World War up until the mid-1970s, linear cities were settled around the world. Whether in the United States, Europe, or Asia, this individuated city seemed to have caught the spirit of the times. What were those cities supposed to achieve in this age, when the welfare state was reaching its apex? What, actually, was their function?

When prompted on the topic of his politics in a 1978 interview, Peter Smithson recalls that the overwhelming spirit of postwar Europe was "to establish a more free, egalitarian government . . . to establish social democracy,"[579] and further affirms that this sentiment was shared by his peers, and specifically Jaap Bakema. Smithson also describes his and partner Alison's work in that period:

> It was an attempt to complement that shared social idea with a form idea. In cities like Bath, Nancy, Karlsruhe or 18th century Berlin one cannot imagine the urban plan of the city without the architecture, without a form language supporting it. . . . What seemed missing in the immediate post-war period was an ideal image of what a new city would look like. We tried to propose an image of what was latently present in social democratic planning.[580]

Under the subject of "urban infra-structure," the Smithsons searched to find this new form. An architectural form for a new kind of society: a machine society[581] of the postwar era that was driven by mass production, mass communication, and mass consumerism.[582] What the Smithsons were looking for was some kind of large-scale structure with the capacity to express the identity of communities in this new paradigm. "Traditionally," they write in the *Team 10 Primer*, "some unchanging large-scale thing—the Acropolis, the River, the Canal or some unique configuration of the ground—was the thing that made the whole community structure comprehensible and assured the identity of the parts within the whole."[583] For their own time, they imagined such large structures containing a new idea: "streets-in-the-air."[584] This was a new space of circulation and of communication updated for the times, an equivalent form as social agent to what the street was in earlier cultures. Their motto: "We must live our lives on different levels."[585]

The Smithsons found the basis of their idea in the work of Louis Kahn. What Kahn's work provided them was an updated definition of the role of the architect in the aftermath of World War

II. In many of their publications they refer to one of Kahn's projects in particular, his Traffic Study of Philadelphia from 1952.[586] What that plan expresses is not the design of a physical structure of a road system. Instead, it proposes a movement pattern for traffic in the form of a diagram with arrows, points, lines, crosses, and brackets. In other words, the plan doesn't represent a physical space, but rather a topological space: a space of communication. Kahn enabled the Smithsons to understand "that the architect can control systems of physical communication and offer new concepts."[587] One such new spatial concept can be seen in Kahn's 1957 project for the Civic Center in Philadelphia, where he redesigned the space of circulation by collecting the flow of automobiles and guiding them into huge parking garages. This redirection of flow liberates the street to become a new void able to be filled with people, an inner-city pedestrian zone. Kahn's projects convinced the Smithsons that the architect has the capacity to produce new human associations and identities[588] for a new mobile society.

The Smithsons referred to "the road as a liberator,"[589] and in many of their projects we find that novel kind of road, the street-in-the-air. In their Golden Lane Housing Project from 1952 or their famous social housing Project Robin Hood Gardens from 1972, linear pedestrian decks with significant width connect the different apartments, providing a new public space just out their front doors. These streets were not typical narrow corridors on every floor. Rather, they were placed on every third floor and were open on one side. The aim was to provide communal densification in order to trigger new associations such as streets are able to do. These public spaces could also take on the shape of elevated plazas. In their proposal for a new Headquarter Building of the Economist Magazine in London, designed between 1959 and 1964, the Smithsons eschewed a single tower an instead splintered the program into three different buildings in order to produce a place in between the buildings. This new in-between space was accessible from the street, and due to being elevated from the common ground of the city, produced a new a space of communication between the citizen and the employees of Economist.

But to return to the notion of this new space of circulation a liberator, in his PhD dissertation on Alison and Peter Smithson Dirk van den Heuvel gives us a hint as to the political aims of their megastructures, specifically in the title of his penultimate chapter, "The Great Society: Between Welfare State Ideals and Consumer Drives." What van den Heuvel presents is the Smithsons' idea that the collective is not larger than the individual. The pair was dissatisfied with the political course of the welfare state in the Great Britain after World War II.[590] What they saw, he explains, was a lack of individual choices:

> In this ideal world of a machine-served society the available "machine energy" is at the service of a "lyricism of control," of "calm as an ideal." It is about "energy ordered and controlled," about ordered flows of traffic too, and about the need to reduce urban densities, all in order to prevent "overcrowding," since overcrowding would mean "violence" and "stress." Ultimately, this late twentieth century world with its "technology and its mechanisms under control" is about enabling "each individual" to "choose his degree of contact … or protection … and thereby pleasure … in the machine-served society," according to the Smithsons in 1973.[591]

This sentiment was stated even more intensely by Peter Smithson in the aforementioned interview: "I believe one should come back from the bureaucratic state to a situation in which the individual is given much more responsibility. Because post-war egalitarianism turned out to be deceptive."[592] What the Smithsons attempted with their linear streets-in-the-air was to produce a space for new individual human associations. It was a space of a certain freedom of choice, liberated from the societal model of the modernist welfare state.

The Smithsons begin their 1970 book *Ordinariness and Light* with a quote by Aneurin Bavin: "The Great Society has arrived and the task of our generation is to bring it under control."[593] Indeed, they saw their work was a critique of the way the Great Society was managed. In his 1914 book, *The Great Society*, Graham Wallas warns that, with the rise of a global network of commercial activities, any new society will face a major challenge, one in which the life of every individual will be affected by this new global phenomenon.[594] As a socialist and member of the Fabian Society, Wallas believed that the only way such a Great Society can be controlled was by state intervention and legislation, "including its driving forces of capitalism and entrepreneurship, as well as other forces of relentless modernization such as the one of technology."[595] This was exactly the task of the welfare state. In *Ordinariness and Light*, the Smithsons include a chapter called "The Great Society,"[596] in which they critique the effects on the individual brought by the welfare state. As van den Heuvel characterizes it, this critique is aimed mainly at "the shift from a society organized around direct personal relations to one of impersonal associations, from a society founded on local and national institutions to one structured by global systems and networks."[597] Or as the Smithsons write themselves, "there can only be a reality where the Individual makes a choice from given and real alternatives."[598]

For me, their aim to generate spaces for the liberated individual puts the Smithsons into dialogue with the ideas of Karl Popper, specifically as he formulated in his book *The Open Society and its Enemies*.[599] In the *Team 10 Primer*, the Smithsons write about "freedom to move," and argue that "an open society needs an open city."[600] Perhaps when they wrote those words they were imagining Popper's idea of a "society in which individuals are confronted with personal decisions, the open society."[601] Popper pulls the individual to the forefront of Western democracy and leaves the collective in the background. His idea of the open society was developed during the Second World War, a time dominated by totalitarian societies like communist Russia and Nazi Germany. He wanted to liberate the critical potential of humans, but what he saw throughout history was the predomination of this totalitarian model, which he calls "the closed society."[602] For him, such closed societies are bound to a form of historicism, an ideology that argues that there exists an ideal societal form toward which every historical development strives. His open society does the opposite. Individual subjects can change their trajectories at any moment. They are not bound to something that is larger than themselves. This is the story, Popper argues, of western civilization, beginning with ancient Greece: "that greatest of all revolutions, a revolution which started just yesterday, as it were, for we are still in its initial stage the transition from the closed to the open society."[603] Popper expounds further on his ideal model of ancient Greece: "The closed society and with it its creed that the tribe is everything and the individual nothing, had broken down. Individual initiative and self-assertion had become a fact. Interest in the human individual as individual, and not only as tribal hero and savior, had been aroused."[604]

I think it was precisely such individualism that arose in postwar England in the minds of Alison and Peter Smithson (and so too in the Netherlands with Jaap Bakema) when they proposed their new linear cities. Perhaps it is this shift in viewpoints between the first and the third CIAM generation that Kenneth Frampton is referring to when he writes: "With the third and final stage of CIAM, liberal idealism triumphed completely over the materialism of the early period."[605]

3.4. The City as an Archipelago

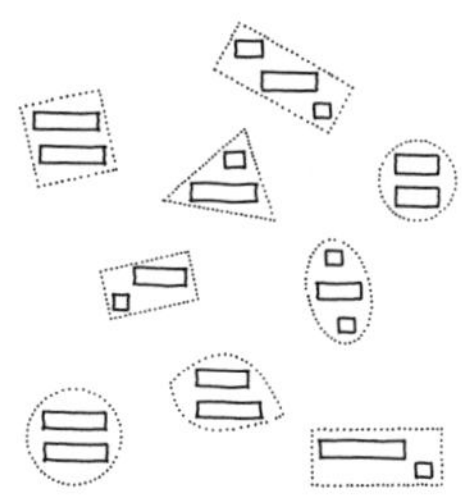

FIGURE 40. THE CITY AS AN ARCHIPELAGO

The city as an archipelago[606] is not to be understood literally as a city of islands in water, like Venice, Stockholm, or Dubai. With the city as an archipelago, what we have understood so far as the city—an enclosure, a grid, or a line—loses its continuity and sees its urban fabric turn into something like confetti, or islands. The city as an archipelago gives rise to a new whole without being a unified form.

We can place the emergence of the city as an archipelago clearly in the first half of the twentieth century, particularly in European cities after World War I, where Social Democrats held political majorities for the first time in history.[607] The welfare policies introduced through their platforms of municipal socialism[608] aimed to accommodate the high demand for housing the working class. To do this, these municipalities sought a new urban model distinct from the grid of the nineteenth-century liberal city. They found it in the archipelago. The two best known examples such new, island-like urban agglomerations were in Vienna and Frankfurt. Although both use the same model of the archipelago, their respective articulations could not be more different. The New Frankfurt of Ernst May was formed by an archipelago of *Siedlungen*, or apartment blocks, which occupied large territories surrounding the nineteenth-century city, while Red Vienna spread its autonomous *superblocks*[609] directly through the existing urban fabric. It should be noted that the idea of urban islands for the working class may have its roots in the English coke towns as well in the garden city movement, but the understanding of the city as an archipelago-like field of architectural agglomerations definitively crystallized later in various Europeans cities, and most significantly in Frankfurt and Vienna.

It was, perhaps, Raymond Hood's fictional proposal for Manhattan 1950[610] that first signaled the success of the city as an archipelago after the Second World War. His idea of thirty-eight gigantic architectural mountains has a surprising similarity to the Viennese superblocks, although predominantly vertical rather than horizontal (not to mention that the two performed completely different social-political ideas).

The city as an archipelago reached some fame by symbolizing postmodern urbanity in the 1970s and '80s as "the city within the city," its appeal confirmed by the multiplicity of similar ideas and manifestos on the city as an archipelago within that brief timespan. Some of these even shared the same name, like OM Ungers' "Cities within the City"[611] and "The City Within the City"[612] by Leon Krier. For Ungers, the concept entails a field of urban islands, which "will have an identity in keeping with their history, social structure and environmental characteristics. The city as a whole will be a federation of all these single towns with different structures, developed in a deliberately antithetic manner."[613] While for Ungers these "mini-cities"[614] can take any morphological shape, for Krier it is the urban quarters that act as an archipelago, the city a collection of autonomous quarters in which the functions of the daily life of citizens are bound territorially to the human scale of walking distances. Krier sees the city within the city as a finite entity, referencing Aristotle: "To the size of cities [states] there is a limit as is the case with everything, with plants, animals, tools; because none of these can retain its natural power if it is too large or too small, for it then loses its nature or it is spoilt."[615]

One image has become possibly the icon of the postmodern archipelago city: Peter Riemann's drawing of the Berlin green archipelago, which he produced under the guidance of Ungers for the exhibition of the Sommerakedmie Berlin in 1977.[616] Yet there is a different drawing that I consider to be more important for the understanding of how the city as an archiplelago individuates: The City of the Captive Globe,[617] made in 1972 by OMA. This axonometric drawing shows how within every plot of the Manhattan grid a fictional reality can emerge. "The City of the Captive Globe,"writes Koolhaas in *Delirious New York*, "is devoted to the artificial conception and accelerated birth of theories, interpretations, mental constructions, proposals and their infliction on the World. . . . The more each 'island' celebrates its different values, the more the unity of the archipelago as system is reinforced."[618] The grid thus contains for Koolhaas an archipelago of cities within the city. In regard to the individuation of the city as an archipelago, what the drawing makes evident is that it is already embedded within the city as a grid. What allows the city as an archipelago to emerge is the specialization, or tuning, of the autonomous quality of each urban plot into territorial architectural islands.

In recent years a new version of the city as an archipelago has emerged within the discipline of architecture. Pier Vittorio Aureli has used the enclosure of the political city to frame a territory—to cut out a space from the endless gridded city. The aim of this new city as archipelago is to use the wall as a political form to counter the fast expansion of our contemporary urbanization.

The Forms of the Archipelago City

As we can see, the city as an archipelago appears in various forms. Furthermore, its formal properties suggest that it was already present within an existing urban fabric. Indeed, throughout history each particular archipelago has used for its island formation a specific urban element, like a piece of land, an urban fragment, or a single building block. Once these elements were extracted from their existing cities, their aesthetic qualities specialized and gave rise to three forms: the territorial, the morphological, and the gridded archipelagos.

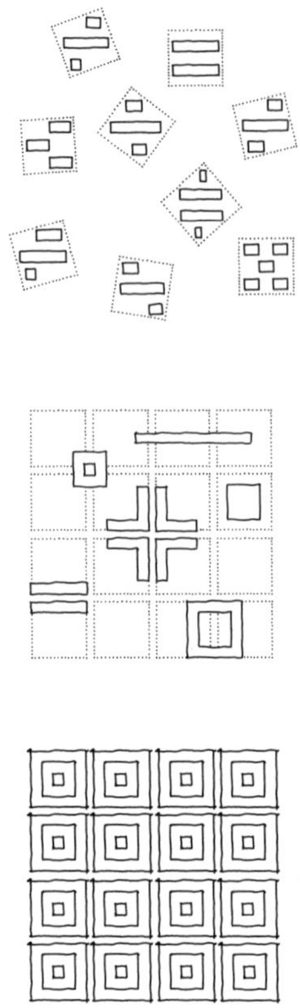

FIGURE 41. THREE FORMS OF THE ARCHIPELAGO CITY: THE TERRITORIAL ARCHIPELAGO(A), THE MORPHOLOGICAL ARCHIPELAGO(B), THE GRIDDED ARCHIPELAGO(C).

a. The Territorial Archipelago

When Ernst May, as head of the urban design department, and his Social Democrat colleagues in the municipal government of Frankfurt asked themselves which form the new metropolitan environment should take, the answer was clear: only an archipelago of housing estates would guarantee the well being of people. "In the next few decades," he wrote, "we will have to restrict our subsidies to suburban satellites only. We will equip them with all the facilities that residents need for daily life."[619] In the years between 1925 and 1930 the city of Frankfurt aimed to extend the nineteenth century liberal city with a ring of housing projects.[620] By 1930 they constructed twenty-six new municipally owned housing estates, called *Siedlung*. While some of them were small infill projects that completed exiting urban islands, the majority of these Siedlungen were placed on large unified territories of five to twenty-five hectares. Most consisted solely of housing, but some had small shops, schools, and workplaces to support their working-class tenants. These housing estates formed an archipelago floating in what May describes as a planned contiguous open space system (*Freiflächensystem*).[621] This green zone accommodated sports facilities and baths for the physical well-being of people.[622] It also was planned to accommodate a small garden for every resident.[623] The city as an archipelago was in this regard the spatial contribution of modern architects and urban designers to the *Lebensreform*[624] movement ongoing at that time in Germany.

The form of these territorial archipelagos was not so radically new. If we understand them to be enclosed territories surrounded by a continuous green space, then it would seem that their topological character is no different from the city as a grid. What is different between the two, however, are their aesthetic properties. The street of the grid city changes its materiality into earthen ground. The shape of its urban block loses its geometric outline and increases its size to an extreme.[625] But what changes the most is the inner structure. While urban blocks are subdivided into smaller properties of land, the territories of the archipelago have no subdivision at all. In Frankfurt, in order for the municipality to lay out rows of standardized, freestanding housing slabs, it required large, unified, singularly owned territories. The city thus bought and expropriated extensive amounts of land[626] for the construction of its territorial archipelago of Siedlungen.

A comparison between the Frankfurt Siedlungen and the garden city movement seems obvious, since Ernst May worked for Raymond Unwin, who designed the first garden city of Letchworth and wrote the introductory essay in the first edition of *Das Neue Frankfurt*, the monthly magazine published by May to accompany the housing program he oversaw. But in terms of scale and form the two are not at all the same. Just how dissimilar the two are can be seen in the largest of the Frankfurt Siedlung projects. Gartenstadt

Goldstein, a 8530-unit housing estate of approximately 1.8 hectares of formerly agricultural land, was small in comparison to the garden cities in England.[627] Furthermore, garden cities in England were singular territories set apart from other cities, while the *Grosssiedlung* of Frankfurt, of which Gartenstadt is one, filled territorial holes in the archipelago of the city. The archipelago of Frankfurt, furthermore, emerged out of the city as a grid by tuning the hypertelic qualities of urban blocks, while the garden city belongs to the formal sequence of the city as an enclosure, by which the material property of a wall was tuned to become a green territory.

This tuning of the inner qualities of an urban block, the specialization of its edges and the fusion of its inner subdivision, falls under Simondon's definition of the first, internal kind of hypertely of technical objects.[628] If the New Frankfurt instrumentalized this first kind of hypertely of technical objects, the archipelago of Red Vienna can be seen to illustrate the second kind, in which objects split into their constituent elements to then fuse newly together and unfold qualities that didn't exist before. Indeed, while the islands of Siedlungen were emerging in the New Frankfurt, a different sort of territorial archipelago was underway in Red Vienna.

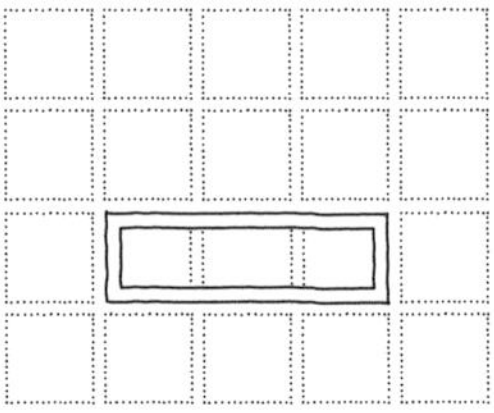

FIGURE 42. THE VIENNESE ARCHIPELAGO

For one thing, it was larger. The construction across Vienna of superblocks serving the same function of municipal housing resulted in the addition of over five times as many units of housing as were built in Frankfurt. More importantly, Vienna split the dependency between the building and its urban property. Once separated, these two city elements saw the specialization of their individual qualities such that their dependence was reversed: the building was not bound by an individual property, but rather the property became bound by the building. In other words, the city of the Austrian Marxists turned the archipelago of the New Frankfurt upside down and inside out.

The difference can be best visualized when we compare the contemporary representations of both archipelago cities. While *Das neue Frankfurt* used a planimetric view, the municipality of Vienna used a central perspectival drawing. When one sees the latter drawing[629] for the first time, the three dimensional aspect of the archipelago jumps off the page. The obvious characteristic of the Vienna archipelago is that it does not surround the existing nineteenth century city. It is placed right into the city. The municipality of Red Vienna also applied a territorial strategy to gain land, but in opposition to Frankfurt, the city did not only buy open agricultural land on the outskirts. It accumulated all kinds of territorial fragments of properties within the existing city. It was not possible to expropriate land, for, as Eve Blau writes, "all of the building land acquired by the municipality had to be bought on the open market, where the city had no control over prices."[630] These urban fragments needed to be attached to other properties within a block, otherwise they could not be united into larger pieces. If this was not possible, the properties needed to be at least adjacent to one another, even if a street divided them. Thus, the land acquired by the municipality appeared as a loose collection of lots, somewhat disjointed from each other and separated by the streets of the city. Instead of placing single buildings on each of these properties, however, the city detached the buildings from the land, unifying the fragments with the new superblocks: megaforms of housing with large inner courtyards that meandered across the urban fabric. Some of these megaforms bridged over a single street to connect a pair of land fragments, like the Professor Jodl-hof,[631] while others more than earned the title of superblock. Am Fuchsenfeld,[632] for example, meandered over four existing urban blocks and formed a series of inner courtyards by bifurcating its mass to bound all its territorial fragments together. One of the most famous Red Vienna superblocks is the Karl Marx Hof.[633] Not only is it one of the largest, but it is also perhaps the superblock in which the split between the building and its ground is most legible. Karl Marx Hof is a truly urban form, bridging five urban blocks and four streets, and framing two courtyards. It hosts a total of 1382 living units. The megaform is an assemblage of traditional nineteenth-century buildings with central staircases each serving between two and four apartments. In a sort of topological fold, these staircases are positioned such that their entrances are located not on the street side, as they would be in the liberal city of the grid, but instead around an inner courtyard that gives access to all the apartments.

When we compare the two territorial archipelagos of Frankfurt and Vienna, it is precisely this topological fold that most distinguishes the latter. It seems as if the same city form has reversed its aesthetic properties: the figurative slabs of Frankfurt turn into the figurative courtyards of Vienna; the green space surrounding the slabs turns into the gigantic megaforms. There is perhaps no better example in the history of architecture and urban design to demonstrate the thesis of the city as a technical object. While both city forms share the same content—functioning as what can be called social-democratic urbanism—their formal articulations are incongruent. Each accelerates a different hypertelic quality of the technical object of the city. Although our two territorial archipelagos individuated from different processes of concretization, they share in the same technical object from which they originated.

b. The Morphological Archipelago

In the late 1970s the discipline of architecture turned its focus to a new form of urban archipelago, one not bound to islands of territories but rather to islands of urban morphologies. In *The Architecture of the City*, Rossi distinguishes between *building typology* and *urban morphology*. For him, typology describes the urban artifact, which has a "permanent character"[634] that is unchanged over time, while morphology describes how the characteristics of such artifacts appear spatially. Morphology, for Rossi, works to identify areas of physical and social homogeneity in the city.[635] What is particularly important for Rossi is the relationship between morphology and typology. While morphology describes the appearance of urban artifacts in space, this space only captures the urban artifact—the typology—at a particular moment in time.[636] Typology and morphology therefore define a relationship of urban forms in time and space.

Cities within the City,[637] Ungers' and Koolhaas' 1977 proposal for Berlin, is such a search into the urban morphology of a city. Ungers and Koolhaas, along with Peter Riemann, Hans Kollhoff, and Arthur Ovaska, sought to identify urban morphologies that would allow them to define Berlin as an archipelago of islands of physical and social homogeneities:

> The first operation of such a project—a Berlin as an archipelago—ought to be the identification and selection of those areas that already have a strong existing identity that deserves to be preserved and reinforced. These enclaves would not be selected on the basis of a particular taste or even for their aesthetic qualities, but only to the extent to which they embody, in a pure and legible form, ideas and concepts, so that the history of architecture would coincide with the history of ideas once more.[638]

In a series of drawings for the final exhibition of the Sommerakedmie program, we can see through the working process how these urban islands were extracted and the existing city was transformed into an archipelago of morphologies. The group's project for the Berlin green archipelago was typified in Peter Riemann's drawing of abstract axonometric objects floating in an abstract grid framed by the boundary of Berlin. It would become the icon of the group's manifesto of "Cities within the City." But it is not the intention here to describe that entire manifesto. Rather, I want to emphasize one aspect of the morphological archipelago, namely its manner of referencing architecture, or what Ungers called "morphological sequence."[639]

In various series of five or six frames, Ungers shows us how he brings the history of architecture back into the realm of the history of ideas. Each morphological sequence starts with an aerial photograph of an area of Berlin. This is followed by a mode of abstraction, whereby the image is converted into a drawing. From this drawing the "useless" urban fabric is erased to make visible a unique morphological structure. The figurative aspect of the urban morphology is emphasized through a figure/ground representation that highlights topological characteristics of the urban fragment. It is at this point in the morphological series that the found urban morphology is linked with the history of architectural ideas. For example, in the series on the Unter den Eichen,[640] a main street in the Berlin district of Lichterfelde, the linear structure of the street becomes linked with the architectural idea of the linear city. Ungers and Koolhaas's choice here to reference Leonidov's linear city proposal for Magnitogorsk is an obvious one, it being perhaps the most noted articulation of an ideal socialist city in the history of urban design.

With his morphological series, Ungers demonstrates a design method that he had formulated a couple of years earlier for an exhibition called "Man Transforms," shown at the Cooper Hewitt Museum in New York in 1976.[641] In an essay accompanying the exhibition Ungers argues that, in order to overcome functionalism on the one hand and expressionism on the other, we should try to understand physical reality "as an analogy to our imagination of that reality."[642] This, in turn, leads him to his morphological design concept:

> If we look at physical phenomena in a morphological sense, like Gestalten in their metamorphosis, we can manage to develop our knowledge without machine or apparatus. This imaginative process of thinking applies to all intellectual and spiritual areas of human activities though the approaches might be different in various fields. But it is always a fundamental process of conceptualizing an unrelated, diverse reality through the use of images, metaphors, analogies, models, signs, symbols and allegories.[643]

Whereas Rossi saw in architectural typologies forms that are determined in time due to being permanent and resistant to change, the urban morphologies of Ungers are determined not in time but in space. But the city as a technical object, in opposition to both concepts, is actually overdetermined: the morphologies of the city have the capacity to turn into buildings *and* buildings have the capacity to turn into urban morphologies.

If we understand the morphological islands of Ungers as elements of a technical object, then this loose urban fabric can be seen as the abstract forms of processes of concretization.[644] Such abstract forms define the early stage of a processes whereby the loose elements—the street, the building, and the landscape—convert over time into a concrete architectural entity. In the case study of the Unter den Eichen, the morphology would have the capacity to become a linear megaform, by melding its elements together and converting the street into an interior corridor. The opposite could happen as well. Take, for example, the morphological sequence of the borough of Neukölln:[645] a building, a form like the Roman amphiteather of Arles, has become concretized into an urban fabric and turned the theater into a city of the Middle Ages.

For Rossi as well as Ungers, architectural forms are permanent. If an archipelago of morphologies is understood as a technical being, then in each urban island lies the capacity to become a new prime architectural object.[646]

c. The Gridded Archipelago

The third form of city as an archipelago is not an altogether different kind of archipelago, but rather it can be seen as the end of a formal sequence in which a territorial archipelago turns into an archipelago of buildings. The reason I call it the gridded archipelago is due simply to the fact that it individuates from a city as a grid that has tuned its blocks, as single pieces of property, to become islands forming a large archipelago of buildings. The single most important image associated with this ultimate stage of that process of concretization is OMA's drawing The City of the Captive Globe.[647]

This drawing represents the fictional conclusion of Koolhaas's idea of Manhattanism.[648] Manhattanism expresses through its form, as Vittorio Gregotti once wrote,"a permissive melting pot of 'isms:' Futurism, Expressionism, Surrealism, Dadaism, Fascism, Marxism, Modernism, etc. In other words Manhattanism is a movement which is in almost every respect the opposite and counterpart of the so-called Modern Movement."[649] What makes Manhattanism possible is the Commissioners Plan that was adopted in 1811, which parceled the island of Manhattan equally into a territory of 2028[650] potential islands unified by a street grid in between them. What OMA emphasize in their drawing is the radical potential of this subdivision of territory. Each individual block, or island, is a world in itself. The character of the city as an archipelago is heightened by showing every block to be as different of a world as possible in comparison to those immediately surrounding it. As Koolhaas writes in *Delirious New York*, the grid of islands has not only given Manhattan its intellectual program, but through pure utilitarian interest it also accelerated its architectural form: "The Grid's two-dimensional discipline also creates undreamt-of freedom for three-dimensional anarchy."[651]

Indeed, *Delirious New York* is more than just a celebration of the emergence of the high-rise. Even as Koolhaas devotes much of the book to such things as the famous diagram of "the theorem of the skyscraper,"[652] the amazing drawings of Hugh Ferriss,[653] the lives within the Waldorf-Astoria Hotel, or—his theoretical highlight—the Downtown Athletic Club,[654] his book reveals another insight on the city as a technical being. That is, namely, that the city as an archipelago was already dormant in all of Manhattan's precursor cities. For Koolhaas, its intellectual program can be found already in an early bird's-eye view plan of New Amsterdam, published by Gerard Jollain in 1672. "Outside the walls on the left," he writes of the plan, "is an extension that seems to promise—after barely fifty years of existence—a new beginning, in the form of a structured system of more or less identical blocks that can extend, if the need arises, all over the island, their rhythm interrupted by a Broadway-like diagonal."[655] Perhaps Koolhaas reimagined in this drawing of New Amsterdam the 400 islands of Indonesia from his childhood, leading him to see the metropolis as an archipelago.[656] Or, by a different argument that I will develop here, it can be shown that the overdetermined city of Manhattan itself accelerated this innate architectural archipelago.

The urban block as an island can be found in the earliest Roman gridded cities. Roman apartment blocks, called *insulae*,[657] were big building masses, up to nine stories high, that covered large portions of the city blocks on which they were built. On the street level were located artisans' workshops and other commercial activities. Above these rose the apartments around an inner courtyard, which gave access to light and air. The term *insula*, in fact, denoted both a city block and an apartment building—a block of flats.[658] And even though these two meanings were separate, the object of the *insula* was a hybrid of both: an assemblage of housing units on a single property.[659] As such, it was an emergent architectural typology, which converged the territorial properties of the grid with the topological properties of the Roman *domus*.

Of course, the gridded archipelago of the metropolis does not end with this hybrid. As an early example, rather, the *insula* broadly suggests that the bounded quality of a city block conditions the appearance of new forms of architectural assemblages, just as enclosed heated aggregates do to matter. If we look at The City of the Captive Globe with such thermodynamic eyes, we see that, in addition to representing an intellectual program, the gridded metropolis also catalyzes a radical, new architectural assemblage. The architectural form that OMA use to present each distinct architectural world can be described as a tower stacked on a plinth. Such building ensembles originated in the metropolis of the early twentieth century. It was this very idea of stacking buildings of different programs that Hilberseimer used for his vertical city project, Hochhausstadt, in which vertical slabs of housing stand atop office buildings as plinths below.[660] The vertical city project was published in Hilberseimer's 1927 book, *Großstadtarchitektur*, in which he presents the findings of his research on the architecture of the metropolis. In the book, Hilberseimer disrcredits the capitalist production of American high-rise towers due to their mismatch between construction and decoration,[661] but he cannot disagree with some of their innovative urban massing. In particular, he gives considerable attention to The Pennsylvania Hotel by McKim, Mead & White, built in Manhattan in 1919, with its street-like voids in the upper floors.[662] The H-plan towers, which contain all the rooms, are placed right on top of a three-story plinth filled with commercial and administrative activities. Occupying nearly the whole urban block, the hotel represents one of the first versions of the architectural assemblage of a tower stacked on a plinth. This metropolitan architectural assemblage was picked up by Hilberseimer for his *Hochhaus* (skyscraper) projects,[663] in particular his design for the Chicago Tribune Tower.[664] In light of this history, the gridded archipelago of OMA's City of a Captive Globe, with its array of towers on plinths, can be seen as an homage to the architecture of the metropolis.

The difference between the city as an archipelago of morphologies and the city as gridded archipelago of buildings can be seen in the contributions by Ungers and OMA, respectively, for the Roosevelt Island Housing Competition of 1974.[665] Ungers applied his morphological concept by taking a piece of the urban fabric of Manhattan and placing a miniature version of it on the island,[666] whereas OMA extended the Manhattan grid between Seventy-First and Seventy-Fourth Streets virtually across the East River and projected four large urban islands, each containing an assemblage of different architectural objects within a single block of the extended grid.[667]

The Functions of the Archipelago City

Throughout the twentieth and twenty-first centuries, the different forms of the city as an archipelago as described above have taken on three distinct functions. The first is its function as a welfare model, as established by social-democratic municipalities before World War II. The second function held by the city as an archipelago is the polycentric urban configuration, which specifically articulates the sociopolitical city paradigms ascendent in the postwar period as described by Lefebvre. The third function of the city as an archipelago looks inward at its own form as being inherently political. This role of the city stands in contrast to the neoliberal mode of urbanization that has predominated globally since the fall of the Berlin Wall. The function of the archipelago as a political form is specifically expounded in the work of Pier Vittorio Aureli.

a. The Welfare State

After World War I Vienna became the first European city with more than a million inhabitants to be governed by Social Democrats. With the majority in the municipal parliament, the Social Democrats allowed the representatives of the workers to execute a housing policy, which became know as Red Vienna by Austrian Marxists.[668] Rather than establishing a social revolution like in Russia, the Austrian Marxists formulated a kind of municipal socialism to support the wellbeing of the working class, in particular their living conditions. "To accomplish this, however," writes Eve Blau in her volume on the topic, *The Architecture of Red Vienna*, "it was necessary not only to transform the city's existing housing system but also to reshape its entire social and economic infrastructure."[669] Under the motto, "Evolution Instead of Revolution,"[670] the Austrian Marxists not only invented but applied the idea of "social realism."[671] What made it possible to establish this new kind of Marxism was a radical intervention into the economic system, in particular tax policy, which aimed to redistribute the flow of capital. This financial *Sozialpolitik*[672] made Vienna, formally expressed as an archipelago of workers, to function as a bastion of social welfare.[673]

In fact, some of the reforms were not as radical as they might seem. The utilities like gas, water, electricity, and public transport companies as well as the city tram system that Red Vienna took over from the previous conservative government were already in the hands of the municipality. The conservative government had brought many previously private infrastructures into the ownership of the municipality, including the Imperial Continental Gas Association. Even the idea of large social welfare housing blocks was not new. In 1896 Kaiser Franz Joseph I established competitions for new housing complexes to house low-income people in apartments of high hygienic standards arranged around a communal courtyard.[674] These *Wohlfahrtsstiftungshöfe*,[674] or "welfare foundation courtyards,"[675] were designed with many functions that can be found later in the superblocks of the Social Democrats. They contained childcare centers with playgrounds, activity rooms for sport, a public bath, a public library with reading rooms, lecture halls, a club for consumption, and rooms for administration.[676]

It was with its tax policies that Red Vienna really was radical. The politicians introduced progressive housing taxes, erased amortization costs, taxed luxury goods, second homes, and cultural events, and waived profits of municipal and public companies.[677] Historian Helmut Weihsman details the major effects these policies had on the housing market:

> Firstly, the local property market stagnated: both owners of small properties and aristocratic and upper-class families who owned extraordinarily large shares of urban land sold their parcels to the city administration due to a lack of offers on the private market. The Social Democrats hit two birds with one fell swoop: They successfully fought private property speculation and found very inexpensive—often larger, contiguous—properties for their large-scale housing projects. Secondly, however, the local construction business was dealt a fatal shock by the rent regulation: the tenant protection provided protection against dismissal, and by separating the rent into basic rent, maintenance costs and operating costs, the rent fell to a minimum, so that private construction activity became unprofitable.[678]

This success allowed the municipality to intervene into Lefebvre's second circuit of capital. As a result of its own reforms of the housing market, the municipality had nearly full control over property prices in the city, allowing the purchase of large amounts of cheap land. By the end of 1931, the municipal government owned a third of the area of Vienna.[679] It was then able to execute one of the largest social housing projects in the world. The resultant welfare archipelago comprised biopolitical islands within the nineteenth-century city fabric of the bourgeoisie.

As intensely focused were the partisans of Red Vienna in achieving their social goals, they were equivalently schizophrenic and contradictory in their elaborations of its form. The formal language of the large superblocks intentionally deviates from the formal language of the garden city movement, and not only because the Viennese islands did not function as cooperatives. More importantly, the Austrian Marxists saw in that English model a conservative, petty-bourgeois settlement ideology—namely, that everyone should own a house on a piece of land.[680] And yet Red Vienna's social megaforms remind us of other conservative architectural examples: the feudal, religious, and bourgeois archetypes of castles, cloisters, and palaces. And this is not to mention the naive facade decorations or the vision for a Ringsstrasse des Proletariats.[681]

Peculiarly, the construction of Red Vienna eschewed industrial modes of production. Its architecture was labor intensive, and perhaps deliberately so, since in times after World War I many were unemployed. It is thus through modes of production that the archipelago of The New Frankfurt can be further distinguished from the Viennese superblocks. While both shared nearly identical functions as archipelago cities, their territorial strategies required very different approaches. In Frankfurt, Ernst May applied a rational mode of housing production.[682] To execute standardized housing units, designed from inside out, required large continuous pieces of property. May thus considered the new territorial islands to be a tabula rasa: a ground clean and without obstacles. And so while *Das neue Frankfurt* introduced similar tax policies to Vienna,[683] the emphasis was much more on the biopolitical aspect of living.[684] That is to say, the rational mode extended beyond just the layout and management the building site and the new process of building in modules.[685] In fact, every daily activity was rationally studied and designed in response to the new planning regime.[686] *Das neue Frankfurt* could not have been executed without the principles of scientific management defined by Frederick Winslow Taylor.[687] What become know as Taylorism is perhaps then the real function behind the social housing project of this neo–garden city.

Certainly, the archipelago of the Siedlungen could not be more different from the archipelago of superblocks. Although both emerged from the same technical object, the nineteenth-century gridded city, and converged with the same function, the politics of welfare, The New Frankfurt tuned to become a city that Red Vienna denounced: a city as an archipelago of cuteness.[688]

b. Polycentrality

"What is actually the essence, or substance, of the urban phenomenon?"[689] This question, which Lefebvre raises in *The Urban Revolution*, echoes throughout his early writings on the city. His extensive answers to the question not only address the functions of the city in general, but also give us a basic explanation of the origination of the city as an archipelago.

Recall Lefebvre's diagram on the history of urbanization from *The Urban Revolution*, in which he identifies the three historical cities—the political city, the mercantile city, and the industrial city.[690] Each of these cities emerged through a different mode of production and, throughout history, intensified the shift from a rural to a completely urbanized society. But for Lefebvre, the mode of production is not alone sufficient for the explanation of the performative qualities of cities. In a chapter of the book called "Urban Form,"[691] he argues that cities are bound by a pair of *double-functionalities*. In the first double-functionality, every city serves its own bounded territory and at the same time expands its modes of production beyond its boundary to form a network with a much larger territory. This could be the territory that immediately surrounds it, its rural hinterland, or a broader one like a network of trade. In the second double-functionality, as Lefebvre explains, the structure of the city is twofold as well: morphologically it consists of spatial elements, like squares, buildings, streets, and quarters; while sociologically it distributes a population composed of different ages, sexes, and households. The city has therefore two qualities in one. It is geometric and plastic at the same time.[692] The former defines its spaces of places, while the latter defines its spaces of flows. These dual properties of cities lead Lefebvre to his argument of the true functionality of the city: its production of centrality.[693]

For Lefebvre, the center or locus is what gives form and identity to all emerging cities, an idea he elaborates in *The Right to the City*: "In the Greek and Roman antique city, centrality is attached to an empty space, the agora and the forum. . . . the medieval city soon integrated merchants and commodities and established them in its centre; the market-place. . . . The capitalist city has created the centre of consumption."[694] While this may be true for all previous cities, the question Lefebvre faced was how to understand the postmodern city after the Second World War. Are such forms of centrality still valuable in a society tending toward total urbanization? What allows Lefebvre to answer this question is the fact that the centrality of the historical city is not static. As easily as it can be produced, it can vanish as well. And more importantly, as he writes, it can emerge anywhere at anytime:

> As we have seen, the essential aspect of the urban phenomenon is its centrality, but a *centrality* that is understood in conjunction with the dialectical movement that creates or destroys it. The fact that any point can become central is the meaning of urban space-time. However, centrality is not indifferent to what it brings together, for it requires a content. And yet, the exact nature of that content is unimportant. Piles of objects and products in warehouses, mounds of fruit in the marketplace, crowds, pedestrians, goods of various kinds, juxtaposed, superimposed, accumulated—this is what makes the urban urban.[695]

What would give rise to the city as an archipelago, then, is not just that every point can become a center, but as Lefebvre further states, that every center "requires another center, a periphery, an elsewhere. An other and different place. This movement, produced by the urban, in turn produces the urban."[696] One is reminded here of Koolhaas's statement in *Delirious New York* that the more these centers are different, the more they reinforce the idea of the city as an archipelago.[697] It seems plausible that Lefebvre's writings might have influenced Ungers and Koolhaas to articulate their archipelago cities. Certainly, their idea of an urban morphological island that can act as a "Mini-City"[698] within a city reinforces this argument.

Lefebvre summarizes his observations on the urban center in his concept of *polycentrality*, which he pairs with the historical understanding of centrality to define his contemporary urban phenomenon. This polycentrality is, for Lefebvre, "omnicentrality, the rupture of the center, dispersion—a trend that can be oriented either toward the constitution of different centers (analogous and possibly complementary) or toward dispersion and segregation."[699] It is as such that we can understand the novel functionality of the city as an archipelago.

Our Lefebvrian framing of the functionality of the city as an archipelago further provides insight into the city as a technical being. While Lefebvre, as a sociologist, argues that the city is a sociopolitical milieu for what we can understand to be technical objects, he indirectly hints—unconsciously or not—toward the idea that the city itself is a technical object as well. When he writes that every urban space can become a "place of convergence," he demonstrates that any morphological entity of the city has the capacity to change and convert its qualities.[700] Similarly, one of the main aspects that allowed Simondon to imagine the mode of existence of technical objects was his finding that machines evolve because a function can be articulated in various forms and the same form can converge various functions. It is this same overdetermined quality of individuated cities that allows them to fuse different urban functions with preexisting urban forms. Therefore, the city as archipelago "doesn't constitute a system,"[701] to borrow Lefebvre's words, even when it might have a social logic. Lefebvre emphasizes that there is no correlation between form and content due to their "(relative) independence."[702] There are no given contents of the urban polycentrality. Rather, every urban center—anywhere, anytime, and even simultaneously—"*accumulates* all content" from "living creatures, the products of industry, technology and wealth, works of culture, ways of living, situations, the modulations and ruptures of the urban everyday."[703]

The city as an archipelago of mini-cities is a city without a continuum. It has individuated into an archipelago of islands. Every island constitutes a world on its own, realizing its polycentric function as one of multiple autonomous points with nothing in between. Perhaps it was this image of the city that stirred Lefebvre to compare the urban materiality in the age of total urbanization with our cosmos:

> Physicists also conceive of a concentration of matter scattered throughout the cosmos at a single point, the density of this matter becoming infinite and the distances (voids and spaces) between molecules and particles canceling one another out. This impossibility clarifies the real. The urban assumes cosmic significance; it is globalized (combining the world as obscure path and cosmos as luminous unity).[704]

c. Political Form

The idea of centrality would seem also to imply its limit. This idea of the limit, or better, the framing of such (poly)centers gives rise to a third function of the city as an archipelago: its function as a political form.

The thesis of the city functioning as a political from was introduced to the discipline of architecture by Pier Vittorio Aureli, in particular in his essay "*Toward the Archipelago*."[705] Written in the late aughts of our current century, in the aftermath of enormous global urbanization driven by means of capitalism from the late 1990s until the economic crash of 2008 caused by the subprime mortgage crisis in the US,[706] the essay includes its aim in its subtitle: "Defining the Political and the Formal in Architecture."[707] Aureli argues that in this process of urbanization, the political aspect, as originated in the ancient Greek city, has vanished. He then argues for the reintroduction of the political aspect of the city back into our contemporary landscape of endless urban sprawl, proposing an archipelago of enclosures—that is, boundaries articulated by the architecture of wall-like buildings. The aim of this "architecture within and against capitalism," as Aureli has elsewhere termed it,[708] can be understood as the convergence of the political function of the city as an enclosure with the formal aspect of the city as an archipelago.

In the essay, Aureli reminds us of the distinction once made by the ancient Greeks between the space of the polis and the space of the house. One represents what Aristotle called *techne politike* and the other what he called *techne oikonomike*.[709] *Techne oikonomike* is concerned, as Aureli writes, "with the administration of the private space par excellence." That is why the Greek called a house *oikos*. The word t*echne oikonomike* refers as well to economy. Thus, economy had a particular location within the Greek city, and that was the private space. Aristotle's definition of the term *techne politike* refers to a different space within the Greek city, which is the space of the city itself:

> What he [Aristole] calls *techne politike* is the faculty of decision-making for the sake of the public interest—decision-making for the common good, for the way individuals and different

> groups of people can live together. Politics in this sense comes from the existence of the *polis*[710] (and not the other way around). The *polis* is the space of the many, the space that exists *in between* individuals or groups of individuals when they coexist.[711]

This distinction in the Greek city is essential for Aureli's version of the city as an archipelago for two reasons: both spaces serve different functions and both also appear in different forms.

We can say that the political and economic function of the polis addresses two very different spatial conditions in the ancient city. The political space of the Greek city was the space of the public and generally included places of social gathering like the agora, the theater, or the Pnyx. On the contrary, the economic space was the space of private habitation, including the house or, more generally, housing.[712] What is significant here is that a particular function is associated with a particular space: the economic function converged with the agglomeration of houses; the political function with the space of the agora.

What Aureli argues is that the political aspect of the city has vanished more and more throughout our urban history, while on the contrary the economic production of the material organization of the city has advanced. This shift can be seen, as he writes, by the meaning of the two Roman words for cities: *urbs* and *civitas*.[713] As Cerdà knew, the word *civitas* is closely associated with the residents of a city. It therefore addresses the citizens of a city and can be seen as the location for the *techne politike*, the space in-between people. The word *urbs* refers to the material aspect of the buildings of the city, or as Cerdà explains, to "everything contained within the limits of the enclosure constituted by the furrow around the perimeter."[714] Here it is clear that Cerdà refers to the construction of the city itself: to buildings and streets rather than inhabitants. It is this distinction that clarifies why he eliminated the word *city* from this theory and replaced it with the word *urbanization*, as the liberal city of the nineteenth century (not just Barcelona) emerged as a construction by means of a capitalist economy. The distinction between *urbs* and *civitas* is thus essential to understanding the loss of the political. "*Urbs*," Aureli writes of the original term, "indicated a city in a different way than the Greek polis. In principle *urbs* was a walled agglomeration of houses without further political qualification."[715] It is a definition of the Roman city of the past that applies just as well to the city of today.

We can say that the political and economical functions of the polis address two different formal principles as well. Already in the Greek polis, the economic function of the city was executed on a grid. The grid became the formal device that has throughout history served the *techne oikonimike* by subdividing land in order to place houses on it. Both of these components became the economic assets of urbanization and constitute the second circuit of capital:[716] the material construction of our cities. Aureli argues that the political function of the city has a form as well. In his essay he clarifies in a note to the word *polis* that, beside its meaning as a city, it also denoted a fortress. This indicates for Aureli that in order for a city to function politically, a boundary has to be articulated, which distinguishes an inside from an outside. Put more abstractly, a space has to be cut out from an endless continuous space.[717] In this sense, Aureli's argument follows that of Carl Schmitt in his *Concept of the Political*.[718] For Schmitt, the cut is a decision about "who is a friend and who is an enemy."[719] To constitute such a political space architecturally, then, would mean to make this limit between and inside and outside tangible. Aureli writes explicitly of the "experience of limit."[720] And if the very ontological foundation of the function of political space is the experience of this limit, then, for Aureli, this limit has an ontologically foundational form as well: the wall.[721]

In a 2011 article Aureli identifies the archipelago of Red Vienna[722] as one of the key archetypes of "the city as political form."[723] What he reads in the gigantic superblocks is the experience of the limit between inside and outside. As at the Karl Marx Hof, the wall-like megaform frames an enclosed courtyard space, its inside, while it detaches, or cuts itself out, from the network of the city fabric, its outside. Although the existing city streets continue underneath the building, this only further emphasizes the experience, here of a different "side" of the wall. This experience makes the form of the archipelago political. In abstract terms, this political form constitutes what Aureli describes as the relationship of an acting subject, the inside, to "the *datum*" in which the subject is situated, its outside.[724] In other words, an enclosed introverted courtyard, the political form of a *city*, is cut out from the endless urban grid, the economic form of *urbanization*.

3.5. The City as a Solid

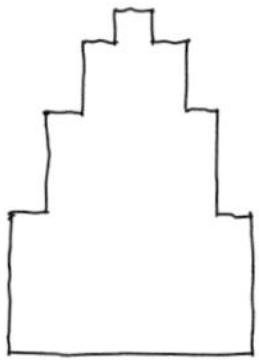

FIGURE 43. THE CITY AS A SOLID

The latest individuated city folds the urban fabric into an interior. The city as a solid can largely be understood as the convergence of a single building mass with the public space of a city. It is a city of pure interiority.

In 1929, Raymond Hood designed a project called Manhattan 1950.[725] It envisioned single buildings covering three or more blocks of Manhattan and containing entire communities within—buildings like mountains, to use the famous words of Hugh Ferriss.[726] An article published that same year in the magazine *Nation's Business*, titled "A City Under a Single Roof," promoted another of Hood's plans for a single building covering three Manhattan blocks. "Whole industries," it describes, "should be united into interdependent developments with clubs, hotels, stores, apartments and even theatres."[727] Like Le Corbusier, Hood imagined that such complexes would be elevated off the ground to allow traffic to flow underneath.[728] Above ground level he proposed a stacking of uses: "From the second to the tenth floors are shops, stores and even theaters, served by connecting arcades at every floor. Office space occupies the level from the tenth to the twenty-fifth floors. From the twenty-fifth to the thirty-fifth are clubs, restaurants and hotels. Above that are the apartments."[729] All work and living spaces would have light and air. Below ground would be as many car parking spaces as the foundations of the gigantic buildings could permit. The qualities for the average working citizen would change radically. Hood imagined the typical resident hardly ever needing to leave: "His business, his lunch, his club and his apartment are all in the same building. The time he saves goes either into recreation or into greater production."[730]

The city under a single roof, a term that I use generally to define Hood's proposals as well as others like them, was one of the first cities as a solid. In his Manhattan 1950 project, Hood located a total of thirty-eight architectural giants at the intersections of roughly every tenth street.[731] Although together these "mountains" look similar to an archipelago city, in fact they are a completely new individuated city, which Koolhaas identifies in Delirious New York as "a new phase of Manhattanism."[732] The city as an archipelago is embedded in the existing city—each island formed by the morphology of the city itself. In contrast, the city under a single roof detaches from the existing city. It becomes autonomous, even producing new city fabric. "Big buildings" observed Hood about Manhattan, "do not merely follow the subways: they now anticipate them."[733] With the city as a solid, it is neither the wall, nor the subdividing grid, nor linear infrastructure, nor the territory that give rise to a new individuated city. Rather, for the first time in the history of our urbanization, it is the agglomeration of buildings into a unified pile. In other words, everything the city has previously originated here converges into a single entity. Architecture no longer exists because of the city, it produces the city. In his seminal 1995 book, S,M,L,XL, Koolhaas introduced the concept of Bigness. "Bigness," he writes, "no longer needs the city: it competes with the city; it represents the city; it preempts the city; or better still, it is the city."[734] The city under a single roof defines the moment when architecture, as an individual object, detaches itself from urbanism.[735]

One of the very first projects with such an agglomeration of buildings was Hood's 1927 design for the Methodist National Cathedral in Ohio.[736] Asked to design a new church, he wrapped the street-level sacred space with classrooms, commercial spaces, and retail facilities. In section, the church is covered with office buildings on top of which stand a hotel, a YMCA, apartments, and a swimming pool. Below the church, in place of a crypt was instead the largest carpark in Ohio.[737] The most famous city as a solid of that time was the proposal for Rockefeller Center in New York from 1930.[738] In many of the early massing studies for his personal scheme for Radio City,[739] Hood employed his ideas from "A City Under a Single Roof," in particular by covering multiple urban blocks with one building scheme. This was the first real attempt to build a mountain-building on three consecutive blocks of Manhattan.[740] Despite what Manfredo Tafuri points out in his *Sphere and the Labyrinth* as the anachronism of proposing such enormous architectural giants—an expression of capitalist spirit—in the New Deal era,[741] the autonomous character of these mountains bore an inevitability that made it possible to imagine the city as a solid anywhere. Indeed, in 1927 Hood used such a scheme of huge solids in his design for a recreation center in Arcady, near Myrtle Beach, South Carolina—the proverbial middle of nowhere.[742] Citing that project, Tafuri concludes on the same page that the city under a single roof "constitutes a prophetic document with respect to the enormous structures that, from the 1970s on, have attempted to install themselves as autonomous islands in the American metropolises."[743]

In the second half of the twentieth century, this city of pure interiority spread all over the planet. Even when it originated in a metropolis, its capacity was to produce autarkic, well-tempered environments—to borrow a term from Banham[744]—in places where cities could not have been imagined before. The city as a solid can be seen as the prototype for Victor Gruen's shopping malls. What started with his project for Northland Shopping Center in Michigan was fulfilled at his Southdale Center in the Minneapolis suburb of Edina. The very first enclosed shopping center, upon completion in 1956, it was the largest indoor public space in the United States.[745] In the beginning, Gruen's shopping malls simply inserted the medieval European marketplace into a huge box, like an instant indoor city.[746] Over the years, however, shopping malls evolved into gigantic interior cities of shopping, containing many kinds of facilities including theaters, offices, housing, and even ice skating rinks, as in the Galleria in Houston.

Further examples of the success of the of city under a single roof are John Portman's atrium buildings, which can be seen as the fusion of a park and a hotel.[747] These buildings, all with gigantic central voids, house apartments, businesses, shops, restaurants, event spaces, bars, spas, jogging paths, and even a lake in Portman's most famous design, the Westin Bonaventure Hotel in Los Angeles. And in Las Vegas a whole world of gambling, with all its complementary functions, has emerged underneath a single roof such that you never need to leave its interior.

The city under a single roof is not only an American phenomenon. In Europe it has fulfilled Tafuri's prophecy by producing new centralities in locations where the investment of capital was previously unimaginable. It is this phenomenon that triggered critical responses like Koolhaas's idea of bigness.[748] In another instantiation that has caught the attention of Koolhaas, the city under a single roof also has become *the* model of the airport. China saw one of the world's largest interiors opened in Chengdu in 2013: the "New Century Global Center," measuring 500 by 500 meters on its sides and 100 meters tall.[749] And today we find a new version of the city as pure interiority, which is not a mountain but rather an iceberg.[750] In cities like Singapore and London, among others around the world, new developments are emerging whereby everything moves underground. These icebergs, like the mountain-buildings, manifest the idea of the city as a building, but there is one truly legal city as building. Whittier, Alaska is an entire community, including schools, shops, and administration, shared within the envelope of the fourteen-story Begich Towers.[751]

The city as a solid further has given rise to an endless amount of utopian fictions in which a building becomes a city or the city turns into pure interiority, like Constant's New Babylon, Hans Hollein's Aircraft-Carrier City, Walter Pichler's Underground City, or Raimund Abraham's Glacier City, to mention just a few.[752] Perhaps the most notable utopian cities as a solid were the No-stop City[753] by Archizoom Associati and The Continuous Monument[754] by Superstudio. Of the former we know only its inside. It is a city of an endless interiority, or a "city without architecture,"[755] as Andrea Branzi once explained. Of the latter we know only its exterior. It is a city of pure exteriority, or as Branzi contrasted, an "architecture without a city."[756]

The city as a solid is the city of what Lieven De Cauter calls "capsular civilization."[757] It is the city of temporary collectives, framed by a spectacle object with a privatized, scripted public-sphere inside. What all cities under a single roof seem to have in common is their particular function within capitalism. The early city under a single roof, as promoted by Hood and others, was conceived in the climate of the rapacious growth of modern capitalism in the so-called Roaring Twenties. Portman's atriums have been identified by Fredric Jameson as the symbols par excellence of postmodernism within late capitalism. Jameson even tagged this new kind of interiority as a new urban spatial experience: *hyperspace*.[758] The same now holds for our contemporary version of this individuated city. Today's icebergs, as well as other forms of large cities under a single roof, perform perfectly within the regime of financial capitalism. For with capitalism always needing to find new outlets for overaccumulation, as David Harvey reminds us,[759] it seems as if it has found a new perfect asset—the city within a huge architectural solid.

The Forms of the City as a Solid

The city as a solid appears as two kinds of mountains.[760] Each can be described as the convergence of a high-rise with an urban element—in one case, the streets of the city as a grid, and in the other, the public space of the city as an enclosure.

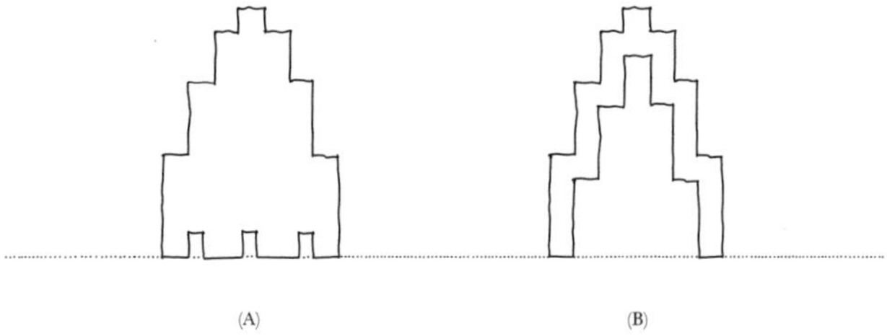

FIGURE 44. TWO FORMS OF THE CITY AS A SOLID.[761] THE GRIDDED MOUNTAIN(A), THE VOIDED MOUNTAIN(B).

a. The Gridded Mountain

We can understand how the gridded mountain takes shape by juxtaposing three images: the model of Raymond Hood's City Under a Single Roof;[762] the drawings of the "Loft & Office scheme on 3 New York Blocks" from proposal for Rockefeller Center by Walter Kilham Jr. from 1929;[763] and Le Corbusier's plan of the cartesian skyscraper.[764] In Hood's model we can recognize that the whole building mass is an agglomeration of various architectural building typologies cohered together. At its center appears to be a high-rise structure, to which thin slabs are attached on each of its four sides. Together these stand on a thick but low solid, similar to a plinth but acting only as a base for the slabs rather covering a whole urban block.

We can similarly deconstruct Le Corbusier's plan of his huge skyscraper. Its outward form of a cross can be seen as the intersection of two central-corridor buildings, with row-house units attached on both sides. It is as if two of the Unité d'habitation intersected. But rather than having L-shape apartments lined up along a corridor every third floor in section, the tower reads more like Le Corbusier's Immeubles Villas,[765] in that the L-shape houses are assembled along the corridor in plan. This gives the corridors a character more like real streets, in that they access individual properties rather than individual rooms as would a mere hallway.

If we now look at the drawings by Walter Kilham Jr., who was at the time an assistant to Hood, we can see that each architectural volume is assembled in such a way that the singular central corridor, which is open on its ends, forms an endless grid. What emerges from this convergence of a street grid with the central-corridor slab-buildings is an internalized urban fabric with the characteristics of the city itself. The internal streets are a scaled-down version of the original Manhattan grid, but the formal capacity changes radically. Instead of being endless, the grid is confined by the boundary of the buildings, a limit which allows this city under a single roof to be completely detached from the existing city.

With the existing urban fabric continuing underneath, the architectural assemblage piles up in section and intensifies its deviation from the surrounding city by forming new internal circulation networks on various levels. These new spaces of flow change their topological characteristics. We find grids above rows of streets and below a rectangular circuit, and more kinds of meshes might be found throughout the vertical expanse of this architectural mountain. Thus we can see how the gridded mountain concretizes—through the specialization of the functional properties of the continuous circulation of streets, which enables the formal properties of the grid to converge with the aesthetic properties of the corridor.

b. The Voided Mountain

If the gridded mountain gives us a glimpse into the mode of existence of a new architectural object—namely by fusing two-dimensional properties of the city with a building—the voided mountain extends this process of concretization. As the fusion of a mountain-building with the volume of an urban public-space, it is a convergence of two three-dimensional properties as well of different material properties. Something as massive and structurally compartmentalized, or cellular, as the single-corridor hotel typology becomes inflated with a huge void of air, or volumetric space. The unified whole that results from the convergence of these city elements is completely new, in terms of its formal, topological, and functional qualities. Portman has said of his atrium buildings that they are the fusion of a park with a traditional hotel slab building.[766] This functional metaphor means something different, however, in terms of their technical being. It is not just that two things are formally added to one another. Rather, as Simondon would say, when technical objects or their parts converge, they effect a concretization process whereby radically new technical objects might appear.

In the case of the voided mountain, in order for a building type with a central corridor to meld with a volumetric public space, it must change its topological character. To allow the exterior public space to inflate, so to speak, inside of the building, the corridor must split down the middle. The straight hallway with a beginning and an end distends into an endless circular balcony encircling the void, the previously double-loaded corridor now single-loaded only on the outside. This new corridor is augmented not just with light and air, but also new functions. On the one hand, the ringed circulation space is quite urban, inviting the occupant to stroll around it as through a city, and on the other hand, it incorporates theatrical qualities, as it makes it possible to watch someone walking through space. The formal and topological properties here are radically changed as well—a void folded into a solid mass and submerged into a torus.[767] Outside becomes inside and inside becomes outside. The vertical section through the hallway, an inner view of the hotel slab that never could be experienced other than in a drawing, here becomes the "outer" facade of the inner public void, the atrium. At the same time, once-exterior public space becomes pure interiority. Yet all these peculiar inversions of reciprocal qualities notwithstanding, Fredric Jameson would not have spent the effort to describe this new interiority in such detail, as we will see, if not for something else radically new. To rehash Simondon, when two entities—here a building and an urban space—exchange their aesthetic properties it allows for qualities to emerge that were foreign to both initial objects. Indeed, for Jameson, in the convergence of the form of a slab building with the function of a hotel with the form of a void with the function of urban public square, a new postmodern space was born: a privatized public space he calls *hyperspace*. In terms of Simondon's thesis on the genesis of technical objects, this suggests that the technical object does not only effect new technical objects, it produces new milieus as well.[768]

c. The Iceberg and the Earth-scraper

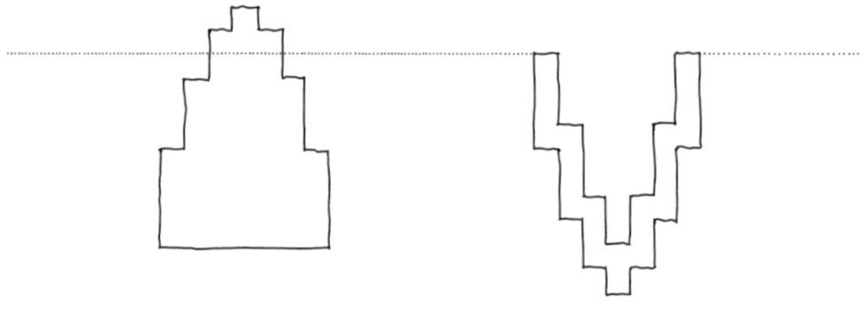

FIGURE 45. TWO MORE FORMS OF THE CITY AS A SOLID: THE ICEBERG(A), THE EARTH-SCRAPER(B).

Today we can find two variations on the theme of the previous two models. The iceberg is simply the mountain submerged, so to speak, in the ground. What is visible is only its top, while the rest of the mountain can be found underground. The building turns into an architectural iceberg.

The second variation, or repetition within the formal sequence, as George Kubler would say, is a mirrored copy of the voided mountain, the building and its void flipped below ground. The void is thus not interiority but rather an excavated exterior space. The building mass, having lost its outside facade, now receives natural light from this subterranean void. Whereas the original skyscraper reaches toward light and air, its flipped variation, the earth-scraper, reaches for the coolness of the caves.

The Functions of the City as a Solid

As described above, the city as a solid has functioned primarily within the second circuit of capital. Indeed, as we will see, the individuated architectural mountain has performed in various phases of twentieth- and twenty-first century capitalism, particular in the laissez-faire city of the 1920s, the late capitalism of the 1970s and '80s, and our contemporary modes of finance capitalism.

a. The Financial Syndicate

It was Alan Colquhoun who said once that architecture will always be made by those with power over money, whether they be a state, government, organization, corporation, or individual.[769] Independent of how the money is earned, architecture as building can only come into existence through the will to spend money for it; or, as it often happens within capitalism, through the will to invest money into "urban assets" in order to gain more capital from them.

The architect who seems to have understood this best was Raymond Hood during the Roaring Twenties in New York. Hood's lifetime (1881–1934) was nearly synchronous with the most significant developments in the American metropolis, which took shape from 1876 until the crash of October 1929. He stood out among the skyscraper architects of America, as Henry-Russel Hitchcock explained: "He is not an idealist and he is not a creative artist."[770] He was, however, the most influential architect of the metropolitan era in New York, because "he accepts the condition under which the Metropolitan architect is expected to work in America."[771] It is therefore no surprise that he worked closely with businessmen, because he needed their knowledge "to cope with the desperate building condition"[772] of the laissez-faire city.[773] Hood thought of himself as a mechanic.[774] He was a mechanic of architecture driven by money—a modern architect who wanted to be honest in regard to how the contemporary city of the 1920s worked. And thus his proposals for the growing metropolis were always presented and argued for as investments. He even designed the financial structures of those investments.

The publication of Hood's "A City Under Single Roof," one of his main proposals for New York, was simultaneous with one of the worst financial crises to ever take place on Wall Street. The stock market collapsed between September 4 and the November 13, 1929. Hood's design ran in the November issue of *Nation's Business* magazine.[775] In his book, *The American City*, Tafuri notes the poor timing of proposing the largest architectural object in the least economical favorable period, but upon closer look we see that Hood's proposal was above all a reaction against the regional planning effort taking place in New York at that time. As we know retrospectively, this de-urbanization process took place up until the early 1980s. Only since then has the city become attractive for its financial assets again. Tafuri points out that Hood's intention was to counter the decentralization of the city, as it was proposed by The Regional Plan of New York committee directed by Thomas Adam.[776] That plan projected some satellite communities and commercial centers being connected into a large infrastructural transportation system to overcome the congestion problem of Manhattan. The actual aim of the plan was the introduction of a "reasonable investment" in the region of New York.[777] Hood proposed the exact opposite: centralization and cooperative investment. His projects aimed to reinstate what, for him, the metropolis always was and should continue to be—that is, the center of agglomeration of large amounts of capital.

In his "City Under a Single Roof," Hood lays out his views on the matter of architecture as investment. Under the current conditions in Manhattan, he claims, the quality of real estate is bad. The reason for this is that each Manhattan block is subdivided into parcels of land that are too small. This causes too many small investments on each block and, furthermore, once an investment is executed it is a bad investment, since all the qualities of these asset-buildings are bad qualities: bad light, bad ventilation, bad backyards, bad views, etc. Hood points out in particular the risk in this kind of small investments. Too many separate ownerships mean an unpredictable future for further investments. Investors have to have their "sails continually trimmed," as he writes, because no one can oversee and coordinate all their individual desires. He concludes:

> This undirected growth has brought about real estate conditions that would not be tolerated in any other industry. The whole tenor of the age is toward consolidation and mutual aid against individual conflict. Building units are too small. They are not sufficiently financed to give themselves even partial protection. Huge investments are at the mercy of chance and the whims of a next-door neighbor. The result is a quarrelsome, competitive, destructive battle into which only the shrewdest opportunist or the most audacious adventurer can afford to put his money.[778]

The only way out of this unregulated growth is, for Hood, not just his architectural solution of a mountain-building containing all the functions of a city over three blocks and fort-five floors, but also a "single enlightened ownership."

For his city under a single roof, Hood imagines that his new magic mountain would not require much more capital than a similar amount of real estate under the status quo system. Instead of up to twenty-five separate interests who would never agree with one another, he calls for replacing them with "a single syndicate." This syndicate would consist of between fifteen and twenty operators who would serve for a time of fifteen to twenty years and would be the only decision makers for the whole development. Not only would this single syndicate overcome the destructiveness of individual, conflictual interest and competitiveness, even more importantly, it would have considerably more financial strength.

Hood anticipated the future of urban real-estate investment.

In the second half of the twentieth century, globalization and multinational investment dominated the landscape of urban real estate. For Hood, this emerging reality of the real estate market and its capital represented governing devices for the well-being of the metropolis: "The central organization endures a form of amalgamation such as occurs every day in the business world. It means the application of farsighted direction to a movement that already has shown itself in the city's growth. Certainly, some such remedy must be applied to prevent New York from strangling itself by its own growth."[779]

The function of the city as a form of large investment through an organization like a syndicate can be found in other city forms as well. The garden city, an articulation of the city as an enclosure, used "trusted" businessmen to lend their money at low interest rates. The linear city of Chambless's Roadtown was unthinkable without the idea that people could invest at 5 percent in the stocks of the Roadtown Corporation. To function as a form of investment syndicate, The city as a solid shows once again that a strict correlation between the form of a city and its function does not exist. What does exist are the hidden potentials—virtually present but not actualized—which, due to their overdetermined qualities, individuated cities have the capacity to bring to the foreground.

b. Hyperspace

At the end of the 1970s, a moment when the map of the world was radically changed for the years to come, a new function of the city as a solid entered the discourse, specifically among urban geographers, philosophers, and critics.[780] In continuity with Lefebvre's work on "the production of space"[781] within the history of urbanization, these Marxist theorists were searching for a new function of the postmodern city that could define postmodern space.[782] What this space came to be identified as was a new form of interiority, which Jameson dubbed hyperspace.[783] Hyperspace was not just a spatial abstraction but actually was manifested in a real building: the Westin Bonaventure Hotel in Los Angeles, a city under a single roof that opened the doors into its hyperspace in 1977.

In his book *A Brief History of Neoliberalism* David Harvey brings up the idea that, in the postwar era, a global compression of space and time took place in our cities.[784] This compression accelerated in the 1970s, due especially to emerging digital technologies. We call this planetary time-space collapse "globalization." The aim of globalization in the '70s was to reach out with greater geographic range for all kinds of investments. But in order for this economic expansion to take shape, new forms had to enter into the institutional traditions of nations—namely, as Harvey outlines, "deregulation, privatization, and withdrawal of the state from many areas of social provision."[785] Neoliberalism, the synonym for this threefold program, became the new form of governance in the age of this globalized world. "Neoliberalism," Harvey explains, "is in the first instance a theory of political economic practices that proposes that human well-being can best be advanced by liberating individual entrepreneurial freedoms and skills within an institutional framework characterised by strong private property rights, free markets, and free trade."[786] Its beginning is typically identified as the period between 1978 and '80, when this form of governance took on specific faces: Margaret Thatcher in Great Britain and Ronald Reagan in the United States. But as Harvey suggests from the beginning of his book, including with the pictures of personalities on the cover, neoliberalism was not just a western idea that forced sociopolitical changes. It was a global phenomenon that perhaps was first started in China by the new paramount leader of the People's Republic after Mao's death: Deng Xiaoping.[787] This new form of governance became the primary political form around the globe and was particularly embraced in the 1990s, even in all the previous welfare states of the European Union.

What the neoliberal economy meant for our cities was that neither the municipalities nor other governmental institutions would design or finance their construction. Instead, this was handed over to private investors. The role that was left for the municipalities and the state in general was, as Harvey writes, "to create and preserve an institutional framework appropriate to such (neo-liberal) practices."[788] It is this shift, from a culture of institutional settings toward this new mode of production, that led theorists, geographers, and philosophers to inquire into its new spatial condition. What was considered in the social sciences as *the spatial turn* had a more general concern, which is summarized by Francois Lyotard in his 1984 book *The Postmodern Condition.*[789] Lyotard observes that within neoliberal globalization the long-term institutional settings became replaced by short-term neoliberal market driven responsibilities. "The temporary contract," he writes, "is in practice supplanting permanent institutions in the professional, emotional, sexual, cultural, family, and international domains, as well as in political affairs."[790]

But what then, specifically, is this postmodern space? It is perhaps useful to first describe modern space. Modernity was, as Marshall Berman writes,

> a mode of vital experience—experience of space and time, of the self and others, of life's possibilities and perils—that is shared by men and women all over the world today. . . . To be modern is to find ourselves in an environment that promises adventure, power, joy, growth, transformation of ourselves and the world—and, at the same time, that threatens to destroy everything we have, everything we know, everything we are.[791]

The architectural translation of this space[792] of the power to transform oneself and the world was the tabula rasa[793] condition of Cartesian space.[794] We can find the application of this architectural space in Le Corbusier's *plan libre* and the empty floor plans of Mies. Both cases allow us to experience the space of modernity, in which the subject is placed in an empty space, the non-quality of the spatial *extensio* exploited for the power or sovereignty of the individual. The ideal form of the architectural space of modernity is therefore the grid.[795] No form better defines this condition of homogeneous, endless Cartesian space without qualities.

Jameson's hyperspace contrasts with that homogeneous modern spatial paradigm. In the 1970s he witnessed the emergence of a new aesthetic sensibility in every form of art—in music, painting, literature, and film, but specifically in architecture—which was neither homogeneous nor perceptional but instead "chaotic and heterogeneous."[796] The aesthetic sensibility of postmodernism, according to Jameson, broke with the modernist tradition to became the aesthetics of late capitalism,[797] in which the city is constructed by a market that produces popular urban spectacles to fulfill the desires of this postindustrial, consumerist, high-tech, information society.

The Westin Bonaventure epitomizes this postmodern sensibility for Jameson. First, it is "popular building," filled with tourists and locals. In contrast to a traditional hotel with an obvious front door, this "populist insertion into the city fabric" has many entrances.[798] One leads from the main street in the back of the building, which brings people to the level of the shops. Another entrance is located on Flower Street and brings people to the level of the reception desk and some restaurants. The other entrance Jameson describes, from the garden terrace in the back, comes in at the building's sixth floor. In addition to the principal entrances he points out, I would note that the lobby continues into the parking garage, an escalator leads from the sidewalk on the opposite side of Fifth Street over a bridge and into the lobby, and there is even a second bridge across Flower Street that gives access to a food court one level higher. Jameson argues that although these many entrances might give the appearance that the building is connected with the city, in fact it is the opposite. It is a mini-city in itself, functionally similar on its exterior, but spatially radically different inside. "The Bonaventure," Jameson writes "aspires to being a total space, a complete world, a kind of miniature city; to this new total space, meanwhile, corresponds a new collective practice, a new mode in which individuals move and congregate, something like the practice of a new and historically original kind of hypercrowd."[799] This hypercrowd gets moved through space at lighting speed, like visitors at a theme park. People shoot through the space with breathtaking speed in chandelier-like escalators. From the within the lobby they move up and outside of the building envelope before entering again from below and into a rotating restaurant. On the way back down they land in a lake within a park-like interior scene. The experience of such a space is topological. It is a permanent spatial folding between inside and outside. Any access, or understanding, of its spatial configuration, is just not there. When, finally, they do want to get out of the elevator, they do not know where they are, since each lift lets off at a different level.

For Jameson, the effect of everything that goes on within this space is a sense of constant busyness. "Emptiness is here absolutely packed,"[800] while any kind of orientation is erased. Crucially for Jameson, the space doesn't enable you to perceive it perspectively. It is a topological experience that is unfamiliar to us—a hyperspace, which withdraws from our human cognitive mapping of space.[801] Even when such attempts were made—for instance, when the elevators were color-coded according to the four axial positions in order to help visitors find a destination like a shop, a restaurant, a hotel room, or a conference space—this was, Jameson notes, an "attempt to restore the coordinates of an older space."[802] This latest mutation of space away from modern Cartesian order transcends human cognition: "Postmodern hyperspace has finally succeeded in transcending the capacities of the individual human body to locate itself, to organise its immediate surroundings perceptually, and cognitively to map its position in a mappable external world."[803] The Westin Bonaventure is a city under a single roof that functions as a space to which we humans have yet no access. Perhaps unsurprisingly, then, Jameson imagines that this new space is further advanced than our own human evolution:

> I am proposing the notion that we are here in the presence of something like a mutation in built space itself. My implication is that we ourselves, the human subjects who happen into this new space, have not kept pace with that evolution; there has been a mutation in the object unaccompanied as yet by any equivalent mutation in the subject. We do not yet possess the perceptual equipment to match this new hyperspace.[804]

c. The Financial Asset

As Harvey observes, "capitalists always produce a surplus product. A healthy capitalism has to grow at 3 percent per year; the problem is to find where you can achieve that 3 percent growth."[805] Sometimes, capitalists cannot find a "healthy" economy. Other times, capitalists produce surplus value and need to store it somewhere. Harvey calls such a situation over-accumulation, a moment in which capitalists are in need of an outlet to store their money.[806] With this in mind, then, what seems to have happened since the 1980s is a shift in the relationship between the architecture of the city and its embedded capitalism. Specifically, as Matthew Soules puts it, "architecture is not [anymore] the result of finance capitalism but rather *is* finance capitalism."[807] As Soules points out in his book *Icebergs, Zombies, and the Ultra Thin*, Jameson saw buildings—even if they were for him an expression of the dominant mode of capitalism—primarily as the outcome of an architectural production based on an aesthetic practice of "symbols, analogies, illustration and expression."[808] In contrast, Soules shares with Reinhold Martin the idea that the emergence of new forms of architecture, like the iceberg, are no longer a representation of capitalism. Rather, for Martin, "architecture . . . does not represent or 'mirror' late capitalism as its cultural equivalent. It *belongs* to late capitalism."[809] What appears to have happened in our current state of capitalism is that architecture no loner fulfills exclusively its historical capitalist role—that is, it is not just storage of wealth for the rich to make a "good life."[810] Architecture has added a new function. It has become a financial asset, and is itself a driving force within finance capitalism.

The role of real estate as a financial asset is perhaps as old as our urban history.[811] The right to own land and to ask for rent could found in many ancient cities, including Rome. When we refer to the fusion of capitalism and architecture today, typically we mean the rise of what Thomas Piketty calls "ownership society."[812] Picketty describes a debate that took place on the eve of the French Revolution, the night of August 4, 1789, the aim of which was to define the word *privilege*. The outcome, he writes, was "to draw a sharp distinction between, on the one hand, the regalian powers (of security, justice, and legitimate violence) henceforth to be monopolised by the centralised state and, on the other hand, property rights, which only individuals could claim."[813] The former indicates what we today refer to as the governmentality of those forces within our city, like capitalism. The latter defines our buildings and apartments, or more specifically, our investments in real estates. As Piketty describes it the debate seemed not have been so easy, but once established it meant that any urban element of the city suddenly had the potential to become part of the second circuit of capital. Individuals could buy and sell any form of real estate. This, more or less, was the beginning of the city of the grid. One is reminded of the images of New York's land auctions right after the subdivision of land was legalized, in which suddenly it was possible to trade parcels of lots.[814] Fast forward and Hood's proposal for a city under a single roof is next to jump into our minds. The driving forces of capitalism demanded larger and larger urban developments. More and more money was needed and new forms of ownership had to be invented to develop these gigantic mountains. Nonetheless, the money for such projects within early or modern capitalism was gained by industrial production and therefore related to the first circuit of capital: the mode of production through labor.

That all shifted in the 1970s when, as Piketty explains, the wealth of the world's richest populations became earned through capital investment rather than through labor. In two diagrams, Piketty shows that the public capital of states has stayed more or less the same over the last 150 years. Meanwhile the private capital in Western countries reached a peak before World War I in Europe and around 1930 in the United States.[815] It declined after World War II and hit its historical minimum around 1950. What the diagrams then show is that, since the beginning of the 1950s in Europe and the '70s in the United States, private capital has increased tremendously. What happened between 1970 and today is that capital assets, particular those earned through real estate and stock shares have continuously increased.[816] As Picketty summarizes:

> At the beginning of the 1970s, the total value of private wealth (net of debt) stood between two and three and a half years of national income in all the rich countries, on all continents. Forty years later, in 2010, private wealth represented between four and seven years of national income in all the countries under study. The general evolution is clear: bubbles aside, what we are witnessing is a strong comeback of private capital in the rich countries since 1970, or, to put it another way, the emergence of a new patrimonial capitalism.[817]

Although it is common to understand financial assets within capitalism as shares in stock markets, less common is to think of architecture playing the same role. In order for a building to be used as a financial asset, it must be turned it into a more liquid asset form. Otherwise it is just a storage space for wealth, as always, rather than able to be used like an *architectural* stock.

In order to meet the Koolhaasian slogan, Architecture = Real Estate,[818] the process of financialization had to break with the historical relationship between architecture and capital. Soules describes the ways that have been used to change the liquidity of an architectural entity, or "the degree to which an asset can be easily exchanged for cash (cash being the ultimate liquid asset)."[819] Usually buildings have a very low degree of liquidity. It takes a while for an apartment, a house, a piece of land, or especially a whole high-rise tower to be bought or sold. This made architecture traditionally an "illiquid asset."[820] From the 1980s onward, Soules explains, new financial instruments have been invented to increase the liquidity of buildings, especially housing. Notable among these instruments are real estate investment trusts (REITs) and mortgage-backed securities (MBS). REITs, which gained quick popularity, "allow investors to buy and sell shares in a company that owns or finances real estate on well-established stock markets,"[821] while MBS "enable investors to trade securitised shares of mortgage debt."[822] The upshot of both of these financial instruments is that investors don't need to own any physical real estate anymore. They can make profits by trading shares of it. Since the '80s architecture has become as lightweight as money. In its function as a financial asset, it has earned $1.8 trillion in profits between 2009 and 2019, according to a FTSE index of global real estate equities.[823]

These new forms of financial liquidity supplied new outlets for the pile of money generated globally by capitalists, especially after the fall of the Berlin Wall in 1989. In turn, this required new forms of liquid architectural assets. In addition to the well-known pencils towers in New York[824] and the "zombie and ghost cities" around the world,[825] there also appeared a new form of city as interiority: the iceberg building, a mountain-like interior below the ground.[826] The premise that architecture could function as a financial asset relies upon the ability to maximize its purely numerical asset of physical space.

Ideally, this space maximization should be exploited with the least possible resistance. In a city like London, for example (and probably in any dense global city), it has become more and more difficult to find that pure asset. Billionaires wishing to build huge new homes in the desirable neighborhoods of Chelsea, Mayfair, Knightsbridge, and Westminster face zoning laws that hinder such development. In these neighborhoods virtually no permissions are given to build upward or outward,[827] those laws having been made to protect the sphere of old Victorian mansions, and with it its stored capital. The super-rich in these quarters were looking for new capital outlets, ideally something with the potential to be absent from any laws. And their "digging in" had literal success. As London architect Ademir Volic told the *Guardian*, "we analysed the planning laws and realized they covered everything about the surface of the ground, but nothing beneath it. There was nothing whatsoever that could stop us from drilling all the way down to the south pole."[828] Money in London had not only found a new financial asset, but a new architectural cave as well. The iceberg home was born. Free of any restrictions underground, these subterranean mansions expanded up to "15 bedrooms, seven bathrooms and 20 toilets, plunging deeper into the earth than the height of neighbouring homes."[829] From the outside, these icebergs appear as old Victorian villas, unassumingly sitting atop gigantic agglomerations of spaces—ballrooms, swimming pools, television rooms, billiards room, tennis courts, gyms, hot tubs, saunas, massage rooms, and garages—sunk many levels deep into the earth. From 2008 to 2012 more than 800 of these mini-cities were built in London.

Architecture, or better, the city as a solid, here again found a new function as a financial asset. It found a new form as well, the iceberg. Both are merely the latest stage of what the individuated city can become. Once again, as presented throughout this chapter, the city demonstrates that technical objects are overdetermined beings with the capacity to permanently mutate into new formal and functional modalities.

Conclusion

These last examples of the fifth individuated city demonstrate what already was introduced in chapter 1—That is, the ways in which theorists, historians, and architects try to define what is *deeper* than the form or use of the architecture of the city. In the work of Fredric Jameson, Rem Koolhaas, and Reinhold Martin we can again identify these deeper aspects as either being a spatial *type*, an idea of how architecture *functions*, or what can be seen as the *matter* of buildings. All three positions ask themselves primarily the same three questions:

- How do buildings appear to us?
- What can buildings do?
- What are buildings made of?

When Jameson sees in the Westin Bonaventure the appearance of a new space, his question addresses the understanding of how buildings appear to us. The answer is an aesthetic one, and it suggests that what can be seen as deeper than the building's form is a new type of space. In his particular case, this is hyperspace. When Koolhaas pens his manifesto on Bigness, his question concerns what architecture can do. When he writes "bigness=urbanism vs architecture" he puts his finger on the fact that architecture has a deeper function than merely its programatic uses. For Koolhaas, buildings are not just containers within cities but themselves function as cities. When Martin writes that architecture *belongs* to late capitalism, he wants to emphasize what is immanent to the architecture of the city.[830] He wants to make clear that capitalism is the life of buildings. He does not discuss how buildings appear to us or how buildings are used, but rather what constitutes their materiality. Buildings are not the outcome of financial capitalism, they are the matter through which financial capitalism operates.

In all three positions we can find an argument for the correlation between the architectural form and the content of the city. It is this correlation through which the discipline of architecture defines the emergence of new architectural types, functions, and materiality. In every case the city is considered as the milieu: as a social, economic, or political force field of which architecture is an expression. But, as the examples of each individuated city have shown, such correlations do not exist in reality. Various cities, once individuated, can be tuned into many forms or functions. Their overdetermined quality allows the same form to take on different social, economic, or political functions, while at the same time various functions can appear in totally different forms. As Simondon wrote about standardization, economic influences or practical requirements do not originate new technical objects.[831] These *extrinsic causes*, as he calls them, never give rise to the new. Rather, the new lies within the technical object itself, or what Simondon calls *internal necessity*.[832] The same can be said about its architecture: The city it is not the milieu for architecture. All the architecture of the city is inherent in the qualities of the technical object, which is the city. It is the city's *innate virtuality* that gives rise to all its architecture. Even if we stretch Martin's argument and say that architecture is immanent to financial assets and this mode of capitalism is immanent to the city, he still cannot explain how the intrinsic qualities of urban elements converge with each other to give rise to new forms of buildings. What is missing is what Simondon did for technical objects. As Schmidgen wrote, he looked under the hood, took a screwdriver, and immersed himself deep into their interiority in order to explain their mode of existence.[833]

That is exactly the intention of the next and final chapter: to look under the hood (or roofs) of buildings, and dive deep into their interiorities to find out how they assemble, fuse, merge, and converge their different qualities. As a result, what become visualized are processes of concretization in which the initial abstract forms of urban elements unify their qualities in a *convergence series*.[834] Each convergence series gives rise to a new kind of individuated architectural prime object as it appeared in our history of urbanization.

[418] Lefebvre, Henri. "The Right to the City" chapter 2-17. In *Writings on Cities*, translated by Eleonore Kofman and Elizabeth Lebas. Cambridge, Mass., USA: Wiley-Blackwell, 2006, 63-181.

[419] Lefebvre, Henri. *The Urban Revolution*. Translated by Robert Bononno. (Originally published in 1970). Minneapolis: University of Minnesota Press, 2003.

[420] Ibid., 165.

[421] Ibid., 1.

[422] Lefebvre, Henri. *The Production of Space*, Translated by Donald Nicholson-Smith, Oxford UK & Cambridge, Mass., USA: Blackwell, 1991.

[423] Merly Paul, Ani. "The Production of Space: Henri Lefebvre." CMS College Kottayam, Department of Sociology, November 27, 2020. Accessed September 24, 2021. https://www.youtube.com/watch?v=BH-p9H43AiA.

[424] Harvey, David. "Senior Loeb Scholar Lecture." Harvard University, Graduate School of Design, March 28, 2016. Accessed September 24, 2021. https://www.youtube.com/watch?v=pm_UgX--ef8.

[425] Lefebvre, Henri (2003) 3-4.

[426] Ibid.,14-15.

[427] Ibid., 8.

[428] Ibid.,10.

[429] Ibid.,13.

[430] Ibid.,16.

[431] Ibid.,17.

[432] Tafuri, Manfredo. "The Disenchanted Mountain: The Skyscraper and the City." In *The American City: From the Civil War to the New Deal*, edited by Giorgio Ciucci, Francesco Dal Co, Mario Manien-Elia, and Manfredo Tafuri, translated by Barbara Luigia La Penta. Cambridge, Mass.: The MIT Press, 1983, 389-503.

[433] Hood, Raymond M. "A City under a Single Roof." In *The Sphere and the Labyrinth: Avant-Gardes and Architecture from Piranesi to the 1970s*, by Tafuri, Manfredo, translated by Pellegrino D'Acierno and Robert Connolly. Cambridge, Mass.: The MIT Press, 1987, 190-195.

[434] Such instances of the city as a grid include the Roman military camp as well as the new cities of ancient Greece like Milet, which used a grid within its surrounding walls. Benevolo, Leonardo. *Die Geschichte der Stadt*. 5th Edition. (Originally published as Storia della Città, 1975) Frankfurt am Main: Campus Verlag, 1990, 146.

[435] The most famous example of such a convergence was in Kowloon Wall City in Hong Kong, which was demolished between 1993 and 1994. https://en.wikipedia.org/wiki/Kowloon_Walled_City.

[436] Benevolo, Leonardo (1990), 19-39.

[437] Ibid., 152-153.

[438] Ibid., 256-263.

[439] Ibid., 59-88.

[440] Ibid., 339-340.

[441] See Howard, Ebenezer, (1902).

[442] Cauter, Lieven de, ed. *The Capsular Civilization: On the City in the Age of Fear*. Rotterdam: nai010 publishers, 2004.

[443] Benevolo, Leonardo (1990), 33.

[444] Ibid., 74-75.

[445] Mumford, Lewis. *The City in History: Its Origins, Its Transformations, and Its Prospects* (1961). San Diego, New York, London: A Harvest/HBJ Book, 1989, 149.

[446] For a deeper reading of the meaning of the Horoi stone in ancient Greek, see Fine, John. Horoi. *Studies in Mortgage, Real Security, and Land Tenure in Ancient Athens*. Athens: American School of Classical Studies, 1951, 41-95.

[447] ASCSA Digital Collections. "Agora Monument: Boundary Stones of the Agora." Accessed September 24, 2021. http://agora.ascsa.net/id/agora/monument/boundary%20stones%20of%20the%20agora.

[448] Fine, John (1951), 41.

[449] Benevolo, Leonardo (1990), 126-127.

[450] Ibid., 218.

[451] Ibid., 349.

[452] Ibid., 703.

[453] Mellaart, James. *Catal Hüyük - A Neolithic Town in Anatolia*, New York: McGraw-Hill Book Company, 1967, 62.

[454] Mumford, Lewis (1989), 120-121.

[455] Benevolo, Leonardo (1990), 376-377.

[456] For a further description of the bastion system, see DeLanda, Manuel. *War in the Age of Intelligent Machines*. New York, NY: Zone Books, 1991, 50.

[457] Mumford, Lewis (1989), 155. Mumford identifies in Howard's *Garden City of To-morrow* the rebirth of the autonomous Greek civilization. In one of his diagrams, Howard includes a key with the words "Science & Religion," from which it seems that he copied not just the content of the Greek city but that of the medieval city as well.

[458] Lefebvre, Henri (2003), 8-9.

[459] Mumford, Lewis (1989), 339.

[460] Lefebvre, Henri (2003), 11.

[461] Braudel, Fernand. *Civilization & Capitalism. 15th-18th Century*. Translated by Siân Reynolds, vol. I. The Structures of Everyday Life - The Limits of the Possible. (Originally published as *Les Structures du Quotidien: Le Possible et L'Impossible*, 1979). London: Collins, 1985, 479-480.

[462] Lefebvre, Henri (2003), 11.

[463] Braudel, Fernand (1985), 501.

[464] The English translation of Braudel's book uses the German term *Weltwirtschaft*. Ibid., 503.

[465] Agamben, Giorgio. *Homo Sacer - Die Souveränität der Macht und das nackte Leben*. Frankfurt am Main: Suhrkamp Verlag, 2002.

[466] Ibid., 175.

[467] Ibid., 175.

[468] In the German edition of Agamben's Book, the term *protection* appears in brackets: *«in Schutz zu nehmen»* Ibid., 176.

[469] Ibid., 176.

[470] This quote is a paraphrase by Agamben of Saint-Bonnet's definition of the state of exception from his book *L' etat d'exception*, Paris: Presses Universitaires de France, 2001, 28. In Agamben, Giorgio. *State of Exception*, translated by Kevin Attell, Chicago and London: The University of Chicago Press, 2005, 1.

[471] See Lefebvre's diagram of the process of urbanization above.

[472] Howard, Ebenezer Howard. *Garden Cities of To-morrow*.

[473] Howard includes a footnote to the cost of an acre: "This was the average price paid for agricultural land in 1898: and, though this estimate may prove far more than sufficient, it is hardly likely to be much exceeded." Ibid., 20-21.

[474] Ibid., 87.

[475] Ibid., 107.

[476] See "The speculative Ground Plan" in Mumford, Lewis (1989), 421-426.

[477] Ibid., 412.

[478] Lefebvre, Henri (2003), 13.

[479] Benevolo, Leonardo (1990), 813-888.

[480] Ibid., 257.

[481] Ibid., 145.

[482] Ibid., 143.

[483] Ibid., 647-700.

[484] Ibid., 66-67.

[485] Ibid., 83.

[486] Ibid., 687.

[487] Wright, Frank Lloyd. "The Disappearing City" (Original edition 1932). In *The Industrial Revolution runs away*, New York: Horizon Press, (1969) 26. Page ten in the original facsimile.

[488] Ibid.

[489] Benevolo, Leonardo (1990), 41.

[490] Ibid., 29.

[491] Ibid., 34.

[492] Ibid., 250.

[493] Ibid., 250.

[494] Ibid., 256.

[495] Krauss, Rosalind. "Grids" October, The MIT Press, Cambridge, Mass., Vol. 9 (Summer, 1979), 50-64.https://www.jstor.org/stable/778321?origin=JSTOR-pdf, Accessed: 24/01/2011 20:39 p.50.

[496] See footnote to Harvey Wiley Corbett's image of "Towers on a Hudson River Bridge

Between New York and New Jersey (1975): "*Very modernized Venice* in full operation: 20-lane streets, pedestrians walking from *island* to *island* in a *system of 2028 solitudes*." In Koolhaas, Rem, (1978), 103.

[497] Benevolo, Leonardo (1990), 675-77.

[498] See William Bridge's map of New York from 1811 in *The Greatest Grid: The Master Plan of Manhattan 1811-2011*. Edited by Hilary Ballon. New York: Co-published by the Museum of the City of New York and Columbia University Press, (2011), 37-38.

[499] Koolhaas writes of Central Park: "A catalogue of natural elements is taken from its original context, reconstituted and compressed into *a system of nature* that makes the rectilinearity of the Mall no more formal than the planned informality of the Ramble. Central Park is a synthetic Arcadian Carpet." In Koolhaas, Rem (1978), 18.

[500] Benevolo, Leonardo (1990), 522.

[501] Ibid., 748.

[502] Wagner, Otto, (1911), 11.

[503] See "The square grid and its diagonals" in Puig, Arturo Soria y, ed. *Cerdà: The Five Bases of the General Theory of Urbanization*. Madrid: Gingko Press, 1999, 130.

[504] Piranesi Variations, the project by Peter Eisenman and designed by Yale architectural students, was presented at the 13th International Architecture Exhibition Venice Biennale, Venice, Italy 2012. https://eisenmanarchitects.com/Piranesi-Variations-2012.

[505] Eisenman, Peter. "Field of Diagrams: The Project of Campo Marzio" In *Zero Piranesi*, SAC Journal 5, edited by Peter Trummer. Baunach: Städelschule Architectural Class (Frankfurt) and AADR Spurbuchverlag, 2019, 21.

[506] The origination of biopolitics goes hand in hand with the origination of the city. See Vitruvius. Book "The Site of a City." In *The Ten Books on Architecture*. Edited by Morris H. Morgan. Unabridged and unaltered republication of the 1914 1st Edition. New York: Dover, 1960.

[507] Bridges, William. "Remarks of the Commissioners for Laying out Streets and Roads in the City of New York, under the Act of April 3, 1807." In *Map of The City of New York and Island of Manhattan with Explanatory Remarks and References*. New York: William Bridges, 1811.

[508] Lefebvre, Henri. "The Right to the City" chapter 2-17. In *Writings on Cities*, translated by Eleonore Kofman and Elizabeth Lebas. Cambridge, Mass, USA: Wiley-Blackwell, (2006), 66.

[509] Mumford, Lewis (1989), 421.

[510] See Howe, Richard. "Notes on 19th Century Lot Sizes." The Gotham Center for New York City History, November 15, 2012. Accessed September 24, 2021. https://www.gothamcenter.org/blog/notes-on-19th-century-lot-sizes.

[511] See Ballon, Hilary (2011).

[512] Mumford, Lewis (1989), 422.

[513] Lefebvre, Henri (2003), 159.

[514] Thomas Piketty's writings on capitalism in the second half of the twentieth century could be summarized in the fact that the real estate market in Europe has been growing much faster than the economy and is therefore responsible for the increase in salaries. For a deeper debate on this subject see: Piketty, Thomas. *Capital in the Twenty-First Century*. Translated by Arthur Goldhammer. Cambridge, Mass.: Harvard University Press, 2014.

[515] Lefebvre, Henri (2003), 159-160.

[516] Lefebvre, Henri (1991), 325.

[517] Ibid., 325.

[518] Ibid., 325.

[519] Sven-Olov Wallenstein defines the term *biopolitical machine* as follows: "(The term *biopolitical machine* is in fact used by Agamben, but my use is different, as I hope will become clear). This means . . . that its primary goal is to *produce subjectivity*, and it should be interpreted in terms of a genealogy of the modern subject". In Wallenstein, Sven-Olov. *Bio-Politics and the Emergence of Modern Architecture*. New York: Princeton Architectural Press, (2009), 20.

[520] Foucault, Michel. *Security, Territory, Population: Lectures at the College De France, 1977-78*. Edited by Michel Senellart. Translated by Graham Burchell. London: Palgrave Macmillan, (2007), 16.

[521] Ibid., 27.

[522] Ibid., 33.

[523] Ibid., 32.

[524] Vitruvius. *The Ten Books on Architecture*. Edited by Morris H. Morgan. Unabridged and unaltered republication of the 1914 1st Edition. New York: Dover, (1960), 17-18.

[525] Foucault, Michel (2007), 33.

[526] Wallenstein, Sven-Olov. "Introduction: Foucault, Biopolitics, and Governmentality." In *Foucault, Biopolitics, and Governmentality*, edited by Jakob Nilsson & Sven-Olov Wallenstein, Södertörn Philosophical Studies 14, Stockholm: Södertörn University, 2013, 11-12.

[527] Cerdà, Ildefons. *General Theory of Urbanization* (1867). Edited by Vicente Guallart. (Originally published as *Teoria General de La Urbanizacion*, 1897) New York, Barcelona: Actar Publishers & the Institute for Advanced Architecture of Catalonia, (2018), 8-9.

[528] Ibid., 18-19.

[529] In Puig, Arturo Soria y, ed. *Cerdà: The Five Bases of the General Theory of Urbanization*. Madrid: Gingko Press, 1999. All five bases of urbanization, which Cerda introduced, are explained in detail. It would go beyond the purpose of this book to describe each of them in detail. What might be important to mention, however, is that all five bases can be seen as functions of the gridded city.

[530] See "The Structure of Man-made Place" in Norberg-Schulz, Christian. *Genius Loci: Towards a Phenomenology of Architecture*. (Originally published as *Genius Loci - Paesaggio, Ambience, Architettura*, 1979). New York: Academy Editions Ltd, 1980, 58-69.

[531] Lefebvre, Henri (2003), 14. In the discourse of architecture, the industrial city has a very specific form. A form once given by the images and plans of Tony Garnier's *Cité Industrielle* (1899-1904), it is a fictional city presented in such a way that all of its functions are separated from each other and located in topographical and infrastructural elements to perform best: the factory is close to the river; the houses are located on a plateau with good infrastructural connection; the hospital is in the hills to gain from the fresh air; and the hydroelectric power station is in the mountains. The *Cité Industrielle* can be considered a fusion of the modern paradigm of separate uses, the Greek polis, and the writings of Émile Zola.

[532] Compañía Madrileña de Urbanización. *Madrid Ciudad Lineal*. 376th Edition. Imprenta

de la Ciudad Lineal, 1911.

533 Chambless, Edgar. *Roadtown*. New York: Roadtown Press, 1910.

534 "I would surround the city worker with the trees and grass and woods and meadows and the farmer with all the advantages of city life—I had invented Roadtown." Ibid., 20.

535 For further explanation of the distinction between these two forms see Frampton, Kenneth "Megaform as Urban Landscape." In *Conflict - The Berlage Cahiers*, edited by Amsterdam The Berlage Institut, 6:102–5. Rotterdam: 010 Publishers, (1999), 102-105.

536 Miljutin, Nikolaj A.. *Sozgorad: Probleme Des Planens Sozialistischer Städte*. Moskau/Leningrad: Staatlicher Verlag, 1930, 29.

537 Hilberseimer, Ludwig. *The Nature of Cities: Origin, Growth, and Decline; Pattern and Form; Planning Problems*. Chicago: Paul Theobald & Co., 1955, 264-265.

538 Feuerstein, Günther. *Urban Fiction: Strolling Through Ideal Cities from Antiquity to the Present Day*. Stuttgart/London: Edition Axel Menges, 2008, 351.

539 Banham, Reyner. *Megastructure: Urban Futures of the Recent Past*. New York: Harper and Row, 1976, 7-12.

540 Ibid., 12.

541 Avery, Dan. *"Saudi Arabia Building 100-Mile-Long 'Linear' City."* Architectural Digest, January 26, 2021. Accessed September 24, 2021. https://www.architecturaldigest.com/story/saudi-arabia-building-100-mile-long-linear-city.

542 Mumford, Lewis (1989), 425.

543 Compañía Madrileña de Urbanización. *Madrid Ciudad Lineal*. 376th Edition. Imprenta de la Ciudad Lineal, (1911), 7. In a later publication from 1913, a new drawing of the layout of manzanas is added. In this plan the measurements of manzanas are sized as 300 by 500 meters. See Compañía Madrileña de Urbanización. *Ciudad Lineal Como Arquitectura Nueva de Ciudades*. First International Congress "Art of constructing cities and the Organization of municipal life", Gant, Belgium, 1913. Imprenta de la Ciudad Lineal, (1913), 8.

544 Frampton, Kenneth.. "Megaform as Urban Landscape." In *Conflict - The Berlage Cahiers*, edited by Amsterdam The Berlage Institut, 6:102–5. Rotterdam: 010 Publishers, (1999), 103.

545 Ibid., 103.

546 Chambless, Edgar, 19.

547 Manuel Martín Rodríguez. *La Ciudad Lineal de Arturo Soria y El Georgismo*. Arquitectura Viva, 2014.

548 Ibid.

549 George, Henry. *Progress and Poverty: An Inquiry into the Cause of Industrial Depressions and of Increase of Want with Increase of Wealth*. Garden City, New York: Doubleday, Page & Co., 1912.

550 Ibid., 425.

551 Soria y Mata, Arturo. "Al entrar en 1910." *In Compañía Madrileña de Urbanización La ciudad Lineal: Revista Científica de Higiene, Agricultura, Ingeniería y Urbanización*, Madrid (Chamartín) 1910, n. 400, 1743.

552 Ibid.

553 See chapter XI, "Roadtown Education and Social Life." In Chambless, Edgar, 123-137.

[554] Ibid., 128.

[555] See chapter V, "Civilisation Through Pipes and Wires,." Ibid., 59-73.

[556] The list is taken from chapter IX, "Industry Returns to the Home." Ibid., 102-115.

[557] Ibid., 110.

[558] Ibid., 134.

[559] Ibid., 127.

[560] Ibid., 123-124.

[561] Ibid., 163.

[562] Ibid., 170.

[563] Ibid., 116-117.

[564] See "The Roadtown Religion." In Ibid., 168-172.

[565] For Milyutin, proposals of archipelagos like the garden city were not radical enough, as he writes: "We understand that these plans, despite some promising aspects, are only a terrible utopia and nurture the illusion that one can escape this situation without smashing the capitalist system. Such illusions undermine the fighting spirit of the proletariat." Miljutin, Nikolaj A.. *Sozgorad: Probleme Des Planens Sozialistischer Städte*. Moskau/Leningrad: Staatlicher Verlag, (1930), 12. My translation.

[566] Ibid., 7.

[567] Ibid., 9.

[568] Ibid., 12.

[569] Ibid., 9.

[570] See foreword by J. Meschtscherjakow. In Ibid., 5.

[571] Ibid., 9.

[572] See part 3 "Urbanisation or De-urbansiation." In Ibid,. 12.

[573] Marx, Karl, and Engels, Friedrich. *Marx and Engels The Communist Manifesto, Crofts Classics*. Edited by Samuel H. Beer and Harvard University. New York: Appleton-Century-Crofts, 1955, 32.

[574] Miljutin, Nikolaj A. (1930), 22. My translation.

[575] See Illustration 11,"Schema: Konzept für Magnitogorsk, nach dem funktionalen Montage-Band-System" (Scheme: Concept for Magnitogorsk, according to the functional assembly line system). In Ibid., 28. My translation.

[576] A detailed description of each of the bands is given in part 5: "Principles of Planning". In Ibid., 22-24. My translation.

[577] See OSA project in Ibid., 51-56, and Stiller, Adolph, and et all. *Leonidov: Ein Architekt des russischen Konstruktivismus*. Salzburg: Müry Salzmann, (2010) 11-13.

[578] Popper, Karl. *The Open Society and Its Enemies*. (First published 1947, reprinted 1947). London; Henley: Routledge & Kegan Paul, 1945.

[579] Dijk, Hans van. *"Wat Is Er Nu Helderder Dan de Taal van de Moderne Architectuur."* In Wonen-TA/BK, Interview met Peter Smithson., 31–34. nrs. 19-20, 1978. (Quoted by Van den Heuvel, D. "Alison and Peter Smithson: A Brutalist Story, Involving the House, the City and the Everyday (Plus a Couple of Other Things)." TU Delft, 2013, 244.)

[580] Ibid., 244.

[581] Smithson, Alison, *Team 10 Primer*, edited by Alison Smithson, (originally published in Architectural Design, December 1962). London/Great Britain: Studio Vista, 1968, 61.

[582] Ibid., 49, and Smithson, Alison, T*eam 10 Meetings 1953-1984*, edited by Alison Smithson, Delft: Publikatieburo, Faculteit der Bouwkunde, Technische Universiteit Delft, 1991, 12.

[583] Smithson, Alison (1968), 48.

[584] The "street-in-the-air" was first formulated by Alison and Peter Smithson in their Golden Lane Project in 1952-53, presented at CIAM 9 in Aix-en-Provence on July 24th, 1953. See Risselada, Max, and Dirk van den Heuvel. *Team 10: In Search of a Utopia of the Present 1953-81*. Rotterdam: NAI Publishers, 2006, 33.

[585] Smithson, Alison, and Peter Smithson. *Ordinariness and Light - Urban theories 1952-1960 and their application in a building project 1963-1970*, London: Faber and Faber, 1970, 63.

[586] Smithson, Alison (1968), 67.

[587] See diagram 51 showing Kahn's Philadelphia study. In Ibid., 53.

[588] Smithson, Alison, and Peter Smithson. *Urban Structuring: Studies of Alison & Peter Smithson*. London, New York: Reinhold Publishing Corporation, (1967), 9-27.

[589] Smithson, Alison (1968), 67.

[590] Van den Heuvel, D. (2013), 242.

[591] Ibid., 249-250.

[592] Dijk, Hans van, (1978). Quoted by Van den Heuvel, D. (2013), 244.

[593] Bevan, Aneurin, *In Place of Fear*, 58. Quoted by Smithson, Alison, and Peter Smithson (1970), 18.

[594] See Wallas, Graham. *The Great Society: A Psychological Analysis*. (Originally published 1914). New York, NY, US: MacMillan Co, 1932.

[595] Van den Heuvel, D. (2013), 247.

[596] Smithson, Alison, and Peter Smithson (1970), 81-83.

[597] Van den Heuvel, D. (2013), 247-248.

[598] Smithson, Alison, and Peter Smithson (1970), 82.

[599] Popper, Karl (1945).

[600] Smithson, Alison (1968), 61.

[601] Popper, Karl (1945), 152.

[602] Ibid.

[603] Ibid., 153.

[604] Ibid., 166. Popper includes footnote to the end of this passage: Cp. Meyer, *Geschichte des Altertums*, III, 443, and IV, 120 f.

[605] Frampton, Kenneth. *Modern Architecture - A Critical History*. London: Thames and Hudson, (1980), 271.

[606] The origin of the city as an archipelago is deeply Eurocentric. See Cacciari, Massimo. "Der Archipelagos." In *Der Archipel Europa*. (Originally published as L'arcipelagos, 1997),

translated by Günter Memmert, 1st Edition, 9–32. DuMont Buchverlag, 1998.

607 One of the first cities to start communal housing projects was Amsterdam through the *Woningwet* law of 1902. Even in the times when the city was governed by liberals, it was the Social Democrat Floor Wibaut who became *Wethouder for volkshuisfesting* in 1914 and commissioned under his leadership the famous Plan Zuid by Hendrik Petrus Berlage. See Wit, Wim de. "Die Amsterdamer Schule und die Städtische Wohnbaupolitik." *In Kommunaler Wohnbau in Wien: Aufbruch 1923 - 1934, Ausstrahlung*, edited by Karl Mang and Eva Mang-Trimmel. Wien: Presse- und Informationsdienst der Stadt Wien, 1977.

608 Blau, Eve. "Against the Idea of Force, The Force of Ideas: Municipal Socialism and the Politics of Austrian-Marxism." In *The Architecture of Red Vienna, 1919–1934*, 18–47. Cambridge, Mass.: The MIT Press, 1999.

609 Schlandt, Joachim, Ungers, Oswald M. "The Viennese Superblocks", translated by Sima Ingberman. In *Oppositions*, Vol. 13, Summer 1978,The MIT Press: Cambridge Mass., London England, 1978, 83-111.

610 See Raymond Hood collage from 1930 called "Manhattan 1950". In Koolhaas, Rem (1978), 148.

611 It is important to note that Rem Koolhaas wrote the first draft of the manifesto, which was called "The City in the City - Berlin: A Green Archipelago." See Ungers, O. M, Rem Koolhaas, Peter Riemann, Hans Kollhoff, Arthur Ovaska, Florian Hertweck, Sébastien Marot, and Ungers Archiv für Architekturwissenschaft. *The City in the City: Berlin: A Green Archipelago: A Manifesto (1977)*. Zürich: Lars Müller Publishers, (2013), 13-23.

612 Krier, Léon. "The City Within the City." *A + U, Tokyo* Special Issue (1977): 69-152. Reprinted in: Architectural Design, vol. 54 (1984), Jul/Aug: 70–105.

613 See thesis 5: Ungers, Oswald M., Rem Koolhaas, Peter Riemann, Hans Kollhoff, and Arthur Ovaska. "Cities within the City. Proposals by the Sommer Akademie for Berlin." *Lotus International 19, no. L'isolato urbano | The urban block* (1978), 86.

614 See handwritten correction by Ungers in "The City in the City - Berlin: A Green Archipelago. In Ungers, O. M, Rem Koolhaas, Peter Riemann, Hans Kollhoff, Arthur Ovaska, Florian Hertweck, Sébastien Marot, and Ungers Archiv für Architekturwissenschaft (2013), 15.

615 Aristotle. *Politics*; Translated by Benjamin Jowett. Batochhe Books Kitchener, (1999), 159. Accessed September 24, 2021. https://historyofeconomicthought.mcmaster.ca/aristotle/Politics.pdf

616 Ungers, O. M., (2013), 50.

617 See "The City of the Captive Globe" from 1972 by OMA in Koolhaas, Rem (1978), 242-243.

618 Ibid., 243-44.

619 May, Ernst. "Fünf Jahre Wohnungsbautätigkeit in Frankfurt." Edited by Ernst May and Fritz Wichert. *Das Neue Frankfurt. Internationale Monatsschrift für die Probleme Kultureller Neugestaltung*, no. 2-3, vol. 4, Februar-März (1930): Verlag Englert und Schlösser, Frankfurt am Main, 28. My translation.

620 See Cover of Gantner, Joseph. "Das Neue Frankfurt - Internationale Monatszeitschrift für die Probleme kultureller Neugestaltung, 11/12" V Jahrgang November/Dezember 1931, "rein-meinische regionalplanung", Verlag Englert und Schlosser, Frankfurt am Main.

621 May, Ernst (1930), 28-29. My translation.

[622] May, Ernst, Joseph Gantner. "Unsere Publikationen - Sport". Edited by Ernst May and Fritz Wichert. Das Neue Frankfurt. Internationale Monatsschrift für die Probleme Kultureller Neugestaltung, no.1, vol. 4, (1930): Verlag Englert und Schlösser, Frankfurt am Main, 1-15.

[623] See image 54. In May, Ernst (1930), 63.

[624] See Linse, Ulrich. "Lebensreformbewegung." In *Metzler Lexikon Religion: Gegenwart — Alltag — Medien: Band 2: Haar — Osho-Bewegung*, edited by Christoph Auffarth, Jutta Bernard, Hubert Mohr, Agnes Imhof, and Silvia Kurre. Stuttgart: J.B. Metzler, 1999, 319-321.

[625] If we take a regular urban block to be approximately 1 to 1.5 hectares, then each of the Siedlungen were five to twenty times larger.

[626] May, Ernst. "Grundlagen der Frankfurter Wohnungsbaupolitik" edited by Ernst May and Fritz Wichert. *Das Neue Frankfurt. Internationale Monatsschrift für die Probleme Moderner Gestaltung*, no. 7-8, vol. 2, Juli-August (1928): Verlag Englert und Schlösser, Frankfurt am Main, 115.

[627] Letchworth was built on an estate of 5300 acres, or just over twenty-one square kilometers, which is still more than ten times the size of the "Goldstein Garden City" of the new Frankfurt, which covered only two. Ebenezer Howard envisioned the need to buy 6000 acres of land for his garden city. See Ebenezer Howard. *Garden Cities of Tomorrow*. London: Swan Sonnenschein & Co., Ltd., (1902), 20. Accessed September 24, 2021. http://archive.org/details/gardencitiestom00howagoog.

[628] See "Hypertely and self-conditioning in technical evolution." In Simondon, Gilbert (2017), 53-59.

[629] See drawing "Die Wohnhausbauten der Gemeinde Wien" by Erich Franz Leischner und Viktor Weixler around 1926. In Tafuri, Manfredo. *Vienna rossa: la politica residenziale nella Vienna socialista, 1919-1933*. Milano: Electa, 1980, 14-15.

[630] Blau, Eve. "Ernst Hein, 'Die Bodenpolitik der Gemeinde Wien,' in Internationaler Wohnungs- Und Städtebaukongress: Vorberichte (1926): 10." In *The Architecture of Red Vienna, 1919–1934*, Cambridge, Mass.: The MIT Press, 1999, 140.

[631] Tafuri, Manfredo (1980), 58.

[632] Ibid., 80.

[633] Blau, Eve (1999), 321-329.

[634] "Sometimes these artifacts persist virtually unchanged, endowed with a continuous vitality; other times they exhaust themselves, and then only the permanence of their form, their physical sign, their locus remains. The most meaningful permanences are those provided by the street and the plan. The plan persists at different levels; it becomes differentiated in its attributes, often deformed, but in substance it is not displaced. . . . I remarked on its permanent character before, but now by permanence I mean not only that one can still experience the form of the past in this monument but that the physical form of the past has assumed different functions and has continued to function, conditioning the urban area in which it stands and continuing to constitute an important urban focus." Rossi, Aldo. *The Architecture of the City*. Translated by Diane Ghirardo and Joan Ockman. Oppositions Books. Cambridge, Mass.: The MIT Press, 1982, 59.

[635] Ibid., 64-65.

[636] Ibid., 32.

[637] Ungers, Oswald M., Rem Koolhaas, Peter Riemann, Hans Kollhoff, and Arthur Ovaska (1978), 82–97.

[638] Ungers, O. M, Rem Koolhaas, Peter Riemann, Hans Kollhoff, Arthur Ovaska, Florian Hertweck, Sébastien Marot, and Ungers Archiv für Architekturwissenschaft (2013), 15.

[639] Ibid., 52-53 and 54-55.

[640] Ibid., 52-53.

[641] Text and images of this exhibition were published in: Ungers, Oswald M. *Morphologie City Metaphors*. Köln: Walter König, 1982.

[642] "If, for instance, designing is understood purely technically, then it results in pragmatic functionalism or in mathematical formulas. If designing is exclusively an expression of psychological experiences, then only emotional values matter, and it turns into a religious substitute. If, however, the physical reality is understood and conceptualized as an analogy to our imagination of that reality, then we pursue a morphological design concept, turning it into phenomena which, like all real concepts, can be expanded or condensed." In Ungers, Oswald M. (1982), 9.

[643] Ibid.

[644] Simondon, Gilbert (2017), 27.

[645] Ungers, O. M., (2013), 52-53.

[646] See Kubler, George (1962), 39.

[647] Koolhaas, Rem (1978), 242-243.

[648] For a detailed description of OMA's work on New York City and in particular the content of each of the islands in the City of the Captive Globe Project, see Koolhaas, Rem, and Zoe Zenghelis. "The City of the Captive Globe (1972)." Edited by Haig Beck. *AD Architectural Design* 47, no. 5 (1977). 331-333.

[649] Gregotti, Vittorio, "OMA- Office for Metropolitan Architecture", In *Lotus International*, 1976, January, No.11, New York City: Rizzoli International Publications, (1976), 34.

[650] Koolhaas, Rem (1978), 13.

[651] Koolhaas, Rem, (1978), 15. On the shaping force of utilitarian interest, see Bridges, William. "Remarks of the Commissioners for Laying Out Streets and Roads in the City of New York, under the Act of April 3, 1807." In *Map of The City of New York and Island of Manhattan with Explanatory Remarks and References*. New York: William Bridges, 1811.

[652] Ibid., 69.

[653] See, Ferriss, Hugh. *The Metropolis of Tomorrow*. USA: Ives Washburn, 1929.

[654] See: Koolhaas, Rem (1978), 127-133.

[655] Ibid., 11.

[656] Koolhaas, Rem. "A: Archipelago. Rem Koolhaas in conversation with Beatriz Colombia: Rem Koolhaas A-Y (A Dictionary)." In *Rem Koolhaas OMA II: 1996-2007*, edited by Richard C Levene and Fernando Márquez Cecilia. Croquis 134/135. Madrid: El Croquis, (2007), 379.

[657] See Fig.: 378-381. In Benevolo, Leonardo (1990), 235.

[658] Storey, Glenn R. "The Meaning of 'Insula' in Roman Residential Terminology." *Memoirs of the American Academy in Rome* 49 (2004), 47.

[659] "If there was a separate meaning of 'apartment house,' it was a species of both meanings of the term, in that such apartment houses were a visibly distinct and separate property within the fabric of the city block (sense 2) and probably took up large portions of a street block, as seen in a number of examples at Ostia (sense 1). Both leading

meanings are thus compatible with the basic meaning of the term as 'island.' In Ibid, 47.

660 Hilberseimer, Ludwig. *Großstadtarchitektur*. Die Baubücher, Band 3. Stuttgart: Julius Hoffmann, 1927, 17-19.

661 Ibid., 63-64.

662 Ibid.,64.

663 See Fig.: 18. and Fig.: 30. In Hilberseimer, Ludwig. *Großstadtbauten*. Hannover: Aposs, (1925), 21 & 27.

664 Fig.: 17. In Ibid., 20.

665 *Lotus International*, 1976, January, No.11, New York City, NY: Rizzoli International Publications, (1976), 38-41.

666 Ibid., 38.

667 Ibid., 40-41 and in OMA edited by Haig Beck. *AD Architectural Design* 47, no. 5, 1977, 348-351.

668 "The Austro-Marxists were committed to developing Marxism as an empirical social science through systematic historical and sociological research. Austro-Marxist sociological theory, as formulated by Max Adler, who elaborated the conceptual and theoretical foundations of Austro-Marxism, was a set of causal statements, open to empirical testing, that dealt with a specific object, 'socialized humanity.' In Blau, Eve (1999), 23-24.

669 Ibid., 37.

670 Weihsmann, Helmut. *Das Rote Wien: Sozialdemokratische Architektur und Kommunalpolitik 1919-1934*. 2., Completely revised Edition. Wien: Promedia, (2002), 93. My translation.

671 Ibid. My translation.

672 See Weber, Anton. "Sozialpolitik Und Wohnungswesen." In *Das Neue Wien*, edited by Städtewerk, unter offizieller Mitw. d. Gemeinde Wien. 1., 1/4:191–310. Wien: Elbemühl Papierfabriken und Graphische Industrie A. G., 1926.

673 See Weihsmann, Helmut (2002), 25-26.

674 See, "Concurs-Ausschreibung der Kaiser Franz Josef I. -Jubiläums- Stiftung für Volkswohnungen und Wohlfahrtseinrichtungen", XIV., XVI., 2. Preis Arch. O. Thienemann, Czeike, Felix. "Wiener Wohnbau vom Vormärz bis 1923." Edited by Karl Mang. *Kommunaler Wohnbau Wien. Aufbruch 1923–1934*, Wien, n.d. 53.

675 See Czeike, Felix. "Wiener Wohnbau vom Vormärz bis 1923." Edited by Karl Mang. *Kommunaler Wohnbau Wien. Aufbruch 1923–1934*, Wien, n.d. 51. My translation.

676 Ibid., 51.

677 See Weihsmann, Helmut (2002), 26-36.

678 Weihsmann, Helmut (2002), 32-33. My translation.

679 Blau, Eve (1999), 141.

680 Weihsmann, Helmut (2002), 94. This difference of land use can be seen in relationship to the social housing estates by Ernst May in Frankfurt, who celebrated the single family row houses. See for example: Schleuning, Johannes. *Die Siedlung Römerstadt in Frankfurt am Main*. von Ernst May. Hamburg: Diplomica, 2000.

681 See cover page of Eugenie Brandl and Paula Hons. Titelblatt: "Die Ringstraße des Proletariats." In "Die Unzufriedene : Eine unabhängige Wochenschrift für alle Frauen",

Eigentümerin, Verlegerin, Herausgeberin und verantwortliche Redakteurin: Eugenie Brandl und Paula Hons. 8. Jg., Nr. 35, 30. August 1930: Titelblatt.

682 See Gropius, Walter. "Der Grosse Baukasten." edited by Ernst May. *Das Neue Frankfurt. Monatschrift für die Fragen der Grosstadt-Gestaltung*, no. 2, vol. 1, Dezember (1926): Verlag Englert und Schlösser, Frankfurt am Main, 25-40.

683 See May, Ernst. "Fünf Jahre Wohnungsbautätigkeit in Frankfurt." edited by Ernst May and Fritz Wichert. *Das Neue Frankfurt. Internationale Monatsschrift für die Probleme Kultureller Neugestaltung*, no. 2-3, vol. 4, Februar-März (1930): Verlag Englert und Schlösser, Frankfurt am Main, 21-51.

684 See Dr. Hagen. "Biologische Und Soziale Voraussetzung Der Kleinstwohnung" edited by Ernst May and Fritz Wichert. *Das Neue Frankfurt. Monatschrift für die Probleme Moderner Gestaltung*, no. 11, vol. 3., November (1929): Verlag Englert und Schlösser, Frankfurt am Main, 222-226.

685 See May, Ernst (1930), 35-44.

686 See Schütte-Lihotzky, Margarete. "Rationalisierung Im Haushalt" edited by Ernst May. *Das Neue Frankfurt. Monatsschrift für die Fragen der Grossstadt-Gestaltung*, no. 5, vol. 1, April-Juni (1927): Verlag Englert und Schlösser, Frankfurt am Main, 120-123.

687 See Taylor, Frederick Winslow (1919).

688 See Sarnitz, August. "Realism versus Verniedlichung: The Design of the Great City." In *Otto Wagner: Reflections on the Raiment of Modernity*, edited by Henry Francis Mallgrave, 85–112. Getty Center for the History of Art and the Humanities, Santa Monica. Chicago: The University of Chicago Press, 1993.

689 Lefebvre, Henri. *The Urban Revolution* (2003), 115.

690 Ibid., 15.

691 Ibid., 115-134.

692 Ibid., 116.

693 See Eleonore Kofman and Elizabeth Lebas. "Lost in Transposition - Time, Space and the City". In *Writings on Cities*, translated by Eleonore Kofman and Elizabeth Lebas. Cambridge, Mass, USA: Wiley-Blackwell, 2006, 3-60.

694 Ibid., Chapter 2-17.

695 Lefebvre, Henri (2003), 116.

696 Ibid., 118.

697 See description of "The City of the Captive Globe." In Koolhaas, Rem (1978), 244.

698 First manuscript of "The City in the City." In Ungers, O. M., et al. (2013), 15.

699 Lefebvre, Henri (2003), 119-120.

700 Ibid., 39.

701 Ibid., 119.

702 Ibid.

703 Ibid.

704 Ibid., 123.

705 Aureli, Pier Vittorio. "Toward the Archipelago - Defining the Political and the Formal in Architecture." *Log*, no. 11, Winter 2008, 91–120. Or "Toward the Archipelago -

Defining the Political and the Formal in Architecture." In *The Possibility of an Absolute Architecture*, 1–46. Cambridge, Mass.: The MIT Press, 2011.

[706] https://en.wikipedia.org/wiki/Subprime_mortgage_crisis

[707] The subtitle characterizes an overarching thesis that was part of Aureli's PhD written in the early 2000's at the Berlage Institute. Since then it has constituted the theoretical background for his ongoing design research project and his research collective called The City as a Project. See Aureli, Pier Vittorio. *The City As A Project*. Berlin: Ruby Press, 2013.

[708] Aureli, Pier Vittorio. *The Project of Autonomy - Politics and Architecture within and against Capitalism*. New York: A copublication of the Buell Center/FORuM Project and Princeton Architectural Press. 2008.

[709] Aureli adds a footnote to both terms: "See Scott Meikle, Aristotle's Economic Thought (Oxford: Clarendon Press, 1995)." In Aureli, Pier Vittorio (2011), 2.

[710] Aureli adds a footnote to the term polis: "Initially the Greek term *polis* indicated a 'fortress.' Later the term was used to name a community organized in the form of a state. The Greek polis is always a city-state." See: Paolo Morachiello, *La Città Greca*, Bari: Laterza, 2003, 51.

[711] Aureli, Pier Vittorio (2008), 2-3.

[712] Aureli uses in his text the term *oikoi*, which he defines as "the agglomeration of houses." Ibid., 4.

[713] See "The Concept of Urb and Urbanisation." In Puig, Arturo Soria y, ed. Cerdà (1999), 79-94.

[714] Cerdà, Ildefons (2018), 67.

[715] Aureli, Pier Vittorio (2008) 93.

[716] See Lefebvre, Henri (2003), 160.

[717] Aureli, Pier Vittorio (2008), 109.

[718] Schmitt, Carl. *Der Begriff Des Politischen*. (8. Auflage. Neusatz Auf Basis Der Ausgabe von 1963. Originally Published 1932). Berlin: Duncker & Humblot, 2009.

[719] Ibid., 26.

[720] Aureli, Pier Vittorio (2008), 111.

[721] Ibid., 119.

[722] Aureli, Pier Vittorio. "City as Political Form: Four Archetypes of Urban Transformation." *Architectural Design* 81, no. Special Issue: Typological Urbanism: Projective Cities (2011), 36.

[723] Aureli clarifies that his use of the word archetype is not as defined by Jung, but rather following Giorgio Agamben's idea of the term: "neither a specific nor a general form, but a singular formal event that serves to define the possibility of a milieu of forms." Aureli adds in a footnote: "This definition is an attempt to adapt Giorgio Agamben's discussion of the idea of example as a method of research. See Giorgio Agamben, *The Signature of all Things*, trans Luca di Santo and Kevin Atell, New York: Zone Books, 2009." Ibid., 36.

[724] Aureli, Pier Vittorio (2008), 111.

[725] Stern, Robert A.M., Catalano Thomas P., *Raymond Hood. Catalogue 15*. Institute for Architecture and Urban Studies. New York, NY: Rizzoli International Publications, 1982, 74.

[726] Ferriss, Hugh. *The Metropolis of Tomorrow*. USA: Ives Washburn, 1929.

[727] Hood, Raymond M. "A City Under a Single Roof" As told to F. S. Tisdale, In *Nation's Business*, Washington D.C: The Chamber of Commerce of the United States, November 1929, 20.

[728] Hood's City Under a Single Roof and Manhattan 1950 proposals were seen by Manfredo Tafuri as the application of the Le Corbusier's Ville radieuse onto Manhattan. See Tafuri, Manfredo. "The Disenchanted Mountain: The Skyscraper and the City." *In The American City: From the Civil War to the New Deal*, edited by Giorgio Ciucci, Francesco Dal Co, Mario Manien-Elia, and Manfredo Tafuri, translated by Barbara Luigia La Penta. Cambridge, Mass.: The MIT Press, 1983, 440, 448. Le Corbusier proposed his own Towers in a Park scheme for Manhattan in When the Cathedrals Were White. Translated by Francis E. Hyslop. (Originally published as Quand les Cathedrales etaient Blanches, 1947). New York London Toronto: McGraw-Hill Book Company, 1964. 186-201.

[729] Hood, Raymond M. (1929), 206.

[730] Ibid., 206.

[731] See paragraph on "Mountains" in Koolhaas, Rem (1978), 147-149.

[732] Ibid., 149.

[733] Hood, Raymond M. (1929), 20.

[734] Koolhaas, Rem. "Bigness, or the Problem of Large. Manifesto (1994)." In *S, M, L, XL,* edited by Bruce Mau, OMA, and Rem Koolhaas, 495–516. New York: Monacelli Press, 1995, 515.

[735] See Kwinter, Sanford. "The Building, the Book, and the New Pastoralism." ANY: Architecture New York, *Urbanism vs Architecture: The Bigness of Rem Koolhaas*, no. 9 (1994), 16–22.

[736] Stern, Robert A.M., Catalano Thomas P., *Raymond Hood. Catalogue 15*. New York, N.Y.: Institute for Architecture and Urban Studies: Rizzoli International Publications, 1982, 56-57.

[737] See Koolhaas, Rem (1978), 142-145.

[738] See Krinsky, Carol Herselle. *Rockefeller Center*. New York: Oxford University Press, 1978.

[739] Kilham, Walter H. *Raymond Hood, Architect - Form Through Function in the American Skyscraper*. New York, Architectural Book Publishing Co., Inc. 1973, 159.

[740] See Koolhaas, Rem (1978), 155-161.

[741] Tafuri, Manfredo. "Introduction to Raymond M. Hood. A City under a Single Roof" *In The Sphere and the Labyrinth: Avant-Gardes and Architecture from Piranesi to the 1970s*, translated by Pellegrino D'Acierno and Robert Connolly. Cambridge, Mass.: The MIT Press, 1987, 190.

[742] Frampton, Kenneth, Kolbowski, Silvia. A. M. *Raymond M. Hood. Catalogue 15.* Institute for Architecture and Urban Studies. New York, NY: Rizzoli International Publications, 1982, 111.

[743] Tafuri, Manfredo (1987), 190.

[744] Banham, Reyner. *The Architecture of the Well-Tempered Environment*. Chicago: Architectural Press, The University of Chicago Press, 1969.

[745] Hardwick, Jeffrey M. "Planning the New Suburbscape." In *Mall Maker - Victor Gruen, Architect of an American Dream*, Philadelphia: University of Pennsylvania Press, 2004,

142–61.

[746] Ibid.,129.

[747] See Riani, Paolo, Paul Goldberger, and John Calvin Portman. “Interview with John Portman by Paul Goldberger.” In *John Portman*. Milan: L’Arcaedizioni, 1990, 31.

[748] Koolhaas, Rem (1994) In Bruce Mau, OMA, and Rem Koolhaas (1995), 495–516.

[749] See: Kate Andrews. *World’s largest Building opens in China*. Accessed September 24, 2021. https://www.dezeen.com/2013/07/10/worlds-largest-building-opens-chengdu-china/

[750] Soules, Matthew. *Icebergs, Zombies, and the Ultra Thin: Architecture and Capitalism in the Twenty-First Century*. New York: Princeton Architectural Press, 2021.

[751] NPR Staff. *Welcome To Whittier, Alaska, A Community Under One Roof*. Accessed September 24, 2021. https://www.npr.org/2015/01/18/378162264/welcome-to-whittier-alaska-a-community-under-one-roof?t=1623143030247

[752] Feuerstein, Günther. *Urban Fiction: Strolling Through Ideal Cities from Antiquity to the Present Day*. Stuttgart/London: Edition Axel Menges, 2008.

[753] See Branzi, Andrea. *No Stop City: Archizoom Associati*. Orléans: Editions HYX, 2006.

[754] Feuerstein, Günther (2008), 306.

[755] Branzi, Andrea (2006), 153.

[756] Ibid., 153.

[757] See Cauter, Lieven de, ed. *The Capsular Civilization: On the City in the Age of Fear*. Rotterdam: nai010 publishers, 2004.

[758] Jameson, Fredric. *Postmodernism, Or, The Cultural Logic of Late Capitalism*. 7th Edition. First Published in 1984 In New Left Review Durham, North Carolina: Duke University Press, 1997, 38-45.

[759] Choonara, Joseph. “Interview: David Harvey - Exploring the Logic of Capital.” *Socialist Review*, no. 335 (April 2009).

[760] Tafuri, Manfredo (1983), 389-503.

[761] The diagrams are inspired by the early skyscrapers of Louis Sullivan. Ibid., 420.

[762] See “City Under a Single Roof” proposal, model variant 2 by (Raymond Hood) Raymond Hood Collection, Architectural Archives, University of Pennsylvania. Local ID #: aaup.022.5.3.

[763] Kilham Jr. produced this scheme while working as an assistant to Hood. See Koolhaas, Rem (1978), 159, 160.

[764] Le Corbusier. *The City of To-Morrow and Its Planning*. (First published in 1929 by Parson & Clarke Ltd. New York). New York: Dover Publications, 1987, 189.

[765] See Le Corbusier. *Vers une Architecture*. 11th Edition. (First Published 1923). Collection de “L’Esprit Nouveau.” Paris: Crès, 1925, 206-207.

[766] Riani, Paolo, Paul Goldberger, and John Calvin Portman. “The Shape of the City.” In *John Portman*, 21–45. Milan: L’Arcaedizioni, 1990, 21-45.

[767] See animation of a torus becoming a sphere. Accessed September 24, 2021. https://en.wikipedia.org/wiki/Torus#/media/File:Sphere-like_degenerate_torus.gif

[768] The reading of architecture as a technical being is not just limited to the city, as presented here. Rather it extends to all architectural elements. A good example is

Portman's Entelechy I house, which consists of a series of hollow columns. Portman described these as exploded cells, and wrote of their effects as voided space entering solid column. The column changes from building structure to building core. It opens an interior for light and air, both natural and artificial. The space can function as either inside or outside and can be programmed as any of the minor functions of the house as well as circulation space. As Portman writes, it was this actualization of virtual potentials that gave the house its name: "Entelechy, an Aristotelian word which means 'that which realizes or makes actual what is otherwise merely potential.'" In Riani, Paolo, Paul Goldberger, and John Calvin Portman (1990), 24. What Portman does not mention, or perhaps he didn't see, is the fact that he actually produced a radically new spatial typology: a fusion of the enfilade with the free plan. It gives rise to a diagonal space, in which one enters rooms at the corner and from each room can access five different spaces: three on the same level and one above and below. Portman thus produced with the fusion of a space into a column what I would call the eighth spatial diagram after the seven introduced by Ungers: the courtyard, the spiral, the poché, the central, the labyrinth, the corridor, the plan libre, plus this new diagonal. See Ungers, Oswald M. *Sieben Variationen des Raumes über die Sieben Leuchter der Baukunst von John Ruskin*. Stuttgart: Hatje Cantz, 1985.

769 Colquhoun, Alan. "The Superblock." In *Essays in Architectural Criticism: Modern Architecture and Historical Change*, Reprint edition. Cambridge, Mass.: The MIT Press, 1985, 83.

770 Barr, Alfred H, Henry-Russell Hitchcock, Philip Johnson, Lewis Mumford, and Museum of Modern Art New York. Modern Architecture. International Exhibition, New York, February 10 to March 23, 1932, Museum of Modern Art. New York: Museum of Modern Art, 1932, 132.

771 Ibid.

772 Ibid.

773 See Manien-Elia, Mario. "Towards an 'Imperial City': Daniell H. Burnham and the City Beautiful Movement" in *The American City: From the Civil War to the New Deal*, edited by Giorgio Ciucci, Francesco Dal Co, Mario Manien-Elia, and Manfredo Tafuri, translated by Barbara Luigia La Penta. Cambridge, Mass.: The MIT Press, 1983, 1-7.

774 See Raymond Hood, "The Spirit of Modern Art," in Architectural Forum, Vol. 51, No.11 November 1924, 445. See quote by Stern, Robert A.M., Catalano Thomas P., *Raymond Hood. Catalogue 15*. New York, N.Y.: Institute for Architecture and Urban Studies: Rizzoli International Publications, 1982, 2.

775 See Hood, Raymond M. (1929), 18-20 and 206-209.

776 Tafuri, Manfredo (1983), 434.

777 Ibid. 439.

778 See Hood, Raymond M. (1929), 209.

779 See Ibid., 209.

780 I refer here in particular to the writings of David Harvey, Edward Soja and Fredric Jameson.

781 Döring, Jörg, and Tristan Thielmann, eds. *Spatial Turn: Das Raumparadigma in den Kultur- und Sozialwissenschaften*. 2nd Edition. Bielefeld: Transcript, 2008, 8.

782 What is meant here by the term space is the intellectual movement, of particular prominence in Europe and the United States, in which theorists emphasize the idea of place and space in the social sciences and the humanities. For a general understanding of these ideas in various disciplines, see Warf, Barney, and Santa Arias. *The Spatial Turn:*

Interdisciplinary Perspectives. London: Routledge, 2008.

[783] See Jameson, Fredric. *Postmodernism, Or, The Cultural Logic of Late Capitalism*. Durham, North Carolina: Duke University Press, 1997, 38-45.

[784] See Harvey, David. *A Brief History of Neoliberalism*. New York: Oxford University Press, 2005.

[785] Ibid., 3.

[786] Ibid., 2.

[787] Ibid., Cover.

[788] Ibid., 2.

[789] See Lyotard, Jean-François. *The Postmodern Condition: A Report on Knowledge*. Translated by Geoffrey Bennington and Brian Massumi. Manchester: Manchester University Press, 1984.

[790] Ibid., 66.

[791] Berman, Marshall. *All That Is Solid Melts into Air*. New York: Simon and Schuster, 1982. Quoted in Harvey, David. *The Condition of Postmodernity - An Enquiry into the Origins of Cultural Change*. Cambridge MA & Oxford UK: Blackwell, 1989, 10.

[792] Recall Mies's assertion, "architecture is the will of the age conceived in spatial terms (Baukunst ist immer raumgefaßter Zeitwille, nichts anderes)." Van der Rohe, Mies. "Baukunst und Zeitwille" In: *Der Querschnitt*, No. 4, 1924, 31-32. My translation.

[793] See Aureli, Pier Vittorio. "The Theology of Tabula Rasa: Walter Benjamin And Architecture in The Age of Precarity." In *Log*, No. 27, 2013, 111–27.

[794] See Descartes, René. "Principles of Philosophy (1644)." Early Modern Texts. Accessed September 24, 2021, 6, point 23. https://www.earlymoderntexts.com/assets/pdfs/descartes1644.pdf.

[795] See Krauss, Rosalind (1979), 50-64.

[796] Jameson refers specifically to the work of Andy Warhol and pop art; photorealism in painting; John Cage, Philip Glass, Terry Riley, punk and new wave in music; Godard and post-Godard in film; and Burroughs, Pynchon, and Ishmael Reed in literature. In architecture, he refers not to the postmodern monumental duck of Robert Venturi and Denise Scott Brown, but to the work of John Portman. See Jameson, Fredric (1997), 1.

[797] Jameson refers to Ernest Mandel's book *Late Capitalism*. In Ibid., 3.

[798] Ibid., 39.

[799] Ibid., 40.

[800] Ibid., 43.

[801] See Soja, Edward W. *Postmodern Geographies: The Reassertion of Space in Critical Social Theory* (1989). London: Verso, 2014. 243–44.

[802] Jameson, Fredric (1997), 44.

[803] Ibid., 44.

[804] Ibid., 38.

[805] See Choonara, Joseph. "Interview: David Harvey - Exploring the Logic of Capital." In *Socialist Review*, no. 335 (April 2009).

[806] See Harvey, David. "The Invisible Political Economy of Architectural Production." In

The Invisible in Architecture, edited by Ole Bouman and Roemer van Toorn. Berlin: Erst & Sohn, 1994, 425.

807 See Soules, Matthew. *Icebergs, Zombies, and the Ultra Thin: Architecture and Capitalism in the Twenty-First Century*. New York: Princeton Architectural Press, 2021, 31.

808 Ibid., 10.

809 Martin, Reinhold. *Utopia's Ghost: Architecture and Postmodernism, Again*. Minneapolis: University of Minnesota Press, 2010,106.

810 See Piketty, Thomas. *Capital in the Twenty-First Century*. Translated by Arthur Goldhammer. Cambridge, Mass.: Harvard University Press, 2014, 113-116.

811 "The law of property and possession," in Britannica. Accessed September 24, 2021. https://www.britannica.com/topic/Roman-law/The-law-of-property-and-possession

812 See Piketty, Thomas. *Capital and Ideology*. Translated by Arthur Goldhammer. Cambridge, Mass.: Harvard University Press, 2020. 99-125.

813 Ibid., 100.

814 Ballon, Hilary. *The Greatest Grid - The Master Plan of Manhattan 1811-2011*. Edited by Hilary Ballon. New York: Co-Published by the Museum of the City of New York and Columbia University Press, 2011, 88-89.

815 Piketty, Thomas (2014),165.

816 See Figure 5.3. "Private capital in rich countries, 1970–2010". In Ibid., 171.

817 Ibid., 173.

818 See Koolhaas, Rem.. "Beijing Manifesto." In Content, 1st Edition., 124. Köln: Taschen Verlag, 2004.

819 See Soules, Matthew (2021), 45-49.

820 Ibid., 45.

821 Ibid., 46.

822 Ibid., 46.

823 Catherine Yoshimoto. "Yield-seekers embrace emerging market real estate" Accessed September 24, 2021. https://www.ftserussell.com/blogs/yield-seekers-embrace-emerging-market-real-estate

824 See Wainwright, Oliver. "Super-Tall, Super-Skinny, Super-Expensive: The 'Pencil Towers' of New York's Super-Rich." *The Guardian*, February 5, 2019. Accessed September 24, 2021. http://www.theguardian.com/cities/2019/feb/05/super-tall-super-skinny-super-expensive-the-pencil-towers-of-new-yorks-super-rich.

825 See Soules, Matthew. "All That Is Solid: Asset Urbanism and the Financial Dynamics of Post-Industrial Space." In *Open Cities: The New Post-Industrial World Order*, edited by Alice Kimm & Jaepil Choi. Washington: ACSA Press, 2014, 343–52.

826 See Soules, Matthew (2021), 82-86.

827 See Wainwright, Oliver. "Billionaires' Basements: The Luxury Bunkers Making Holes in London Streets." *The Guardian*, November 9, 2012. Accessed September 24, 2021. http://www.theguardian.com/artanddesign/2012/nov/09/billionaires-basements-london-houses-architecture.

828 Ibid.

[829] Ibid.

[830] I assume Martin refers in his writing to the Deleuzian concept of immanence. "We will say of pure immanence that it is A LIFE and nothing else. It is not immanence to life, but the immanent that is in nothing is itself a life. A life is the immanence of immanence, absolute immanence: it is complete power, complete bliss." See, Deleuze, Gilles. "Immanence: A Life." In *Pure Immanenca. Essays on A Life*, edited by John Rajchman, translated by Anne Boyman. New York: Zone Books, 2001, 27.

[831] See Simondon, Gilbert (2017), 29.

[832] Ibid.

[833] See Schmidgen, Henning. "Das Konzert Der Maschinen. Simondons Politisches Programm." In *Zeitschrift Für Medien- und Kulturforschung*, no. 2, Felix Meiner Verlag: Leipzig, 2012, 117–34.

[834] Simondon, Gilbert (2017), 29.

Chapter 4: The Architecture Tuned by the City

In his book *A History of Architecture*, Spiro Kostof gives a general definition of the city:

> The city is an involved organism under constant change.[835] In its living mesh, public structures are bonded to the places where people live, and these, in turn, are bonded to each other, in a rich artifice of contiguity. The city presents us with a new set of environmental ideas, such as the street, the public square, the defensive wall and its gates. It crowds our discussion with a score of building inventions—for example, the canal and the granary, the palace and the bath, the market, the bakery, shops, restaurants, and libraries.[836]

For Kostof, the city can clearly be defined as the milieu in which those new functions and buildings appear. And if we understand Kostof's living mesh as the technical being-ness of the city, then the city not only defines a milieu for his artifice of contiguity, but it originates new technical objects as well. This means that the architecture of the city is not shaped externally. As Mumford explains in *The Myth of the Megamachine*, the social, political, and economic functions of the city are not external either. Rather, they originate through the city, shaped by overdetermined qualities embedded within.

In their analysis of the essential forces shaping the city, both Kostof and Mumford approximate Simondon's explanation of what drives the concretization of technical objects. "Extrinsic causes," he writes, "are not more powerful than those that tend toward the multiplication of types, appropriated for an infinite variety of needs. If technical objects do evolve toward a small number of specific types then this is by virtue of an internal necessity and not as a consequence of economic influences or practical requirements."[837] So, too, for the architecture of the city. Architecture exists due to an *internal necessity* of the city.

One question remains: How does architecture come alive through internal necessities of the city? Or, to put it differently: How can we define the mode of existence of architecture as a technical object? To begin to answer this question requires that we identify what Simondon describes as the "essential aspect of the abstract technical object: namely, that it is grounded in an analytical organization that always leaves the path open for new possibilities; these possibilities are the external manifestation of an internal contingency."[838] It is precisely such internal contingencies, or internal necessities, of the city as a technical object that will be the focus of this final chapter. And as an introduction to such a mechanological approach we will look to one of the most famous examples of an early urban typology: the Greek theater.

The Theater: In Which a Public Space Converges with a Hill and a Stairway

Greek theater is unquestionably an outcome of Greek city cultures. History is not fully clear about when and how the idea of Greek drama emerged.[839] It is known, however, that theatrical culture was linked to the ritual performances at the Dionysia, one of the festivals to worship the god Dionysus. The name of the ancient Theater of Dionysos in Athens today still reminds us of these events.[840] Perhaps evolved from pre-urban or later rituals, the drama—as a tragedy or a comedy—is understood to have originated through Greek urban culture, as opposed to having been received from outside. It is a Greek invention. Its specific theatrical forms originated within ancient Greek cities as a result of those cities' internal necessities.

If such is the case for the origin of the content of the Greek theater, can the same not be said about its built form—that the theater arose through the internal necessities of urban forms, and that this building typology is the outcome of a process of concretization whereby several urban elements converged and formed a new technical object called the theater? We know from Simondon that technical beings have hypertelic qualities, by which elements within technical objects can specialize their individual performances or at other times can splinter apart in order to fuse with other parts in new ways. Such a mechanological reading can be applied to the Greek theater as well. But instead of cylinders heads or cooling fins as in motors, for the theater the elements are (public) *space*, (convex) *ground*, and (urban) *stairway*. All three are manifested as specific objects of the Greek city.

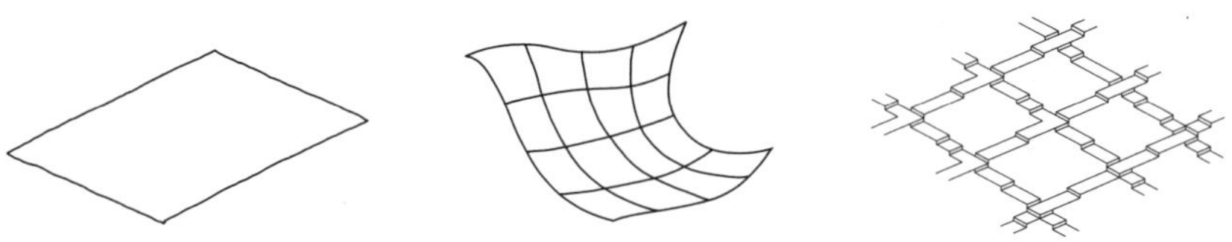

(A) (B) (C)

FIGURE 46. THREE ELEMENTS OF A CITY: A PUBLIC SPACE(A), A HILL(B), AND A STAIRWAY(C)

As a specific hypertelic element, *public space* mostly refers to the Greek agora. This was considered a place for gatherings or just "to meet,"[841] as the literal translation of the word suggests. It was the social, political, and religious center of the polis, as well as a marketplace for economic activities including the exchange of goods with people from outside the polis. The agora had no boundary wall. Instead, as described in Roger Caves' *Encyclopedia of the City*, "the agora was surrounded by buildings used for special functions such as civic meetings in the bouleterion (council chambers) or the tholos (a circular committee meeting building), a variety of activities in the stoas (long rectangular colonnaded buildings), and religious activities (temples and shrines)."[842]

Convex ground refers to a slope or a hill. The hill is a characteristic element of the topographical landscape of the Greek archipelago in the Aegean Sea. Hills provided the landmarks where Greek cities were located—either on top, below, between, or sometimes along the slopes. The word acropolis literally suggests a city built on a hill.[843] The acropolis in Athens consists of four hills: the Likavitos Hill, the Hill of the Nymphs, the Pnyx Hill, and the Philapappos Hill. An important aspect of Greek city planning is that the Greeks were not interested in leveling the natural ground. The polis thus was not built on an artificial tabula rasa. The natural ground of the hills was, rather, treated as untouchable. Topography was seen as an opportunity for placemaking.[844]

The *urban stairway* is the outcome of this ancient Greek treatment of the natural ground. The placement of an urban grid onto the ungraded existing topography of the hills had the effect of a blanket landing on a piece of furniture and taking on the contours of that underlying surface.[845] In a new polis, like Priene, streets were therefore not planar. They were more like urban stairways, with steps of varying dimensions and slopes to accommodate the natural ground conditions of the landscape.[846]

To apply Simondon's mechanological method to query the genesis of the Greek theater, first, as he showed in his mechanical examples, we must imagine our individual urban elements as abstract forms. In this way, each abstract form—agora (public space), hill (convex ground), and stairway—is extracted from its embedded context, the better to visualize its formal or functional properties that converge with other objects. In this process not all properties of the urban elements will be exchanged, only those properties that are useful to fulfilling the internal necessity for the new architectural typology to become concrete.

We can visualize the process of concretization abstractly as well. In what Kubler calls a *formal sequence*[847] and Simondon refers to as a *convergence series*,[848] we can imagine how the public space of the agora first mutates into a democratic space, the Pnyx of the ecclesia, and then ends with the space of the drama, the Greek theater.[849] There is of course no historical proof for such a formal sequence. The Pnyx in Athens might have appeared after the theater, or at least after early wooden ones. But the convergence sequence is didactically useful. It allows us to introduce, or to bring on stage, each different urban element one after the other. This staging helps to demonstrate the common capacity these technical objects carry within, namely that when the aesthetic qualities of different parts fuse, the abstract forms vanish and new formal and functional qualities appear. The outcome is a newly individuated, overdetermined technical being, or what Kubler would call a new architectural prime object.[850] The process of concretization of the Greek theater, then, would consist of the following sequence:

1. The wall meets the ground and turns into the agora;
2. the agora meets the hill and turns into the Pnyx;
3. the Pnyx meets the stair and originates the theater.

1. Agora: In Which the City Wall Meets the Urban Ground

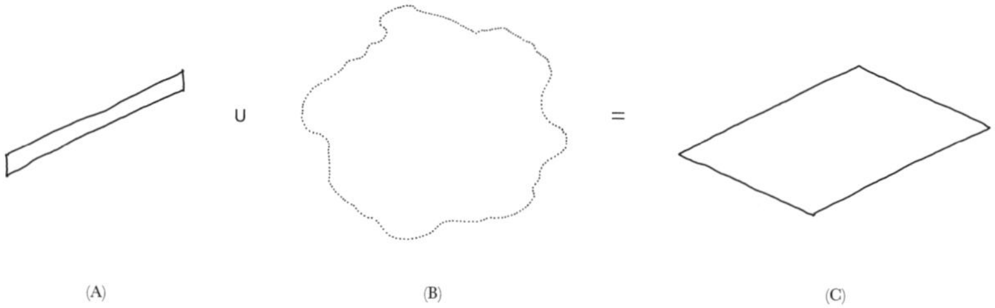

FIGURE 47. AGORA(C): THE CITY WALL(A) MEETS THE URBAN GROUND(B).

Benevolo mentions in his book *The European City* that in the early stages of our urban history the primary element of the city, the wall, was used to articulate the first building environments.[851] The agora is no exception. The agora can be described as the fusion of the qualities of the city wall with the urban ground. When the wall fuses with the ground of a city, an enclosed space appears. This is a very particular space: a space for public use only. This new space gives rise to all kinds of new public activities in the ancient polis. Not only is this a collective meeting space, it is also collectively owned. The qualities of this public space have fused with the surrounding "wall" as well. In some cases, the public void of the agora literally moves into the wall and becomes a wall-like building or a wall formed by multiple buildings.[852] In ancient Greece these buildings took on new public uses and extended the collective qualities of the public space into the interiority of the abstract form of the city wall. One of the best examples of such a wall building that frames the agora is the stoa. The stoa defines a new kind of public architecture: a covered walkway open on one side.

2. Pnyx: In Which the Public Space of the Agora Meets the Topography of a Hill

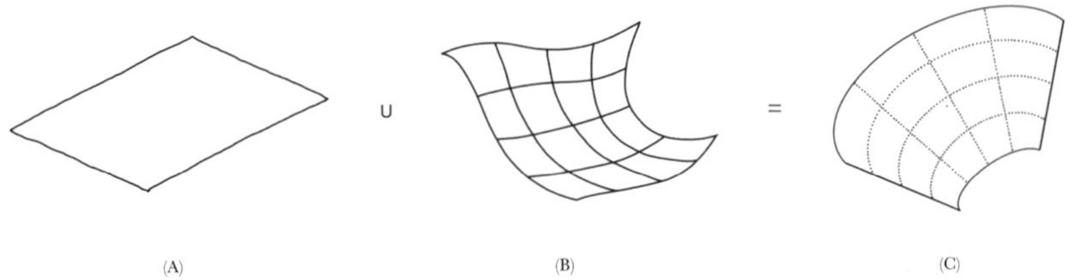

FIGURE 48. PNYX(C): THE PUBLIC SPACE(A) MEETS THE HILL(B).

What we know from the city of Athens is that at a certain moment some of the functions in the agora separated from the public space. The polis seems to have needed a new architectural object[853] for its democratic assembly, the ecclesia.[854] Around the fifth century B.C.E., this function was extracted from the agora and moved to the Pnyx.

In the Pnyx, the enclosed void space of the agora meets the topography of the hill, and a technical object with manifold new properties emerges. Due to the topography, this new space of democracy becomes directional. That directionality divides the space, which was previously dominated by the relationship between the boundary and the void space within, into a new dual relationship of up and down, or front and back. This directional duality is further distinguished by a topographically marked its edge. Historically, the edge was first emphasized by a natural cut in the rock of the hill, while in a second stage the addition of artificial topography made a clear demarkation line.[855] This hard division in the topography is the location of the bema, the speaking platform of the Pnyx.[856] Thus the fusion of the hill with the qualities of the agora results in a new public space, which bifurcates the public into the side of the speaker, a flattened part for a podium, and the side of the audience, an inclined part for the auditorium. The boundary of this new architectural object changes its formal properties as well. Due to the directionality of the space and its division between *one* (speaker) and *many* (assembly), a form is needed to emphasize this quantitative difference in its qualitative spatial character. What emerges is a semicircular shape. The hard dividing line of the half circle, its diameter, is coincident with the topographic edge line where the bema is located, while the curve of the semicircle becomes the weak edge of the audience.[857] This semicircular prime object emphasizes one further aspect, namely the unidirectionality between the single center point of the speaker and the multiplicity of points in the audience.

3. Theater: In Which the Public Space of the Agora Meets Convex Ground and Urban Stairway

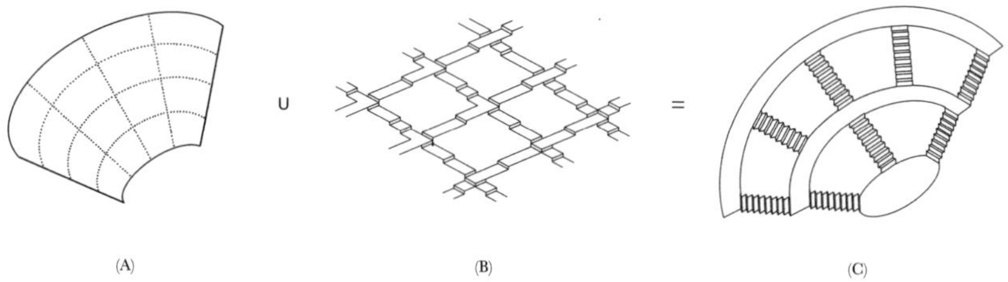

FIGURE 49. THEATER(C): THE PUBLIC SPACE MEETS THE HILL(A) AND THE STAIRWAY(B)

In the last stage of the concretization process, the qualities of duality that appeared when the public space fused with the hill ultimately specialize in the Greek theater, with its final concrete characteristics given by the addition of the qualities of the urban stairway. Akin to we saw in the Pnyx, when the hill converges with the public space of the polis, two qualities become tuned into the theater. First, in addition to the directional quality of the slope, the form of the hills introduce a curvature in the perpendicular axis to the directionality of the Pnyx. This curvature is found in the declivities of the convex-concave topography of the Greek hills. A good example of such a territorial specificity can be seen in a drawing of the ancient city of Pergamon,[858] where the theater is placed exactly at the point, moving across slope, where the hill folds inward and forms a natural convex or cone-like ground. With the orientation of the slope reversed from the

Pnyx[859] such that the audience occupies the upslope side, this quality intensifies each individual viewpoint toward the podium, which here is called the orchestra, as its function is not only for words but for the performance of dance as well.[860] The second tuned quality of the hill increases the separation of auditorium, called the theatron, from the orchestra.[861] Instead of being placed *in* the hills like the Pnyx, the orchestra's circular stage is placed right at the foot of the hill where the slope meets the horizontal ground plane. Thus, through an internal contingency in the convergence of territorial elements, the theater enforces a clear division between the performers and the audience.

The final phase in the genesis of the new technical object is the convergence of the public space of the agora and the convex ground of Greek hillside with the third element: the urban stairway. The obvious aspect here is the fusion of the stairway with the topography of the slope as contour lines to articulate the theatron with steps for seating. In early Greek theaters this was further articulated with wood seating, which later became stone. The delineated contours of the seating rows produce a conical geometry for every location to perform this new "democratic" space, in which every spectator is treated as an individual, given the right to view the spectacle equally.[862]

Fused with the newly stepped theatron is a second quality of the urban stairway: the gridded layout of the city streets. In the plan of a theater like the famous Epidaurus,[863] we can see how the gridded form of the urban stairway merges with the conical surface of the theatron, giving rise to a radial grid. This grid segments the auditorium into trapezoidal blocks of seating, similar to how an urban grid subdivides it territory with blocks and streets, a layout which can be found in a polis like Milet.[864] The radial grid is a space of circulation like in the polis, but with a hierarchical distinction between the flat and wide horizontal paths and the up or down aisles of stairs.

Through the convergence of the qualities of three antecedent urban elements, the Greek theater becomes a new architectural entity. Its concretization was not driven by an outside force, but rather by an internal necessity of the Greek city—its function as well as its type. As thus a prime object it is able to be multiplied, as we find throughout the history of architecture.[865]

With this introductory example of the theater, I have demonstrated how a mechanological reading of the architecture of the city might be made accessible. It is such processes of concretization, in which properties of urban elements converge, that will be defined as the mode of existence of architecture. The re-origination of Simondon's theory into architecture does not end with the Greek theater. It is only one of the beginnings of the long arc of emergence of many new technical objects called architecture: the stoa, the agora, the temple, the insula, the basilica, the forum, the monastery, the hotel, the housing slab, the housing block, the high-rise, the mat-building, the megaform and megastructure, the shopping mall, the atrium building, up until the pencil tower which just recently emerged in Manhattan. Today a radical, new individuated architectural object has emerged in our metropolis, which I call *the city on a single roof*.[866]

4.1 The City on a Single Roof

Whereas the theater can be considered as an emergent architectural prime object of the ancient Greek city, in the last decade we have witnessed the rise of a new kind of architectural entity in the global metropolis. The city on a single roof is a strange built-agglomeration. It is a new typology with yet unseen topological properties.

Four Villas on the Roof of a Shopping Mall

In 2012 the online newsmagazine *China Daily* reported that four villas built on top of a shopping mall in the city of Zhuzhou, in China's Hunan province, had been deemed legal by city planners.[867] A developer built the villas on the roof of the Jiutian International Square shopping mall. The roof of this huge eight-story mall looks like a park, with the planted green terrain containing four rectangular plots of around 500 square meters. On each of these pieces of real estate stands a large villa with an approximate footprint of one hundred square meters and a floor area around twice that. The villas host the office workers of the real-estate developer of the shopping mall, who can enjoy the unobstructed unobstructed views from the rooftop site. Built with permission from the authorities and fulfilling all building codes, one detail that may be different from a conventional home on a so-called real piece of land, i.e., terra firma, is the presence of industrial-scale air-conditioning machines in the villas' gardens.

Twenty-five Villas on a Shopping Mall[868]

In August 2013 *China Daily* reported a similar story. This time it involved twenty-five luxury villas built on the roof of a four-story furniture mall in the city of Hengyang, in Hunan province.[869] On

20,000 square meters of this flat "land," a developer had built the small housing project without official permission. Although it was illegal, the government decided that the villas can remain, however they were not allowed to be sold. Thus, as in Zhuzhou, the houses do not host the rich or upper middle class. Instead they are used like dormitories for employees and immigrant workers. The twenty-five villas are laid out in a rectangular grid with streets and alleys. Each street gives access to four or five plots on either side, on which sit a variety of three-story high villas, each with a bright blue roof and yellow walls. Porches are placed at the front and balconies face the rear. Each property is planted with trees and bushes and framed by a white fence. And while there are some air-conditioning machines in the gardens, compared to Zhuzhou this project has one more important element attached to it: the street that runs in front of each property.[870]

A Suburb on a Shopping Center with a Carpark[871]

FIGURE 50. A SUBURBAN VILLAGE ON A SINGLE ROOF. COSMO PARK, JAKARTA, 2010.

In 2019 the *Guardian* reported on an entire suburban village on the roof of a shopping center and parking garage, which had recently been the topic of a viral tweet: "What type of person thinks about developing a housing complex on top of a building?" Cosmo Park, as it is called, was built in 2009 in Jarkata, a city of more than ten million people, located within a broader metropolitan area with a total population three times that. In addition to townhouses with gardens and streets, the village of Cosmo Park has a tennis court, jogging track, and swimming pool. A gym, shopping, and food are just a few floors below. The apartments range from 120 to 300 square meters and have private carports.[872] Cosmo Park has seemingly all the features of a suburb: roads with traffic markings for cars, separate pedestrian paths, public rubbish pins, public space, individual properties, apartments equipped with alarms and a twenty-four-hour security system, etc. What is radically different from a typical suburb, however, is that it is built not on natural ground but instead on an already existing real estate. And this is not a unique project. The *Guardian* report mentions a second such project in Jarkarta. This means that the city has already tuned its elements to give rise to this new typology—the city on a single roof, ready to be multiplied and repeated.

The City on a Single Roof

This newly individuated prime object emerged in the city and has entered the discipline of architecture as well. Today we can find even more developments with the same characteristics described above. Many of these newer cities on a single roof are not extensions onto existing shopping malls, parking garages, or other roofs, but are whole urban entities, for example the 2018 mixed-use development in Shenzhen called Shum Yip UpperHills Loft.[873] Designed from the ground up, these new developments use the form of the city on a single roof as an urban archetype and apply it as an abstract architectural typology.

What, exactly, makes the city on a single roof a new individuated object? What kind of topological properties does this urban archetype contain that evidence the emergence of a new prime object, for our cities as well as for the discipline of architecture?

This new urban articulation marks a radical shift in the relationship between two previously distinguishable forms of real estate: a piece of land property and a building. With this new architectural object the two become interchangeable. The building is not standing on a piece of land anymore. Nor is it understood as the vertical repetition of pieces of property, like with the early skyscraper. The building itself becomes the ground of the city. The subdivision of private and public is now drawn on an individual urban asset. The city has tuned its architecture to become the ground of city: a real estate built on land becomes land itself.

Concretization of the City on a Single Roof
We can visualize this convergence, as above with the Greek theater, through a speculative process of concretization in which the qualities of the ground of the city merge stepwise with the roof of a building. Any process of concretization of a city will always start with a given natural terrain, a kind of wilderness. Often this is a terrain that has been exploited for other uses before, especially agricultural production.[874] Put simply, the base for every city is its ground: the skin of the earth.

FIGURE 51. A NATURAL GROUND

Once a city has defined its territory, either by a wall or another boundary, its inner ground is fused with an abstract geometry. This rationalizing device might be rigid like a grid or irregular, like the curvilinear plan of Riverside designed by Olmsted, Vaux & Co.[875] The aim is always to subdivide the ground into public properties and private properties: a space for circulation and a space for inhabitation.

FIGURE 52. SUBDIVISION OF THE GROUND INTO PRIVATE AND PUBLIC LAND PROPERTIES

As we have seen from the diagram of the theorem of the skyscraper, as presented by Koolhaas in his *Delirious New York*, every floor of a building can be seen as endless multiplication of "virgin sites" on a single urban locus.[876] The building fuses the qualities of a single piece of land with its floor plates and generates a vertical stacking of empty properties for whatever uses are to come.

FIGURE 53. VERTICAL STACKING OF PRIVATE LAND PROPERTIES AS FLOOR

With advances in building technology, the traditional pitched roof is no longer needed to keep rain out. A building's roof can thus be horizontal, like one of its floor plates, except outside. For Le Corbusier this was a new datum that could be fused with the qualities of the site that were sacrificed in the placement of building. This fusion of qualities of that lost skin of the earth and the roof reproduced a new "natural" ground. Of course, this is in fact an engineered nature, which we know as the second of Le Corbusier's famous five points—namely, *les toits-jardins*, the roof gardens.[877]

FIGURE 54. REAPPEARANCE OF THE LOST NATURAL GROUND ON THE ROOFTOP

Up to this point, the speculative process of concretization toward the city on a single roof seems familiar to what the discipline of architecture witnessed with the emergence of the modernist high-rise building in the early twentieth century. On the basis of this modernist idea, Ludwig Hilberseimer developed his Hochhausstadt (Vertical City) in the late 1920s, which OMA used as the basis of the City of the Captive Globe in the 1970s. In all of these works, the modernist diagram of the horizontal roof is treated as a new ground on which to add and place extended constructions. In other words, what became referred to generally by OMA's term, *hyperbuilding*,[878] did not really change its inner topological features since El Lissitzky's Wolkenbügel of 1924. Stacked or not stacked, the agglomeration of these buildings can still be seen as belonging to the same formal sequence of the city under a single roof—continuous interiority, elevators connecting all floors, the assemblage of volumes owned by either a single person or a financial syndicate, and built under a single form of investment.

What can be seen as the radical shift with the city *on* a single roof is that the roof datum, the engineered "natural" ground, is fused with an abstract geometry. It is the same sort of geometry that subdivides the ground in the origination of cities. This subdividing device likewise segments the constructed roof datum into two kinds of property: private property as a multiplicity of pieces of land, united by public property as a single network of streets.

FIGURE 55. SUBDIVISION OF THE ROOFTOP INTO PRIVATE AND PUBLIC LAND PROPERTIES

With this new layout on the roof of an existing building, the city can be constructed on top. The plots of private property can be multiplied again, as with the high-rise, while the remaining areas fuse with the quality of the public space of the city. The roof has become an urban datum, but the whole building has changed its function. In order for the city on a single roof to emerge atop an existing building, the building must incorporate qualities of the natural ground on which cities are built. It must accommodate cars driving through the building to be able to park in front of the rooftop properties, it must give each new piece of real estate the same infrastructural resources as though it were on the ground, and its physical structure needs to be able to carry the new city.

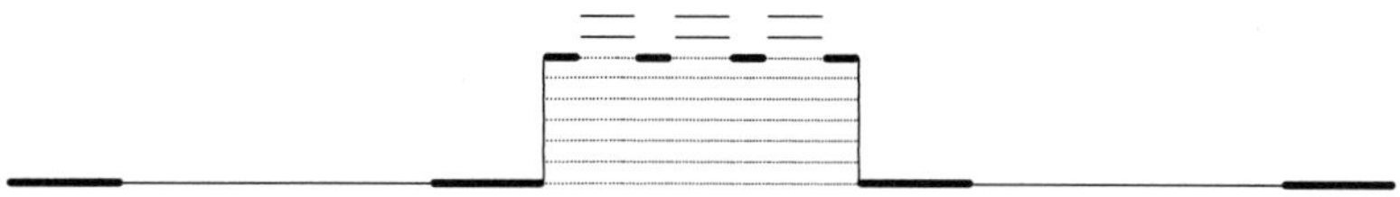

FIGURE 56. VERTICAL STACKING OF PRIVATE ROOFTOP PROPERTIES AS FLOORS

In its final stage of concretization, with buildings surrounded by private gardens and properties fronting onto streets, the city on a single roof deviates from any previous architectural agglomerations. Emerging out of a series of convergences, it has become a new prime object of architecture, and it is ready to be repeated and multiplied. Not only that: with its emergence in our cities it gives rise to ever new formal sequences and processes of concretization. One can imagine a pattern in which the roofs of the buildings of this rooftop city become the new "natural" ground on which the layout of further cities on a single roof could emerge. If Le Corbusier's Maison Dom-Ino is considered *the* architectural typology of the twentieth century, perhaps this radical new diagram will be that of the twenty-first.

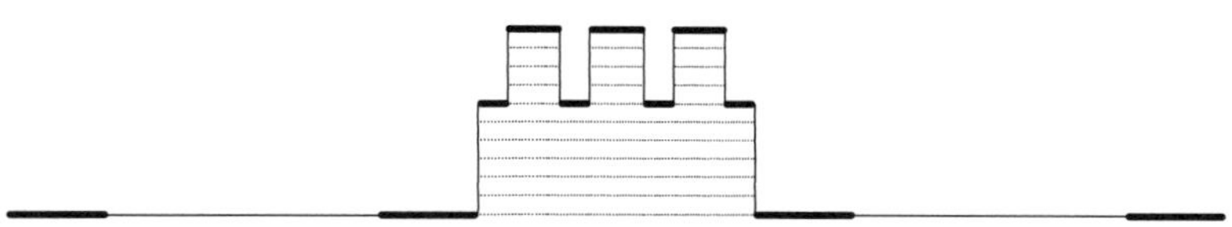

FIGURE 57. THE CITY ON A SINGLE ROOF

What is radical about this new architectural object is that what is constructed on land has become land itself. What was a private financial asset becomes a new public asset, albeit privately owned. And it is this that makes it an architectural entity of the twenty-first century: The common infrastructures that once were owned by the state are now owned by individuals or companies.[879]

As in ancient cities, the contemporary city has tuned its elements according to internal necessity, which has given rise to a new technical object. In the example of the Greek theater, the city used its hypertelic potential to fuse some of its elements—the framed public space, topographic ground of the hill, and stepped streets or stairways—to form a new architectural archetype. In the contemporary city, the hypertelic potential of a basic urban architectural form led to its fusion with the subdivision of the city's ground and the emergence a new urban archetype. Both examples demonstrate that the city is not only a milieu for buildings, but also a technical object in itself. Due to its innate overdetermination the city is perpetually separating and specializing its inner parts, giving rise to new ensembles. As new architectural wholes, what is unique to all of these is that new typological forms and functional performances have been concretized.

To what extent does such a mechanological reading of the agglomeration of buildings differ from other theoretical positions on the built matter of the city? This is the question addressed in the following subchapter, in which I discuss my re-origination of Simondon's idea, as an assertion on the mode of existence of architecture, in comparison with the ideas by which five key thinkers—Alberti, Kaufmann, Muratori, Benevolo, and Rowe—defined the architectural ensembles of the city.

4.2. The Architectural Ensembles of the City: From Alberti to the Re-origination of Simondon

From the point of view of architecture, a city is simply the assemblage of buildings with space in between. If, as has been shown, architecture originates by the convergence of urban elements due to what I refer to, following Simondon, as their internal necessity, then every building is a new architectural entity and the city an *ensemble* of these individuated objects.[880]

How does this idea of reading the city as a technical being differ from other disciplinary viewpoints? How can other readings of the urban agglomeration of buildings be seen now through the lens of the mode of existence of architecture as described by the earlier examples in this chapter?

The Architectural Ensembles of Leonardo Benevolo

Benevolo argues that as the city was coming into existence in the third and second millenniums BCE, it separated the world into an inside and an outside. Inside was the city enclosed within a boundary, typically defined by a wall, and outside was the countryside. For Benevolo, the consequence of this division effected across our planet was not just the separation between the space of history (city) and the space of the myth (wilderness). More importantly, it produced a new knowledge. This knowledge was from then on what we call architecture.

In his book on the European city, Benevolo writes: "The City is an enclosure, or a series of enclosures, in which the art of manipulating medium and short distances—that which from then on would be described as 'architecture'—reached maturity, while the older art, which aimed at the occupation and modification of the unlimited landscape, was gradually forgotten."[881] He then goes a step further in his argument, claiming not only that the manipulated medium inside the city wall is called architecture, but also that the elements of the city—its enclosing walls and the space inside the walls—act as the formal originators of all its emergent buildings. "Within the city," he continues, "the house, palace, and temple of the city are each partial enclosures which gain importance according to their degree of segregation."[882] What is interesting in Benevolo's argument here is that the formal idea of a building emerges neither by an architect nor from an exteriority, but comes into existence due to the inner formal properties of the object that contains it—the city.

FIGURE 58. THE CITY BECOMING ARCHITECTURE (THE BENEVOLO ENSEMBLE)

This link between architecture and the city has many theoretical offspring in the disciplinary history of architecture. Especially the idea of *separation*, which unites both the city and its buildings. As already discussed, this quality was most recently used by Aureli in his argument for an architecture as a political form.[883] For him, the formal and the political are the basis of the architecture of the city. We can hear the ideas of Benevolo in the background when Aureli states, "the very condition of architectural form is to separate and to be separated. Through its act of separation and being separated, architecture reveals *at once* the essence of the city and the essence of itself as a political form: the city as the composition of (separate) parts."[884]

But it seems as if a mechanological detail is missing in Benevolo's reading of the city becoming architecture. If we take the enclosed city wall with its void space inside, we do not arrive at the typology of the Greek house or the basilica, for example, by just copying this relationship. As we saw above in the description of the buildings surrounding a Greek agora, those two elements of the city—the massive wall and void space—had to exchange some of their properties for specific building types, like the stoa, to emerge. It is very similar in the case of the Greek house[885] and the basilica as well.

If we follow a speculative convergence series beginning with a rectangular wall framing a piece of land, a few exchanges of qualities are necessary to see this through to a house as a concrete object. The qualities of the void, for example, have to fuse with the massive city wall to allow a room to appear inside. These include the volumetric envelope around the void, which when within the wall provides for the articulation of interior volumes that become inhabitable spaces, or rooms. At the same time, the massive quality of the enclosed wall fuses with the void space of the city. When the solidness of the wall expands around the voided volume, it gives rise to a partially roofed courtyard space. Or we can imagine this volume fully covered by the "wall" such that a public indoor space appears, as we find in a Vitruvian basilica, for example.[886] In this mechanological reading of Benevolo, nothing more than the melding of the formal properties of the two elements of the city—that is, no external objects—is needed to give rise to the Greek house or the basilica.

These architectural prime objects, or new building typologies, contain formal and functional qualities that were absent in the original two objects of the city. Formally, the continuous, enclosure form of the wall turns into a new topological organization. Instead of a single figurative built object, it turns into a torus-like building with a series of cellular volumes inside. The exterior void space of the city becomes a form of interiority that includes inside-outside spaces, as we find in all kinds of courtyard types. Functionally, in the case of the house, the city as the place of the polis, a place of collective democratic and collectively owned space, mutates into a private property and becomes the place of *oikos*, the locus of the family household with its hierarchical organization. In contrast, the basilica tunes this new space into collective interiority and begins to insert functions like a courtyard house or a place of commerce. Later it gives rise to a radically new collective functionality, tuning its interiority into a religious meeting place. Once the basilica fuses with Christian liturgy a new prime object is born: the church.

The Architectural Ensembles of Leon Battista Alberti

In the ninth chapter of the first book of *De re aedificatoria*, his ten books of architecture from 1452, Alberti places an intriguing thought about the city and its buildings into the discipline of architecture: "if a City, according to the Opinion of Philosophers, be no more than a great House, and, on the other Hand, a House be a little City; why may it not be said, that the Members of that House are so many little Houses; such as the Courtyard, the Hall, the Parlour, the Portico, and the like?"[887] In defining the city as a large house and the house as a small city, Alberti introduces a twofold reading of urban buildings. On one hand, he defines the parts of the building in relationship to its whole. Since each room in the house should be seen as a miniature building, the whole house can be seen as an assemblage of various parts. On the other hand, when Alberti defines the city as a house, he implies that the city is actually a unified single object. In effect, Alberti is defining the city as a technical object.

Indeed, the title of this ninth chapter, "Of the Compartition, and of the Origin of Building," suggests Alberti can give us further detailed ideas for a mechanological reading of buildings. For Alberti, technical objects do not only consist of formal properties, like Benevolo's wall and space geometries. In his example material properties can be exchanged as well. When he argues that each room in a house can be seen as a house in the city, he implies the idea that the material substance of each part of a technical object can be tuned: the void of a room becomes the massing of an architectural ensemble of a city. Thus, to use the language of thermodynamics, in a mechanological reading of Alberti's city-architecture each part can be specialized through the sublimation or deposition of their states of matter. Instead of just the city wall being the origin of architectural entities, all elements of the city have the capacity to converge into each part of a building. At the same time, each of the individual elements of buildings can specialize and fuse back into the city.

But what kind of city might Alberti have had in mind where all architectural elements have such hypertelic qualities?

If the rooms of Alberti's house form the ensemble of buildings within a city and the walls of the house form its streets, it would give rise to a slightly unfamiliar yet real city. At first the convergence of all of the parts of the house remind us of any premodern city fabric. If a room is a house and the walls are streets, then each house is surrounded by a kind of pedestrian alley, or even a street in cases where the room reaches the size of an urban block. It is a somewhat strange city. Indeed, no city comes to my mind where literally each house is surrounded by a space of circulation (A). But what makes this city of Alberti's house even stranger is when we consider the doorways as another distinct element (B). If the voids of the rooms are houses, what then are the voids of the thresholds that connect them? It seems that in Alberti's city-as-house all the buildings would connect by some

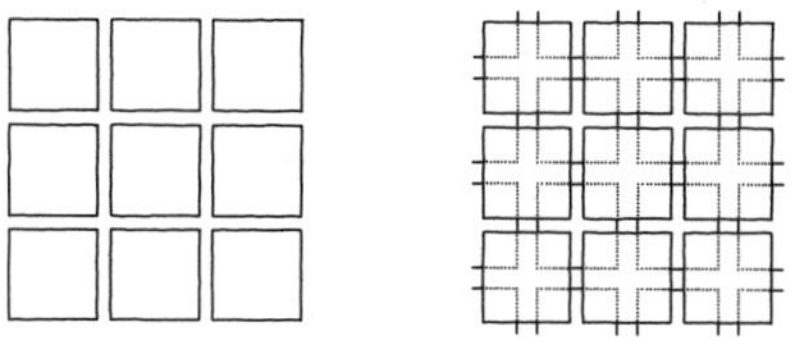

(A) (B)

FIGURE 59. THE CITY OF ALBERTI'S HOUSE (THE ALBERTI ENSEMBLE)

kind of raised walkway, as we can find in many medieval cities, and in particular in Venice.[888] Today this emergent quality has become a concrete architectural prime object—namely, the megastructure, wherein a series of buildings are united by an infrastructural element detached from the ground of the city.[889]

In abstract terms we could say that when the city takes the shape of a large house, in return this house gives rise to a new city: a city where a continuous ensemble of buildings (the void of rooms) intersects with a continuous urban space of circulation (the mass of walls). Once again, without the help of any external object, the house of the city originates into a new city itself due to the hypertelic capacity of both as overdetermined technical beings.

The Architectural Ensembles of Emil Kaufmann

According to Emil Kaufmann's historical reading of buildings, in the second half of the eighteenth century, between the period of the Baroque and classicism, a second hypertelic quality of technical objects gave rise to a new understanding of the architectural ensembles of cities. As Kaufmann writes of the formation of buildings at that time, "the autonomy of the parts is the most important result of the architectural regeneration process from the beginning of the eighteenth century. The new principle of autonomy does not tolerate that architectural entities are dominated by alien, extra-architectural laws."[890] In that time of the Enlightenment, the French Revolution, the appearance of Kant's philosophy, and the beginning of industrialization, Kaufmann argues, the architecture of the city shifted its focus toward the interiority of each of its architectural components: whether a single column, which detached itself from the wall; or each room within a floor plan,[891] which liberated itself from its poché to become a single isolated form; or a whole architectural ensemble, which exploded its composition into individual architectural objects. "The new joining of the parts," he writes,

> means the free union of individuals who do not need to sacrifice their own life, whose form obeys only their own purpose. Their inner law determines their shape. This is how the new anti-baroque ground plan is to be understood, this is how a completely new relationship of all parts, of the parts to each other and of the parts to the whole results, until at the end of the logically progressing development there are no more parts, but only independent units.[892]

Kaufmann's focus on the inner laws of all architectural

elements makes two kinds of architectural ensembles distinguishable. The first one, called "baroque association,"[893] dominated our cities before the nineteenth century. The second is the "pavilion system,"[894] a radically new, emergent formation of the nineteenth century that determined the architecture of our cities from then on, even until today.

Within baroque association, each architectural element is not at all

FIGURE 60. HETERONOMOUS & AUTONOMOUS ARCHITECTURE (THE KAUFMANN ENSEMBLE)

autonomous. Each part within the ensemble has lost its individuality by being joined together to form a architectural compositional-whole, like an urban block in the case of a city. Kaufmann considers such architecture as heteronomous, meaning that each part of a building, or each building in an urban fabric, sacrifices its individuality to serve the purpose of an overall composition. Each house in a city may have its own site and stand on its own property, but it is joined together with every other house and land property to form an urban unity. Kaufmann clearly places this form of heteronomous architecture in the time of the European empires, but generally speaking it is *the* architectural ensemble from the birth of our cities. However, Kaufmann argues that the single elements of such heteronomous ensembles evolved, through what we could identify as their internal necessity, toward autonomy. In other words, the individual element was extracted or pulled out of the architectural composition to turn into an individual entity. The resulting ensemble of these autonomous elements is what Kaufmann defines as the pavilion system, in which every part of a building, or buildings themselves, are liberated from their embedded context and form an ensemble of autonomous architectural elements. In the case of the city at large, the individual buildings then are freestanding entities floating in their plots of land without touching one another.[895] Each and every architectural entity reaches its autonomous Dasein. As the title of this book *From Ledoux to Le Corbusier* suggests, this new architectural ensemble became the expression of the modern city, and found perhaps its *prime* moment in Le Corbusier's freestanding towers in the park from his 1924 proposal for La ville radieuse.

Kaufmann's distinction between the two different architectural ensembles is best summarized in his own words:

> In the pavilion system there are basically no more parts, it is an association of independent elements. If one wants to reduce the two principles of composition to the most concise formulas, then one could characterize the baroque association with the words: One part is above all, and yet all parts are one. The deepest sense of the pavilion system, however, might be paraphrased as follows: The part is free within the framework of the whole.[896]

This difference between the two ensembles demonstrates the difference between Simondon's two kinds of hypertely of technical objects.[897] Baroque association illustrates the first: in the ensemble each architectural entity is fine-tuned without breaking the unity of technical object. The pavilion system, in contrast, demonstrates the second: the technical object, or the (baroque) ensemble, breaks apart and each element becomes an autonomous technical being. While in the baroque ensemble the whole is autonomous, the pavilion system sacrifices the autonomy of the compositional whole, giving rise to the concretization of each of its newly autonomous elements.

This process toward architecture as autonomous entities by means of an internal necessity of convergence has accelerated throughout modernity. Soon after the unity of the larger urban fabric was broken the same began to happen to the building as well.[898] Each individual apartment and each of its rooms drove toward autonomy by specializing the demands of its interiority. It is therefore no surprise that we can find in the work of Le Corbusier buildings like the Immeubles Villas,[899] or blocks of dwellings on the *cellular system*, as it is typically translated, for his vision of a contemporary city in the proposal for Une ville contemporaine from 1922.[900]

Perhaps this striving toward the interiority of homes, on one hand, and the question of how the new modern city should look, on the other, demanded an understanding of the architectural ensemble of the city as more like an aggregation of inhabitable cells. Hilberseimer formulated this very concern in a 1927 essay titled "Grossstadtarchitektur":

> Metropolisarchitecture is considerably dependent on solving two factors: the individual cell of the room and the collective urban organism. The solution will be determined by the manner in which the room is manifested as an element of buildings linked together in one street block, thus becoming a determining factor of the city structure, which is the actual objective of architecture. Inversely, the constructive design of the urban plan will gain considerable influence on the formation of the room and the building as such.[901]

Hilberseimer's call to understand the association between the various elements of the architecture of the city also evokes another quality of technical beings, specifically that they are not enclosed entities. Simondon describes the technical object as having what he calls "reticular structure," which for him means that it is not a closed machine but rather an "*open* object."[902] The architect whose work perhaps focused the most on these kinds of building qualities is Saverio Muratori, whose research on the association of architectural ensembles transcends a multiplicity of scales and milieus.

The Architectural Ensembles of Saverio Muratori

Simondon further elaborates his concept of the *open object* with a set of norms of what he refers to as "technical mentality." And to define this technical mentality, he uses an architectural example:

> To construct a building according to the norms of the technical mentality means to conceive of it as being able to be enlarged, continued, amplified without disfiguration or erasure. The 'Le Corbusier monastery' at Eveux-l'Arbresle is a beautiful example of the contribution of the technical mentality in architecture; it includes within its plan its proper line of extension for a further enlargement. And this is possible not only because of the architectural conception of the whole, but also because of the pairing down that manifests itself in

the choice of forms and the use of materials.[903]

Muratori would appear to be anything but related to something like a modern, technical mentality. His work ran counter to the modernist paradigm. He saw his research as critique of the idea of reducing architecture to a problem of tectonics.[904] He and his so-called Italian school of architects were not concerned with fulfilling the promise of modern architecture in the age of industrial production.[905] More specifically, Muratori did not want to break with history in search of the new. Quite the opposite, he wanted to find an argument for historical continuity in the architectural ensembles of the city to link the past with the present. He found this link in those architectural elements whose qualities stayed permanent throughout time.

Muratori and his colleagues referred to the built continuity of the city as "typological processes."[906] The permanent architectural element they looked for was the "building type."[907] Most famously, Muratori demonstrated these ideas in his 1959 *Studi per una operante storia urbana di Venezia, [Studies for an operative urban history of Venice]*.[908] In the book, Muratori redraws the built layers of the historical city in several of Venice's districts. One of his examples is the Quartiere di Campo due Pozzi, a neighborhood in the eastern part of the sestiere of Castello.[909] Using archival building plans Muratori reconstructs the area around the Campo due Pozzi for the fifteenth, sixteenth, and eighteenth centuries as one continuous urban ground plan. Muratori's aim with this fictional but accurately redrawn *quartiere* was not only to demonstrate the morphological growth of a part of Venice, but also to search for the architectural unit, the elementary cell, which could be defined as the permanent building type on which the city fabric was based and by which it evolved. This idea of basic architectural types and their variations is illustrated in Muratori's book with drawings of Florence, Rome, and Genoa produced by his pupil Gianfranco Caniggia. The drawings show how basic cellular building types are extracted from the historical layers of the city fabric, and visualize their mutations in a progressive typological process.[910]

Muratori and the followers of his school of urban morphology and building typology were not interested in contributing to a Semperian tectonic history, as asked for by Kenneth Frampton. In this sense it is indeed accurate to say that their work has nothing in common with the technical mentality of architecture that Simondon locates in Le Corbusier's La Tourette. They understood the architecture of the city more along the line of a biological metaphor than a technical one. The morphology of a city was thought as an organic organism,[911] not as a technical object. Furthermore, their idea of type was not understood as the outcome of a concretization involving the convergence of the inner parts of the city or architecture, but rather was seen as a priori, as something given to builders at their respective times in the form of a spontaneous consciousness.[912] This meant for Muratori's school that "basic building types" could only be discovered a posteriori by empirical research of the city's morphology through critical consciousness. As Caniggia and Gian Luigi Maffei write in *Architectural Composition and Building Typology*, "type . . . inevitably owes its existence to being 'a priori synthesis,' 'concept.' That is to say, it exists in the builder's mind before producing a house and is not a prefiguration of one or several aspects of the building but all of them together: a real organism, bringing the whole house to life before it exists physically."[913]

Even while Muratori's research on architectural typology may not align with Simondon's statement on technical mentality, his work on how urban morphology evolves does contain viable disciplinary aspects for understanding the city as an *open object*. The idea that the city can grow and is "able to be enlarged, continued, amplified without disfiguration or erasure," as Simondon writes, points toward Muratori's insight on urban architectural ensembles. To read his work from the viewpoint of an open technical object, then, would not focus on the idea of type, but rather on the mode of aggregation of a type's

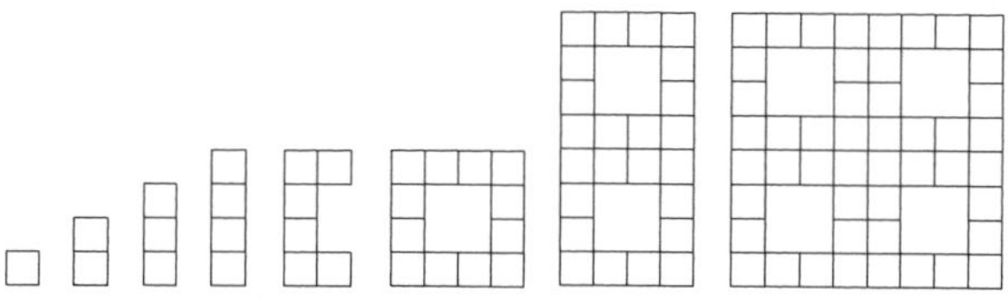

FIGURE 61. CELLULAR AGGREGATES (THE MURATORI ENSEMBLE)

mutations.[914] I therefore refer to Muratori's architectural ensembles as a research on cellular aggregates, or aggregates of architectural population.

In a series of drawings published in Giorgio Pigafetta's 1990 monograph of Muratori's work under the title "General outline of the consciousness-reality process,"[915] Muratori provides insight into how urban fabric can be thought through various scales. These drawings reveal that, for Muratori, any urban morphology is based on the aggregation of cellular units, whereby each unit is informed by its inhabited interiority and grows according to the condition of its embedded territory. Muratori's cellular aggregates can be understood as an associative model between all the various scales as well as the various materials at each scale. Muratori distinguishes between five main scales: the scale of furniture, the architectural room (cell), the building, the urban field, and the territory. Each associative model starts with the scale of furniture and its distribution in space, then moves to the scale of architecture with its various structural building principles, to the scale of the cellular room and its relationship to building type, and to the urban scale by bringing the cellular building type in relationship with the urban fabric, then moves to the scale of the territory by first relating it to pre-urbanized layouts of farmland and finally ending up at the scale of territorial layouts of various historical forms of urban civilizations. What one can imagine is that Muratori's cellular aggregates contain qualities that Simondon attributed to the postindustrial technical object. Postindustrial objects form, for Simondon,

> unity [out] of two layers of reality—a layer that is as stable and permanent as possible, which adheres to the user and is made to last, and a layer that can be perpetually replaced, changed, renewed, because it is made up of elements that are similar, impersonal, mass-produced by industry and distributed by all networks of exchange.[916]

Similarly, on one hand Muratori's chain of associativity between the various scales provides the kind of permanence of any urban morphology, while on the other hand each scale belongs to different material organization, or *regime*,[917] which becomes perpetually replaced, either by individuals who renew their homes or city administrations that replace their infrastructure. It is this rhizomatic, reticular structure that allows us to think Muratori's architectural ensemble as an open technical object. Not only because of its formal structure, but because for Simondon all open objects are regimes as well.[918]

The Architectural Ensembles of Colin Rowe

Colin Rowe would perhaps have been surprised to find his ideas on the architecture of the city in a book that presents those things as technical objects. His work is generally recognized as belonging to the tradition of formalism within the discipline of architecture. His work, especially that formulated with Fred Koetter in their book *Collage City*, became known as an investigation into a form of postmodern contextualism,[919] meant to "repair" the city after modernist urban planning, through pure formal devices, which gestalt theorists would call figure-ground relationships. As Anthony Vidler has pointed out, Rowe was seen as an "outdated formalist,"[920] and was added by cultural theorists to the same list as Wöllfin and Hildebrandt. Perhaps this view of Rowe as being detached from his times became even more obvious after the 1968 revolution in Europe. His devotion to the discourse of rationalism with its idea "that the ratio of architecture is architecture itself,"[921] had no chance to reach the ears of the young generation of students at that time.[922]

In an essay titled "Who's Afraid of Formalism?"[923] written for the 1994 issue of ANY Magazine on Rowe, Sanford Kwinter suddenly pointed the work of *Collage City* in the direction of a kind of formalism which had been denied in the discourse of architecture until then. What Kwinter claims is that there are two kinds of formalism. The first he calls "poor formalism." This formalism is nothing more than "parodic analytical methods derived from the great and genuine aesthetic and epistemological innovations of modern, avant-gardist tradition, but which have simply forgotten that that is what they are."[924] According to Kwinter, the discourse had almost exclusively employed this degenerate formalism, which reduces the problem of form to being nothing more than the image of an object. What he refers to as "true formalism" doesn't reduce or conflate meaning between objects and their formation. In other words, form is seen from this viewpoint as being generative, instead of just an ordering action, or as typologists[925] think of it, as just a variation on a theme. As he points out, "the form of the object (or the form of the expression) and the form of the theme (form of the content) are, in truth, in continual dynamic resonance."[926] We can hear Simondon's critique of the hylomorphic model here in Kwinter's words. But Kwinter's critique is oriented toward the discipline of architecture as well. If architecture wants to talk about formalism in the work of architects or historians, it should look at the work through the eyes of true formalism. This would mean an attempt to formulate the dynamic resonances, communications, and transmissions which cause the emergence of the plans of buildings, urban fabric, or, as in this book, architectural ensembles of the city. In short, true formalism concerns the way in which objects historically emerge. What Kwinter sees in the work of Colin Rowe is a cornerstone within the discipline of architecture in the twentieth century for the possibility of the emergence of a true formalism. What Rowe does in his writings on architecture is what all great formalists do. They all, as Kwinter writes, "demonstrate first and foremost that form is resonance and expression of embedded forces,"[927] which causes the formation of any kind of object.

While this might count for all of Colin Rowe's writings, Kwinter's essay does not mention how his idea of true formalism can be found in Rowe's work as an architect, in particular his analytic methodological approaches to the formation of architectural ensembles in cities. I would argue that what makes Rowe a true formalist is that he reinvented a figure-ground relationship that had been traditionally a sort of poor formalism of gestalt theory. This invention was his particular use of urban poché.[928] As Simondon argues in *On the Mode of Existence of Technical Objects*, traditional formal-analysts have focused on the figuration of forms and have thus missed the fact that it is their dynamic (back)ground whereon these figurative forms are activated and which generates their appearance. As he writes:

Gestalt psychology, while recognising the function of totalities,

> attributed force to form; a deeper analysis of the inventive process would no doubt show that what is determinant and plays an energetic role are not forms but that which carries the forms, which is to say their ground; the ground, while perpetually marginal with respect to attention, is what harbors the dynamisms; it is that through which the system of forms exists; forms do not participate in forms, but in the ground.[929]

Rowe's work on architecture as poché is exactly that: he incorporates the qualities of the backgrounds into the forms they host. More specifically, he allows the resources and expressions of the forces of the urban milieu to migrate into the architectural ensembles of their cities.

On the cover of *Collage City* is a black and white drawing

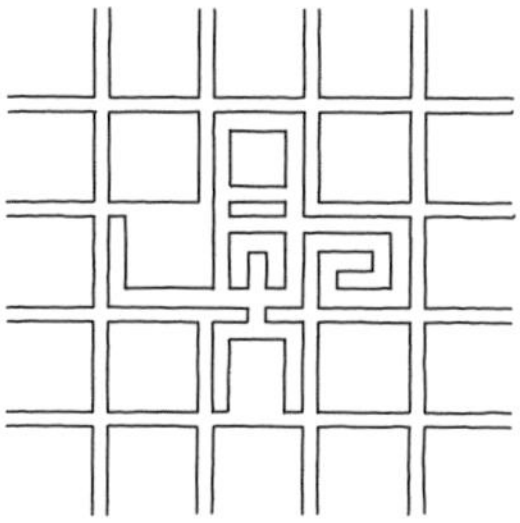

FIGURE 62. THE BUILDING AS POCHÉ (THE ROWE ENSEMBLE)

of the city of Wiesbaden around 1900.[930] I imagine that the image was chosen for the book's cover because it is the most immediate visualization of its content. What Rowe and Koetter address with this diagram is that the material articulation of the architecture of the city can be defined as two different formations: the premodern and the modern cities, each the result of two radically different sociopolitical processes. Each condition is expressed in one half of the figure-ground diagram, which has been split down the center. The left half of the diagram defines the premodern city. It is the expression, as we heard from Lefebvre above, of the city of politics and trade. Its figurative elements represent the public spaces of the city like the square. The buildings are an anonymous architectural mass that forms the ground for these public-space figures. The right half of the diagram defines what would become the modernist city. Again according to Lefebvre, this is the city of industrialization. In this city the figurative elements represent the mass-produced freestanding buildings and their ground is the void space that surrounds buildings, which is used for various modes of transportation and the circulation of air.

What Rowe and Koetter show in this dual figure-ground diagram is that in the two different cities the content of the figurative objects and the background simply reverse. In both, the background seems irrelevant. In the premodern city no single building can be identified while the void space in the modern city shows no qualities at all. The reason is obvious. In both cities the figure—public spaces in the premodern city and freestanding buildings in the modern city—were the essential expressions of their zeitgeist. If the constitution of political collectives needed public squares, then, as we learned from Kaufmann, industrial production with its new interiority demanded autonomy.

In his contextualist projects[931] Rowe proposes to activate the forgotten qualities of both backgrounds. This is similar to Simondon's reading of the ground as the necessary milieu without which the figures could not exist. Without the houses of the people framing the voids of the city there would not be a public space, and without the circulation of air and the space for vehicles around buildings there would not be a modernist floor plan. Rowe brings to the fore those lost qualities of the background and moves them into the form of the figures. What emerges is a new kind of building. This building performs both qualities of the figure-ground relationship, as Rowe writes: "It seems that the general usefulness of poché in a revived and overhauled sense, comes by its ability, as a solid, to engage or be engaged by adjacent voids, to act as both figure and ground as necessity or circumstance might require."[932] The qualities of the background in premodern architecture move into the figure of modern architecture, while the figurative qualities of the premodern public space merge with the anonymous void of the modern city. Emerging from the convergence of the background qualities into the figurative forms is this new architectural *poché object*, which performs as urban background and urban figure at the same time. It is this convergence of the formal and functional qualities that gives rise to a whole new world of urban formations to come.

Perhaps it is this idea of activating the qualities lost in the background that makes Rowe a true formalist, not only as a historian but as an architect as well. At the very least, to borrow some of Kwinter's words on true formalism, this reading of Rowe's figure-ground forms is an attempt to access their "dynamic inner intelligibility,"[933] which allows us finally to see Rowe's work on the architectural ensembles of the city "transition from the generic view to the genetic view of organic nature."[934]

Architectural Ensembles According to Simondon's Mechanology.
As specifically described above, the notions of architectural ensembles formulated by Benevolo, Alberti, Kaufmann, Muratori, and Rowe are attempts to read the architecture of the city through the eyes of the mode of existence of the technical being. This position holds that building objects arise due to the city's overdetermined formal and functional qualities, or what I refer to as their internal necessity. What was for Benevolo the city-wall was for Alberti the whole city fabric, for Muratori its historical layers, for Kaufmann the pursuit of autonomy pulling buildings out of their urban composition, and for Rowe the qualities of the background—in every case the properties of the city define the articulation of its architectural ensembles.

But can these five kinds of convergences explain all architecture? How is it possible to explain buildings like a high-rise, El Lissitzky's Wolkenbügel, or the city on a single roof?

The above five readings of the architectural ensembles of the city all stay within the qualities of the two-dimensionality of the city. Perhaps this is due to the fact that the city is mostly a two dimensional artifact: a technical object of horizontal, rhizomatic reticular-structure. But if we unpack Simondon's claim that technical objects are the milieu for new technical objects, then those new objects are also overdetermined and hypertelic. This means, then, that once a building appears in a city it is a new individuated technical object itself, holding a multiplicity of virtualities waiting to be concretized.

Thus we can speculate through the lens of Simondon's mechanology on how buildings can give rise to new architectural ensembles through the hypertelic qualities within the elements of the buildings themselves. Such a mechanological reading of the history of architecture of the city would not be limited to the horizontal dimension and would give us access to understanding various prime objects as they have emerged throughout the history of the city until today.

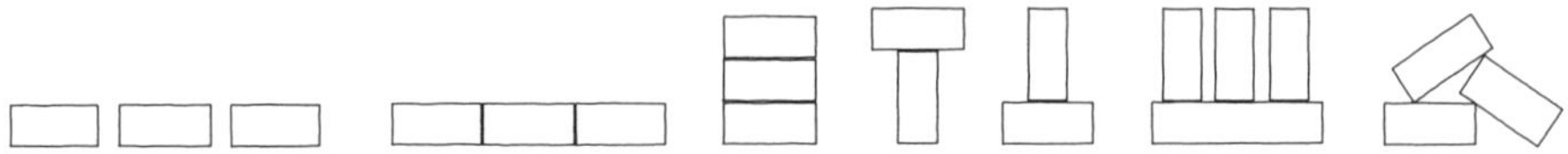

FIGURE 63. ARCHITECTURAL ENSEMBLE OF THE HYPERTELIC QUALITIES OF ITS ELEMENTS (THE SIMONDON ENSEMBLE)

The Ground Ensemble

FIGURE 64. ARCHITECTURAL ENSEMBLE OF THE HYPERTELIC QUALITIES OF ITS GROUND

The first architectural ensemble can be seen as a specialization of the ground on which buildings stand. Many things have already been said about the beginning of our urbanization. We know from Mumford that the retreat of ice caps and the liberation of the earth's skin brought a planetary spring with its newly fecund plant life. The following agricultural revolution and its resultant need for management of this productive new skin of the earth led to the emergence of our urban settlements in the form of our prime object: the city. It is only obvious that the ground was the first element to be specialized.

At the shift from nomadic to farming communities, human settlements started by marking a location. As Aureli has noted, the placing of a limestone disc at the center of our first circular buildings was the beginning of the use of abstract models to configure our floor plans.[935] And let us not overlook some of our prehistoric settlements, like the rectangular layout of that from the fifth millennium BCE in Sittard, in the Netherlands, where the excavations of the post holes look as if the houses were hybrids of a wall and a territory.[936] It is therefore no surprise that, for Alberti, building a house does not start by just choosing a region, but by determining a particular platform on which to walk on and place walls.[937] And perhaps this is the reason why Le Corbusier begins his chapter on "Regulating Lines" with a description of "primitive man" preparing the ground and then framing it with an enclosed palisade.[938] (Note that the actual door of the house is the gate in the fence of its surrounding territory.) We can see this in all kinds of suburban projects on this planet, including the early garden cities by Raymond Unwin,[939] the Levittowns by the Levit Brothers, Wright's Broadacre City, and up to the recent Ascaya developments in Las Vegas,[940] as well as in many others around the planet. It is always the same. Their layout is governed by the subdivision of land into parcels as equal as possible to enhance the success of their architectural objects. The specialization of the ground, its floor-making capacity, thus causes our loose first type of architectural ensemble of the city, and of the suburban city in particular.

The Wall Ensemble

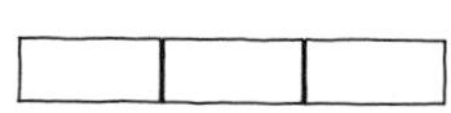

FIGURE 65. ARCHITECTURAL ENSEMBLE OF THE HYPERTELIC QUALITIES OF THE WALL

The second architectural ensemble of the city can seen as a specialization of the wall. By this I mean not only the city wall to which Benevolo referrs as the prototype for our first urban architecture, but also the walls of buildings. What I mean by the specialization of the wall is the capacity of walls to merge into each other to produce something that did not exist before: an articulated public space. What we saw in the drawing of the Mousgoum village from Benevolo's book was that at a certain point in our urban history individual freestanding buildings started to converge, their walls fusing together. As we read from many formalists there have always existed two different models of architectural ensembles:[941] the acropolis model with its loose assemblage of buildings on an empty piece of land and the Roman forum model, for example in Pompeii, where buildings stand wall to wall and generate a figurative space. It is the latter ensemble that requires the specialization of the wall.

Such specialization of the walls of buildings, their fusing together, is a demonstration of an internal necessity of convergence: public and commercial spaces demand a new continuous formal articulation; buildings line up one after the other, supporting themselves with newly shared walls that define their individual interior organizations while their facades now articulate the new public space.[942] Beyond ancient poleis that suddenly were laid out on a street grid, a famous example of this continuous straight line of a street front produced by lining up buildings can be found in the Via Giuseppe Garibaldi in Genoa, or Strada Nuova, as it was originally called.[943] The same can be said about the public squares where buildings formed perfect geometric voids, such as the plan of Paris by Pierre Patte.[944] The irregular geometrical perimeters of the Piazza del Campo in Siena are no different. Their continuity was guaranteed by the sequence of buildings built wall-to-wall as well. What seems to have happened at a particular moment in the history of the city as a technical being is that buildings converged their walls together to give shape to a new exteriority, a form larger than the individual buildings themselves. This is what Kaufmann's heteronomous architecture means according to a mechanological approach. Buildings gave up their autonomy and specialized one of their elements. The wall unlocked this hypertelic quality because of the changes in its political and economical milieu, which occurred as such in cities until the end of the eighteenth century.

The Floor Ensemble

The third architectural ensemble can seen as a specialization of the floor. Kaufmann considers the pursuit of an autonomous architecture

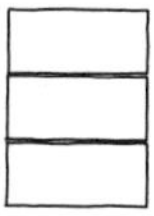

FIGURE 66. ARCHITECTURAL ENSEMBLE OF THE HYPERTELIC QUALITIES OF THE FLOOR

as a consequence of the changes in the political milieu in European capitals around 1800. While someone like Rowe sees the appearance of freestanding individual buildings as a consequence of the need for a new modern living condition, both hold that the emergence of this new architectural ensemble is the effect of an exteriority—something forced onto architecture from the outside. From a mechanological viewpoint, however, the opposite is the case. It is an inner mutation of technical objects, the hypertely of their elements, that allows freestanding buildings to emerge. In this case the internal specialization took place within the floor plate.

As I have already discussed in regard to the diagram of the theorem of the high-rise printed in *Delirious New York*, individual towers emerged in the growing metropolis because the qualities of the city moved into the architectural elements of the building. In part this was possible because new construction methods cleared the floor area of columns and walls. What further enabled this capacity—and resultant demand—for more density was the fusion of pieces of land, or property, with the floor plate. Once again a shift in the milieu of the city led to the specialization of a technical object, which itself was possible because of its overdetermination. Specifically, the convergence between the subdivision of private properties and the section of a building begot the stacking of lots. From a mechanological viewpoint, then, such autonomous architecture did not emerge through industrialization, but rather through the hypertelic capacity of the floor.

If we are to be precise, it was not only the floor that specialized in order to give rise to this new kind of vertical ensemble. As noted in the caption of that 1909 theorem diagram, the elevator became an inner street, the effect being that the high-rise was a vertical repetition of not merely land but of developed urban blocks served by infrastructure. As vertical circulation, elevators do not provide access to every floor in the same way as streets do to every house. After a certain height, vertical circulation thus comprises stacks of elevators with sky lobbies in between. After several levels of private floors, these public spaces are inserted. This public platform allows people to change their vertical transportation analogously to how street intersections allow them to change directions. Through the insertion of this public function into the autonomous building, a new specialization has taken place. A piece of public property enters the diagram of the high-rise tower. A new architectural ensemble is in the becoming.

The Roof Ensemble

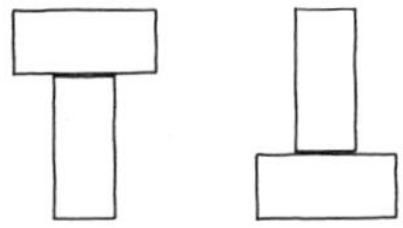

FIGURE 67. ARCHITECTURAL ENSEMBLE OF THE HYPERTELIC QUALITIES OF THE ROOF

The fourth architectural ensemble can be seen as a specialization of the roof. As we have seen in Le Corbusier's work, one aspect of the specialization of the horizontal floor is the concurrent liberation of the roof. What became known as his second point, *le toit-jardin*, is actually the lost piece of land on which a building stands, only reproduced on its top. The first time such a roof functioned as a public terrain was perhaps within the garden-housing schemes of Corbusier's proposal for A Contemporary City for Three Million People, whereby the roofs of the immeubles villas act as a public recreation area.[945] It was the eventual work of Hilberseimer through which we can witness the true virtuality of the roof as a new datum. What Hilberseimer showed was not just a repositioning of this piece of land on the top of a building, but also that this new datum has the innate potential to place a building with a radically different function right on top of it. This new kind of architectural ensemble became known as the *stacked building*. Its purest diagrammatic articulation was formulated by Hilberseimer in his proposal of a Hochhausstadt,[946] in which a housing slab is placed on the roof of a rectangular office building. However, what Hilberseimer proposed was actually not new at all. He found this archetypical building already in the metropolis of the early twentieth century, in particular New York. This new kind of building emerged due to the innate inner potential of cities to compress various functions on one site by distinguishing them vertically, a vertical stacking that is possible due to their different needs for access. Hilberseimer stated that this demand of the new architecture of the city, the stacking of functions on one another, is perhaps as old as cities themselves: "The idea of combining the workplace with the home in one building is not new. Medieval houses had workshops on the ground floor and flats on the upper floors. We find the same thing in some large hotels. It is possible to live in a hotel and have one's place of work in it at the same time."[947] What is new in Hilberseimer's diagram of his metropolitan architecture, in comparison to the typical Manhattan hotel, where a more-or-less single building is split into a commercial plinth with a hotel building on top, is that it makes this split explicit in a twofold manner. For one, the separation is driven by the different internal necessities of the various specific functions, and secondly, the roof of the building is literally treated as a piece of land hosting a freestanding building. Hilberseimer showed this accelerated hypertely of a roof in one of his proposals for Berlin: a design for a *Geschäftsviertel*, or business district, from 1929.[948] His vertical stack of buildings, each carrying a specific function and appearing in its most rational formal type, gives us a hint of how this ensemble became prototypical for the the twentieth century metropolis. Underneath the street level is a parking garage with storage space. On the roof of this earth-building stands a two-story-high commercial building with shops, businesses, warehouses, and an inner market-hall. Its roof is a gigantic platform where the office buildings are placed, and which today would likely be adorned with a park. The roofs of these office buildings are proposed as roof gardens, and we can imagine that today this datum could provide the land for housing projects or urban farms.

The example of the stacked architectural ensemble demonstrates the radical consequence of the specialization of the roof as a datum for a new building. This new emerging architectural ensemble probably found its masterpiece in El Lissitzky's 1924 Wolkenbügel design: a horizontal building placed on three roofs.

The Building Ensemble

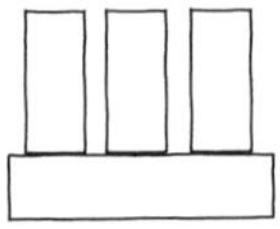

FIGURE 68. ARCHITECTURAL ENSEMBLE OF THE HYPERTELIC QUALITIES OF THE BUILDING

In the previous ensemble the roof is tuned to a piece of land for a new, freestanding building. In order for the city on a single roof to emerge, however, it is not only the roof of a building that specializes its performance. Here the whole building takes on the qualities of the urban ground in order for a building to function as a ground for an entire city. The building, which usually is served by the infrastructure of the city, has to become infrastructure. It is this hypertelic quality of the building to converge with the qualities of the "real" ground of the city that gave rise to this very recently emerging architectural ensemble.

In order for the ensemble to function, various ground conditions converge with all kinds of architectural elements. The roof has to fuse with the legal apparatus of property and subdivide its surface into the two kinds of legal properties of cities: private real estate, which can bought and sold, and public real estate, which can serve as roads and gives access to each lot. In order to enable access to the city on the roof, the entire building has to take on the performative quality of a street. The structure of the building needs to behave like the soil of the city to structurally carry the added built mass, and the building as a whole has to provide infrastructures, which are usually underground, within the building itself—various energy resources like electricity, a sewage system, and public waste management. Indeed, while there are several kinds of single buildings to have submerged within them one or more elements of the urban ground condition, what is unique with this architectural ensemble is that the building serves as the *infrastructural* ground of a city.

The Multiple-Element Ensemble

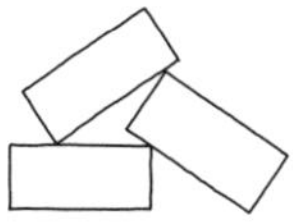

FIGURE 69. ARCHITECTURAL ENSEMBLE OF THE HYPERTELIC QUALITIES OF MULTIPLE ELEMENTS

The last architectural ensemble in this formal sequence is a purely speculative one. The assertion here is that the city on a single roof, in tuning the building to become the ground for a city, does not exhaust its hypertelic qualities. That a single building can be specialized toward multiple city elements—whether a street, a boulevard, or a whole district—and at the same time its entire three-dimensional agglomeration can have subway system–like qualities, was once proposed by OMA in a project called Hyperbuilding.[949] This speculative design project from 1996 for the city of Bangkok was never built. Perhaps it was not even intended to be built. It is an urban collection of all kinds of building typologies fused with urban elements. While, formally speaking, each individual building appears discretely, it actually functions as a piece of the city. What we find in a series of drawings of the project are buildings being used as the ground for other buildings, like stacked assemblages. At other times buildings lean onto each other and function like a boulevard, megastructures in which buildings are fused with a piece of urban infrastructure. In other cases buildings have become streets with houses and lots around their cores as in the example of the high-rise theorem. We even find large volumetric buildings with gigantic public void spaces hosting different programs inside, which perform as their own city districts, like the Manhattan hotels, cities within cities. What is unique and new in the Hyperbuilding is that the whole agglomeration of buildings functions as something more than the sum of its parts. Its overall performance is as an urban metro network, but with one difference: the trains run not underground but inside buildings or outside along their facades.

The significance of the Hyperbuilding isn't that it contains buildings that are unfamiliar to the city. Nor is it just a collection to demonstrate that within the properties of the city lie all kinds of new prime objects. More importantly, it suggests that the agglomeration itself, as a technical object, harbors a new city. A city that seems familiar, but which yet only existed in the hypertely of this overdetermined architectural ensemble.

I have called this kind of city *the pile city*.[950] Pile cities contain a new form of expression and a new form of content. Each building within the agglomeration carries a double functionality: it functions as a building and an urban element at the same time. Each also carries a binary form: it is an autonomous architectural element and it needs the other autonomous elements to become a whole. In other words, this new ensemble of multiple elements cannot be characterized with Kaufmann's dualism. It is neither autonomous nor heteronomous architecture. It is a amphinomous.

Conclusion: The Role of the Architect

One question that is left to answer is to what extent the architect contributes to the technical being of architecture. If it is true that the architect is neither the genius creator of buildings nor the slavish copyist, then is the role of the architect within this mechanological understanding of the mode of existence of buildings? The answer comes from Simondon himself, when he compares the human-machine relationship with that of musicians and their conductor:

> Man is the permanent organizer of a society of technical objects that need him in the same way musicians in an orchestra need the conductor. The conductor can only direct the musicians because he plays the piece the same way they do, as intensely as they all do; he tempers or hurries them, but

> is also tempered or hurried by them; in fact, it is through the conductor that the members of the orchestra temper or hurry one another, he is the moving and current form of the group as it exists for each of them; he is the mutual interpreter of all of them in relation to one another. Man thus has the function of being the permanent coordinator and inventor of the machines that surround him. He is *among* the machines that operate with him.[951]

Here we can easily imagine replacing *orchestra* with *the architecture of the city* and *conductor* with *architect*. And when, on the same page, Simondon adds, "man's presence to machines is a perpetuated invention,"[952] we can see how this can be applied to architecture as well. We humans live in buildings; this is our architecture. We humans also live between buildings; this is our city. Today buildings live with us; this is our zeitgeist.[953] What this means is that architects are part of these technical ensembles.[954] Architects do not invent them as just external ideas or things, for example as a useful thing like a shelter. Nor are architects slaves to their existence. What architects do is participate in the mode of existence of the technical ensembles, by tuning the hypertelic qualities within them.

To visualize such an operation, and how architects throughout history have picked up the signals sent by various city elements in order to reveal qualities contained within their overdetermination, here at the close of this final chapter I present three fictional processes of concretization. In each process an urban element—a street, a square, and a ground—converges with a building. Each process starts with the most abstract form, meaning the moment when both objects present themselves in their purest singular appearance. Through these processes I speculate on how architects have participated in this formal sequence and contributed to the rise of new prime objects for architecture, with the understanding that what architects do is simply to tune the hypertelic qualities that became liberated in each earlier phase of the convergence series. Kubler writes that such formal sequences "exceed the ability of any individual to exhaust their possibilities. An occasional person, born by chance into a favoring time, may contribute beyond the usual measure of a single life-span, but he cannot alone simulate in his life the corporate activity of a whole artistic tradition."[955] Therefore we must understand that such processes of concretization go beyond any architect's individual lifetime and also proceed in nonlinear fashion as well. Even where it seems that a process of concretization is chronological in time, this is an exception and not the rule.

The three processes of concretization to follow:

- A building converges with a street.
- A building converges with a square.
- A building converges with a ground.

4.3. Concretization One: In Which a Building Converges with a Street

To think of a building converging with a street we might generally refer to a building like the ancient Greek stoa, or its unfolding multiplications in cities in the form of colonnades, gallerias, or *Passagen*—the arcades famously studied by Walter Benjamin.[956] These buildings represent a fusion in terms of a mechanological method, since attributes of the street merge with attributes of the building. But this kind of convergence, which takes place mainly on the ground floor—sometimes becoming stacked on multiple floors, as in what Le Corbusier called the "street" in his Unite d' Habitation or the Smithson's "street in the sky"—is essentially an additive intersection of the street and the building. Here I want to present more than just the urban element of the street moving into the floor plan of the building, to show a process of concretization in which those two elements truly converge and produce a new architectural prime object. I will chart this process through a series starting from an origin, or "0," to the prime object.

0. A Street and a Building

FIGURE 70. A STREET AND A BUILDING

As a point of origin, we could begin with the street and the building as two separate entities in their most abstract form, as we can find anywhere on the planet: the linear, flow-oriented public street and the enclosed, inhabitation-oriented private building. Cerdà already hints at the opening of a space of convergence between these two abstract elements when he addresses the fact that, in its origin, the street was not detached from buildings but was actually a "connective entity," which shared all the flows that were needed for the exchange between that which needs to go into a building and that which needs to go onto the "way."[957]

1. Strada Nuova, Genoa, Italy, 1558–1583

FIGURE 71. A STREET NEXT TO A BUILDING

The first stage in this fictional convergence might occur at the moment when the building and the street fuse their boundaries—that is, when the edge of the building is placed just on the property line and marks the edge of a section of the street. The edge of the street at the same time converges one after the other with all the building facades lining both sides of the street. The effect of this convergence of boundaries, or edges, is to produce a new aesthetic property of the street that did not exist before: it becomes space. As a three-dimensional urban element, it leaves behind its two-dimensional existence as an object only for the function of transportation. Meanwhile the private building tunes its facade toward the new public space in front of it and also folds Cerdà's "connective entity," or interface between the building to the street, into its interior, such as we can find in the plans of the palazzi along the Strada Nuova in Genoa.

2. Spangen Quarter Housing, Rotterdam, Netherlands. 1919

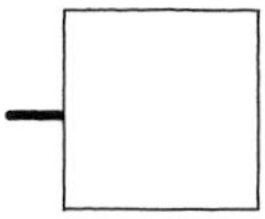

FIGURE 72. A STREET ON A BUILDING

In this project from 1919 designed by Michiel Brinkman, a previously unknown quality of the building envelope is revealed. Once the property line of the street has merged with the edge of the building, the wall undergoes further specialization, wherein the street climbs up the exterior facade in the form of wide, cantilevered walkway. What suddenly emerges here is the street without its old relationship to the ground. It takes off into the air and becomes part of the building. This specialization is not merely a structural attachment to the wall. The effect of this merging of street and facade is to turn the building from a single independent object and into a multiplication of buildings on top of each other. At the same time, the elevated street is more than a thoroughfare for the general public, it is a container for a particular collective of residents. The fusion of street with the facade thus converges formal and functional characteristics. The street takes on elements of inhabitation, becoming a public balcony, while the building takes on urban qualities, where houses now stand on top of one another.

3. Narkomfin Housing, Moscow, Russia, 1928–32

FIGURE 73. A STREET MOVES INSIDE A BUILDING

Once the street loses its relationship to the ground and is stuck on the facade, this liberates its fusion with other building elements.

Narkomfin brings a new kind of interiority to the forefront where the street moves into the interior. On the third floor of the building the street converges with the floor and turns into a stoa-like interior public street, now functioning exclusively as the *social condenser* for its inhabitants. On the first floor the street fuses with the floor plate as well, but instead of just a shared surface this gives rise to a new volumetric interiority, which was so far unactualized. When the street met the facade, as at Spangen, the space of the street framed by the buildings on either side was lost. But it returns here at Narkomfin, where the street moves inside and becomes even more articulated, since the new internal street is now an enclosed linear volume two stories high.

For the first time in this series, both abstract forms of the street and the building share their qualities within the same elements: the space of flow and the space of inhabitation are shared within the floor plate, while the volumes of both of those spaces are shared within the interiority of the building.

4. Petersschule, Basel, Switzerland, 1926

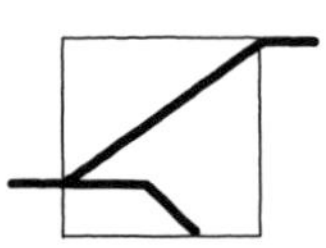

FIGURE 74. A STREET SPIRALS UP AND AROUND A BUILDING

There are many replicas and derivative ideas of Narkomfin's interior streets, especially the one on its third floor. But for this process of concretization toward a new prime object between the qualities of a street and a building, a novel kind of hypertely needs to be gained. This new quality is to relate the street with more than one floor.

Where the boundary of the street and the hidden floor plates meet on the facade, as at the Spangen, the street and the building have qualities like an urban fabric. Hannes Meyer's Petersschule reveals a quality between the street and the building that is foreign to both. Instead of the street just running horizontally along the facade, it spirals around it vertically. In doing so it connects the ground floor with the first floor. The street becomes partially an extension of the interior spatial volumes and in other parts an exterior extension of the floors as well.

There is one more quality this wrapped street reveals, which is not only that it loses its planar character and becomes a stair in some parts, but that this so-called street bifurcates and connects other parts, like the roof, as well. This topological quality is essential, since its distinguishes this particular process of concretization from that of spiralled street-buildings like the Guggenheim Museum in New York.

5. Carpenter Center for Visual Arts, Cambridge, Mass., United States, 1961

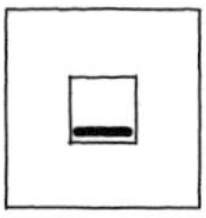

FIGURE 75. A STREET THROUGH A BUILDING

The contribution of the Carpenter Center to the present concretization can be summarized by the fact that the street literally enters into the core of the building. The Carpenter unifies the street and the floor in a twofold manner. First, the street—tuned toward a ramp, in which the planar continuity of the street is unified with the vertical directionality of the stair—runs here through the middle of the building volume. It extends the street mesh of the city into the inner core of the building. This topological outside-inside condition tunes every floor to contain the virtual potential to be, effectively, the ground floor. Crucially, this potential exists not just on the perimeter but at every point on the floor plate, since the building can now be entered anywhere. Second, the interior floors are connected with a ramp as well, meaning that every point on each floor plate has the potential to be connected to every other point on a different floor. The Carpenter Center thus tunes the floor, such that every location on each floor, independent of its hierarchy within the building, has the same potentiality as the ground floor, and every location on each of these "ground floors" can be connected to every other location on each other floor.

6. Palais des congrès, Strasbourg, France, 1964

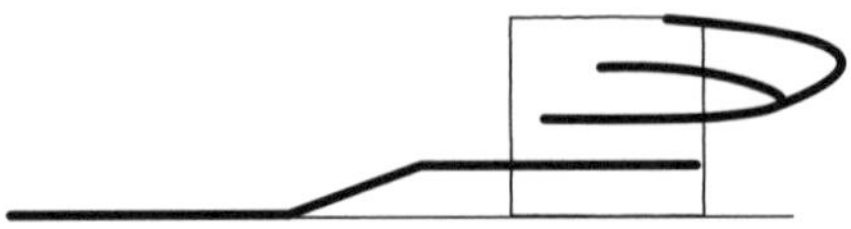

FIGURE 76. A STREET AS A PART AND EXTENSION OF A FLOOR OF A BUILDING

Le Corbusier's Carpenter Center erases the distinction between the two abstract forms of the street and the floors of a building by demonstrating that the inner qualities inherent in their forms as well as in their expressions can be unified at every particular location within the building. In his project for the Palais des congrès in Strasbourg, we a new emerging spatial element that fuses all those qualities. Here multiple ramps enter the building on multiple levels. There is not just one entrance, but many. One particular floor-like ramp takes off from the urban ground and unites with the third floor of the building. There, it expands and bifurcates horizontally, one of the branches wrapping inward while the other extends outward as a giant outdoor ramp before curving back toward the building and again bifurcating, with one of its branches turning back toward the third floor while the other continues upward and unites with the smooth curve of the roof of the building. Although none of the drawings of this project include any cars, the whole topological unity is similar to a parking garage. United in this continuum are a multiplicity of floor expressions: a corridor, a gridded path, a courtyard square, a balcony, a ramp, a staircase, an escalator, a gallery, an arcade, or simply a *plan libre* hosting rooms of all kinds. This unification of many hypertelic qualities in one spatial expression gives rise to the emergence of a new prime object.

7. Fundação Iberê Camargo, Porto Alegre, Brazil, 2008

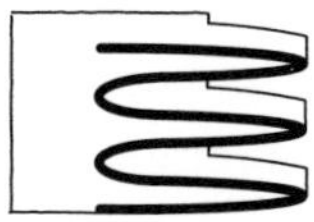

FIGURE 77. A STREET OVER MULTIPLE FLOORS OF A BUILDING

While the Palais des congrès gives access to the qualities of a new emergent prime object, it is only expressed partially throughout the building. Many floors remain untouched by the new qualities described above. While the ramps in particular take on properties of the floor in terms of their size, they are predominantly attached exterior elements, not part of the interiority of the building itself. This missing specialization can be found in Alvaro Siza's building for the Iberê Camargo Foundation in Porto Alegre, Brazil. The building falls out of the linear historical time of our concretization process, as it was built much later than the rest of the projects. But it inherits the signal of a missing specialization needed for the final prime object. What can be found in this project is the unification of a multiplicity of street-like volumes with a multiplication of floors defining together one continuous interiority. Even while parts of the initial abstract forms are visible on the outside, its interior reveals a new unified whole.

Concretization of a New Prime Object: Jussieu Library, Paris, France, 1992

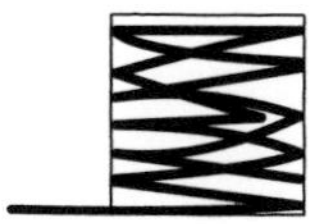

FIGURE 78. A STREET FUSED WITH THE FLOORS OF A BUILDING

The convergence series ends once a new technical object concretizes. In the words of George Kubler, it is the moment when all possibilities have been accelerated or, in Simondon's words, when an associative milieu defines the "condicio sine qua non"[958] for this new individuated object. The concretization of this particular series ends with the Jussieu Library in Paris, designed in 1992 by OMA.[959] The building has lost the quality of being just a street as well as the quality of being just a building with multiple stacked floors. It has turned into a single topological object, an extension of the ground of the city into its interior, and an interior extended to its exterior. It becomes a new type of building, or rather a condensed field,[960] in which any point within the building no longer belongs to one single datum. It is a topological surface, on which every location has its own specificity of being city and building, inside and outside, topological, geographical, architectural, and urban at the same time. It has no set function and is not a measurable space, or *striated space*, to use Deleuzian terms. It is, rather, a field of events, a space of flux, a Deleuzian *smooth space*.[961] The Jussieu Library is perhaps the single clearest example of what at the time was known as "folding in architecture,"[962] or, the prime object of single-surface buildings.

4.4. Concretization Two: In Which a Building Converges with a Public Square

0. The Public Square and Its Building(s)

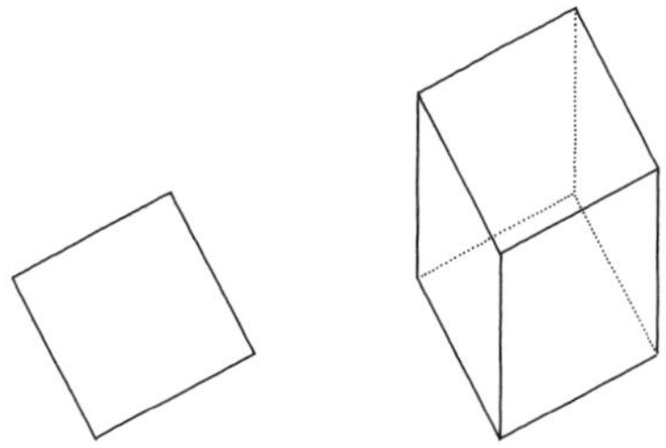

FIGURE 79. A PUBLIC SQUARE AND ITS BUILDING

A point of origin for the process of concretization between the public square and the building might be found in two historical models that often are juxtaposed to define a difference in planning ideas. As Camillo Sitte presents it, this the difference between "The Forum Romanum" and "The Acropolis in the time of Pericles."[963] The former defines the relationship between the square and the building on the basis of buildings enclosing the public space, while in the latter buildings are hosted within the framed space.

1. Basilica & Piazza di Santa Croce, Florence, 13th to 15th century

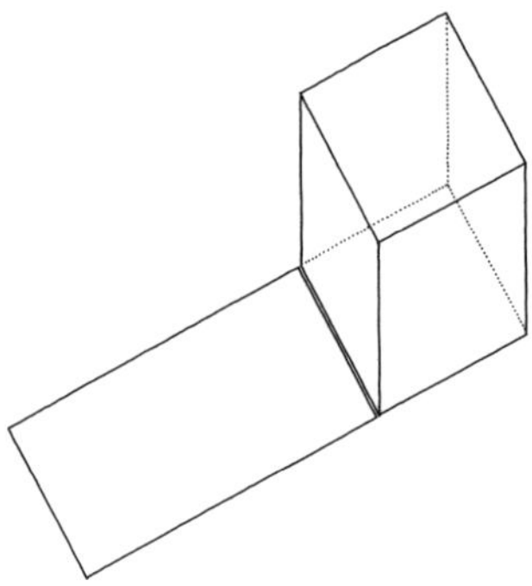

FIGURE 80. A PUBLIC SQUARE AND ITS BUILDING

As Sitte once pointed out, there was no better place than the podium of the Temple of Jupiter from which to oversee the public spectacle of Pompeii's Forum. Sitte's observation hints toward the notion that at a certain moment in the history of the relationship between the building and the square, the randomly oriented buildings started to specialize their directionality. Perhaps what Sitte saw in the Temple of Jupiter is what he explained later about the layout of the Basilica di Santa Croce and the Piazza di Santa Croce in Florence, where the geometry of the facade of the basilica is merged with the geometry of plan of the piazza. They are congruent, the short edge of the piazza fused with the width of the facade. The outline of the plan of the square can be rotated up vertically to define the bounding box of the building, while the outline of the basilica can be rotated down horizontally to mark the length of the piazza. At the time, this fusion between a plan and an elevation produced a novel performative experience in which tall churches could be experienced perspectively through deep plazas. Such settings increased in the baroque period when palace designs would include their own framed space in front of the building. The relational qualities were the same, but the effect was radically different, as horizontal baroque palazzi demanded wide and shallow forecourts.[964]

2. Seagram Building, New York City, United States, 1958 & Centre Pompidou, Paris, 1971–77

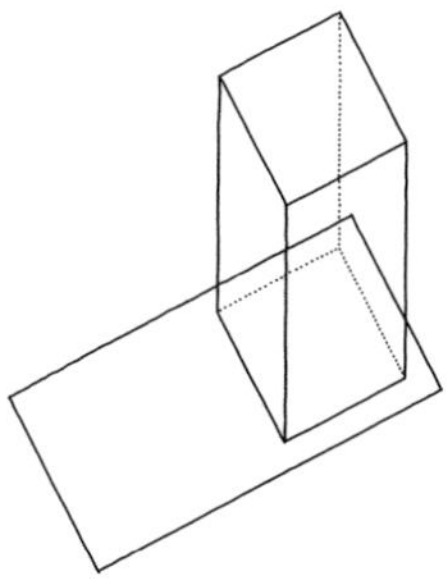

FIGURE 81. A PUBLIC SQUARE AS A PLINTH FOR A BUILDING

From the specialized directionality between the building and the square, the fusion of their common territory begins. At this moment the process toward a new prime architectural object could bifurcate into two different series. Perhaps it is due to the different sociopolitical milieus[965] that we can find two spatial models of how this common territory is defined, even while the hypertelic elements stay the same. As we can see in both the Seagram Building in New York and the Centre Pompidou in Paris, the territorial perimeter, the outline that unites the building and the public square, becomes articulated by a height difference between the ground of the common territory and the rest of the city. At Seagram this articulation is tuned toward a plinth, while at Pompidou the height difference is sunk into the ground: a negative plinth. This negative plinth may cause its own process of concretization, but it is the former case that gives rise to the process unfolded further here, as its articulation upward allows the common territory to dissociate from the ground and merge into the building.

3. S.R. Crown Hall, Chicago, 1950–56 & An Anonymous Campus Building, University of Innsbruck, Austria, 1966

At the entrance of Crown Hall, the territorial plinth becomes reformulated as a platform. A public ground-plate in between the common ground of the campus and the building, this specialization of the public square as a singular, floating mini-square seems to have

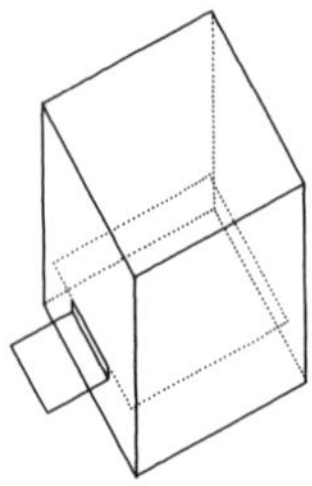

FIGURE 82. A SQUARE BECOMING A FLOOR OF A BUILDING

been necessary in order for the public square to merge into its adjacent building. We can find such a fusion of the floating public square with the ground floor of a building in an anonymous building on the campus of the University of Innsbruck. In this multiple-story building, the public square partially replaces the ground floor, slicing into it from the outside. As seen in section, the square does not fully replace the floor. It takes only as much of the floor as is needed for its public performance, while one third of its area remains on the exterior. The effect of such an insertion of the public square into the building is that this previously floating plate now carries two public spheres within its one single platform. One of these is the articulated interior volume of the platform area inside of the building, while the other is the volume of the outdoor part of the platform covered by the cantilever of the building.

4. Piranesi's Carceri, 1750 & UFA Cinema Center, Dresden, Germany, 1998

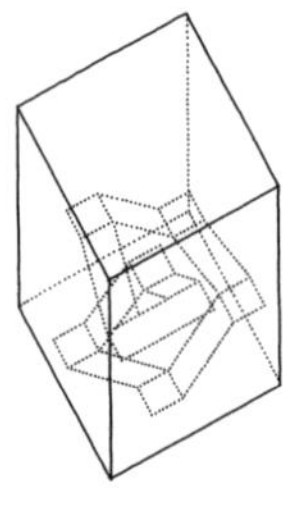

FIGURE 83. PUBLIC CIRCULATION MEETS A BUILDING VOLUME

The hypertelic qualities of this emergent interior public square lead it to take on three-dimensionality and to no longer be exclusively a horizontal space of circulation. The result is a new kind of interiority, which can take on the characteristics of a multiplicity of urban experiences. Once within the building, the internal necessity of the public square demands it to perform as a dynamic urban space of flows, but in the vertical direction. In order to fuse the qualities of urban movement into the spatial volume of the building, something as simple as vertical, volumetric extrusion with some kind of escape staircases would not sufficiently provide the circulation patterns of the public urban square. Rather, it is necessary to bend the multiplicity of urban flows vertically to form a new volumetric public sphere. The lobby of the UFA Cinema Center in Dresden is just such a tuned three-dimensional urban plaza. What can be found in this interior public space is the fusion of a rhizomatic pattern of circulation with a multiplicity of destinations. The result is a new kind of public volume, a space similar to the one we can find in Piranesi's *Carceri d'invenzione* etchings of imaginary prisons[966]—a void with multiple ramps, stairs, bridges, and elevators. This new kind of interiority produces a new kind of inner public square, one that is not empty like an urban void, but to the contrary is utterly occupied with objects and full of flows.

5. Ford Foundation Building, New York City, United States, 1968

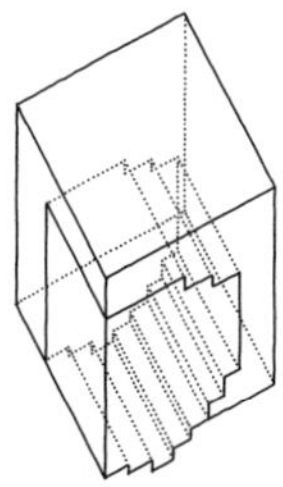

FIGURE 84. A PARK ENTERS THE INTERIOR OF A BUILDING

The Piranesian space of the UFA, although an interior public space, is still articulated formally as a separate volume attached to the building and performs functionally according to a convention that has long been specialized, namely to orchestrate the circulation of people. The Ford Foundation building tunes both of those aspects. Not only does it converge the volume of the building and the volume of the public square into one unified entity, it also fuses its interiority with a radically new public function: the urban oasis.

Having already done so with their directional, territorial, and spatial properties, here for the first time in this process of concretization the two objects, building and public square, have merged their different volumetric properties as well. A slightly blobby, spherical void[967] and a L-shaped stack of stepped floor plates form what appears from the outside a unified cube. Both volumes partially fuse their envelopes to become a new whole of which both share the same amount of cubic air. The functional specialization at this stage is the fusion of the public interior with the urban program of the park, resulting in what I am calling the urban oasis. The public sphere tunes the function of urban circulation by filling its void with an urban program that was previously unknown to buildings. This is not Le Corbusier's garden on the roof. The building has fused with its antithesis and allowed it to enter into its core.

6. Westin Bonaventure Hotel, Los Angeles, California, 1976

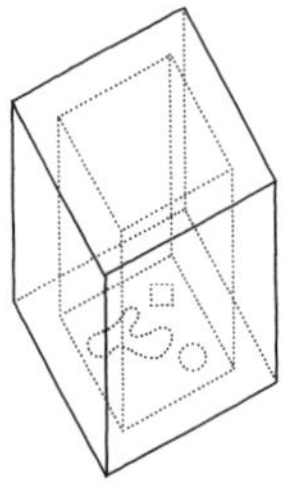

FIGURE 85. A CITY UNDER A SINGLE ROOF

The above specializations have given rise to a multiplicity of urban functions within this special public interiority. As already described in the previous chapter, the city under a single roof merges all functions surrounding the historical inner-city square on the inside of the building. The Bonaventure Hotel in Los Angeles, perhaps the best articulated representative of the city under a single roof, shows how the compression of public activities such as eating, shopping, swimming, strolling, "nature-gazing" at an indoor pond, or people watching from spectacular elevators can be unified within a gigantic common void. The hyperspace that Jameson observed in the Bonaventure emerged through this fusion of an urban piazza with a building, and it remained unknown, or inaccessible, not only to the discipline of architecture but to the building's occupants as well.

At this juncture it is important to point out that the present process of concretization also made a new legal space tangible—specifically, a public space that is privately controlled. It is the associated milieu of the neoliberal economy, as Simondon would say, which has individuated this particular prime object of architecture.

Concretization of a New Prime Bbject: The Lloyd's Building, London, England, 1986

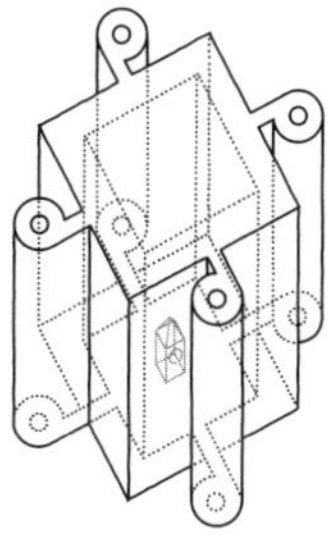

FIGURE 86. COMPLETION OF THE NEW PRIME OBJECT THROUGH THE BENEDICTINE BLESSING

The concretization would be finished here if not for one building, which, in addition to the formal and functional qualities of the public square, fuses with its machinic behavior as well. The Lloyd's building in London converges each of its architectural elements with an equivalent urban component of a medieval square. If we take the generic plan of this atrium building and place it next to a plan view of the Piazza Navona in Rome or Piazza del Campo in Siena, we can easily see such fusion. The center of the plan with the rectangular void of the atrium has fused with the qualities of the public space of the city. The open-plan floor-plates around this void are not merely stacked floors but rather carry similar properties as the buildings surrounding an urban piazza. This fusion can be seen especially from the outside, where the whole massing surrounding the atrium space consists of what looks like a multiplicity of high-rise buildings. The most intriguing aspect of this convergence of a building and a medieval urban fabric happens with the staircases placed on the outside of those built volumes. This strange spiraling vertical circulation space is not just an egress. It fuses with the medieval street pattern and its meandering shape, leading back toward the inner center of trade, just as the streets from the countryside intersect at the medieval marketplace in the city center.

With its metal cladding the building hints to the outside of a kind of machine aesthetic. What is really machinic is not its look, however, but its operational apparatus, which is indicated by the Lutine Bell hung from the rostrum of the ground-floor Underwriting Room, the clock on top visible from vantages throughout the atrium. Regardless of the particular meaning of this bell for the Lloyd's insurance company,[968] one cannot deny its functional symbolism: the fusion of a monastastic mode of behavior with the daily operations within the building. To recall Mumford on the monastery's significance in the history of the city:

> The order and regularity that was introduced into the monks' day—with every office performed in due succession at stated intervals, the seven 'canonical hours'—was timed and paced by the hour-glass, the sun-dial, and eventually, the clock. From the monastery, this time-keeping habit spread back to the marketplace, where in the classic era it had perhaps originated: so that from the fourteenth century on a whole town would time its activities to the ringing of the tower clock's bells.[969]

What has been fused into the Lloyd's building, then, is not just a nostalgic ship's bell, but rather the regularities and efficiencies with which the cloisters laid way to the mechanization of life in the city and specifically, as Mumford concludes, to its capitalist organization.[970]

4.5. Concretization Three: In Which a Building Converges with a Ground

0. A Building and Its Ground

FIGURE 87. A BUILDING ON THE GROUND

The origin point of a concretization process in which the ground merges with the building might begin with a diagram in which a building is placed on or anchored to the existing natural terrain. For while the cave was a geological fold inward and the house in the trees a biological fold outward, both still were modifications of the ground itself. The technicity, to use Simondon's term, of how the building came to be placed on the ground has its own concretization processes. Alberti argues in *De Re Aedificatoria* that the building needs a platform from which to extrude its walls.[971] To reach Palladio's Villa Rotonda, one must first climb a huge staircase to arrive at the platform where the house with its loggias is located.[972] Ledoux employed negative and positive extrusions of the ground to host nearly all his buildings.[973] And of course there are the buildings of Mies van der Rohe, which lead perhaps to the individuation of the emergent architectural element of the plinth. All these examples, however, still belong to a formal sequence of the ground itself. With the plinth there may have arisen a new prime object, but this element as well as the building still appear in their abstract forms. Thus, while the projects might be useful to understanding the uniqueness of the city on a single roof, they do not necessarily belong to its process of concretization. It is Le Corbusier's Maison Dom-ino with which we can mark perhaps the first building to start this convergence series of building and ground.

1. Les maisons "Dom-ino," 1914[974]

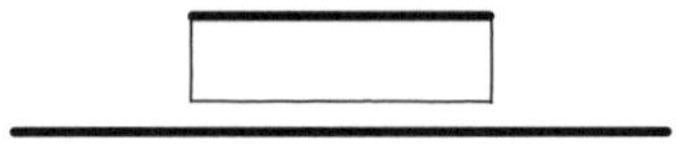

FIGURE 88. REAPPEARANCE OF THE LOST GROUND ON THE ROOF OF A BUILDING

The roof garden as one of the five points of Le Corbusier's new architecture might be the first fusion of a building element with the natural ground. In a diagram of his five points,[975] Le Corbusier shows the relationship between a building and its ground through his proposed roof gardens. The pre–Maison Dom-ino section in the diagram expresses the building as sunken into the ground, basically a carved-out hole that is filled with a building. The Maison Dom-ino section suggests the opposite, placing the building on *pilotis* to elevate it off the ground. Furthermore, it implies that the lost ground on which the building stands becomes replaced on the roof—the ground fuses its properties into the roof of the building. This convergence of the lost ground with the building is visualized in Le Corbusier's diagram through the sectional continuation of plants from the ground around the building up onto the roof. From an aerial photograph, such a building would perhaps not even be identifiable. What would be identifiable are new forms of plants or ecologies, due to the artificiality of the constructed soil.

2. House of Industry, Moscow, Russia, 1929

In a 1929 project called House of Industry, the Russian architect Ivan Leonidov tuned the potentiality of this new ground in a twofold manner. First, he introduced onto the roof not a private garden but public greenery: a park. This tuning of the

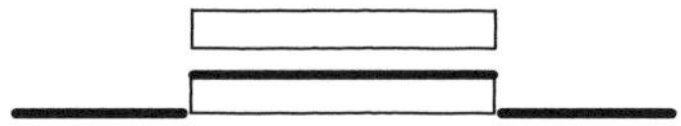

FIGURE 89. FUSION OF THE NEW GROUND WITH A PARK

function allowed for public programs on this datum. Like all the other programs on each floor of this office building, the park was an *antithetical zone*: " an area," as Koolhaas writes about the project, "for non work that included a swimming pool, a sauna and high-pressure shower, a kiosk for news and announcements, a lavish arrangement of chaises-longues, a small library, an acoustic console, and a TV-like screen."[976] Secondly, and not unimportant for our convergence series, Leonidov's placement of this new ground hints toward its own distinct reading. Rather than being formally in the middle of the building, this new ground can be seen as embedded between buildings, since spaces of inhabitation emerge below and above its new public terrain.

3. Casa Malaparte, Isle of Capri, Italy, 1937

FIGURE 90. MERGING OF THE NEW GROUND AND ITS NATURAL ORIGIN

There is perhaps no architectural representation to better depict this fusion of the new ground on the roof of a building with its surrounding natural terrain as the 1961 film *Le Mépris* by Jean-Luc Godard, which was filmed at Adalberto Libera's Casa Malaparte on Capri. What emerges in the process of concretization between a building and its site is a new architectural element, which links the roof back to nature. It is the floor plate of the roof itself that folds like stair downward to the ground. This is not simply a stair attached onto a facade that climbs up to the roof, as in Le Corbusier's Maison Citrohan from 1920.[977] Crucially, at Casa Malaparte the convergence works in both other directions. The property of the stair also merges into the existing terrain of the island, forming for the first time in our convergence series a continuous connection between the building and the natural terrain, which is not an internal extension onto the roof garden but an extension of two kind of exteriorities. The effect, as we see in a scene of Godard's film, is a new kind of promenade whereby a couple can go from the new built datum directly down the stairs and into the wilderness of the island.

4. Walkable Department Store, St. Louis, MO, USA, 1963

FIGURE 91. THE WALKABLE BUILDING

That emergent stepped connection between the building and the ground tuned its hypertelic qualities with Hans Hollein's proposal for a walkable department store in St. Louis. What was a link between two objects becomes an autonomous object itself and gives form to a new kind of building: a building as a walkable topography. If Godard had used Hollein's sketch of the Begehbares Kaufhaus as the stage for his movie, Brigitte Bardot and Michel Piccoli wouldn't walk up onto and down off of a building, but on the building itself. Hollein once used a formal sequence of his own to describe this new kind of building. In studies titled "digging, piling up, forming,"[978] he demonstrates how architecture's relationship to the ground changes in each cultural area: from digging into the ground to make a place to the liberation of the building from the ground to produce a new public space underneath. The walkable department store saw its further development in Hollein's 1972 Städtische Museum Abteiberg[979] in Mönchengladbach, Germany, defining the end of his series. Hollein's end point articulates for the first time the true fusion of our two main abstract elements. The outcome is a building as stepped topography, or as Hollein would call it, an inclined building.

5. The Oakland Museum, Oakland, CA, USA, 1968

FIGURE 92. BUILDING AS GROUND

Kevin Roche and John Dinkeloo's Oakland Museum project exploits the precedent of the building as a walkable topography, and in the process adds to our convergence series both a formal and a functional specialization. On a functional level, the building is not just a walkable object. Due it its walkability, in fact, it fuses back into its accessible topography features of the building itself, in particular, entrances and windows. What we find in the section of the project is that entry into the building is guaranteed through the walkable topography. Door-like holes emerge in the topography where the inner floors bifurcate and unite with the modulations of the exterior landscape. The same occurs with the windows, which are not placed in walls but appear as cuts in the topographical contour lines. On a formal level, the building has submerged itself into the ground. From the outside no building-like entity is recognizable. The building is embedded between two surfaces resulting from the bifurcation of the given urban ground of the city. The building as a figurative object disappears and in its place the building as ground appears.

This new kind of building-as-ground reproduces from this moment onward into a multiplicity of replicas. Those replicas represent a formal sequence on its own, of which the best articulations include the complete works of Zaha Hadid, starting with the unbuilt project for the Peak Leisure Club in Hong Kong from 1982; Foreign Office Architects' 1995 Yokohama International Port Terminal in Yokohama, Japan; and many projects by Peter Eisenman, such as the City of Culture of Galicia in Santiago de Compostela, Spain and especially his Rebstockpark Masterplan in Frankfurt am Main, Germany.

FIGURE 93. BUILDING AS A FIELD OF GROUNDS. EXAMPLE: THE PEAK PROJECT BY ZAHA HADID, 1992.

FIGURE 94. BUILDING AS A BIFURCATED GROUND. EXAMPLE: THE YOKOHAMA PORT TERMINAL BY FOREIGN OFFICE ARCHITECTS, 1995.

FIGURE 95. BUILDING AS A FOLDED GROUND. EXAMPLE: REBSTOCKPARK MASTERPLAN BY PETER EISENMAN ARCHITECTS, 1992.

FIGURE 96. BUILDING AS A TOPOLOGICAL GROUND. EXAMPLE: SKETCH BY PETER TRUMMER. 1996

6. Milliron's Shopping Centre, Westchester, Los Angeles, USA, 1950

FIGURE 97. FUSION OF THE STREETS WITH A BUILDING

As early as 1950, at Milliron's Department Store in Los Angeles designed by Victor Gruen,[980] the new ground on the roof of the building fused with the function of the street. At Million's, it was not a stepped plate that linked the building with the urban terrain but two gigantic ramps, which gave access to a parking lot on top of the shopping mall. Gruen's diagrams of the evolution of the shopping mall[981] offer the speculation that all floors of a building have the potential to fuse with the qualities of the street. Gruen's diagrams show the urban fabric bifurcating into the multiple floor plates, similarly to the Oakland Museum. Instead of just giving access to pedestrians, the shopping center tunes all floor areas to carry all kinds of urban flows. He would apply this speculation to reality in many of his projects, like the early-1970s design for Center Glatt in Switzerland. As we can see in the model and the section for the project,[982] the floors are entered directly from the highway, its flows transforming into the parking garage's organization, from whence they mutate into flows of pedestrians, and then continue by reversing outward: the shoppers turn into drivers and get spit out on the other side back into the city fabric. Malls such as this do not just carry qualities of the urban ground on the outside. They specialize the whole building, on all floors, to fulfill the conditions of the city—namely, to provide a space of circulation and give access to spaces of inhabitation.

7. The "Hilberseimer" Buildings of Chongqing, China

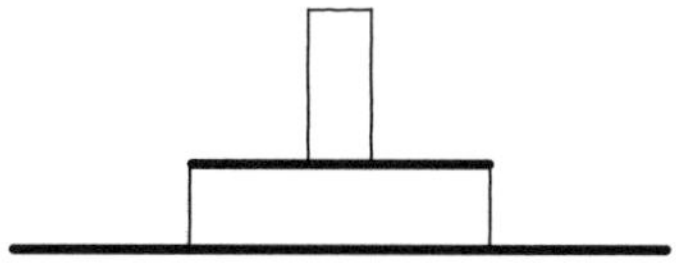

FIGURE 98. A BUILDING ON TOP OF THE BUILDING WITH A STREET

What Hilberseimer once proposed as a visionary idea for a vertical city in the 1920s is realized today in the Chinese city of Chongqing in Sichuan province. Known for its hilly topography, the city is full of infrastructural bridges and streets, between and through the middle of buildings. Perhaps its most famed example is the Liziba Railroad Station.[983] Line 2 of the Chongqing Metro stops in the middle of a nineteen-story residential tower, the station occupying the sixth through eighth floors.

Another building, a four-story multifunctional structure, not only has a roof that is fused with a street, but it has also tuned it to become a stepped topography. What the building adds to this convergence series is that it specializes its rooftop ground to host an entire building with apartments and balconies on it.[984] There is nothing strange about this building. The natural terrain of the hills extends onto the roof and continues its functions as an urban fabric. It should come as no surprise, as argued in the present book, that the building's architect is unknown or that, perhaps, whoever built it has never heard or read anything about Hilberseimer. For it is the city as a milieu and its element of the (back)ground that give rise to such technical entities.

8. Competition for the Tiergarten Quarter, Berlin, Germany, 1973[985]

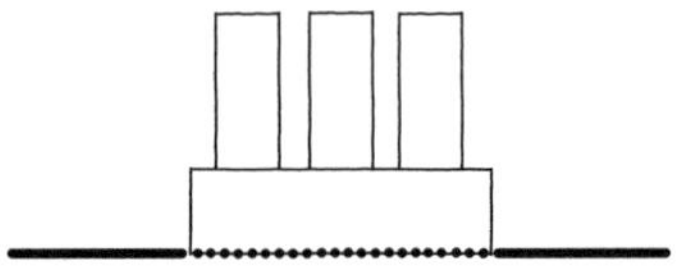

FIGURE 99. FUSION OF HIGH-RISE TOWERS TO A BUILDING

In his sketch for Ungers' competition entry for the Landwehrkanal Tiergartenviertel in Berlin in 1973, Rem Koolhaas accelerates what OMA presented in their work for New York. While in their drawing of the City of the Captive Globe[986] a building covering a whole city block acts as a plinth for another hosting one "world," the proposal for Berlin projects the idea that a building can be the site of an entire segment of a city. The drawing shows a series of towers laid out on the roof of a building, with spaces in between and a boardwalk edged by railings from which to watch the city below. The lower floors of this city are curiously enclosed within a glass-like envelope. This new pedestrian area between the buildings looks more like a shopping mall or hotel lobby than urban streets. Thus, while the project formally fuses an entire urban fabric with the roof of the building, it does not contain all the functionalities of the urban fabric. This last hypertelic quality becomes specialized with the final outcome of this process of concretization: in today's *emergent cities on a single building.*

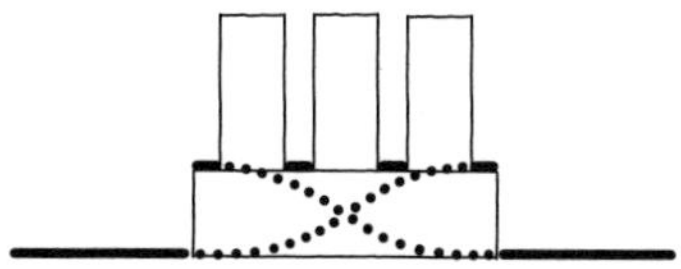

FIGURE 100. THE CITY ON A SINGLE BUILDING

As already described above in regard to the city on a single roof, the final outcome of the fusion of the building with the ground of the city is that the *entire building* acts as the urban infrastructure on which a city can be built. What takes place in this final fusion is not only that the building as a ground carries all the urban qualities within, but also that a complete prime object with radically new qualities emerges. In particular, this is the legal fact that a constructed real estate[987] can act as a common ground for a new kind of real estate.

A new overdetermined technical being emerges with its own hypertelic qualities, a new architectural prime object with ever-emergent replicas.

[835] Kostof refers here to Figure 3.2 in his book, which is a bird's eye view of Hamadan in Iran. Kostof, Spiro. *A History of Architecture - Settings and Rituals*. Revisions by Greg Castillo, Original Drawings by Richard Tobias, New York, Oxford: Oxford University Press, 1995, 45.

[836] Ibid., 43.

[837] Simondon, Gilbert (2017), 29.

[838] Ibid.

[839] "Greek Theatre." Accessed September 24, 2021. https://www.worldhistory.org/Greek_Theatre/

[840] Kostof, Spiro (1995), 153.

[841] Caves, Roger, W. *Encyclopedia of the City*, 1st Edition, London and New York: Routledge Taylor & Francis Group, 2005, 7.

[842] Ibid., 7.

[843] Ibid., 3.

[844] See: Le Corbusier. *Vers une Architecture*. 11th Edition. (First published 1923). Collection de "L'Esprit Nouveau." Paris: Crès, 1925, 182. See also: the location of the holy district in Olympia with its concave topography. In Benevolo, Leonardo (1990), 99.

[845] See: Plan of Milet with the underlying contour lines of the topography. In Benevolo, Leonardo (1990), 147.

[846] See: Image of Pirene with the urban streets as stairways of irregular steps. In Ibid., 152-153.

[847] Kubler, George (1962).

[848] Simondon, Gilbert (2017), 29.

[849] The formal sequence might be fictional, but not so from the point of view of its function. The ecclesia, or assembly, which gathered for political debates and decision making, moved from the Agora to the Pnyx and from there to the Theater of Dionysos. See Lawrence, Arnold Walter, and Richard Allan Tomlinson. *Greek Architecture*. New Haven, London: Yale University Press, 1996, 205-211.

[850] I want to recall here that Kubler's idea of the formal sequence was not to reinforce the idea of reading the history of an artifact through a biological metaphor—that is, as a chronological historical development. Prime objects, including what I am here calling individuated architectural objects, instead appear for him intermittently. The agora, the Pnyx, or the theater thus can be expressed according to Kubler's reading of the history of artifact through a physical metaphor—namely, that of electrodynamics. Such a reading of history would mean that all three Greek typologies would potentially incorporate signals from other artifacts, independently from each other and independent of any sequential time. Each typology has it own "historical time," which for Kubler "is intermittent and variable. Every action is more intermittent than it is continuous, and the intervals between actions are infinitely variable in duration and content." See: Kubler, George. *The Shape of Time. Remarks on the History of Things*. New Haven, London: Yale University Press, 1962, 13.

[851] Benevolo, Leonardo. *The European City. The Making of Europe*. Series Editor: Jacques Le Goff. Translated from the Italian by Carl Ipsen. Oxford UK, Cambridge USA: 1993, 2.

[852] This is understood as the difference between the two kinds of Agora: the Archaic and the Ionic. See: https://www.britannica.com/topic/agora

[853] It would seem that the Greek polis's internal contingency was to produce a more compact or tight space, as the translation of the Greek word Pnyx suggests: tightly packed together. See https://www.stoa.org/athens/sites/pnyx.html

[854] See: Article "Ecclesia ancient Greek assembly" in Britannica. Accessed September 24, 2021. https://www.britannica.com/topic/Ecclesia-ancient-Greek-assembly

[855] See: drawing of the three phases of the Pnyx in https://archaeology-travel.com/greece/athens-and-attica/pnyx-hill/ Accessed September 24, 2021.

[856] See: the enforced cut in the natural rook with the embedded bema (speaker platform). Accessed September 24, 2021. https://www.stoa.org/athens/sites/pnyx.html

[857] In its first phase, the edge of the audience area was hardly defined, while in the third phase of the Pnyx, the edge of the audience was delineated by a wall, thus becoming tuned more and more toward the form of the theater. See: https://archaeology-travel.com/greece/athens-and-attica/pnyx-hill/ Accessed September 24, 2021.

[858] See: Fig 8.33. In Kostof, Spiro (1995), 186.

[859] Arnold Walter Lawrence, in his writing on open structures in Greek cities, indicates that the Pnyx was the prototype for the theater. See: Lawrence, Arnold Walter, and Richard Allan Tomlinson. *Greek Architecture*. New Haven, London: Yale University Press, 1996, 205.

[860] Ibid., 205.

[861] Ibid., 206.

[862] "The ancient Greek theatre is often quoted as an example of 'democratic' seating. Only the first rows were reserved for priests and public officials. Yet there was some kind of organisation in the audience space. The central part of the auditorium, right behind the seat for priest of Dionysos, was used by guests of honour and at the sides of the auditorium foreigners and latecomers were seated." In http://www.kvl.cch.kcl.ac.uk/THEATRON/theatres/sabbioneta/assets/text/sabtxt08.html Accessed September 24, 2021.

[863] Benevolo, Leonardo (1990), 100.

[864] See: Figure 7.5 In Kostof, Spiro (1995), 142.

[865] See: Pevsner, Nikolaus. *A History of Building Types*. Princeton, New Jersey: Princeton University Press, 1979, 63-90.

[866] I use the term *city on a single roof* as an overt allusion to Raymond Hood's "City Under a Single Roof." The difference being that the building does not host a city in its interior, as in the case of Hood, but instead becomes the new ground for the city.

[867] Article "Rooftop villas are legal, officials say," by Li Yao in Beijing and Feng Zhiwei in Changsha (China Daily) 2012. https://www.chinadaily.com.cn/china/2012-08/16/content_15679402.htm Accessed September 24, 2021.

[868] Article "Villas on roof of mall waiting in the wings," by Zhao Lei in Beijing and Wen Xinzheng in Changsha (China Daily) 2013. https://www.chinadaily.com.cn/china/2013-08/06/content_16872572.htm Accessed September 24, 2021.

[869] For images of villas on the rooftop of the shopping mall in Hengyang, see https://www.alamy.com/villas-are-seen-on-the-rooftop-of-a-shopping-mall-in-hengyang-central-chinas-hunan-province-30-july-2013-the-developer-who-built-25-villas-on-the--image263752009.html Accessed September 24, 2021.

[870] These streets seem not to be for cars, just for circulation.

[871] Article "Suburb in the sky: how Jakartans built an entire village on top of a mall,"

by Kate Lamb, The Guardian, August 2019. https://www.theguardian.com/cities/2019/aug/05/suburb-in-the-sky-how-jakartans-built-an-entire-village-on-top-of-a-mall Accessed September 24, 2021.

872 See "Cosmo Park Apartment for Rent/Sale)" in Jakarta-Apartment.net. https://www.jakarta-apartment.net/category/apartment/cosmo-park/ Accessed September 24, 2021.

873 For images of SHUM YIP UpperHills LOFT in Shenzhen, see https://www.archdaily.com/919939/shum-yip-upperhills-loft-urbanus and https://www.designboom.com/architecture/urbanus-shum-yip-upper-hills-loft-shenzhen-china-06-26-2019/ Accessed September 24, 2021.

874 See: Bernoulli, Hans. *Die Stadt und ihr Boden*. (Original 1946, Verlag Architektur AG, Erlenbach-Zürich). Birkhäuser Architektur Bibliothek. Basel, Berlin, Boston: Birkhäuser Verlag, 1991, 14-17.

875 See Image: "General Plan of Riverside" by Olmsted, Vaux & CO. Landscape Architects, 1869. https://www.olmstedsociety.org/wp-content/uploads/2008/11/general-plan-of-riverside.jpg Accessed September 24, 2021and Adams, Thomas. *Metropolitan America/ The Design of Residential Areas-basic Considerations, Principles, and Methods*. Harvard City Planning Studies VI, (originally published by Cambridge: Harvard University Press, 1934) reprint New York: Arno Press, 1974, 201-219.

876 See: Koolhaas, Rem (1978), 69.

877 "Les 5 points d'une architecture nouvelle." In Le Corbusier & Pierre, Jeanneret. *Oeuvre Complète Volume 1, 1910–1929*. Zürich: Les Editions d'Architecture Artemis, 1964, 128-129. Corbusier's five points were triggered by his development of the Maison Dom-Ino system diagram. See ibid., 21.

878 Despite OMA's use of city metaphors for their hyperbuilding concept—towers = streets, parks = horizontal elements, building volumes = districts, diagonal buildings = boulevards—it still belongs to the same the diagram of stacked buildings that remained unchanged since Hilberseimer or Lissitzky. See: https://www.oma.com/projects/hyperbuilding Accessed September 24, 2021.

879 Google, Facebook, and Amazon, to name just the three most notable of such companies.

880 I refer here to Simondon's definition of the ensemble as one of three distinct kinds of technical object: the element, the individual, and the ensemble. In Simondon, Gilbert (2017), 53-81.

881 The quote by Benevolo is perhaps the single most important disciplinary antecedent of the present book. The wall of the city can be seen as one of the first originations of architecture, whereby a quality of the city converges into an architectural object. In Benevolo, Leonardo (1993), 2.

882 Benevolo continues: "One need only recall the common structure of the temple and the entombment in Egypt, both characterised by multiple protective layers to ward off a hostile and feared outside world." Ibid., 2.

883 See: Aureli, Pier Vittorio (2008), 91–120.

884 Aureli, Pier Vittorio. *The Possibility of an Absolute Architecture*, Cambridge, Massachusetts: The MIT Press, 2011, ix-x. Aureli gives a further explication of the word separation when he writes, "I use absolute not in the conventional sense of 'purity' but in its original meaning as something being resolutely itself after being 'separated' from its other. In the pursuit of the possibility of an absolute architecture, the other is the space of the city, its extensive organization, and its government." Ibid., ix.

885 See Image of "A Greek House in Delos", Book VI, Chapter 7. In Vitruvius. *The*

Ten Books on Architecture. Edited by Morris H. Morgan. Unabridged and unaltered republication of the 1914 1st Edition. New York: Dover, 1960, 187.

[886] See image of plan and interior perspective of "Vitruvius Basilica at Fano", Book V, Chapter 1. In Ibid., 135.

[887] Book I, Chapter IX. In Alberti, Leon Battista. *The Ten Books of Architecture*: The 1755 Leoni Edition. Translated by James Leoni. New York: Dover Publications, 1986, 13.

[888] See: Ponte dei Sospiri in Venice: https://en.wikipedia.org/wiki/Bridge_of_Sighs Accessed September 24, 2021.

[889] See: Steven Holl's Bridge of Houses projects (1979-1982), especially his Bridge of Houses for Manhattan. https://socks-studio.com/2015/04/19/steven-holls-bridge-of-houses-1979-1982/ Accessed September 24, 2021.

[890] Original German: "*Die Verselbständigung der Teile* ist das wichtigste Ergebnis des architektonischen Regenerationsprozesses vom Ausgang des 18. Jahrhunderts. Das neue Prinzip der Autonomie duldet nicht, daß architektonische Gebilde von fremden, außerarchitektonischen Gesetzen beherrscht werden." In Kaufmann, Emil. *Von Ledoux bis Le Corbusier - Ursprung und Entwicklung der Autonomen Architektur*. (Unchanged reprint of the 1933 Edition published in Verlag Dr. Rolf Passer, Wien/Leipzig). Stuttgart: Verlag Gerd Hatje, 1985, 43.

[891] See floor plans of House "21" by Louis Ambroise Dubut. In Ibid., 57.

[892] Original quote: "Die neue Fügung der Teile bedeutet den freien Zusammenschluss von Individuen, die ihr Eigenleben nicht z opfern brauchen, deren Form nur dem eigenen Zweck gehorcht. Ihr inneres Gesetz bestimmt ihre Gestalt. So ist der neue antibarocke Grundriss zu verstehen, so ergibt sich eine völlig neue Beziehung aller Teile, der Teile untereinander und der Teile zum Ganzen, bis es am Ende der logisch fortschreitenden Entwicklung keine Teile mehr gibt, sondern nur unabhängige Einheiten." In Kaufmann, Emil (1985), 43.

[893] See Ibid., 3-23.

[894] See Ibid., 17-19.

[895] Kaufmann refers in particular to Claude Nicolas Ledoux's 1788 project for a Discount Bank on the rue d'Artois in Paris, a commission of Minister Necker. Ibid.,19.

[896] Original quote: "Im Pavillonsystem gibt es im Grunde keine Teile mehr, es ist ein Verein unabhängiger Elemente. Will man die beiden Kompositionsprinzipien auf knappste Formeln bringen, dann könnte man den Barocken Verband mit den Worten charakterisieren: Ein Teil ist über allen, und dennoch sind alle Teile eins. Den tiefsten Sinn des Pavillon systems aber mag man etwa so umschreiben: *Der Teil ist frei im Rahmen des Ganzen*." Ibid., 19.

[897] See: Simondon, Gilbert (2017), 54.

[898] See, for example, Le Corbusier's five points. "Les 5 points d'une architecture nouvelle" (The 5 points of a new architecture). In Le Corbusier & Pierre, Jeanneret (1964), 128-129.

[899] Ibid., 40-41.

[900] Le Corbusier. *The City of To-Morrow and Its Planning*. (First published in 1929 by Parson & Clarke Ltd. New York). New York: Dover Publications, 1987, 221.

[901] Hilberseimer, Ludwig. "Metropolisarchitecture." In *Ludwig Hilberseimer - Metropolisarchitecture and Selected Essays*, edited by Richard Anderson, GSAPP Books, Columbia University, New York, 2012, 270. Originally published in Hilberseimer, Ludwig. *Großstadtarchitektur*. Die Baubücher, Band 3. Stuttgart: Julius Hoffmann, 1927, 98.

902 Simondon introduced this concept in an unpublished text written in the 1970s, which was finally published in 2006 and later translated into English and published in 2009 in the journal *Parrhesia*. His idea of *open objects*, to understand objects as a network or a rhizome as Deleuze would say, is the more common idea with which Simondon has influenced the architectural discourse. For the present research, however, his idea of a process of concretization from *On the Mode of Existence of Technical Objects* is more relevant to the argument of the origin of new architectural ensembles. See: Simondon, Gilbert. "Technical Mentality." In *Gilbert Simondon: Being and Technology*, edited by Arne De Boever, Alex Murray, and Jon Roffe. Edinburgh: Edinburgh University Press, 2012, 12.

903 Ibid., 14.

904 See Gian Luigi Maffei's critique of Kenneth Frampton's definition of tectonic. In Caniggia, Gianfranco, and Gian Luigi Maffei. *Architectural Composition and Building Typology: Interpreting Basic Building*. Translated by Susan Jane Fraser. Firenze: Alinea Editrice, 2001, 11.

905 See Cataldi, Giancarlo, Gian Luigi Maffei, and Paolo Vaccaro. "Saverio Muratori and the Italian School of Planning Typology." *Urban Morphology*, no. 1, vol. 6, 2002 3–14.

906 See Caniggia, Gianfranco, and Gian Luigi Maffei (2001), 54-56.

907 Ibid., 50-55.

908 Muratori, Saverio, "Studi per una operante storia urbana di Venezia." Roma: Instituto poligrafico dello Stato, Libreria dello Stato, 1960.

909 See Ibid., 106-109, In Pigafetta, Giorgio. *Saverio Muratori Architetto: Teoria e Progetti*. Marsilio, 1990.

910 Ibid., 101.

911 See Caniggia, Gianfranco, and Gian Luigi Maffei (2001), 70-74.

912 Ibid., 75.

913 Ibid., 53.

914 I refer to a methodological approach I have described as population thinking in architecture. See: Trummer, Peter. "Associative Design: From Type to Population." In *Computational Design Thinking*, edited by Sean Ahlquist and Achim Menges. *AD Reader*. Chichester: John Wiley & Sons, 2011, 179-197.

915 Original Italian title: "Schema generale del processo coscienza-realtà (il cosiddetto «tabellone»)." Each of the seven drawings, 29a-g, include captions: a) "Example on the furniture scale: setting up the relationship between typical furniture elements and typical distribution forms." b) "Example on the scale of architecture: systematization of the relationship between typical structures and architectural organisms." c) "Example on the scale of architecture: systematization of the relationship between typical structures and historically determined architectural languages." d) "Example on the urban scale: systematization of the relationship between cell type and building type." e) "Example at the urban scale: systematizing the relationship between building type and building fabric." f) "Example on a territorial scale: systematization of the relationship between the natural constitution of the land and the typical organization of the farm." g) "Example on the territorial scale: systematization of the relationship between typical territorial layouts and historically determined civilisations." In Pigafetta, Giorgio. *Saverio Muratori Architetto: Teoria e Progetti*. Marsilio, 1990, folio insert. My translation.

916 Simondon, Gilbert. "Technical Mentality." In Gilbert Simondon (2012), 13.

917 Regime is a difficult word to translate, as Michael Cuntz mentions in his German translation of Simondon's "Technical Mentality" (Die technische Einstellung). Cuntz

describes regime as a dynamic operation. It is not used as a static idea of political or economical organizations, but rather as simply the operational mode of maintaining and running machines, like to guide or steer their behavior. See footnote 1 in Simondon, Gilbert. "Die technische Einstellung," in *Die technologische Bedingung-Beiträge zur Beschreibung der technischen Welt*. Edited by Erich Hört. Berlin: Suhrkamp Verlag: 2011, 73.

[918] Ibid.

[919] See: Schumacher, Thomas L. "Contextualism: Urban Ideals and Deformations (1971)." In *Theorizing a New Agenda for Architecture: An Anthology of Architectural Theory 1965 - 1995*, edited by Kate Nesbitt, 2nd Edition. New York: Princeton Architectural Press, 1996, 294–306.

[920] Vidler, Anthony. "Reckoning with Art History: Colin Rowe's Critical Vision." In *Reckoning with Colin Rowe: Ten Architects Take Position*, edited by Emmanuel Petit. New York: Routledge, 2015, 42.

[921] Ungers, Oswald M. "He who did not understand the Zeitgeist," in Ibid., 65-66.

[922] Ungers describes the scene of the storming of the final review panel by students at the International Congress in Berlin in 1967. Ibid., 69.

[923] Kwinter, Sanford. "Who's Afraid of Formalism?" In *ANY 7/8, Form Work: Colin Rowe*. Edited by Cynthia C. Davidson and R.E. Somol (1994), 65.

[924] Ibid.

[925] I assume Kwinter intended his argument to point toward even contemporary architects like Greg Lynn, who just used generative computational techniques to produce variations of self-similar objects. See: Ibid., 38-43.

[926] Ibid., 65.

[927] Ibid.

[928] While *poché* literally means the blackened parts within a sectional plan of a building, Bernhard Hoesli gives an elaborate insight into the deeper meaning of the word in his essay "Transparent Form-Organisation as an Instrument of Design," in *Reckoning with Colin Rowe: Ten Architects Take Position*, edited by Emmanuel Petit, 127–137. New York: Routledge, 2015, 136.

[929] See: Simondon, Gilbert (2017), 60-61.

[930] In contrast to the conventional black-and-white representation of urban fabric, in this plan of Wiesbaden the white represents built mass and the black those areas considered as voids.

[931] See Rowe, Colin. "Roma Interrotta Project" with Peter Carl, Judith di Maio, Steven Peterson, in Roma *Interrotta, Incontri Internazionali d'Arte*. Roma: Officina Edizioni 1978, 136-150.

[932] Rowe, Colin and Fred Koetter. *Collage City*. Cambridge, Mass., and London, England: The MIT Press, 1983, 79.

[933] Kwinter, Sanford (1994), 65.

[934] Ibid.

[935] Aureli gives a detailed description of a Natufian dwelling—Shelter 51, Eynan (AinMallaha), Israel—in Aureli, Pier Vittorio. "Life, Abstracted: Notes on the Floor Plan." In *E-Flux Architecture, Architecture and Representation*, October 2017. Accessed September 24, 2021. https://www.e-flux.com/architecture/representation/159199/life-abstracted-notes-on-the-floor-plan/.

[936] See: Figure 2.12. In Kostof, Spiro (1995), 29.

[937] In the English translation the word seat or platform is used to describe the ground on which buildings stand on. See Alberti, Leon Battista.. *The Ten Books of Architecture*: The 1755 Leoni Edition. (Chapter II, Book I) Translated by James Leoni. New York: Dover Publications, 1986, 2. In the German translation the word "Grund (die Baustelle)" is used instead. See: Alberti, Leon Battista. *Zehn Bücher über die Baukunst*: Ins Deutsche übertragen, eingeleitet und mit Anmerkungen und Zeichnungen versehen von Max Theuer. Translated by Max Theuer. The new edition follows the Wien & Leipzig 1912 edition. (Originally published as De re aedificatoria, 1521). Tegernsee: Boer Verlag, 2020, 61.

[938] See: Le Corbusier (1986), 69.

[939] See Unwin, Raymond. *Town Planning in Practice; An Introduction to the Art of Designing Cities and Suburbs*. London: T. Fisher Unwin, 1909.

[940] See "Aerial image, taken 2015, of the incomplete Ascaya development in metropolitan Las Vegas." In Soules, Matthew (2021) 38.

[941] As Rowe and Koetter wrote in their chapter on the "Crisis of the Object": "Ultimately, and in terms of figure-ground, the debate which is here postulated between solid and void is a debate between two models and, succinctly, these may be typified as acropolis and forum." In Rowe, Colin and Fred Koetter (1983), 83.

[942] Shopping malls are a good example of this. Neither dead-end streets nor gaps within a street are allowed, as this form of shopping only works through continuous (or endless) forced circulation.

[943] Benevolo, Leonardo (1990), 654.

[944] See "Plan for Paris (1765)," D.O. Garden Stories, Accessed February 1, 2022, http://images.doaks.org/garden-histories/items/show/166.

[945] As Le Corbusier wrote: "On the roof of the building there is a 1000-yard track on which to run in the fresh air, and there also are the gymnasiums, where instructors would direct parents as well as children; there are sun parlours too, which have proved so successful in the United States in combating tuberculosis." In Le Corbusier (1987), 216.

[946] See: Figure 22-24 "Schema einer Hochhausstadt". In Hilberseimer, Ludwig (1927), 17-19.

[947] Original German quote: "Die Idee, die Arbeitsstätte mit der Wohnstätte in einem Gebäude zu vereinigen, ist nicht neu. Die mittelalterlichen Häuser hatten Werkstätten in Erdgeschoß und Wohnungen in den oberen Geschossen. Dasselbe finden wir auch in manchen großen Hotels. Es ist möglich, in einem Hotel zu wohnen und in ihm zugleich seine Arbeitsstätte zu haben." In Hilberseimer, Ludwig. *Entfaltung einer Planungsidee*. Bauwelt Fundamente 6. Berlin, Frankfurt, Wien: Ullstein Verlag, 1963, 22.

[948] The German title of the project is called "Planning eines Geschäftsviertel." See: fig. 5-7. Ibid., 17-19.

[949] See: Koolhaas, Rem. "Hyperbuilding." In Rem Koolhaas *OMA I: 1996-2006*, edited by Richard C. Levene and Fernando Márquez Cecilia, 60–69. Croquis 131/132. Madrid: El Croquis, 2006.

[950] See: Trummer, Peter. "Pile City." *Offramp*, SCI-Arc, 08 (2014), 64-71.

[951] Simondon, Gilbert (2017), 17-18.

[952] Ibid., 18.

[953] See Bryant, Levi R. R. *The Democracy of Objects*. Ann Arbor: Open Humanities Press, 2011.

[954] As Simondon writes, "[the] desire for change, however, does not happen directly within the technical being; it happens within man as inventor and user." In Simondon, Gilbert (2017), 71.

[955] Kubler, George (1962), 34.

[956] Benjamin, Walter. "Passagen Werk" In *Walter Benjamin Gesammelte Schriften* V. I. Herausgegeben von Ralf Tiedemann. Frankfurt am Main: Suhrkamp Verlag, 1982.

[957] "If we go back to the origins of building, we shall find that before being a public way, the street was the private or personal way or path to the house to which it is attached . . . (1861, TVU, §710)." See the chapter "The Concept of Street", In Puig, Arturo Soria y, ed. Cerdà (1999), 104-105.

[958] Simondon, Gilbert (2017), 63.

[959] The project's associative milieu of smooth space included the rise of globalization, with its flow of capital and flows of data. And Polo, Alejandro Zaera. "Kapitalflüsse, Datenströme, Drive-Thru und andere Strömungen." *ARCH+*, vol. 117, Rem Koolhaas, June 1993, 56–58.

[960] Ibid., 57.

[961] See "The Smooth and the Striated" Deleuze, Gilles, and Félix Guattari. T*housand Plateaus: Capitalism and Schizophrenia*, translated by Brian Massumi. (Originally published in French 1980). Minneapolis: University of Minnesota Press, 1987, 474-500.

[962] See Lynn, Greg (ed.) *Folding in Architecture*: Revised Edition. 1st Edition. (Originally published in 1993). Hoboken, New Jersey: John Wiley & Sons, 2004.

[963] See Figure 2 and Figure 4. In Sitte, Camillo "City Planning according to Artistic Principles" from 1889, In *Camillo Sitte. The Birth of Modern City Planning* by George R. Collins and. Christiane Crasemann Collins, Mineola, New York: Dover Publications, 1986, 147-149.

[964] See: Ibid., 217-220.

[965] What is referred to here as a milieu is specifically the fact the Seagram Building is placed on a private land, with the legal consequence that the public space is on private property, while at Centre Pompidou it is assumed that when it was built the property of the square and the building were both owned by the municipality of the city.

[966] See: "Imaginary Prisons: Giovanni Battista Piranesi Prints" from1749-1750 in the collection of Princeton University Art Museum. https://artmuseum.princeton.edu/object-package/giovanni-battista-piranesi-imaginary-prisons/3640 Accessed February 1, 2022.

[967] This volumetric differentiation can be seen best in the section of the building. See "The Ford Foundation" by Kevin Roche John Dinkeloo and Associates in New York, 1968. https://www.archdaily.com/436653/ad-classics-the-ford-foundation-kevin-roche-john-dinkeloo-and-associates Accessed February 1, 2022.

[968] See "The Lutine Bell" in the history of the Lloyds Corporation. https://www.lloyds.com/about-lloyds/history/catastophes-and-claims/hms-lutine Accessed February 1, 2022.

[969] Mumford, Lewis. *The Myth of the Machine: Technics and Human Development*. San Diego, New York, London: A Harvest, HBJ Book, 1967, 265.

[970] Ibid., 266.

[971] Alberti, Leon Battista (1986), 2.

[972] Palladio, Andrea. *I Quattro Libri dell'Architettura di Andrea Palladio*. Apresso Bartolomeo Carampello, 1581, B.2, 13.

[973] See "Quarters for the Rural Caretakers", and "Palace of Concord." Lemagny, Jean-Claude. *Visionary Architects - Boullee, Ledoux, Lequeu*, Exhibition Catalogue for the traveling exhibition originated in University of St. Thomas, Houston, Santa Monica: Hennessey+Ingalls, 2002, 93 and 114.

[974] Le Corbusier & Pierre Jeanneret (1964), 23.

[975] Ibid., 129.

[976] Koolhaas, Rem. "The Future's Past." *The Wilson Quarterly* 3, no. 1, 1979, 135.

[977] Le Corbusier & Pierre Jeanneret (1964), 31.

[978] See 'DIGGING, PILING UP, FORMING' by Hans Holllein in his studies in Berkeley, California, from 1958-1960, https://www.hollein.com/eng/Architecture/Chronology/early-projects/Digging-Piling-up-Forming Accessed February 1, 2022.

[979] See "Städtisches Museum Abteiberg" in Mönchengladbach, Germany by Hans Hollein 1972-1982. https://www.hollein.com/index.php/eng/Architecture/Chronology/1980-1989/Staedtisches-Museum-Abteiberg Accessed February 1, 2022.

[980] See: Figure18 and Figure19, Hardwick, Jeffrey M. *Mall Maker. Victor Gruen, Architect of an American Dream*. Philadelphia: University of Pennsylvania Press, 2004, 97-98 and Banham, Reyner (1971), 153.

[981] See Gruen, Victor, *Centers for the Urban Environment - Survival of the Citie*s, van Nostrand Reinhold Company, New York, Cincinnati, Toronto, London, Melbourne: Litton Educational Publisher Inc., 1973, 61.

[982] Ibid., 140-146.

[983] See "Liziba Station" of Line 2 of the Chongping Rail Transit in Chongqing China from 2004. https://en.wikipedia.org/wiki/Liziba_station Accessed February 1, 2022.

[984] See Video "Road across a rooftop in China" 2017. https://www.stuff.co.nz/motoring/news/94205259/road-across-a-rooftop-in-china Accessed February 1, 2022.

[985] Rem Koolhaas, Sketch for O.M. Ungers, Competition for Tiergarten Quarter, Berlin, Germany, 1973-1974. In Ungers, Oswald M. *10 Kapitel Über Architektur - Ein visueller Traktat*, DuMont Reiseverlag, Ostfildern, 1999.

[986] Koolhaas, Rem (1978), 242-243.

[987] Whereas the term real estate can mean land or building, by constructed real estate I mean exclusively buildings.

Conclusion:

Citology; or, How the City Tunes Architecture

In this book I have attempted to re-originate Simondon's theory of mechanology within the discipline of architecture. Simondon's work is concerned with the mode of existence of technical objects. I have posited the architecture of the city to be a technical object in order to search for its mode of existence. In opposition to other disciplinary traditions, this means not thinking architecture in terms of its *form* or its *function*, or even what it is made of, its *matter*. It means not thinking the buildings of the city in terms of living in or among them. What it does mean, as I have tried to demonstrate, is thinking architecture in terms of its internal necessity: its being as a technical object.

This idea, of thinking the architecture of the city as a technical object, also means not thinking the city as something external to human beings, but rather as something of which we humans are part. The city is therefore a technical ensemble of human and nonhuman entities, which coexist together on a democratic, flat-ontological[988] plain. Simondon tells us that as humans we will never fully access what happens inside the hylomorphic schema—that is, we will never know the way matter fuses with form or how a form merges with matter.[989] When as architects we design our buildings, when as engineers we construct our infrastructures, when as politicians we plan our urban environment, when as developers we try to build all these for profit, or even when as citizens we renovate our homes, we only engage *with* the form and matter of our spaces but we are not *in* them. However we might care about the hylomorphic schema in our engagements with the city, this relationship between form and matter will be ever inaccessible to us. "Attention is given to form and matter," Simondon writes, "not to the process of taking form as operation."[990] The hylomorphic schema, as such, is clear to us and part of our long history, but how matter meets form, or in our case how the city meets architecture, will always be dark and obscure.[991]

What is it, then, that we do, as *Gestalter* of our built environment? If we wanted to truly to understand the relationship of the city and its architecture we would need to become their matter and with it enter into their form. We would need to transform into their formal and material properties. We would need to become buildings and cities. Simondon uses a brick as an example to describe such relational distinctions:

> It would be necessary to be able to enter the mold with the clay, to be both mold and clay at once, to live and feel their common operation in order to be able to think the process of taking form in itself. For the worker elaborates two technical half-chains that prepare the technical operation: he prepares the clay, makes it malleable, without lumps, without air bubbles, and correlatively prepares the mold; he materializes the form by making it into a wooden mold, and makes matter pliable, capable of receiving information; then, he puts the clay into the mold and presses it; but it is the system constituted by the mold and the pressed clay that is the condition of the process of taking form; it is the clay that takes form according to the mold, not the worker who gives it its form.[992]

Yet we, as architects, engineers, politicians, developers, and citizens, are not wholly external to this technical process. What we do is prepare the mediation between form and matter when we *gestalten*, or "design," our city. We are therefore a part within this technical apparatus. "Through technical activity," Simondon writes further,

> man creates mediations, and these mediations are detachable from the individual who produces and thinks them; the individual expresses himself in them, but does not adhere to them; the machine has a sort of impersonality which allows it

> to become an instrument for another man. . . . The technical object, which is thought and constructed by man, is not limited to simply creating a mediation between man and nature; it is a stable mixture of the human and the natural, it contains human and natural aspects; it gives its human content a structure comparable to that of natural objects, and allows for the integration of this human reality into the world of natural causes and effects.[993]

Simondon's philosophy thus takes a step further, naturalizing the technical object as a structure that would seem to be innate in nearly all of the physical objects available, if not accessible, to us humans.

The hylomorphic schema between form and matter is the inner mode of the technical object itself. Simondon refers to this as *technicity*, and attributes it as what causes the evolution of technical beings. What can we learn form this idea of technicity when we think our buildings as the internal necessity of the city?

To be immediately clear, the answer to the question has nothing to do with how Simondon imagined an ideal building should look or perform under the premise of being a technical object. In his text "Technical Mentality," in which he praises the work of Le Corbusier, he argues, "to construct a building according to the norms of the technical mentality means to conceive of it as being able to be enlarged, continued, amplified without disfiguration or erasure."[994] Le Corbusier's monastery at Eveux-l'Arbresle is for Simondon the best contribution of architecture in terms of this technical mentality. His reason is simple: in its original plan it already incorporates all the proper forms and material settings so that the cloister could extend and enlarge in its possible future.

It is this idea of the never complete, of the permanently evolving and in constant flux, embedded within a rhizome of forces, which became perhaps the most attractive to the discipline of architecture. Indeed, through the writings of Deleuze, Simondon entered the discipline through the back door. It was thus that the city and the building were seen as *becoming* an individuated object, through folds and foldings,[995] rather than as being one.

The line of thought from Simondon that I have followed in this thesis is that a technical object such as the city is not undetermined and in a permanent state of becoming, but rather, as we have seen, is overdetermined and individuates along processes of concretization. What we have learned is that the city appears due to an internal necessity to converge the formal and functional qualities of its elements. This process has given rise to completely unique new kinds of cities throughout our history of urbanization. We saw how once a new city emerges containing qualities which did not exist before, there is no direct correlation between the form—the topological qualities of the city's spatial layout—and the content—its sociopolitical functions. Rather, various sociopolitical functions can occur within the same form while one particular function can spread into a multiplicity of urban forms.

We can conclude: Cities individuate through a process of concretization by converging their nonhuman and human entities and give rise to new forms and contents due to their being overdetermined technical objects loaded with hidden qualities.

If we can agree that the city as a technical object is the largest human artifact, then it should be no surprise that we find a similar reading on the evolution of human artifacts in the work of Henri Focillion and George Kubler. In particular, Kubler shows us that these artifacts have sent out signals into the nonlinear time of history, as though it were an electromagnetic field. These signals have been carried throughout history within the artifacts until being extracted and fused within what he calls formal sequences, which end in the rise of new prime objects in our cultures. Similar to Simondon's individuated technical objects, these prime objects precede their individual qualities and contain radically unique ones.

In addition to their overdetermination, we have examined the hypertely of technical beings such as the city. This is the capacity to specialize each of their individual parts, either by extracting one element, like a street, a wall, a piece of land, or a public space, in order to autonomously specialize its properties, or by way of the parts within technical objects accelerating their qualities and transforming ensembles of the city itself. We have seen this from the origin of our built environment, as represented by the Mousgoum village; we saw it in our first urban buildings like the theater and the Pynx; we found it in the city under a single roof as well as in the city on a single roof; and we identified it in the diagram of the high-rise. Cities converge the properties of each of their inner elements and give rise to new qualities, which we call buildings. The city tunes its qualities to effect the mode of existence of its architecture. This tuning that happens in the city is the same as it happens inside a trumpet in a jazz ensemble. "Like in jazz", Timothy Morton explains, "a better solo would reveal *something* about the metal and the curvature and the size and the spittle of a trumpet."[996] Independent of any human playing the object-instrument, the solo, Morton continues, "bring[s] out strange hidden properties of that object."[997] A property that was unknown to us and the trumpet—it didn't exist before—became tuned. The same can be applied to our cities. When the city, with or without the involvement of an architect, tunes its hidden qualities, it gives life to a new kind of architecture, just as a trumpet gives us a new tone. When new buildings emerge in the city, this tells us something about its "molten core,"[998] its internal necessity as a technical object. We witness the moment when that *something*, in our case a building, that was virtually present within the city, suddenly becomes actualized and tangible.

As we are told by contemporary philosophers of object-oriented-ontology, or OOO, like Graham Harman, not only will we humans never have full access to that inner molten core of objects, but those objects also will never fully be able to access other objects. Harman uses the example of how fire burns cotton.[999] When fire burns cotton, it never engages all of its properties, only those it meets in order to burn, while others like smell are untouched. The same can be said about the architecture of the city. Buildings will never fully be able to engage in all the qualities of the city. They only ever meet with the properties of the city that can give rise to their existence, only with those by which they are tuned.

This brings me here at the end back the initial fourfold diagram of architecture that I used at the outset to contextualize the thesis.

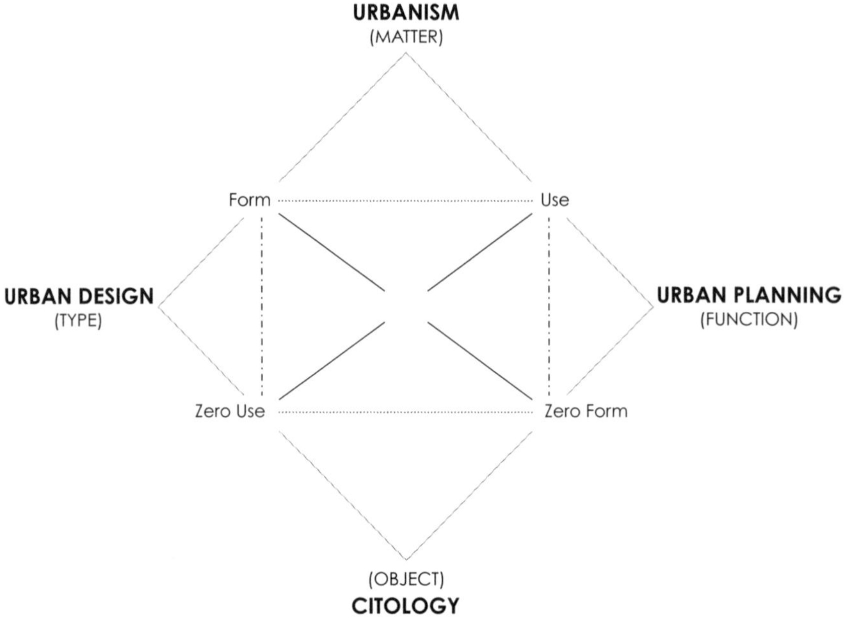

FIGURE 101. THE FOURFOLD DIAGRAM OF THE ARCHITECTURE OF THE CITY AND ITS DISCOURSES

What I would like to propose in conclusion is the engagement of a new disciplinary discourse. What we need today is not a discipline of urban design, which considers abstract *form* as being deeper than the real city. Nor do we need urbanism, which considers the *matter* of the city as being deepest. Furthermore we do not need urban planning, whose representatives consider the *function* of the city as the deepest concern. What I think we do need in our contemporary world is to engage our understanding of the internal necessity, of the inner molten core of our cities and how these cities, as a technical beings, constitute our world. I therefore propose here a new disciplinary discourse: *citology*. Citology, as presented in this book, concerns how the city meets its architecture—that is, the *being*, or the mode of existence of the architecture of the city.

Because all that is written here would not exist without the ideas of Simondon, I would like to end with one of his key thoughts on why it was necessary for him to invent his mechanology for our understanding of the world of technical objects:

> In order to restore to culture the truly general character it has lost, one must be capable of reintroducing an awareness of the nature of machines, of their mutual relations and of their relations with man, and of the values implied in these relations. This awareness requires the existence of a technologist or mechanologist alongside the psychologist and the sociologist.[1000]

I would now add a new agent to this list: the *citologist.*

[987] See DeLanda, Manuel. *Intensive Science and Virtual Philosophy*. London, New York: Continuum, 2002, 47.

[988] Simondon, Gilbert (2017), 248.

[989] Ibid., 248.

[990] Ibid.

[991] Ibid., 248-249.

[992] Ibid., 250.

[993] Simondon, Gilbert (2012), 14.

[994] See Rajchman, John. “Out of the Fold.” In *Folding in Architecture: Revised Edition*, edited by Greg Lynn, (2004), 77-79.

[995] Morton, Timothy. *Realist Magic: Objects, Ontology, Causality*. Ann Arbor, Michigan: Open Humanities Press, 2013, 22-23.

[996] Ibid., 23.

[997] See: Harman, Graham. *Prince of Networks: Bruno Latour and Metaphysics*. Melbourne: re.press, 2009, 215. In many of his writings Harman uses this expression, which he arrives at through his explanation of Ortega y Gasset’s ontology of metaphors: “When they [the cypress and a flame] collide with one another their hard carapaces crack and the internal matter, in a molten state, acquires the softness of plasm, ready to receive a new form and structure.” In Graham Harman (2018), p.73.

[998] See: Harman, Graham. *Guerrilla Metaphysics: Phenomenology and the Carpentry of Things*. Chicago: Open Court, 2005, 170.

[999] Simondon, Gilbert (2017), 19.

Bibliography

Abraham, Raimund. "Nine Houses, Triptych, 1972-1976." In *Postmodern Visions: Drawings, Paintings, and Models by Contemporary Architects*, edited by Heinrich Klotz and Volker Fischer, 18–20. (Originally published 1984). New York: Abbeville Press, 1985.

———. [UN]BUILT. 2nd revised and enlarged edition by Brigitte Groihofer. Wien, New York: Springer, 1996.

Abrams, Charles. "The Economy of Cities by Jane Jacobs." *New York Times*, June 1, 1969, sec. Book Review, 3.

Adams, Thomas. *Metropolitan America/The Design of Residential Areas-bassic Considerations, Principles, and Methods*. Harvard City Planning Studies VI, (Original published by Cambridge: Harvard. University Press, 1934) reprint New York: Arno Press, 1974.

Agamben, Giorgio. *Homo Sacer - Die Souveränität der Macht und das nackte Leben*. Frankfurt am Main: Suhrkamp Verlag, 2002.

———. *State of Exception*, translated by Kevin Attell, Chicago and London: The University of Chicago Press, 2005.

ASCSA Digital Collections. "Agora Monument: Boundary Stones of the Agora." Accessed September 24, 2021. http://agora.ascsa.net/id/agora/monument/boundary%20stones%20of%20the%20agora.

Alberti, Leon Battista. *The Ten Books of Architecture: The 1755 Leoni Edition*. Translated by James Leoni. New York: Dover Publications, 1986.

———. *Zehn Bücher über die Baukunst: Ins Deutsche übertragen, eingeleitet und mit Anmerkungen und Zeichnungen versehen von Max Theuer*. Translated by Max Theuer. The new edition follows the Wien & Leipzig 1912 edition. (Originally published as *De re aedificatoria*, 1521). Tegernsee: Boer Verlag, 2020.

Andrews, Kate. "The New Century Global Centre. World's Largest Building Opens in Chengdu, China." Dezeen, 2013. Accessed September 24, 2021. https://www.dezeen.com/2013/07/10/worlds-largest-building-opens-chengdu-china/.

Ansari, Iman. "Eisenman's Evolution: Architecture, Syntax, and New Subjectivity." ArchDaily, 2013. Accessed September 24, 2021 https://www.archdaily.com/429925/eisenman-s-evolution-architecture-syntax-and-new-subjectivity.

ArchDaily. "SHUM YIP UpperHills LOFT / URBANUS." ArchDaily, 2019. Accessed September 24, 2021. https://www.archdaily.com/919939/shum-yip-upperhills-loft-urbanus.

Arendt, Hannah. *The Human Condition: A Study of the Central Dilemmas Facing Modern Man*. Garden City, New York: Doubleday Anchor Books : Doubleday & Company, 1959.

Aristotle. *Politics*. Translated by Benjamin Jowett. Batochhe Books Kitchener, 1999. Accessed September 24, 2021. https://historyofeconomicthought.mcmaster.ca/aristotle/Politics.pdf

Aßländer, Michael S. "Freiheit als Grundlage der Ökonomie." In *Adam Smith Zur Einführung*. Hamburg: Junius Verlag, 2007.

Augustine, Saint. *The City Of God (de Civitate Dei)*. London: J. M. Dent & Sons LTD. New York: E.P. Dutton & Co. Inc. 1945.

Aureli, Pier Vittorio. "Toward the Archipelago - Defining the Political and the Formal in Architecture." *Log*, no. 11 Winter (2008): 91–120.

———. "City as Political Form: Four Archetypes of Urban Transformation." *Architectural Design* 81, no. Special Issue:Typological Urbanism: Projective Cities (2011): 32–37.

———. "Toward the Archipelago - Defining the Political and the Formal in Architecture." In *The Possibility of an Absolute Architecture*, 1–46. Cambridge, Massachusetts: The MIT Press, 2011.

———. *The Possibility of an Absolute Architecture*, Cambridge, Massachusetts: The MIT Press, 2011.

———. *The City As A Project*. Berlin: Ruby Press, 2013.

———. *The Project of Autonomy - Politics and Architecture within and against Capitalism*. New York: The Temple Hoyne Buell Center for the Study of American Architecture at Columbia University and Princeton Architectural Press, 2008.

———. "The Theology Of Tabula Rasa: Walter Benjamin And Architecture in The Age of Precarity." *Log*, no. 27 (2013): 111–27.

———. "Life, Abstracted: Notes on the Floor Plan." e-flux Architecture, Architecture and Representation, October 2017. Accessed September 24, 2021. https://www.e-flux.com/architecture/representation/159199/life-abstracted-notes-on-the-floor-plan/.

Avery, Dan. "Saudi Arabia Building 100-Mile-Long 'Linear' City." Architectural Digest, January 26, 2021. Accessed September 24, 2021. https://www.architecturaldigest.com/story/saudi-arabia-building-100-mile-long-linear-city.

Ballon, Hilary. *The Greatest Grid - The Master Plan of Manhattan 1811-2011*. Edited by Hilary Ballon. New York: Co-Published by the Museum of the City of New York and Columbia University Press, 2011.

Banham, Reyner. *The Architecture of the Well-Tempered Environment*. Chicago: Architectural Press, The University of Chicago Press, 1969.

———. *Los Angeles: The Architecture of Four Ecologies*. 1st Edition. London: Allen Lane Penguin Books, 1971.

———. *Architecture Documentary: Reyner Banham Loves Los Angeles*, 1972. Accessed September 24, 2021. https://www.youtube.com/watch?v=ymg0e4g7qeQ.

———. *Megastructure: Urban Futures of the Recent Past*. New York: Harper and Row, 1976.

———. *Theory and Design in the First Machine Age*. Originally published 1960. London: Architectural Press, 1977.

———. *Architecture of the Well-Tempered Environment*. Revised edition. Chicago: University of Chicago Press, 1984.

Barr, Alfred H, Henry-Russell Hitchcock, Philip Johnson, Lewis Mumford, and Museum of Modern Art New York. *Modern Architecture: International Exhibition, New York, February 10 to March 23, 1932, Museum of Modern Art*. New York: Museum of Modern Art, 1932.

Barthes, Roland. *Writing Degree Zero* (Originally published as *Le Degré Zéro de l'écriture*, 1953). London: Jonathan Cape, 1967.

———. "The Death of the Author (1967)." In *Roland Barthes. Image, Music, Text*, translated by Stephen Heath, 142–48. Great Britain: Fontana Press, 1977.

Bedford, Joseph, ed. *Is There an Object Oriented Architecture?: Engaging Graham Harman*. Bloomsbury Academic, 2020.

Benevolo, Leonardo. *Die Geschichte der Stadt*. 5th Edition. (Originally published as *Storia della Città*, 1975) Frankfurt am Main: Campus Verlag, 1990.

———. *The European City*. The Making of Europe: Series Editor: Jacques Le Goff. Translated from the Italian by Carl Ipsen. Oxford UK, Cambridge USA: 1993.

Benjamin, Walter. *Das Kunstwerk im Zeitalter seiner technischen Reproduzierbarkeit* (1935). 6th Edition. Berlin: Suhrkamp Verlag, 2010.

———. "Passagen Werk" In Walter Benjamin *Gesammelte Schriften Band: V· I.* Herausgegeben von Ralf Tiedemann. Frankfurt am Main: Suhrkamp Verlag. 1982.

Bernoulli, Hans. *Die Stadt und ihr Boden*. Birkhäuser Architektur Bibliothek. Basel, Berlin, Boston: Birkhäuser Verlag, 1991. (Original 1946, Verlag Architektur AG, Erlenbach-Zürich.)

Bernstein, Conord, Dahou, Debord, Fillon, Wolman. "The Minimum Life" in potlatch #4, 13 July 1954, translated by Gerardo Denis and Reuben Keehan, Accessed September 24, 2021. https://www.cddc.vt.edu/sionline/presitu/potlatch4.html.

Blau, Eve. *The Architecture of Red Vienna, 1919–1934*, 18–47. Cambridge, Massachusetts: The MIT Press, 1999.

———. "Ernst Hein,'Die Bodenpolitik der Gemeinde Wien,' in Internationaler Wohnungs- Und Städtebaukongress: Vorberichte (1926):10." *In The Architecture of Red Vienna, 1919–1934*, 140. Cambridge, Massachusetts: The MIT Press, 1999.

Boever, Arne De, Alex Murray, and Jon Roffe, eds. *Gilbert Simondon: Being and Technology*. New Edition. Edinburgh: Edinburgh University Press, 2012.

Böhm, Gottfried. "Kunst versus Geschichte: Ein unerledigtes Problem." In *Die Form der Zeit*, edited by George Kubler, translated by Bettina Blumenberg. Frankfurt am Main: Suhrkamp, 1982.

Brandl Eugenie/Paula Hons. Titelblatt: "Die Ringstraße des Proletariats." In *Die Unzufriedene : Eine unabhängige Wochenschrift für alle Frauen*, Eigentümerin, Verlegerin, Herausgeberin und verantwortliche Redakteurin: Eugenie Brandl und Paula Hons. 8. Jg., Nr. 35, 30. August 1930: Titelblatt.

Branzi, Andrea. *No Stop City: Archizoom Associati*. Orléans: Editions HYX, 2006

Braudel, Fernand. *Civilization & Capitalism. 15th-18th Century*. Translated by Siân Reynolds, vol. III. The Perspective of the World. (Originally published as *Le Temps Du Monde*, 1979). London: Collins, 1984.

———. *Civilization & Capitalism. 15th-18th Century*. Translated by Siân Reynolds, vol. I. The Structures of Everyday Life - The Limits of the Possible. (Originally published as *Les Structures du Quotidien: Le Possible et L'Impossible*, 1979). London: Collins, 1985.

Bridges, William. "Remarks of the Commissioners for Laying out Streets and Roads in the City of New York, under the Act of April 3, 1807." In *Map of The City of New York and Island of Manhattan with Explanatory Remarks and References*. New York: William Bridges, 1811.

Britannica. "Ecclesia," n.d. Accessed September 24, 2021. https://www.britannica.com/topic/Ecclesia-ancient-Greek-assembly.

Bryant, Levi R. R. *The Democracy of Objects*. Ann Arbor: Open Humanities Press, 2011.

Cacciari, Massimo. "Der Archipelagos." In *Der Archipel Europa*. (Originally published as *L'arcipelagos*, 1997), translated by Günter Memmert, 1st Edition, 9–32. DuMont Buchverlag, 1998.

Caniggia, Gianfranco, and Gian Luigi Maffei. *Architectural Composition and Building Typology: Interpreting Basic Building*. Translated by Susan Jane Fraser. Firenze: Alinea Editrice, 2001.

Castells, Manuel. *The Rise of the Network Society*. Reprint of the 1996 First Edition. Chichester: Wiley-Blackwell, 1997.

Cataldi, Giancarlo, Gian Luigi Maffei, and Paolo Vaccaro. "Saverio Muratori and the Italian School of Planning Typology." *Urban Morphology*, no. 1, vol. 6, (2002): 3–14.

Cauter, Lieven de, ed. *The Capsular Civilization: On the City in the Age of Fear*. Rotterdam: nai010 publishers, 2004.

Caves, Roger, W. *Encyclopedia of the City*, Edition 1st Edition, London and New York: Routledge Taylor & Francis Group, 2005.

Cerdà, Ildefons. *General Theory of Urbanization* (1867). Edited by Vicente Guallart. (Originally published as T*eoria General de La Urbanizacion*, 1897) New York, Barcelona: Actar Publishers & the Institute for Advanced Architecture of Catalonia, 2018.

Chambless, Edgar. *Roadtown*. New York: Roadtown Press, 1910.

Choonara, Joseph. "Interview: David Harvey - Exploring the Logic of Capital." *Socialist Review*, no. 335 (April 2009).

Colquhoun, Alan. "The Superblock." In *Essays in Architectural Criticism: Modern Architecture and Historical Change*, Reprint edition. Cambridge, Massachusetts: The MIT Press, 1985, 83-103.

Compañía Madrileña de Urbanización. *Madrid Ciudad Lineal*. 376th Edition. Imprenta de la Ciudad Lineal, 1911.

———. *Ciudad Lineal Como Arquitectura Nueva de Ciudades*. First International Congress "Art of constructing cities and the Organization of municipal life," Gant, Belgium, 1913. Imprenta de la Ciudad Lineal, 1913.

Czeike, Felix. "Wiener Wohnbau vom Vormärz bis 1923." Edited by Karl Mang. *Kommunaler Wohnbau Wien. Aufbruch 1923–1934*, Wien, n.d.

DeLanda, Manuel. *War in the Age of Intelligent Machines*. New York, NY: Zone Books, 1991.

———. *A thousand years of non-linear history*. Edited by Jonathan Crary, Sanford Kwinter, and Bruce Mau. New York: Swerve Editions, 2000.

———. *Intensive Science and Virtual Philosophy*. London, New York: Continuum, 2002.

———."Deleuze and the use of the genetic algorithm in architecture", In *AD-Architectural Design* 72(1) January 2002, 9-12.

Deleuze, Gilles. *The Fold: Leibniz and the Baroque*. Foreword and translation by Tom Conley. London: The Athlone Press, 1993.

———. "Immanence: A Life." In *Pure Immanenca. Essays on A Life*, edited by John Rajchman, translated by Anne Boyman, 25–34. New York: Zone Books, 2001.

Deleuze, Gilles, and Félix Guattari. *Anti Ödipus - Kapitalismus and Schizophrenie*. Translated by Bernd Schwibs. (Original titel: *L'Anti-Oedipe*, 1972). Frankfurt am Main: Suhrkamp, 1977.

———. *Anti-Oedipus - Capitalism and Schizophrenia*. Preface by Michel Foucault. Tenth. Printing 2000. Minneapolis: University of Minnesota Press, 1983.

———. *Thousand Plateaus: Capitalism and Schizophrenia*, translated by Brian Massumi. (Originally published in French 1980). Minneapolis: University of Minnesota Press, 1987.

Delevoy, Robert L., Anthony Vidler, Leon Krier, Massimo Scolari, Rita Wolff, Karl Gruber, R. Krier, and Rodrigo Perez De Arca. *Rational Architecture. The Reconstruction of the European City*. Bruxelles: AAM Editions, 1978.

Demetri Krier, Leon; Porphyrios. *Leon Krier: Houses, Palaces, Cities*. Architectural Design AD Editions. London: Academy Publications, 1984.

Descartes, René. "Principles of Philosophy (1644)." Early Modern Texts. Accessed September 24, 2921. https://www.earlymoderntexts.com/assets/pdfs/descartes1644.pdf.

Designboom | Architecture & Design. "URBANUS Completes SHUM YIP UpperHills LOFT in Shenzhen," June 26, 2019. Accessed September 24, 2021. https://www.designboom.com/architecture/urbanus-shum-yip-upper-hills-loft-shenzhen-china-06-26-2019/.

Dijk, Hans van. "Wat Is Er Nu Helderder Dan de Taal van de Moderne Architectuur?" In *Wonen-TA/BK*, Interview met Peter Smithson., 31–34. nrs. 19-20, 1978.

Döring, Jörg, and Tristan Thielmann, eds. *Spatial Turn: Das Raumparadigma in den Kultur- und Sozialwissenschaften*. 2nd Edition. Bielefeld: Transcript, 2008.

Dumbarton Oaks Research Library. "Plan for Paris (1765)." D. O. Garden Stories. Accessed September 24, 2021. http://images.doaks.org/garden-histories/items/show/166.

Egerton, Frank N. "History of Ecological Sciences, Part 47: Ernst Haeckel's Ecology." *The Bulletin of the Ecological Society of America* 94, no. 3 (2013), 222–44.

Eisenman, Peter. "Post-Functionalism." In *Oppositions Reader: Selected Readings from a Journal for Ideas and Criticism in Architecture, 1973-1984*, edited by K. Michael Hays, 9–12. New York: Princeton Architectural Press, 1998.

———. "Aspects of Modernism: Maison Dom-Ino and the Self-Referential Sign" In *Eisenman Inside Out: Selected Writings, 1963-1988*, 111–20. New Haven, CT: Yale University Press, 2004.

———. "Field of Diagrams: The Project of Campo Marzio." In *Zero Piranesi*, SAC Journal 5, edited by Peter Trummer. Baunach: Städelschule Architectural Class (Frankfurt) and AADR Spurbuchverlag, 2019.

———. *Eisenman Inside Out: Selected Writings, 1963-1988*. New Haven, CT: Yale University Press, 2004.

———. "Project or Practice?" Architecture Fall 2011 Lecture Series, Grant Auditorium, Syracuse University School of Architecture, September 30, 2011.

Eisenman, Peter, with Matt Roman. *Palladio Virtuel*. New Haven/London: Yale University Press, 2015.

Ellis, William. "Type and Context in Urbanism: Colin Rowe's Contextualism." In *Oppositions Reader: Selected Readings from a Journal for Ideas and Criticism in Architecture, 1973-1984*, edited by K. Michael Hays, 225–52. New York: Princeton Architectural Press, 1998.

Feher, Michel, Sanford Kwinter, and Jonathan Crary, eds. *Zone 1/2: The Contemporary City*. 1st Edition. New York: Zone Books, 1985.

Ferriss, Hugh. *The Metropolis of Tomorrow*. New York City: Ives Washburn, 1929.

Feuerstein, Günther. *Urban Fiction: Strolling Through Ideal Cities from Antiquity to the Present Day*. Stuttgart/London: Edition Axel Menges, 2008.

Fine, John. *Horoi. Studies in Mortgage, Real Security, and Land Tenure in Ancient Athens*. Athens: American School of Classical Studies, 1951

Fishman, Robert. *Urban Utopias in the Twentieth Century, Ebenezer Howard, Frank Lloyd Wright, and Le Corbusier*. Fourth printing. Cambridge, Massachusetts, London, England: The MIT Press, 1991.

Focillon, Henri. *The Life of Forms in Art*. Translated by George Kubler. Revised 3. Edition (1996). (Originally published as *La Vie des Formes*, 1934). New York: Zone Books, 1992.

———. *Das Leben der Formen* (Originally published as *Vie des Formes*, 1934). Translated by Gritta Baerlocher. 1st Edition. Göttingen: Steidl Verlag, 2019.

Foucault, Michel. *Power/Knowledge: Selected Interviews and Other Writings, 1972-1977*. Edited by Colin Gordon. 1st American Edition. New York: Pantheon Books, 1980.

———. *Aesthetics, Method, and Epistemology: Essential Works of Foucault, 1954-1984*. Edited by James D. Faubion. Translated by Robert Hurley, vol. 2. Paul Rabinow Series. New York: The New Press, 1998.

———. *The Birth of Biopolitics: Lectures at the Collège de France, 1978-1979*. Edited by Michel Senellart. Translated by Graham Burchell. New York: Palgrave MacMillan, 2004.

———. *Security, Territory, Population: Lectures at the College de France, 1977-78*. Edited by Michel Senellart. Translated by Graham Burchell. London: Palgrave Macmillan, 2007.

Frampton, Kenneth. *Modern Architecture - A Critical History*. London: Thames and Hudson, 1980.

———. "Megaform as Urban Landscape." In *Conflict - The Berlage Cahiers*, edited by Amsterdam The Berlage Institut, 6:102–5. Rotterdam: 010 Publishers, 1999.

Friedell, Egon. *Kulturgeschichte der Neuzeit*. 15th Edition. (1st Edition published 1976). München: Deutscher Taschenbuch Verlag, 2003.

Gantner, Joseph. *Das Neue Frankfurt - Internationale Monatszeitschrift für die Probleme kultureller Neugestaltung, rein-mainische regionalplanung*, 11/12 V Jahrgang November/Dezember 1931, , Verlag Englert und Schlosser, Frankfurt am Main.

Garnier, Tony. *Une Cite Industrielle*, Edited by Riccardo Mariani, Rizzoli International Publications, New York, 1990.

George, Henry. *Progress and Poverty: An Inquiry into the Cause of Industrial Depressions and of Increase of Want with Increase of Wealth*. Garden City, New York: Doubleday, Page & Co., 1912.

Glendon, M. Ann. "Roman Law." In *Encyclopedia Britannica*. Accessed September 24, 2021. https://www.britannica.com/topic/Roman-law.

Goodman, Elyssa. "Soldier, Sailor, Stable Boy, Spy: 100 Years of Tom of Finland's Legacy." InsideHook, July 27, 2020. Accessed September 24, 2021. https://www.insidehook.com/article/art/tom-of-finland-legacy.

Gregotti, Vittorio, "OMA- Office for Metropolitan Architecture." In *Lotus International*, 1976, January, No.11, New York City: Rizzoli International Publications, 1976, 34-37.

Gries, John M., and James Ford. *Planning for Residential District - City Planning, Subdivisions, Utilities, Landscape Planning*. Publication of the President's Conference on Home Building and Home Ownership-Final Reports of Committees. Washington D.C.: National Capital Press, 1932.

Gropius, Walter. "Der Grosse Baukasten." Edited by Ernst May. *Das Neue Frankfurt. Monatschrift für die Fragen der Grosstadt-Gestaltung*, no. 2, vol. 1, Dezember (1926): Verlag Englert und Schlösser, Frankfurt am Main, 25-40.

Groys, Boris. *Über das Neue - Versuch einer Kulturökonomie*. Edition Akzente. München: Carl Hanser Verlag, 1992.

———. *In the Flow*. London; New York: Verso, 2016.

———. "On The New." *RES: Anthropology and Aesthetics* 38 (Autumn 2000), 5–17.

Gruen, Victor, *Centers for the Urban Environment - Survival of the Cities*, van Nostrand Reinhold Company, New York, Cincinnati, Toronto, London, Melbourne; Litton Educational Publisher Inc. 1973.

Guattari, Félix. "Regimes, Pathways, Subjects." In *Incorporations*, edited by Jonathan Crary and Sanford Kwinter, translated by Brian Massumi. Zone 6. New York: Zone Books, 1992, 16-35.

———. "On Machines." In *Complexity*, Architecture/Art/Philosophy, edited by Andrew Benjamin. *JPVA Journal of Philosophy and the Visual Arts* 6, no. AD Academy Editions, London: Academy Group, 1995,, 8–12.

———. "Über Maschinen." In *Ästhetik und Maschinismus: Texte zu und von Félix Guattari*, edited by Henning Schmidgen, 115–32. Berlin: Merve Verlag, 1995.

———. "Regimes, Pathways, Subjects." In *The Guattari Reader - Pierre-Félix Guattari*, edited by Gary Genosko, Cambridge Massachusetts: Blackwell Publishers Inc. 1996, 95-108.

———. *The Three Ecologies*. Translated by Ian Pindar and Paul Sutton. London, New York: Continuum, 2000.

Dr. Hagen. “Biologische Und Soziale Voraussetzung Der Kleinstwohnung.” Edited by Ernst May and Fritz Wichert. *Das Neue Frankfurt. Monatschrift für die Probleme Moderner Gestaltung*, no. 11, vol. 3., November (1929): Verlag Englert und Schlösser, Frankfurt am Main, 222-226.

Hardwick, Jeffrey M. *Mall Maker - Victor Gruen, Architect of an American Dream*. Philadelphia: University of Pennsylvania Press, 2004

———. “Planning the New Suburbscape.” *In Mall Maker - Victor Gruen, Architect of an American Dream*, 142–61. Philadelphia: University of Pennsylvania Press, 2004.

Harman, Graham. *Tool-Being: Heidegger and the Metaphysics of Objects*. Chicago and La Salle, Illinois: Open Court, 2002.

———. *Guerrilla Metaphysics: Phenomenology and the Carpentry of Things*. Chicago: Open Court, 2005.

———. “Zero-Person and the Psyche.” In *Mind That Abides: Panpsychism in the New Millennium*, edited by David Skrbina, 253–82. Amsterdam: John Benjamins Publishing, 2009

———. *Prince of Networks: Bruno Latour and Metaphysics*. Melbourne: re.press, 2009.

———. *The Quadruple Object*. Winchester, UK, Washington, USA: Zero Books, 2011.

———. “Form and Its Rivals.” SCI-Arc, October 5, 2012. Accessed September 24, 2021. https://www.youtube.com/watch?v=fqLEmyjlq1M. (Lecture)

———. quotes Husserl, in Kimbell, Lucy. “The Object Fights Back: An Interview with Graham Harman.” *Design and Culture* 5(1), 2013, 103-117.

———. “Materialism Is Not the Solution: On Matter, Form, and Mimesis.” *The Nordic Journal of Aesthetics* 47 (2014), 94–110.

———. *Object-Oriented Ontology. A New Theory of Everything*. Pelican Books. New York: Penguin Random House, 2018.

———. “What Objects Mean for Architecture.” In *Is There an Object Oriented Architecture? Engaging Graham Harman*, edited by Joseph Bedford. London, New York: Bloomsbury Academic, 2020, 15-24.

———. *Architecture and Objects. Art after Nature.* Minnesota: University of Minnesota Press, 2022.

Harvey, David. “The Invisible Political Economy of Architectural Production.” In *The Invisible in Architecture*, edited by Ole Bouman and Roemer van Toorn, 420–27, 1994.

———. *A Brief History of Neoliberalism*. New York: Oxford University Press, 2005.

———. “Senior Loeb Scholar Lecture.” Harvard University, Graduate School of Design, March 28, 2016. Accessed September 24, 2021. https://www.youtube.com/watch?v=pm_UgX--ef8.

———. *The Condition of Postmodernity - An Enquiry into the Origins of Cultural Change*, Blackwell, Cambridge MA & Oxford UK,1989.

Hays, K. Michael, ed. *Architecture Theory since 1968*. Cambridge, Massachusetts: The MIT Press, 1998.

———. *Oppositions Reader: Selected Essays 1973-1984*. New York: Princeton Architectural Press, 1998.

Hegel, Georg Wilhelm Friedrich. *Vorlesungen über die Ästhetik*, 1835-1838, https://www.lernhelfer.de/sites/default/files/lexicon/pdf/BWS-DEU2-0170-04.pdf

Heidegger, Martin. *Hebel- der Hausfreund*. Günter Neske Verlag: Pfullingen, 1957.

Herrmann, Friedrich-Wilhelm v., ed. *Heidegger, Martin: Der Ursprung des Kunstwerkes. Mit der "Einführung" von Hans-Georg Gadamer und der ersten Fassung des Textes* (1935). Rote Reihe 48. Frankfurt am Main: Vittorio Klostermann, 2012.

Hilberseimer, Ludwig. *Großstadtbauten*. Hannover: Aposs, 1925.

———. *Großstadtarchitektur*. Die Baubücher, Band 3. Stuttgart: Julius Hoffmann, 1927.

———. *The Nature of Cities: Origin, Growth, and Decline; Pattern and Form; Planning Problems*. Chicago: Paul Theobald & Co., 1955.

———. *Ludwig Hilberseimer - Metropolisarchitecture and Selected Essays*, edited by Richard Anderson, GSAPP Books, Columbia University, New York, 2012.

———. *Entfaltung einer Planungsidee*. Bauwelt Fundamente 6. Berlin/Frankfurt/Wien: Ullstein Verlag, 1963.

Hildebrand, Adolf von. *Das Problem der Form in der Bildenden Kunst*. Straßburg: Heitz & Mündel, 1893.

Hillings, Valerie L., Daniel Birnbaum, and Margriet Schavemaker. *ZERO: Countdown to Tomorrow, 1950s - 60s*. 1st Edition. New York: Guggenheim Museum Publications, 2014.

Hoesli, Berhard. "Transparent Form-Organisation as an Instrument of Design" In *Reckoning with Colin Rowe: Ten Architects Take Position*, edited by Emmanuel Petit, 127–137. New York: Routledge, 2015.

Hollein, Hans. "Digging, Piling up, Forming. Studies. (1958-1960)." Accessed September 7, 2021. https://www.hollein.com/eng/Architecture/Chronology/early-projects/Digging-Piling-up-Forming.

Hood, Raymond M. "A City under a Single Roof." In *The Sphere and the Labyrinth: Avant-Gardes and Architecture from Piranesi to the 1970s*, by Tafuri, Manfredo, translated by Pellegrino D'Acierno and Robert Connolly. Cambridge, Massachusetts: The MIT Press, 1987. 190-195.

———. "A City Under a Single Roof" As told to F. S. Tisdale, In *Nation's Business*, Nov.1929, Washington D.C: Published by the Chamber of Commerce of the United States, 1929, 18-20 (continued on 206-209).

———. "The Spirit of Modern Art," *Architectural Forum* vol.51, no.11 November 1924).

Hookway, Branden. *Pandemonium: The Rise of Predatory Locales in the Postwar World*. 1st Edition. Princeton Architectural Press, 2000.

Howard, Ebenezer. *Garden Cities of Tomorrow*. London: Swan Sonnenschein & Co., Ltd., 1902. Accessed September 24, 2021. http://archive.org/details/gardencitiestom00howagoog.

———. *Garden Cities of To-Morrow*. Edited by Frederic J. Osborn. (Originally published in 1902 and in 1898 as *To-Morrow: A Peaceful Path to Real Reform*). London: Faber and Faber, 1946.

Howe, Richard. "Notes on 19th Century Lot Sizes." The Gotham Center for New York City History, November 15, 2012. Accessed September 24, 2021. https://www.gothamcenter.org/blog/notes-on-19th-century-lot-sizes.

Huizinga, Johan. *Homo Ludens - A Study of the Play-Element in Culture*. London, Boston and Henley: Routledge & Kegan Paul, 1949.

Jacobs, Jane. *The Death and Life of Great American Cities*. New York City: Random House, 1961.

————. *The Economy of Cities*. The Vintage Book edition, New York City: Random House,1970

————. *The Nature of Economies*. The Modern Library. New York City: Random House, 2000.

Jakarta Apartments. "Cosmo Park Apartment for Rent." Accessed September 24, 2021. https://www.jakarta-apartment.net/category/apartment/cosmo-park/.

Jameson, Fredric. *Postmodernism, Or, The Cultural Logic of Late Capitalism*. 7th Edition. First Published in 1984 in "New Left Review." Durham, North Carolina: Duke University Press, 1997.

Jeanneret, Pierre, and Le Corbusier. *Le Corbusier et Pierre Jeanneret: Oeuvre Complete 1910-1929*, vol. 1, edited by Willy Boesiger and Stonorov (Ohio). Zurich: Les Editions d'Architecture, 1964.

Jencks, Charles. *The Language Of Post-Modern Architecture*. 2nd Edition. London: Academy Editions, 1978.

Johnson, Philip C., and Mies van der Rohe, eds. "Architecture and the Times (1924)." In *Mies van Der Rohe*, 186–87. New York: The Museum of Modern Art New York, 1947.

Jung, Carl Gustav. *Archetypen*. München: dtv Deutscher Taschenbuch Verlag, (first published in 1934), 14th Edition, 2008.

Kant, Immanuel. *Critique of Judgment*. Edited by Werner S. Pluhar and Mary J. Gregor. (Originally published in Prussia in 1790). Indianapolis/Cambridge: Hackett Publishing, 1987.

————. "Prolegomena to Any Future Metaphysics (1783)." Translated by Paul Carus. The Project Gutenberg E-Book, 2016. Accessed September 24, 2021. https://www.gutenberg.org/files/52821/52821-h/52821-h.htm.

Kaufmann, Emil. *Architecture in the Age of Reason; Baroque and Postbaroque in England, Italy, and France*. Cambridge: Harvard University Press, 1955.

————. *Von Ledoux bis Le Corbusier - Ursprung und Entwicklung der Autonomen Architektur*. (Unchanged reprint of the 1933 Edition published in Verlag Dr. Rolf Passer, Wien/Leipzig). Stuttgart: Verlag Gerd Hatje, 1985.

Kilham, Walter H. *Raymond Hood, Architect - Form Through Function in the American Skyscraper*. New York City: Architectural Book Publishing Co., Inc. 1973.

Kimbell, Lucy. "The Object Strikes Back: An Interview with Graham Harman." *Design and Culture* 5(1) (2013), 103–17.

Kipnis, Jeffrey. *A Question of Qualities: Essays in Architecture*. Edited by Alexander Maymind. New edition. Cambridge, Massachusetts: The MIT Press, 2013.

Kofman, Eleonore and Lebas, Elizabeth. "Lost in Transposition: Time, Space and the City." In *Writings on Cities*, translated by Eleonore Kofman and Elizabeth Lebas, 3-60. Cambridge, MA: Wiley-Blackwell, 2006.

Koolhaas, Rem. *Delirious New York. A Retroactive Manifesto for Manhattan*. New York: Oxford University Press, 1978.

————. "The Future's Past." *The Wilson Quarterly* 3, no. 1 (1979): 135–40.

———. "Bigness, or the Problem of Large. Manifesto (1994)." In *S, M, L, XL*, edited by Bruce Mau, OMA, and Rem Koolhaas, 495–516. New York: Monacelli Press, 1995.

———. "Beijing Manifesto." In *Content*, 1st Edition, 124. Köln: Taschen Verlag, 2004.

———. "Hyperbuilding." In *Rem Koolhaas OMA I: 1996-2006*, edited by Richard C. Levene and Fernando Márquez Cecilia, 60–69. Croquis 131/132. Madrid: El Croquis, 2006.

———. "A: Archipelago. Rem Koolhaas in conversation with Beatriz Colombia: Rem Koolhaas A-Y (A Dictionary)." In *Rem Koolhaas OMA II: 1996-2007*, edited by Richard C Levene and Fernando Márquez Cecilia. Croquis 134/135. Madrid: El Croquis, 2007.

Koolhaas, Rem, and Zoe Zenghelis. "The City of the Captive Globe (1972)." Edited by Haig Beck. *AD Architectural Design* 47, no. 5 (1977).

Kostof, Spiro. *A History of Architecture - Settings and Rituals*. Revisions by Greg Castillo, Original Drawings by Richard Tobias, New York, Oxford: Oxford University Press, 1995.

Krauss, Rosalind. "Sculpture in the Expanded Field." *October*, The MIT Press, Cambridge, Massachusetts, Vol. 8 (Spring 1979), 31–44.

———. "Grids" *October*, The MIT Press, Cambridge, Massachusetts, Vol. 9 (Summer, 1979), 50-64.

Krier, Léon. "The City Within the City." *A + U*, Tokyo Special Issue (1977): 69-152. Reprinted in: *Architectural Design*, vol. 54 (1984), Jul/Aug: 70–105.

Krinsky, Carol Herselle. *Rockefeller Center*. New York: Oxford University Press, 1978.

Kubler, George. *The Shape of Time. Remarks on the History of Things*. New Haven/ London: Yale University Press, 1962.

Kuhnert, Nikolaus, and Marc Fester, eds. *Der Tod in der Architektur*. Arch+, vol. 37, 1978.

Kuhnert, Nikolaus, and Stefan Reiß-Schmidt. "Thesen zur 'Rationalen Architektur.'" *Der Tod in der Architektur*. ARCH+, vol. 37, 1978, 28–38.

Kuhnert, Nikolaus, and Philipp Oswalt, eds. *ChaosStadt*. ARCH+, vol. 105/106, 1990.

Kwinter, Sanford. "Landscapes of Change: Boccioni's 'Stati D'animo' as a General Theory of Models." *Assemblage* 19 (1992): 50–65.

———. "Der Genius der Materie: Eisenmann Project für Cincinnati." *Die Architektur des Ereignisses. ARCH+*, vol. 119/120, (Dezember 1993), 44–49.

———. "The Genius of Matter: Eisenman's Cincinnati Project." In *Re:working Eisenman*. London: Academy Editions, Ernst & Sohn, 1993, 90-97.

———. "Who's Afraid of Formalism?" Edited by Cynthia C. Davidson and R.E. Somol. *ANY* 7/8, no. Form Work: Colin Rowe (1994), 65.

———. "The Building, the Book, and the New Pastoralism." *ANY: Architecture New York, Urbanism vs Architecture: The Bigness of Rem Koolhaas*, no. 9 (1994), 16–22.

———. "The Eisenman Wave." In *The Master Architect Series: Eisenman Architects, Selected and Current Works*. Mulgrave, Victioria: The Images Publishing, 1995, 7-15.

———. "Flying the Bullet, or When Did the Future Begin?" Translated by Dieter Hoffmann-Axthelm. *ARCH+*, vol. 132, Rem Koolhaas / Projekte und Texte

1993-1996 (June 1996): 80–85.

———. "The Complex and the Singular." Kwinter, Sanford. *Architectures of Time-Toward a Theory of the Event in Modernist Culture*, Cambrigde, Massachussetts, London, England: The MIT Press, 2001, 3-31.

Lamb, Kate. "Suburb in the Sky: How Jakartans Built an Entire Village on Top of a Mall." *The Guardian*, August 5, 2019. Accessed September 24, 2021. http://www.theguardian.com/cities/2019/aug/05/suburb-in-the-sky-how-jakartans-built-an-entire-village-on-top-of-a-mall.

Latour, Bruno, Graham Harman, and Peter Erdelyi. *The Prince and the Wolf: Latour and Harman at the LSE*. Winchester: Zer0 Books, John Hunt Publishing, 2011.

Laugier, Marc-Antoine. *An Essay on Architecture*. London, Printed for T. Osborne and Shipton, 1755. Accessed September 24, 2021. http://archive.org/details/essayonarchitect00laugrich.

Lawrence, Arnold Walter, and Richard Allan Tomlinson. *Greek Architecture*. New Haven/London: Yale University Press, 1996.

Le Corbusier. *Vers une Architecture*. 11th Edition. (First Published 1923). Collection de "L'Esprit Nouveau." Paris: Crès, 1925.

———. *When the Cathedrals Were White*. Translated by Francis E. Hyslop. (Originally published as *Quand les Cathedrales etaient Blanches*, 1947). New York, London, Toronto: McGraw-Hill, 1964.

———. *Towards a New Architecture*. Edited by Frederick Etchells. (First published by John Rodker, 1931). New York: Dover Publications, 1986.

———. *The City of To-Morrow and Its Planning*. (First published in 1929 by Parson & Clarke Ltd. New York). New York: Dover Publications, 1987

Le Corbusier & Pierre, Jeanneret. *Oeuvre Complète Volume 1, 1910–1929*, Les Editions d'Architecture Artemis, Zürich, 1964.

Lefebvre, Henri. *The Urban Revolution*. Translated by Robert Bononno. (Originally published in 1970). Minneapolis: University of Minnesota Press, 2003.

———. "The Right to the City" Chapter 2-17. In *Writings on Cities*, translated by Eleonore Kofman and Elizabeth Lebas. Cambridge, MA: Wiley-Blackwell, 2006, 63-181

———. *The Production of Space*. Translated by Donald Nicholson-Smith, Oxford UK & Cambridge: Blackwell, 1991.

Lemagny, Jean-Claude. *Visionary Architects - Boullee, Ledoux, Lequeu*, Exhibition Catalogue for the traveling exhibition originated in University of St. Thomas, Houston, Santa Monica: Hennessey+Ingalls, 2002.

Levy, Pierre. "Fraktale Faltung oder wie Guattaris Maschinen uns helfen können, heute das Transzentale zu denken." In *Ästhetik und Maschinismus: Texte zu und von Félix Guattari*, edited by Henning Schmidgen. Berlin: Merve Verlag, 1995, 95-114.

———. *Technologies de l'intelligence. l'avenir de la pensee a l'ere informatique*. Paris: POINTS, 1990.

Linse, Ulrich. "Lebensreformbewegung." In *Metzler Lexikon Religion: Gegenwart — Alltag — Medien: Band 2: Haar — Osho-Bewegung*, edited by Christoph Auffarth, Jutta Bernard, Hubert Mohr, Agnes Imhof, and Silvia Kurre, Stuttgart: J.B.

Metzler, 1999, 319-321.

Lloyd's. "HMS Lutine." Lloyd's. Accessed September 24, 2021. https://www.lloyds.com/about-lloyds/history/catastophes-and-claims/hms-lutine.

Lucarelli, Fosco. "Steven Holl's Bridge of Houses (1979-1982)." Socks Studio. Accessed September 7, 2021. https://socks-studio.com/2015/04/19/steven-holls-bridge-of-houses-1979-1982/.

Lynn, Greg. *Folds, Bodies & Blobs: Collected Essays*. Books-by-architects, Bibliotheque Royale de Belgique, Bruxelles: La Lettre Volee, 1998.

———. *Animated Form*, New York: Princeton Architectural Press, 1999

———. ed. *Folding in Architecture: Revised Edition*. 1st Edition. (Originally published in 1993). Hoboken, New Jersey: John Wiley & Sons, 2004.

———. "New Variations on the Rowe Complex." Edited by Cynthia C. Davidson and R.E. Somol. *ANY* 7/8, no. *Form Work: Colin Rowe* (1994), 38-43.

Lyotard, Jean-François. *The Postmodern Condition: A Report on Knowledge*. Translated by Geoffrey Bennington and Brian Massumi. Manchester: Manchester University Press, 1984.

Manien-Elia, Mario. "Towards an Imperial City": Daniel H. Burnham and the City Beautiful Movement:" In *The American City: From the Civil War to the New Deal*, edited by Giorgio Ciucci, Francesco Dal Co, Mario Manien-Elia, and Manfredo Tafuri, translated by Barbara Luigia La Penta. Cambridge, Massachusetts: The MIT Press, 1983, 1-142.

Manuel Martín Rodríguez. *La Ciudad Lineal de Arturo Soria y El Georgismo*. Arquitectura Viva, 2014.

Martin, Reinhold. *Utopia's Ghost: Architecture and Postmodernism, Again*. Minneapolis: University of Minnesota Press, 2010

Marx, Karl, and Friedrich Engels. *Marx and Engels The Communist Manifesto, Crofts Classics*. Edited by Samuel H. Beer and Harvard University. New York: Appleton-Century-Crofts, 1955.

May, Ernst. "Fünf Jahre Wohnungsbautätigkeit in Frankfurt." Edited by Ernst May and Fritz Wichert. *Das Neue Frankfurt. Internationale Monatsschrift für die Probleme Kultureller Neugestaltung*, no. 2-3, vol. 4, Februar-März (1930): Verlag Englert und Schlösser, Frankfurt am Main, 21-51.

———. "Grundlagen der Frankfurter Wohnungsbaupolitik" edited by Ernst May and Fritz Wichert. *Das Neue Frankfurt. Internationale Monatsschrift für die Probleme Moderner Gestaltung*, no. 7-8, vol. 2, Juli-August (1928): Verlag Englert und Schlösser, Frankfurt am Main, 113-124.

May, Ernst, Joseph Gantner. "Unsere Publikationen - Sport." Edited by Ernst May and Fritz Wichert. *Das Neue Frankfurt. Internationale Monatsschrift für die Probleme Kultureller Neugestaltung*, no.1, vol. 4, (1930): Verlag Englert und Schlösser, Frankfurt am Main, 1-15.

McDonough, Tom, ed. *The Situationists and the City: A Reader*. New York: Verso Books, 2009.

Mellaart, James. *Catal Hüyük - A Neolithic Town in Anatolia*, New York: McGraw-Hill Book Company, 1967.

Merly Paul, Ani. "The Production of Space: Henri Lefebvre." CMS College Kottayam,

Department of Sociology, November 27, 2020. Accessed September 24, 2021. https://www.youtube.com/watch?v=BH-p9H43AiA.

Miljutin, Nikolaj A.. *Sozgorad: Probleme Des Planens Sozialistischer Städte*. Moskau/ Leningrad: Staatlicher Verlag, 1930.

Moneo, Rafael. "On Typology." *Oppositions. A Journal for Ideas and Criticism in Architecture* 13 (Summer 1978): 23–45.

Morton, Timothy. *Hyperobjects: Philosophy and Ecology After the End of the World*. Minneapolis: University of Minnesota Press, 2013.

———. *Realist Magic: Objects, Ontology, Causality*. Ann Arbor, Michigan: Open Humanities Press, 2013.

Mumford, Lewis. *Technics and Civilization*. Originally published 1934. New York: Harcourt, Brace & World, 1963.

———. *The Myth of the Machine: Technics and Human Development*. San Diego, New York, London: A Harvest/HBJ Book, 1967

———. *The Culture of Cities* (1938). San Diego, New York, London: A Harvest/HBJ Book, 1970.

———. *The Myth of the Machine: The Pentagon of Power*. San Diego, New York, London: A Harvest/HBJ Book, 1970.

———. *The City in History: Its Origins, Its Transformations, and Its Prospects* (1961). San Diego, New York, London: A Harvest/HBJ Book, 1989.

Muratori, Saverio. "Studi per una operante storia urbana di Venezia." Roma: Instituto poligrafico dello Stato, Libreria dello Stato, 1960.

Murawski, Michał. "The Social Condenser: A Century of Revolution through Architecture, 1917–2017." *The Journal of Architecture* 22, no. 3 (April 3, 2017): 369–71.

Nelson, Steven. *From Cameroon to Paris. Mousgoum Architecture In & Out of Africa*. Chicago/London: The University of Chicago Press, 2007.

Nesbitt, Kate, ed. "Chapter 5: Typology and Transformation." In *Theorizing a New Agenda for Architecture. An Anthology of Architectural Theory 1965-1995*, 2nd Edition, 239–63. New York: Princeton Architectural Press, 1996.

Neumeyer, Fritz. *Quellentexte zur Architekturtheorie*. München Berlin: Prestel, 2002.

Noebel, Walter A., ed. "Das Thema Der Transformation oder die Morphology der Gestalt." In *Oswald Mathias Ungers - Die Thematisierung der Architektur*, 17–34. (Originally published as *Architettura Come Thema*, Electa, Milan, 1982). Sulgen: Verlag Niggli, 2011.

Norberg-Schulz, Christian. *Genius Loci: Towards a Phenomenology of Architecture*. (Originally published as *Genius Loci - Paesaggio, Ambience, Architettura*, 1979). New York: Academy Editions Ltd, 1980.

NPR. "Welcome To Whittier, Alaska, A Community Under One Roof." NPR, 2015. Accessed September 24, 2021. https://www.npr.org/2015/01/18/378162264/welcome-to-whittier-alaska-a-community-under-one-roof.

Oechslin, Werner, ed. *Das Große / On Bigness*, vol. September. DAIDALOS 61. Gütersloh: Bertelsmann Fachzeitschriften, 1996.

Olmsted Society. "General Plan of Riverside." Olmsted Society. Accessed September 24, 2021. https://www.olmstedsociety.org/wp-content/uploads/2008/11/general-plan-of-riverside.jpg.

OMA. "Hyperbuilding." OMA. Accessed September 7, 2021. https://www.oma.com/projects/hyperbuilding.

———. *AD Architectural Design* 47, no. 5. edited by Haig Beck, 1977.

Oxford University Press. "Parti." Encyclopedia.com. Accessed September 24, 2021. https://www.encyclopedia.com/education/dictionaries-thesauruses-pictures-and-press-releases/parti.

Palladio, Andrea. *I Quattro Libri dell'Architettura di Andrea Palladio*. Apresso Bartolomeo Carampello, 1581.

———. *The Four Books of Architecture*. Edited by Adolf K. Placzek. Republication of the Isaac Ware English Edition of 1738. (First published 1570). New York: Dover Publications, 1965.

Peirce, Charles Sanders. "Logic as Semiotic: The Theory of Signs." In *Philosophical Writings of Peirce*, Revised Edition, 98–119. With an Introduction by Justus Buchler. New York: Dover Publications Inc., 1986.

Pevsner, Nikolaus. *A History of Building Types*. Princeton, New Jersey: Princeton University Press, 1979.

Pigafetta, Giorgio. *Saverio Muratori Architetto: Teoria e Progetti*. Marsilio, 1990.

Piketty, Thomas. *Capital and Ideology*. Translated by Arthur Goldhammer. Cambridge, Massachusetts: Harvard University Press, 2020.

———. *Capital in the Twenty-First Century*. Translated by Arthur Goldhammer. Cambridge, Massachusetts: Harvard University Press, 2014.

Polo, Alejandro Zaera. "Kapitalflüsse, Datenströme, Drive-Thru und andere Strömungen." *ARCH+*, vol. 117, Rem Koolhaas (June 1993): 56–58.

Popper, Karl. *The Open Society and Its Enemies*. (First published 1947, reprinted 1947). London; Henley: Routledge & Kegan Paul, 1945.

Prigogine, Ilya. "The Physics of Becoming." Part II in *From Being to Becoming - Time and Complexity in the Physical Sciences*, New York: W.H. Freeman and Company, 1980: 73-150.

Princeton University Art Museum. "Imaginary Prisons: Giovanni Battista Piranesi Prints." Princeton University Art Museum. Accessed September 24, 2021. https://artmuseum.princeton.edu/object-package/giovanni-battista-piranesi-imaginary-prisons/3640.

Quincy, Quatremère de. "Type." In *Oppositions Reader: Selected Readings from a Journal for Ideas and Criticism in Architecture, 1973-1984*, edited by K. Michael Hays, 616–20. New York: Princeton Architectural Press, 1998.

Quincy, Quatremère de, and Samir Younés. "Type." In *Encyclopédie Méthodique*. vol. 3. Reprinted in The Historical Dictionary of Architecture of Quatremère de Quincy. London: Papadakis Publisher, 2000.

Rajchman, John. "Out of the Fold." In *Folding in Architecture: Revised Edition*, edited by

Greg Lynn, 1st Edition, 77–79. (Originally published in 1993). Hoboken, New Jersey: John Wiley & Sons, 2004.

Rancière, Jacques. “Problems and Transformations of Critical Art.” In *Aesthetics and Its Discontents*, 45–60. Cambridge, UK: Polity Press, 2009.

Raunig, Gerald. *A Few Fragments on Machines*. Translated by Aileen Derieg, 10/2005. Accessed September 24, 2021. https://transversal.at/transversal/1106/raunig1/en.

Riani, Paolo, Paul Goldberger, and John Calvin Portman. “Interview with John Portman by Paul Goldberger.” In *John Portman*. Milan: L’Arcaedizioni, 1990.

———. “The Shape of the City.” In *John Portman*, 21–45. Milan: L’Arcaedizioni, 1990.

Riegl, Alois. *Spätrömische Kunst-Industrie*. (Originally published 1901). Bremen: Unikum Verlag, 2011.

Riemann, Peter. “Urban Design Strategies for Berlin, with a Case Study on Berlin/Südliche Friedrichstadt.” Cornell University, 1979.

Risselada, Max, and Dirk van den Heuvel. *Team 10: In Search of a Utopia of the Present 1953-81*. Rotterdam: NAI Publishers, 2006.

Rossi, Aldo. *The Architecture of the City*. Translated by Diane Ghirardo and Joan Ockman. Oppositions Books. Cambridge, Massachusetts: The MIT Press, 1982.

Rowe, Colin. “Roma Interrotta Projects” with Peter Carl, Judith di Maio, Steven Peterson, in *Roma Interrotta*, Incontri Internazionali d’Arte, officina edizioni. Roma, 1978, 136-150.

Rowe, Colin and Fred Koetter. *Collage City*. Cambridge, Massachusetts, and London, England: The MIT Press, 1983.

Sarnitz, August. “Realism versus Verniedlichung: The Design of the Great City.” In *Otto Wagner: Reflections on the Raiment of Modernity*, edited by Henry Francis Mallgrave, 85–112. Getty Center for the History of Art and the Humanities, Santa Monica. Chicago: The University of Chicago Press, 1993

Schlandt, Joachim, Ungers, Oswald M. “The Viennese Superblocks”, translated by Sima Ingberman. In *Oppositions*, Vol. 13, Summer 1978,The MIT Press: Cambridge Massachusetts, London England, 1978, 83-111.

Schleuning, Johannes. *Die Siedlung Römerstadt in Frankfurt am Main*. von Ernst May. Hamburg: Diplomica, 2000.

Schmarsow, August. “Das Wesen der Architektonischen Schöpfung (1894).” In *Quellentexte zur Architekturtheorie*, edited by Fritz Neumeyer. München: Prestel, 2002.

Schmidgen, Henning. “Das Konzert Der Maschinen. Simondons Politisches Programm.” *Zeitschrift Für Medien- und Kulturforschung*, no. 2, Felix Meiner Verlag, Leipzig (2012): 117–34.

———. “Thinking Technological and Biological Beings: Gilbert Simondon’s Philosophy of Machines.” *Revista Do Departamento de Psicologia* UFF, no. 17 (n.d.): 11–18. Accessed September 24, 2021.https://www.researchgate.net/publication/262626849_Thinking_technological_and_biological_beings_Gilbert_Simondon%27s_philosophy_of_machines.

Schmitt, Carl. *Der Begriff Des Politischen*. 8. Auflage. Neusatz Auf Basis Der Ausgabe von 1963. Originally Published 1932. Berlin: Duncker & Humblot, 2009.

Schumacher, Patrik. *The Autopoiesis of Architecture, Volume I: A New Framework for Architecture*. London: John Wiley & Sons, 2011.

Schumacher, Thomas L. "Contextualism: Urban Ideals and Deformations (1971)." *In Theorizing a New Agenda for Architecture: An Anthology of Architectural Theory 1965 - 1995*, edited by Kate Nesbitt, 2nd Edition, 294–306. New York: Princeton Architectural Press, 1996.

Schütte-Lihotzky, Margarete. "Rationalisierung Im Haushalt." Edited by Ernst May. *Das Neue Frankfurt. Monatsschrift für die Fragen der Grossstadt-Gestaltung*, no. 5, vol. 1, April-Juni (1927): Verlag Englert und Schlösser, Frankfurt am Main, 120-123.

Simondon, Gilbert. *Simondon, In L'individu et sa genèse physico-biologique (L'individuation à la lumière des notions de forme et d'information)*. Presses Universitaires de France - PUF, coll. "Epiméthée," 1964.

———. "The Condition of Individuation." from Chapter One: Form and Matter, 27-29. In *L'individu et sa genèse physico-biologique (L'individuation à la lumière des notions de forme et d'information)*. Presses Universitaires de France - PUF, coll. "Epiméthée," 1964. Original translation by Taylor Adkins, 2007. Accessed September 24, 2021. http://topologicalmedialab.net/xinwei/classes/readings/Simondon/Physico-BiologicalGenesisIndiv.pdf: 1-16.

———. "The Genesis of the Individual." In *Incorporations*, edited by Jonathan Crary and Sanford Kwinter, translated by Mark Cohen and Sanford Kwinter, 297–319. New York, NY: Zone Books, 1992.

———. "Technical Mentality." In *Gilbert Simondon: Being and Technology*, edited by Arne De Boever, Alex Murray, and Jon Roffe. Edinburgh: Edinburgh University Press, 2012.

———. *On the Mode of Existence of Technical Objects*. Translated by Cecile Malaspina and John Rogove. (Originally published 1958). Minneapolis: Univocal Publishing, 2017.

———. "Die technische Einstellung." In *Die technologische Bedingung - Beiträge zur Beschreibung der technischen Welt*. Edited by Erich Hört, Suhrkamp Verlag Berlin 2011, 73-92.

Sitte, Camillo. "City Planning according to Artistic Principles" from 1889, In *Camillo Sitte: The Birth of Modern City Planning* by George R. Collins and Christiane Crasemann Collins, Dover Publications, Mineola, New York.1986.

Smithson, Alison. *Team 10 Primer*, edited by Alison Smithson, (originally published in Architectural Design, December 1962). London/Great Britain: Studio Vista, 1968.

———. *Team 10 Meetings 1953-1984*, edited by Alison Smithson, Delft: Publikatieburo, Faculteit der Bouwkunde, Technische Universiteit Delft, 1991.

Smithson, Alison, and Peter Smithson. *Ordinariness and Light - Urban theories 1952-1960 and their application in a building project 1963-1970*, London: Faber and Faber, 1970.

———. *Urban Structuring: Studies of Alison & Peter Smithson*. London, New York: Reinhold Publishing Corporation, 1967.

Soja, Edward W. *Postmodern Geographies: The Reassertion of Space in Critical Social Theory*. (1989). London: Verso, 2014.

Soria y Mata, Arturo. “Al entrar en 1910.” In Compañía Madrileña de Urbanización *La Ciudad Lineal: Revista Científica de Higiene, Agricultura, Ingeniería y Urbanización*, Madrid (Chamartín) 1910, n. 400.

Soria y Puig, Arturo. *Cerdà: The Five Bases of the General Theory of Urbanization*, Madrid: Electa, 1999.

———. “Layouts for the Network of Ways.” In *Cerdà: The Five Bases of the General Theory of Urbanization*, 117–38. Madrid: Electa, 1999.

———. “The Square Grid and Its Diagonals.” *In Cerdà: The Five Bases of the General Theory of Urbanization*, 130–31. Madrid: Electa, 1999.

Soules, Matthew. “All That Is Solid: Asset Urbanism and the Financial Dynamics of Post-Industrial Space.” Edited by Alice Kimm & Jaepil Choi. *Association of Collegiate Schools of Architecture, no. Open Cities: The New Post-Industrial World Order* (2014), 343–52.

———. *Icebergs, Zombies, and the Ultra Thin: Architecture and Capitalism in the Twenty-First Century*. New York: Princeton Architectural Press, 2021.

Stern, Robert with Thomas Catalano in *Raymond M. Hood*. Catalogue 15 Institute for Architecture and Urban Studies, edited by Kenneth Frampton, Silvia Kolbowski, New York: Rizzoli International Publications, 1982, 2-27.

Stevens, Philip. “URBANUS Encloses Mixed-Use Shenzhen Development with ‘Artificial Mountain Volumes.’” *Designboom | Architecture & Design*, 2019. Accessed September 24, 2021. https://www.designboom.com/architecture/urbanus-shum-yip-upper-hills-loft-shenzhen-china-06-26-2019/.

Stiller, Adolph, and et al. *Leonidov: Ein Architekt des russischen Konstruktivismus*. Salzburg: Müry Salzmann, 2010.

Storey, Glenn R. “The Meaning of ‘Insula’ in Roman Residential Terminology.” *Memoirs of the American Academy in Rome* 49 (2004), 47–84.

Stromberg, Joseph. “What Is the Anthropocene and Are We in It?” Smithsonian magazine, January 2013. Accessed September 24, 2021. https://www.smithsonianmag.com/science-nature/what-is-the-anthropocene-and-are-we-in-it-164801414/.

Tafuri, Manfredo. *Vienna rossa: la politica residenziale nella Vienna socialista*, 1919-1933. Milano: Electa, 1980.

———. “The Disenchanted Mountain: The Skyscraper and the City.” In *The American City: From the Civil War to the New Deal*, edited by Giorgio Ciucci, Francesco Dal Co, Mario Manien-Elia, and Manfredo Tafuri, translated by Barbara Luigia La Penta. Cambridge, Massachusetts: The MIT Press, 1983, 389-503.

———. Introduction to Raymond M. Hood. “A City under a Single Roof.” In T*he Sphere and the Labyrinth: Avant-Gardes and Architecture from Piranesi to the 1970s*, translated by Pellegrino D’Acierno and Robert Connolly. Cambridge, Massachusetts: The MIT Press, 1987, 190-191.

Taylor, Frederick Winslow. *The Principles of Scientific Management*. Harper & Brothers, 1919.

Trummer, Peter. “Associative Design: From Type to Population.” In *Computational Design Thinking*, edited by Sean Ahlquist and Achim Menges, 179–97. *AD Reader*. Chichester: John Wiley & Sons, 2011.

———. "Pile City." *Offramp*, SCI-Arc, 08 (2014), 64–71.

———. "The City in the Age of Hyperobjects," in: *Log*, No. 45. New York: Anyone Corporation 2019, 35-42.

Tschumi, Bernard. *The Manhattan Transcripts*. (First published 1981 by *Architectural Design*). London: Academy Editions, 1994.

———. *Architecture and Disjunction*. Cambridge, Massachusetts: The MIT Press, 1996.

Twombly, Robert C., ed. *Frank Lloyd Wright Essential Texts*. New York: W.W. Norton & Company, 2009.

Ungers, Oswald M. *Morphologie. City Metaphors*. Köln: Walter König, 1982.

———. *Sieben Variationen des Raumes über die Sieben Leuchter der Baukunst von John Ruskin*. Stuttgart: Hatje Cantz, 1985.

———. "Was ist Architektur?" *ARCH+*, vol. 179, O. M. Ungers – Berliner Vorlesungen 1964-65 (July 2000): 12–19.

———. "He who did not understand the Zeitgeist." In *Reckoning with Colin Rowe: Ten Architects Take Position*, edited by Emmanuel Petit, 65–71. New York: Routledge, 2015.

———. *10 Kapitel Über Architektur - Ein visueller Traktat*, DuMont Reiseverlag, Ostfildern, 1999.

Ungers, O. M, Rem Koolhaas, Peter Riemann, Hans Kollhoff, Arthur Ovaska, Florian Hertweck, Sébastien Marot, and Ungers Archiv für Architekturwissenschaft. *The City in the City: Berlin: A Green Archipelago: A Manifesto* (1977). Zürich: Lars Müller Publishers, 2013.

Ungers, Oswald M., Rem Koolhaas, Peter Riemann, Hans Kollhoff, and Arthur Ovaska. "Cities within the City. Proposals by the Sommer Akademie for Berlin." *Lotus International* 19, no. L'isolato urbano | The urban block (1978): 82–97.

Unwin, Raymond. *Town Planning in Practice: An Introduction to the Art of Designing Cities and Suburbs*. London: T. Fisher Unwin, 1909.

Valéry, Paul. "Eupalinos or The Architect (1921)." In *Paul Valery: Dialogues*, translated by William Stewart, 56–152. Bollingen Series: 45.4. New York: Pantheon Books, 1956.

———. *The Collected Works of Paul Valéry: Dialogues*. Translated by William Stewart. Bollingen Series, 45.4. New York: Princeton University Press, 1956.

Van den Heuvel, D. "Alison and Peter Smithson: A Brutalist Story, Involving the House, the City and the Everyday (Plus a Couple of Other Things)." TU Delft, 2013.

Van der Rohe, Mies. "Baukunst und Zeitwille." In *Der Querschnitt* - (1924); 4. 31-32. trashttps://www.cloud-cuckoo.net/openarchive/Autoren/Mies/Mies1924b.htm.

Venturi, Robert. *Complexity and Contradiction in Architecture*. With Introduction by Vincent Scully. Museum of Modern Art Papers on Architecture. New York: Museum of Modern Art, 2002.

Venturi, Robert, Denise Scott Brown, and Steven Izenour. *Learning from Las Vegas, The Forgotten Symbolism of Architectural Form*. 2nd Revised Edition. Cambridge, Massachusetts: The MIT Press, 1977.

Vidler, Anthony. “The Third Typology.” In *Oppositions Reader: Selected Readings from a Journal for Ideas and Criticism in Architecture, 1973-1984*, edited by K. Michael Hays, 13–17. New York: Princeton Architectural Press, 1998.

———. “The Third Typology (1975).” In *Theorizing a New Agenda for Architecture. An Anthology of Architectural Theory 1965-1995*, 2nd Edition, 239–63. edited by Nesbitt, Kate, New York: Princeton Architectural Press, 1996.

———. “Reckoning with Art History: Colin Rowe’s Critical Vision.” In *Reckoning with Colin Rowe: Ten Architects Take Position*, edited by Emmanuel Petit, 41–56. New York: Routledge, 2015

Vitruvius. *The Ten Books on Architecture*. Edited by Morris H. Morgan. Unabridged and Unaltered Republication of the 1914 1st Edition. New York: Dover, 1960.

Wagner, Otto. *Die Groszstadt: eine Studie über diese*. Wien: Anton Schroll, 1911.

Wainwright, Oliver. “Billionaires’ Basements: The Luxury Bunkers Making Holes in London Streets.” *The Guardian*, November 9, 2012. Accessed September 24, 2021. http://www.theguardian.com/artanddesign/2012/nov/09/billionaires-basements-london-houses-architecture.

———. “Super-Tall, Super-Skinny, Super-Expensive: The ‘Pencil Towers’ of New York’s Super-Rich.” *The Guardian*, February 5, 2019. Accessed September 24, 2021. http://www.theguardian.com/cities/2019/feb/05/super-tall-super-skinny-super-expensive-the-pencil-towers-of-new-yorks-super-rich.

Wallas, Graham. *The Great Society: A Psychological Analysis*. (Originally published 1914). New York, NY: MacMillan Co, 1932.

Wallenstein, Sven-Olov. *Bio-Politics and the Emergence of Modern Architecture*. New York: Princeton Architectural Press, 2009.

———. “Introduction: Foucault, Biopolitics, and Governmentality.” In *Foucault, Biopolitics, and Governmentality*, edited by Jakob Nilsson & Sven-Olov Wallenstein, Södertörn Philosophical Studies 14, Stockholm: Södertörn University, 2013, 7-34.

Warf, Barney, and Santa Arias. *The Spatial Turn: Interdisciplinary Perspectives*. London: Routledge, 2008.

Weber, Anton. “Sozialpolitik Und Wohnungswesen.” In *Das Neue Wien*, edited by Städtewerk, unter offizieller Mitw. d. Gemeinde Wien. 1., 1/4:191–310. Wien: Elbemühl Papierfabriken und Graphische Industrie A. G., 1926.

Weber, Max. *Economy and Society: An Outline of Interpretive Sociology*. University of California Press, 1978.

Weihsmann, Helmut. *Das Rote Wien: Sozialdemokratische Architektur und Kommunalpolitik 1919-1934*. Completely revised Edition. Wien: Promedia, 2002.

Wiener, Norbert. *Cybernetics or Control and Communication in the Animal and the Machine*. New York: Wiley, 1948.

Wit, Wim de. “Die Amsterdamer Schule und die Städtische Wohnbaupolitik.” In *Kommunaler Wohnbau in Wien: Aufbruch 1923 - 1934*, Ausstrahlung, edited by Karl Mang and Eva Mang-Trimmel. Wien: Presse- und Informationsdienst der Stadt Wien, 1977.

Wittkower, Rudolf. *Architectural Principles in the Age of Humanism*. New York: W. W.

Norton & Company, 1971.

Wolfe, Ross. “Dom Narkomfin in Moscow, 1929 - Moisei Ginzburg & Ignatii Milinis’ Iconic Constructivist Masterpiece.” The Charnel-House, 2013. Accessed September 24, 2021. https://thecharnelhouse.org/2013/10/05/dom-narkomfin-in-moscow-1929/.

Wölfflin, Heinrich. *Kunstgeschichtliche Grundbegriffe: Das Problem der Stilentwicklung in der neueren Kunst*. 19th Edition. Basel: Schwabe Verlagsgruppe AG Schwabe Verlag, 2004.

Wright, Frank Lloyd. “The Disappearing City” (Original edition 1932). In *The Industrial Revolution Runs Away*, New York: Horizon Press, 1969.

Yao, Li, and Feng Zhiwei. “Rooftop Villas Are Legal, Officials Say.” *China Daily*, August 16, 2012. Accessed September 24, 2021. https://www.chinadaily.com.cn/china/2012-08/16/content_15679402.htm.

Yoshimoto, Catherine. “Yield-Seekers Embrace Emerging Market Real Estate | FTSE Russell.” FTSE Russell. Accessed September 7, 2021. https://www.ftserussell.com/blogs/yield-seekers-embrace-emerging-market-real-estate.

Illustration Credits

Cover. Layout by author. Original Photograph: Shahrir Bahar/instagram/@shahrirbahar1. Published in Lamb, Kate. "Suburb in the Sky: How Jakartans Built an Entire Village on Top of a Mall." *The Guardian*, August 5, 2019. Accessed September 24, 2021. http://www.theguardian.com/cities/2019/aug/05/suburb-in-the-sky-how-jakartans-built-an-entire-village-on-top-of-a-mall.

Figure 1. Cartoon by A. B. Walker, originally published in Life, March 4, 1909, https://www.architakes.com/wp-content/uploads/2009/08/walker21.jpg. Republished without its original caption in *Delirious New York* with the added caption: "1909 theorem: the Skyscraper as utopian device for the production of unlimited numbers of virgin sites on a single metropolitan location." See: Koolhaas, Rem. *Delirious New York: A Retroactive Manifesto for Manhattan*. New York: Oxford University Press, 1978, 69.

Figure 2. Drawing by author. © Peter Trummer

Figures 3–5. Image: Wikimedia Commons

Figure 6. Original caption: Entwerfen mit Invarianzen und Vorstellungsbildern, Thesen zur rationalen Architektur, Montage: Werner Wigenfeld. Published in *Arch+* 37, Zeitschrift für Architekten, Stadtplaner, sozialarbeiter und Kommunalpolitische Gruppen, Editors: Nikolaus Kuhnert, AAchen: Klenkes Druck und Verlag Gmbh, April 1978, p.28–29.

Figure 7. Original caption: Morphological sequences: Unter den Eichen, pictures of the Exhibition of the Summer School on the topic of the Urban Villa Supervised by Ungers in Berlin for Cornell students in 1977. Published in Ungers, O. M., Rem Koolhaas, Peter Riemann, Hans Kollhoff, Arthur Ovaska, Florian Hertweck, Sébastien Marot, and Ungers Archiv für Architekturwissenschaft. *The City in the City: Berlin: A Green Archipelago: A Manifesto* (1977). Zürich: Lars Müller Publishers, 2013: 52–53.

Figure 8. Original caption: Entwerfen mit Invarianzen und Vorstellungsbildern, Thesen zur rationalen Architektur, Montage: Werner Wigenfeld. Published in *Arch+* 37, Zeitschrift für Architekten, Stadtplaner, sozialarbeiter und Kommunalpolitische Gruppen, Editors: Nikolaus Kuhnert, AAchen: Klenkes Druck und Verlag Gmbh, April 1978, p.28–29.

Figure 9. Published in Colin Rowe and Fred Koetter, *Collage City*, The MIT press, Cambridge, Massachusetts, and London, England, 1978, p.82.

Figure 10: Published in *Learning from Las Vegas: The Forgotten Symbolism of Architectural Form*. Robert Venturi, Denise Scott Brown, Steven Izenour, The MIT Press Cambridge, Massachusetts, and London, England, 1977 (original 1972), 88–89, figs. 75 & 76.

Figure 11. Published in *The Manhattan Transcripts*, London: Academy Edition, 1994, 17. First published in Great Britain in 1981 by Architectural Design.

Figure 12. Published in *The Manhattan Transcripts*, London: Academy Edition, 1994, 46. First published in Great Britain in 1981 by Architectural Design.

Figure 13. Published in *Delirious New York: A Retroactive Manifesto for Manhattan*. Rem Koolhaas, New York: Oxford University Press, 1978, 128.

Figure 14. Published in *Delirious New York: A Retroactive Manifesto for Manhattan*. Rem Koolhaas, New York: Oxford University Press, 1978, 132.

Figure 15. Published in *I quattro libri dell'architettura*. Andrea Palladio, Venedig 1570, Tavola 3:2-06.

Figure 16. Published in *On the Mode of Existence of Technical Objects*. Gilbert Simondon. Translated by Cécile Malaspina and John Rogove, First Edition, Minneapolis, Univocal, 2017, 88, plate 4. (original: Du mode d'existence des objets techniques by Gilbert Simondon © Aubier (department of Flammarion) Paris, 1958 and 2012: 33–34.

Figure 17. From Socks-Studio, "Musgum mud huts," http://socks-studio.com/img/blog/musgum-01.jpg, or *Die Geschichte der Stadt*, Leonardo Benevolo, Frankfurt/New York: Campus Verlag, 5. Auflage 1990, 17.

Figures 18–23. Drawings by author. © Peter Trummer

Figure 24. From Socks-Studio, "Musgum mud huts," http://socks-studio.com/img/blog/musgum-02.jpg.

Figures 25-30. Drawings by author. © Peter Trummer

Figure 31. Published in Lefebvre, Henri. *The Urban Revolution*. Translated by Robert Bononno. (Originally published in 1970). Minneapolis: University of Minnesota Press, 2003, 7.

Figure 32. Published in Lefebvre, Henri. *The Urban Revolution*. Translated by Robert Bononno. (Originally published in 1970). Minneapolis: University of Minnesota Press, 2003, 15.

Figures 33-49. Drawings by author. © Peter Trummer

Figures 50. Photograph: Shahrir Bahar/instagram/@shahrirbahar1. In *The Guardian*, (2019). Accessed September 24, 2021. http://www.theguardian.com/cities/2019/aug/05/suburb-in-the-sky-how-jakartans-built-an-entire-village-on-top-of-a-mall.

Figures 51-101. Drawings by author. © Peter Trummer

Thanks to *SARS-CoV-2*

ORO Editions
Publishers of Architecture, Art, and Design
Gordon Goff: Publisher

www.oroeditions.com
info@oroeditions.com

Published by ORO Editions.

Author: Peter Trummer
Book Design: Peter Trummer
Text Editor: Lude Studebaker
Project Manager: Jake Anderson

10 9 8 7 6 5 4 3 2 1 First Edition

ISBN: 978-1-957183-55-8

Color Separations and Printing: ORO Group Inc.
Printed in China

ORO Editions makes a continuous effort to minimize the overall carbon footprint of its publications. As part of this goal, ORO, in association with Global ReLeaf, arranges to plant trees to replace those used in the manufacturing of the paper produced for its books. Global ReLeaf is an international campaign run by American Forests, one of the world's oldest nonprofit conservation organizations. Global ReLeaf is American Forests' education and action program that helps individuals, organizations, agencies, and corporations improve the local and global environment by planting and caring for trees.